POWER RPG IV

*Advanced Concepts, Tips,
and Techniques, Including ILE*

*Doug Pence
and Ron Hawkins*

First Edition, June 1996

DISCLAIMER

© 1996 Midrange Computing

ISBN: 1-883884-32-2

Midrange Computing
5650 El Camino Real, Suite 225
Carlsbad, CA 92008

Acknowledgments

Doug would like to extend a special thanks to his wife, Cathy, and their kids, John, Rachel, and Sarah.

Ron would like to thank his wife, Darla, and their kids, Daniel, Nicholas, and Rebecca.

Without all of their patience, sacrifice, and support, this project would have never been possible.

We would also like to extend a special thank you to our editor, Anita Craig, and her team at Midrange Computing. She has a special talent that makes us look better than we really are.

And finally, we would like to thank the gang at CPU (Computer Processing Unlimited). Your help, tolerance, and support is greatly appreciated.

Doug Pence and Ron Hawkins
San Diego, California

TABLE OF CONTENTS

Power RPG IV

Preface

If a man empties his purse into his head no one can take it away from him. An investment in knowledge always pays the best interest.

—Benjamin Franklin

The authors of this book have spent the better part of the last two decades accumulating tips, tools, and techniques that will benefit any AS/400 programmer. Their objective was to put together a collection that would serve all RPG/400 programmers, whether a junior programmer right out of school, or a seasoned veteran with 10 years of experience.

Along with the announcement of V3R1 of the AS/400 operating system came RPG IV and a virtual avalanche of new information and capabilities. This book will open doors and unlock that information, helping you take full advantage of the full range of AS/400 capabilities.

From designing software to attain maximum performance, to learning how to use advanced problem-solving tools, this book presents a wide range of important topics. It offers in-depth coverage of basic subjects—like data structures, string handling, and subfiles—and also tackles the more intricate areas like APIs (Application Program Interfaces), the Integrated Language Environment (ILE), and using journaling as a debugging tool. There are numerous tools designed to improve programmer productivity and efficiency. The book also contains tools and a strategy to help deal with the upcoming millennium.

Often, knowing the best way to do the job is a direct result of being familiar with all of the tools at your disposal. It is for this reason that this book should find its way into every RPG/400+ reference library.

Chapter 1

Performance Starts with Program Design

Throughout this chapter, we focus on reducing I/O and maximizing the use of main memory. We discuss how the Integrated Language Environment (ILE) affects performance and how it should affect your design considerations. We compare the pros and cons of *dynamic* program calls and *static* program calls. And we give you numerous tips on how to maximize your system resources.

A THOUSAND MILE JOURNEY BEGINS WITH A SINGLE STEP...

To understand how to write programs that perform well on the AS/400, you must understand which functions most degrade system performance. The primary bottleneck on most midrange systems is related to I/O processing or memory management. Creating, deleting, opening, closing, reading, and writing to data files drain system performance, making your software appear to run slowly. Over utilization of system memory causes the system to "thrash" and spend the majority of its resources moving objects from memory to disk and vice versa. Most software on the AS/400 and its predecessors falls victim to one or the other of these problems.

I/O AND ITS EFFECT ON AS/400 PERFORMANCE

I/O processing is slow because it is still slave to a mechanical process. The data is stored on some form of magnetic media and must be retrieved or written using the moving parts of whatever the storage device happens to be.

Despite major technical achievements in this area within the last decade, I/O processing remains the culprit of most performance problems on the AS/400. Features like *journaling* and *mirroring* have been added to the operating system for stability and to allow us to make software systems more reliable, but their use can further amplify the I/O processing bottleneck problem. The good news is that there are a number of things that you can do as a programmer to help alleviate this problem. Let's begin with the basics.

Don't Need It? Don't Use It!

From a performance standpoint, opening and closing files are two of the most time-consuming events that take place on the AS/400. When an RPG program is called, the data files are usually opened automatically by the system. If the programs you are working with have a large number of files (sometimes this is unavoidable), program initiation can seem to take forever while the program is loaded and all of the files are opened.

This delay can be reduced if the file opens are *user-controlled*, if the files are already open with a *shared data path*, or *both*.

User-controlled File Opens

User-controlled file opens give you the option of only opening a file when you intend to use it. As you can see by the example in Figure 1.1, you can code your program to open files as you need them instead of when the program loads. You can either set a flag in the program indicating that the file has been opened already so you will not attempt to open it again, or you can use an error indicator on the open statement, as shown in Figure 1.2. Failure to perform one step or the other results in a nasty little RPG error.

Figure 1.1: User-controlled Opens Using Conditional Flags

```
FFilename++IPEASFRlen+LKlen+AIDevice+.Keywords++++++++++++++++++++++Comments++++++++++
FCUSTOMER  IF   E          K DISK      USROPN


DName++++++++++ETDsFrom+++To/L+++IDc.Keywords++++++++++++++++++++++Comments++++++++++
D OpenCust        S              1A


CL0N01Factor1+++++++Opcode&ExtFactor2+++++++Result+++++++Len++D+HiLoEq....Comments++++++
 * Open the file, if it is not already open
C                   If        OpenCust <> *On
C                   Open      Customer
C                   Eval      OpenCust = *On
C                   Endif
C        CustKey    Chain     Customer                               99
```

Figure 1.2: User-controlled Opens Using Error Indicators

```
FFilename++IPEASFRlen+LKlen+AIDevice+.Keywords++++++++++++++++++++++Comments++++++++++
FCustomer  IF   E          K DISK      USROPN

CL0N01Factor1+++++++Opcode&ExtFactor2+++++++Result+++++++Len++D+HiLoEq....Comments++++++
C                   Open      Customer                               99
C        CustKey    Chain     Customer                               99
```

If you code your file opening routines at strategic points within your program, it is possible that certain files may never be opened at all. For example, if the program contains multiple screens that are processed conditionally depending upon user response, the program could be coded to open only those files associated with the selected screens. There is a double bonus in this situation because files that are never opened obviously need never be closed.

Secondly, but perhaps more importantly from an overall performance standpoint, user-controlled files offer an excellent opportunity to distribute program overhead so that it is less noticeable to the user.

The example in Figure 1.3 illustrates how you can code the program so that the files are being opened at the same time the program is waiting for a response from the user. While EXFMT was a wonderful addition to the RPG language, those of us who have been in the midrange market for a while remember when we had to code the display file as a primary or demand file. Separate steps were required to write and read each screen format.

Figure 1.3: User-controlled Opens between Writing and Reading Display File Format

```
FFilename++IPEASFRlen+LKlen+AIDevice+.Keywords+++++++++++++++++++++++++++Comments++++++++++
FDisplay    CF   E              WORKSTN
FCustomer   IF   E              K DISK      USROPN
FSalesmen   IF   E              K DISK      USROPN


DName+++++++++++ETDsFrom+++To/L+++IDc.Keywords+++++++++++++++++++++++++++Comments++++++++++
D OpenCust           S              1A
D OpenSales          S              1A


CL0N01Factor1+++++++Opcode&ExtFactor2+++++++Result++++++++Len++D+HiLoEq....Comments++++++
 * Write Display Format
C                    Write     Format
 * Open files
C                    If        OpenCust <> *On
C                    Open      Customer
C                    Eval      OpenCust = *On
C                    Endif
C                    If        OpenSales <> *On
C                    Open      Salesmen
C                    Eval      OpenSales = *On
C                    Endif
 * Wait for input from the display file
C                    Read      Format                                    99
```

In this example, the WRITE and READ op codes replace Execute Format (EXFMT). Notice that several user-controlled file opens have been placed in between the WRITE and the READ. When this program executes, the screen panel displays and then the files open while operator attention is focused on the screen. Coding the program this way creates a condition where the files are being opened while the program is waiting on the user, instead of the other way around.

When using this particular technique of writing and reading the display formats, you must compile your display file as DFRWRT(*NO) so it does not defer writing a screen until a read operation is encountered. Failure to comply with this requirement results in a condition where the screen does not appear until the read operation is executed.

When using user-controlled file opens, you may choose to ignore the closing of the files and let the program handle that part of it when the last record indicator is encountered. If the delay caused when the program ends is causing you problems, you may want to try using the RETRN op code instead of setting on LR (this is discussed in further detail later in this chapter, "RPG Program Calls").

The Shared Data Path

Another technique that helps to reduce program initiation overhead uses a method called *shared data paths*. This method can be very useful when programs and subprograms use the same data files. By opening the data or display files using shared open data paths, subsequent high-level language (HLL) programs can be opened in about half the time.

The example in Figure 1.4 is a sample initial program that is called when a user first signs on to the system. The Override Database File (OVRDBF) command specifies that the open data path is to be shared, and the Open Database File (OPNDBF) command opens the data files that are used by the application most often. The monitor message (MONMSG) command was added to prevent error messages from appearing if the files in question already had an open data path when the program was run.

When the sample program in Figure 1.4 is run, the files are opened with a shared data path and the menu is displayed. Program calls to application programs within this same session will then use the existing open data path instead of creating a new one.

Figure 1.4: Sign-on CL Program to **Pre-open** *Files and Display Initial Menu*

```
PGM
MONMSG      CPF0000
            OVRDBF      FILE(CUSTOMER)   SHARE(*YES)
            OVRDBF      FILE(SALESMEN)   SHARE(*YES)
            OPNDBF      FILE(CUSTOMER)   OPTION(*ALL)
            OPNDBF      FILE(SALESMEN)   OPTION(*ALL)
            GO          CUSTMENU
ENDPGM
```

Another method of employing the open data path methodology is to build or change the file so that the data path is always shared. Notice that the Create Physical File (CRTPF), Change Physical File (CHGPF), Create Display File (CRTDSPF), and Change Display File (CHGDSPF) commands give you the option of compiling the objects in such a manner that the data path is always shared.

You may want to share the open data path of a display file when you have several programs within a single job stream that happen to use the same display file. Employing this technique gives you the same advantages as if used with a database file.

RPG IV, the Next Generation

Now that ILE is available with Version 3, Release 1 (V3R1), you are allowed to read a record with one program and update it with another (as long as the open data path is shared). Another change with this release is that it allows you to share open data paths within a job or an activation group.

To summarize, if your application uses the same physical or display files over and over, those files may be opened and closed many times within a single job stream. This can cause big delays in application program initiation and help to create a situation where overall system performance is degraded significantly. You may also have applications that open files that never get closed (for one reason or another), creating a condition where your job has multiple open data paths for the same file. Using shared data paths can help alleviate these problems and help to improve overall system throughput.

Words of Caution

The term *shared* may be somewhat misleading because not all sessions have access to the open data paths. Only programs within the same session share the open data path.

There is also a warning to heed if you use the library list to manipulate which file on the system is to be used. When a file has been pre-opened with a shared open data path, an application program uses that file whether it is currently in your library list or not. The program simply uses the open data path of the shared file. If you do not have files with the same name in multiple libraries, this is not a problem for you.

Another thing to remember when using open data paths is that the file is always in use as long as the session exists. It does not matter whether or not a program is actually running. This can be a potential problem at times when a job needs dedicated access to a file (e.g., file saves). Files with shared data paths remain "in use" until the files are closed or the session is terminated.

Also, you can not assume that the file pointer will be where you want it when a program is initiated. If you are going to do any type of sequential read operation, remember to set your file pointer appropriately. You do not need to worry about this when the open data path is not shared because each program in the job stream will open and keep its own independent file pointer.

You also need to pay attention to how you open the file. In other words, you will experience problems if you open a file as *input only* and then try to update the file in a subsequent program.

There are other security and operational issues to consider before trying this particular method. More information on this technique is offered in the IBM AS/400 *Database Guide*, the *CL Reference Manual*, and the *ILE RPG/400 Programmers Guide*.

THE PATH YOU CHOOSE MAY BE THE MOST IMPORTANT PART OF YOUR JOURNEY

The path through your data is often the most critical decision you can make with regard to how an application performs. As stated earlier in this chapter, I/O has a dramatic effect on performance.

For example, if you choose to read a file by index instead of arrival sequence, you are making a choice to greatly increase the amount of work the system has to do. The AS/400 HLLs do not perform as well when reading a file by index as they do when they read data in arrival sequence. This is because, when a program reads a data file by an index key, the system must first read the key and then go out to get the physical data. So the HLL program must double the I/O processing right off the bat. Also, because the physical data is being accessed in a random fashion, the data can not be blocked (retrieving multiple records on every I/O operation) as it would be when the file is processed in arrival fashion. This increases the system resources that are used when the HLL program is run.

When running one of your RPG programs, you may have noticed a message in your job log stating that the key was to be ignored and the data was being processed in arrival sequence. This occurred because, at compile time, the system noticed that there was nothing in your RPG program that required the file to be processed randomly. In other words, there were no I/O operations, like CHAIN or SETLL, that required a key. Consequently, the system decided that, to be more efficient, the HLL program should process the data in arrival sequence and assigned a minimal blocking factor (more on blocking when we discuss reading files by the index).

Design Considerations with Regard to I/O Processing

When designing a new program, the choice is whether to read records in arrival sequence, to read by an index, or to use OPNQRYF or FMTDTA (sort) to sequence the data into the desired path. Unfortunately, the answer is: It depends. Answer these two, key questions before you decide which method to employ:

- Is the program interactive or will it run in batch?

- How big is the file that is being processed?

Most of the time when coding an interactive program, you do not have much of a choice. You will have a tough time trying to convince your salespeople that they are better off working with a subfile of their prospects in arrival sequence. He or she will want the subfile presented in a sequence that makes him or her more productive, with little or no regard to system performance. Who can blame them? Addressing system performance is your job, not theirs.

Batch programs should almost always be written to use FMTDTA or OPNQRYF. Even if there is already an index available for the sequence you desire, the program is likely to run faster if you get the data into the proper arrival sequence prior to processing it.

Avoid Reading Files by the Index Whenever You Can

If the program you are writing involves a data file with a handful of records (in the hundreds), it may be more efficient to read the file by keyed index. This is because there is a certain amount of overhead required to run FMTDTA or OPNQRYF. However, if the file you are reading has 250,000 records, you will notice a definite performance improvement if you put the data into the appropriate sequence first. Two options available to perform this task are either Format Data (FMTDTA) or Open Query File (OPNQRYF).

We should mention here that both of these options apply only to batch jobs. Interactive jobs that include Format Data or Open Query File can severely impact performance. Any job requiring these tools (generally where a large number of records are to be read) should be run in batch.

Since the addition of the ALLWCPYDTA(*OPTIMIZE) to the OPNQRYF command, there are few reasons to use the FMTDTA (sort) command. This new option allows the system to decide whether or not it is more efficient to sort the data.

Using OPNQRYF can range from the very simple to the very complex. Let's say, for example, that you have a daily sales report that has been written to read a logical file over your 250,000-record customer file by customer name. The code in Figure 1.5 could be embedded into a CL driver program to put the customer file (CUST) into customer name sequence prior to running the RPG program. The RPG program could then be changed to read the CUST file in arrival sequence.

Figure 1.5: Using OPNQRYF to Sequence Data into the Appropriate Arrival Sequence

```
OVRDBF FILE(CUST) SHARE(*YES)
OPNQRYF FILE((CUST)) ALWCPYDTA(*OPTIMIZE) KEYFLD((CUSNAM))
```

The net result of this change is a significant performance improvement. I/O is reduced because the system does not need to read the index first and then go out and get the data. The system also automatically blocks the data and multiple records are read each time the system has to go to the disk.

LOGICAL FILES ARE A VALUABLE TOOL, BUT DON'T OVERUSE THEM

The logical file is one of the most treasured gems in our toolbox, but most of us have abused the privilege of using it at one time or another. Why shouldn't we? The Sales Department asked us for a new report and we do not seem to have a data path that puts the data in the exact sequence they are looking for. It would be so easy to add that new logical file over the Customer Master file, write the report, and get the request off our desk.

DON'T DO IT!

Before adding a new logical file, consider the consequences of your actions. Depending upon the DDS and compile options you use when you create the logical file, you are potentially creating additional system overhead for your AS/400 every time that the physical file is updated. Even if you build the file so that the index maintenance is delayed, the index still has to build at some point.

The decision to create a new logical file should be based upon the run-time environment (batch or interactive) for which it is required. Logical files should not be created for programs that will run in a batch environment.

There are other disadvantages to logical files as well. Logical files require disk space for the index. File backups and restores take longer because they either have to save or rebuild the access path. There is also a certain amount of system overhead that the system incurs when keeping track of logical files and the physical files with which they are associated.

USING *SETOBJACC* TO REDUCE I/O AND MAXIMIZE MEMORY USAGE

Throughout this chapter, we have encouraged you to reduce the impact of the mechanical process of reading disk as it pertains to your application. One way to do this is to maximize use of your system memory.

The Set Object Access (SETOBJACC) command is used to pull objects (primarily programs, database files, and their access paths) into memory to reduce the amount of disk I/O required by the system. If a database file's index and data can be processed from memory rather than disk, the mechanical part of the task is removed from the equation and the processing is performed significantly faster. Obviously, how well this works depends upon the amount of main memory you have on your system, the time of day the job runs, and the size of the files or programs with which you are working.

The benefits of moving a physical file that must be processed randomly (by key) into memory will far outweigh the benefits of doing the same for a file that will be read in arrival sequence for two reasons:

- When you compile your RPG program, the compiler checks to see if you are processing a file in arrival sequence. If so, the system automatically *blocks* records when the program is run. *Blocking* is a term used to describe when the system retrieves multiple blocks of your data on each I/O request because the system determined the order in which you will be reading the records. How many blocks of data are retrieved depends upon algorithms within the operating system.

  Blocking is not effective on randomly accessed files because the system must work overtime to load records into memory that are not in the sequence the program expects. In fact, blocking can actually degrade the performance when applied to randomly accessed files.

- When you are reading a file by an index key, the system must first read the index record and then go out to seek the physical data.

The maximum advantage is attained if you can put both the physical file and its access path into main memory simultaneously. All of the I/O requests from within your program occur in memory rather than on disk.

Using the SETOBJACC command to put a file into memory is like record blocking, except that you can bring the entire file into memory at once. In the case of randomly accessed files, you want to bring both the data and the access path into memory, if you can. This can have a tremendous impact on program performance because the mechanical process of the disk I/O has been eliminated. The SETOBJACC command may be run interactively, or from within a program.

It should be noted here that the SETOBJACC command is not useful when the file is specified as output only. This is because the output operations are already "buffered" in memory (remember that all records are added to the end of a file unless you are reusing deleted records) and do not cause high levels of I/O activity.

There are basically two flavors to the SETOBJACC command: plain vanilla and tutti-frutti. Plain vanilla is very simple and great to use when your system is dedicated to a single task (like month end or daily startup). Tutti-frutti is a little more involved, but the benefits derived can be substantial.

Make Mine Vanilla, Please

Most AS/400 shops have certain times of the day, week, or month when dedicated processing can occur. If you have this luxury, you may want to look at this flavor of the SETOBJACC command to speed up the dedicated jobs that run at such times.

For our example in Figure 1.6, we take our customer physical file (CUST) in our library (FILES) and place it into main memory. Our job is to process the file randomly by key, so we also specify the MBRDATA parameter so that both the data and the access path are pulled into main memory (we could have indicated that just the access path or data be brought in).

Figure 1.6: Using SETOBJACC to Put Objects into Main Storage

```
SETOBJACC OBJ(FILES/CUST) OBJTYPE(*FILE) POOL(*JOB) MBRDATA(*BOTH)
```

When the SETOBJACC command is run, the system takes a "snapshot" of memory just prior to pulling your object into memory. It then sends a message to your job log that lets you know how much benefit you will gain from running the command. Figure 1.7 is an example of what the message looks like.

Figure 1.7: Message Sent When Running the SETOBJACC Command Showing Object Size and Space Available in the Memory Pool

```
19K of CUST brought to pool with 996K unused.
```

The message states that, prior to bringing 19K of the CUST file into memory, 996K of memory was available. Memory may not be available because main storage is not cleared of your objects just because a job ends. The objects in memory are left there until the space is needed for something else. If the message tells you that 0K was available prior to attempting to bring your object into memory, clear the memory pool first.

Clear the Pool!

For our example, let's assume the job is running interactively. In this case, the parameters for the Clear Memory Pool (CLRPOOL) command are very simple (Figure 1.8).

Figure 1.8: Clearing the Memory Pool

```
CLRPOOL POOL(*JOB)
```

The Clear Memory Pool (CLRPOOL) command clears all objects out of the main storage pool so there is plenty of room for the objects that we want to place there. The down side is that your job will be moved out of the main storage pool as well. We recommend signing off to end your job after running the Clear Memory Pool (CLRPOOL) command. When you sign back on, the memory pool is cleared and you will have initiated a new job.

With a clear memory pool, you are free to run the SETOBJACC command to put the objects you will be using into main memory. You can then run the rest of your job as you would normally. The only step left is to clear your objects from memory once your job is completed. There are two ways to do this. You can use the Clear Memory Pool (CLRPOOL) command as we did prior to placing objects into memory, or you can use the SETOBJACC command with slightly different parameters (Figure 1.9).

Figure 1.9: Clearing Objects from Main Storage After Using SETOBJACC to Put Them There

```
SETOBJACC OBJ(FILES/CUST) OBJTYPE(*FILE) POOL(*PURGE)
```

Time for Tutti-frutti

The tutti-frutti method would be used in nondedicated environments, but the same basic principles and advantages we experienced in the plain vanilla version apply. The difference is that, in the tutti-frutti version, you set up your own memory pools to store your most heavily used objects.

Memory Pools

Memory pool is simply a term used to describe the segregation of memory. When you install memory on the AS/400, it is automatically placed into the memory pool designated *BASE. If you leave your default system configuration alone, all of your subsystems will get their memory from this pool.

When processing in a nondedicated environment, it is best to create your own subsystem. When you create a subsystem and allocate memory to it, the memory the new subsystem uses is taken from the *BASE storage pool. The command to allocate 500K to pool number 2 in the SETOBJS subsystem is shown in Figure 1.10. Ensure that you have enough memory in the *BASE memory pool before executing the command. If there is not enough, decrease the size of some other subsystem that will return the memory to the *BASE pool. This can be done while working in the Work with System Status (WRKSYSSTS) command display.

Figure 1.10: Creating a Subsystem for SETOBJACC

```
CRTSBSD SBSD(QGPL/SETOBJS) POOLS((1 *BASE)(2 500K 1))
```

The 500K figure is for example only. You need to adjust it based on the size of the objects you are going to put in it. When you run the SETOBJACC command, it displays a message (like that shown in Figure 1.7) telling you the size of the object put into memory as well as the available space in the pool before the object was put in.

The example in Figure 1.7 shows that the object CUST has a size of 19K and was put into a memory pool that had 996K available prior to executing the SETOBJACC command. If there is not enough space available for the whole file, it might still be advantageous to bring in as much of the file as you can. Obviously, it's better to fit the whole object in the pool if possible. But remember, it's not the size of the object that is important, it's the number of times the file is being accessed. You can still improve response time by bringing a 20K file (or half of a 40K file) into memory if that file is accessed a jillion times a day.

The next step is to start the subsystem and initialize the memory pool. You should automate this process by making it part of your daily startup routine. The command in Figure 1.11 starts the subsystem and clears pool 2 in our SETOBJ subsystem, which is where we are going to load our files. Do not become confused by the numbering system of the pools. The AS/400 operating system divides memory into pools and numbers them. Pool 1 is the machine pool and pool 2 is the *BASE pool. All other pools are numbered consecutively from there. In addition, each pool can be segregated up to 10 times. We segregate ours twice, and put the memory in pool 2.

Figure 1.11: Clearing the User-created Private Main Storage Memory Pool

```
STRSBS SBSD(QGPL/SETOBJS)
CLRPOOL POOL(SETOBJS 2)
```

We can now bring the file into memory using the command in Figure 1.12. The SETOBJACC command executes extremely quickly, taking no more than a few seconds for most files.

Figure 1.12: Using SETOBJACC to Put Objects into a Private Main Storage Pool

```
SETOBJACC OBJ(FILES/CUST) OBJTYPE(*FILE) POOL(SETOBJS 2) MBRDATA(*BOTH)
```

Memory is Fast, Disk I/O is Slow

Bringing a file or program into memory (which is done with relatively few I/Os) can eliminate thousands of disk accesses throughout the day and prove to be a tremendous savings in transaction throughput. It requires some planning as to which objects should be in memory, but the rewards can far exceed the effort.

As you can see, the difference between plain vanilla and tutti-frutti is not all that great. Enjoy the improved performance and *bon appétit*.

TOO MUCH OF A GOOD THING CAN KILL YOU

We stress that you should concentrate on reducing I/O and maximize utilization of your system memory. But, like many good things in life, it is easy to go overboard.

If your system does not have enough memory or you are over-utilizing it in an effort to reduce I/O, your overall system performance can be degraded because your system is thrashing. In this case, there are too many objects contending for system memory and the system is trying to keep up by expending all of its resources moving pages temporarily from memory to disk and vice versa. This is similar to the drop-off in performance you notice on your PC when you do not have enough memory to run a job and "virtual memory" is used.

There are a variety of tools that can help you analyze if this is a problem on your system. We recommend that you take a class on Work Management if you think this may be an issue on your system.

REUSING DELETED RECORDS

The odds are pretty good that most of the physical files on your system can be broken down into three categories:

- Files that almost never change.

- Files that have records written to them regularly, but records never get deleted.

- Files that frequently have records written and deleted from them.

We concern ourselves with the second and third types in this section. Because the information in these types of files is not static, they can reach conditions that adversely affect performance if they are not maintained properly.

When you must read a file randomly by key, system performance is better when the physical data in the file is in the same order as the key by which you are reading it. This is because a single I/O operation is more likely to get a block of data that holds more than one record that must be processed. If the sequence of the data and the index do not match, the I/O operation will likely result in only a single record being processed before the system must go out and get another block (and the same block may need to be read later). The end result is that many more I/O operations may need to take place for the job to complete.

When a record is added to a file, the data normally is added to the end of the file, unless the REUSEDLT parameter was specified for the file. When REUSEDLT has been specified for a physical file, the system attempts to "reuse" records that were previously deleted whenever you add new records to the file. This parameter must be specified when the file is built (CRTPF), or you can change the file using the Change Physical File (CHGPF) command.

Using the REUSEDLT parameter can adversely affect system performance. The system has to search for deleted records every time a new record is added. This may or may not be a big deal, depending upon the size of the file as well as the percentage of deleted records. Secondly, because new records may be inserted into spots where deleted records previously existed, programs that were designed to process the file in arrival sequence may perform differently than what was intended initially.

THE RGZPFM COMMAND

Regardless of how records get added, if the index is added to randomly, the index and the data will not be in the same sequence after the add is performed. As we have repeatedly discussed, the greatest bottleneck for system performance is I/O. One way to combat this is to perform maintenance on files that experience heavy traffic. The Reorganize Physical File Member (RGZPFM) can be used to put the data and index back into the same sequence and, at the same time, remove any records that are flagged for deletion. Any programs that process the file randomly benefit from this process because the I/O is likely to be reduced (record size can affect this too because it directly relates to how many records are retrieved on a single I/O process).

The primary functions of the RGZPFM command are to remove deleted records from a physical file and to change the sequence of the records to match a selected index (usually this is the primary key to the physical file). If you have a physical file that is usually read by a specific logical file, it may be advantageous to reorganize the records in the file so they match the key of that particular logical file.

It can be surprising how much disk space gets tied up in deleted records if your data files never get reorganized. When a record gets deleted on the AS/400, it still takes up the same amount of space on disk until the record gets reused (if the file was designated to use the Reuse Deleted Records option, REUSEDLT) or the RGZPFM command is run. The file must not be in use when the RGZPFM command is run, so it may be a problem in some shops that do not have scheduled down time to perform system maintenance tasks.

If you do not specify any additional parameters, the RGZPFM command simply removes the deleted records from the physical file. If you choose to use the KEYFILE parameter, it can be used to resequence the data to match the key of the physical file or to match the path of a selected logical file. The examples in Figures 1.13 through 1.15 show our customer file being reorganized to remove deleted records only, to remove the deleted records and resequence the file into physical file key order, and so the data will be in customer name order (that is the path of the CUSBYNAM logical file), respectively.

Figure 1.13 : Using RGZPFM to Remove Deleted Records from a File

```
RGZPFM FILE(CUST)
```

Figure 1.14: Using RGZPFM to Remove Deleted Records and Resequence the Data to Match the Key to the Physical File

```
RGZPFM FILE(CUST) KEYFILE(*FILE)
```

Figure 1.15: Using RGZPFM to Remove Deleted Records and Resequence the Data to Match the Key of a Logical File

```
RGZPFM FILE(CUST) KEYFILE(CUSBYNAM)
```

Note: You do not want to use the KEYFILE parameter on a file that has no key. You will end up with an error message or a file that is not reorganized.

The *RGZPFFLTR* Command

The Reorganize Physical File Filter (RGZPFFLTR) command (explained in more detail in Chapter 11) can be a valuable tool if your shop has the luxury of being able to schedule unattended down time to perform system maintenance. The command can be setup as an autostart job that automatically reviews all of the files on your system to determine which files need to be reorganized. How it determines whether the RGZPFM process is required or not is based upon a percentage value you use when you call the RGZPFFLTR command.

The percentage refers to the level of deleted records in a file that you deem to be acceptable. For example, if you think that all files that have at least 10 percent of the records in them deleted should be reorganized, you would set the parameter at 10 percent.

In any case, the files that meet the prescribed percentage criteria are reorganized automatically into the order of the key of the physical file. This utility could take some time to run, depending upon the number of files that meet the specified criteria and the speed of your system, but the overall impact on system performance and DASD utilization could be appreciable.

Performance and the Dynamic Program Call

The ability to break down job streams into smaller subprograms is one of the wonderful things about the AS/400. RPG and CL can be used to break down larger jobs into smaller, more manageable components that can be used elsewhere. These modular components can be thought of as *reusable code*. They can be called from a variety of places to perform the same function. We think it is a good idea to code your programs with this thought in mind!

One example of this type of module is our window subfile program, used to decide to which printer a report should be sent (this sample program is in Chapter 2). You can call this program from any RPG or CL program and the operator is able to select a printer. The selection values are returned to the calling program parameters.

The program can be called from any other program that has been designed to request printed output. The fact that the same program can be called from many different places makes the code reusable. The greatest value to reusable code is that every time you enhance the reusable code, you are enhancing the utilization of all programs that call it.

As with most good things, however, there is a price to pay. Breaking down longer job streams into smaller, more manageable components can have an adverse effect on system performance. IBM announced ILE in V3R1, and for the first time, they gave us a choice between *dynamic* program calls and *static* program calls.

Pandora's Box

A *dynamic* call is a call to another program whose address is resolved at run time. This is the type of call we have always used in Original Program Model (OPM) programs. It is very flexible in that it can use the library list to locate the actual program to run, which means that it can be changed at run time. It is also very slow to initiate, especially if you are calling a program written in a different language. You execute a static call with the standard CALL op code.

A *static* call is a call to another program whose address is resolved when the program is created. This type of call initiates very quickly, as much as four times faster than a dynamic call. In fact, it initiates almost as fast as if the called program were coded as a subroutine in the calling program. You execute a static call with the new ILE Call Bound (CALLB) op code.

While static calls are much faster than dynamic calls, that speed can come with a heavy price tag. Static calls to programs other than service programs are *bound by copy*. That means a copy of the program being called is made in the calling program when it is compiled. That's why the called program can run almost as fast as if it were a subroutine in the calling program. Basically, it is!

Even given the dramatic performance improvement, binding by copy should be avoided unless you are in a very stable operational environment. It can indeed be the Pandora's Box of programming. It looks beautiful on the outside, but if you open it up, it can release plagues for the body and sorrow for the mind.

Making changes to programs that have been bound by copy to other programs can quickly become a cascading nightmare of never-ending changes. Each time you change a *module* (which we formerly referred to as a program) that happens to be bound by copy into multiple programs, each of those programs must be recompiled. Worse yet, some programs that call the changed program may be missed, causing different levels of the same program to exist on your system.

We have given you some tools in Chapter 11 to help you avoid this problem, but if your system is still being updated on a regular basis, you can easily end up with a very volatile situation. Visions of your tired old body being dragged out of bed in the middle of the night to fix a program that you already corrected but somehow the changes did not make it into the client's version should flash before your eyes anytime you consider opening this box.

As you may know, there was one redeeming quality in Pandora's Box, that of Hope. There is hope in the CALLB op code in that it sets the stage for fast, multilanguage programming. If you need a system function that is best coded in C, go ahead and use the CALLB. By performing the static call, you won't lose in the call overhead what you gained by coding in C in the first place.

Even without static program binding, a number of techniques can be employed to help reduce the impact on dynamic call performance. In the next section, we discuss changes you can make to your CL and RPG programs to reduce the effect of program calls.

The bottom line is this: Even though there is hope in the box, we recommend you keep the lid at least partially on it unless you are in a very stable operating environment.

CL Program Calls

CL program calls have a few downsides that RPG does not have, so here are a few tips to keep in mind when you are working with CL programs.

- If your CL program is designed to contain a loop where a program is called multiple times, use a qualified program name (indicating the library and program name) on your call instead of letting the library list determine where the program resides. Unlike RPG, the CL program does not keep internal pointers telling it where the program was found originally.

- If you have a choice of calling a CL program or an RPG program that both perform the same function, choose the RPG program. A CL program requires more overhead to call than an RPG program.

- If programs within the job stream will use the same files, seriously consider sharing open data paths (as discussed earlier). Reduced I/O nets you the greatest gain in performance.

RPG Program Calls

There are also several tips you can use to reduce system overhead when performing program calls from RPG. Here are a few we have come up with.

- If an RPG program is going to be dynamically called more than once in the job stream, consider using the RETRN op code instead of setting on LR. This keeps the program resident in memory so it does not need to repeatedly incur the overhead required for program initialization and file open and close operations. In making this change, however, you need to pay attention to file pointers, field usage, and indicator settings. Because the program does not terminate, these values are going to be what they were when you last exited the program.

- If you elect to employ this method, you should code a "last call" routine, which will call the program one last time to set on last record (LR) and release the resources it is hanging on to. This will prevent you from having rogue programs hanging around, sucking up valuable system resources.

- As previously mentioned, if you have a choice of calling a CL program or an RPG program that both perform the same function, choose the RPG program. A CL program requires more overhead to initiate than an RPG program.

Again, focus on the reduction of I/O operations. User-controlled file opens and shared open data paths can be used to reduce the effect of file open and close operations. Appropriate use of the SETOBJACC command or sharing open data paths can be used to minimize the effect of I/O on your programs.

ILE PERFORMANCE ISSUES

All of the performance issues raised so far in this chapter also apply to the ILE environment. But with ILE, there is even more to consider.

Never Buy at Retail Prices

The first thing you should consider when compiling an ILE program is the optimization level. The definition of the word optimization is performance! More specifically, it means maximizing the run-time performance of an object. The compiler does this amazing feat for you via the optimization techniques of the optimizing translator. These techniques look for processing shortcuts to reduce the amount of system resources used to produce the same output. Think of optimization as buying wholesale, not retail. You spend less money (resources) to get the same product (output).

You control the optimization level via the optimize parameter on the Create RPG Module (CRTRPGMOD), Create Program (CRTPGM), or Create Service Program (CRTSRVPGM) commands. Although you can specify optimizing on the Create Program commands, the actual optimizing techniques are applied to the modules. The values allowed for the optimize parameter are as follows:

> *NONE — minimal optimizing

> *BASIC — some optimizing

> *FULL — maximum optimizing

When testing and debugging your programs, you should first compile with optimization *NONE. This is the fastest compiling option (we don't know anybody who actually gets a program up and running, bug free, in production on the first compile). Once you have the program debugged, compile it again with the *FULL optimization option and then run through your final testing before putting it into production.

There is another reason, aside from the lengthy compile time, that you do not want to compile with the *FULL (or *BASIC) option while debugging a program. Because of the optimization techniques applied, you can not change the value of a variable while in debug. Worse yet, you may not be able to display the value of a variable! And even if it shows you a value, you can not rely on it being the correct, current value. We use debug 90 percent of the time to check on the value of a variable, so this negates the whole value of the debug process.

The reason for this inaccuracy is that the optimizer might have caused the current value of a data variable to be in a hardware register and the debugger can not access hardware registers. The factors used in making the determination to put a variable in a hardware register include how it is used, its size, and where in the code you have stopped. In short, you can not rely on the value shown for a variable if you are running it with an optimization level other than *NONE.

Activation Group Therapy

The next parameter on the create commands that needs our attention is the activation group parameter, ACTGRP. (See Chapter 13, "Integrated Language Environment (ILE) Concepts" for an in-depth look at activation groups). This parameter accepts three options:

- ACTGRP(you name it) — You give the system the name of the activation group in which it is to run. If the activation group exists, it is used. If not, a new one is created. The activation group is not destroyed when the program ends.

- ACTGRP(*NEW) — The system creates an activation group when the program is called, and deletes it when the program ends.

- ACTGRP(*CALLER) — The program runs in the activation group in which the calling program runs.

Given the fact that creating and deleting activation groups is resource intensive (and therefore a big performance hit), which option should you use? It seems pretty obvious that the *NEW option is the last one you would want to use for performance reasons. Guess which option is the default. You guessed it! The *NEW option is the default for the ACTGRP parameter on the create commands. No single individual at IBM would be allowed to make such a damaging decision. This one must have been made by committee, probably during group therapy. Everyone involved in this decision should seek help immediately!

You should *almost never* use the *NEW option. Use the user-named option instead.

The reason we say almost never (and not never) is that the *NEW option does provide a method of simulating recursive calls in RPG. If Program A calls Program B, and Program B then calls Program A, the system would normally generate a recursive call error condition. If, however, Program A were compiled with the *NEW option, the call to Program A would generate a new activation group for the second copy of Program A to run in. No error message would be generated.

This feature in itself, however, is not enough of a reason to justify making *NEW the default. Most programs should use the user-named option for the ACTGRP parameter.

REDUCING THE SIZE OF YOUR PROGRAMS

One way to reduce memory utilization on your system is to reduce the size of the programs that are being run. Logic tells us that, if the programs being loaded into memory were half the size, twice as many could fit in memory at once. There is a simple way to attain this goal without reprogramming or reducing the functionality of your system—remove program observability in your programs.

When a program is compiled, the system takes your source member and translates it into a program object that the machine can read and execute. As part of the compile process, the system automatically adds in program overhead to allow the program to be debugged. This extra program overhead that the compiler automatically built in is called *observability*.

Observability is a very valuable part of your toolbox when you are writing, implementing, and beta testing a new system. Without it, you would not be able to run Debug and it would take much longer to diagnose problems. But, once a system goes into production, you are not as likely to be running Debug all of the time. Why not use the Change Program (CHGPGM) command to remove the observability and cut the size of your programs in half? You can always restore observability by recompiling the program.

The results from removing observability vary, but we have seen some programs shrink to 40 percent of their original size. To run a test for yourself, simply display the size of a program by running the Display Program (DSPPGM) command. Then use the CHGPGM command to remove observability. Running the DSPPGM command again reveals how much you were able to reduce the size of your program. In our example in Figure 1.16, we remove observability from the CUSPGM program in library TESTLIB by keying the CHGPGM command.

Figure 1.16: Remove Program Observability and Reduce Program Size with CHGPGM

```
CHGPGM   PGM(TESTLIB/CUSPGM) RMVOBS(*ALL)
```

REDUCING SCREEN I/O IN YOUR INTERACTIVE PROGRAMS

Another way to improve overall system performance is to minimize the amount of data that must be passed to and from display panels from within your interactive programs. Rather than reduce the amount of information on the screens, you can move toward this goal by reducing redundant data.

Many interactive programs are designed to send an entire display panel full of data on every output to the screen. Sometimes the data being sent to the screen is almost identical to the information that is already displayed, with only one or two fields or display attributes changing from the previous display. This can create a situation where there is a lot more system traffic than is necessary. It is particularly noticeable if these programs are being run on terminals that are running over remote lines, where you can actually see the terminal "paint" the lines on the screen.

When a display panel is sent to the screen, display attributes must be sent as well as the data. These attributes control which fields are high-intensity, reverse-image, underline, nondisplay, input-capable, and much more. There is a lot of data beyond what you see that must be sent for every screen operation.

There is a way you can code your interactive programs so only the data and attributes that have changed since the previous screen I/O operation are sent to the screen. This method consists of utilizing the Put with Explicit Override (PUTOVR), Override Data (OVRDTA), and Override Attribute (OVRATR) DDS keywords.

PUTOVR is a DDS record-level keyword that essentially allows the system to "look" before presenting a display panel to see what needs to be sent to the screen. If the system determines that the display panel being sent is not already on the screen, the entire panel is displayed. On the other hand, if the display panel is already displayed, only fields that have the OVRDTA or OVRATR keywords in effect are sent to the screen. Using this technique can have a significant impact on how much data needs to be sent to the screen.

Using the example in Figure 1.17, we have used the PUTOVR keyword on the FORMAT1 display panel. Note that our customer number and customer name fields both have been coded to utilize the OVRDTA keywords. The CUSNBR field also has been coded with the OVRATR keyword.

Figure 1.17: Using the PUTOVR, OVRDTA, and OVRATR DDS Keywords

```
AAN01N02N03T.Name++++++RLen++TDpBLinPosFunctions++++++++++++++++++++++++++++++
A           R FORMAT1
A                                         PUTOVR
A                                       1 35'Customer Lookup'
A             PGMNAM        35    B  4 25DSPATR(RI)
A                                       4  5'Customer Number:'
A             CUSNBR         5    B  4 22OVRDTA
A                                         OVRATR
A  40                                     DSPATR(HI)
A             CUSNAM        35          +2OVRDTA
```

When FORMAT1 is initially written to the screen, the entire display panel is sent because the system detects that FORMAT1 is not already on the screen. On subsequent output operations to the screen, only the CUSNBR and CUSNAM fields are sent because they have been coded with the OVRDTA fields. Note that the PGMNAM field has not been coded with the OVRDTA keyword because it will not change after the initial output to the screen.

Also in our example, only the CUSNBR field has been assigned the OVRATR keyword. This means that the only field on the screen with display attributes that may change after the initial display is the CUSNBR field. If the indicator controlling the High Intensity attribute (indicator 40) is turned on, the field is updated on the following output to the screen. If the OVRATR keyword was not coded with the CUSNBR field, the display attributes do not change and the attributes in effect on the initial output operation remain in effect as long as the screen is displayed.

Both the OVRDTA and OVRATR keywords may be conditioned by indicators. You may want to go a step further than this example and condition these keywords so they are only active when the data or attributes are going to change.

DO NOT OVERLOOK THE OBVIOUS

If your system is experiencing performance problems (and whose isn't?), there are a number of things you should look for prior to changing programs. Some of the same things that make the AS/400 such a wonderful computer to work on can also lead to degraded performance. Just a few of the things that can cause degraded performance are the following:

- DASD (disk storage) that is over 80-percent utilized. Check your utilization with the WRKDSKSTS command. The AS/400 operating system needs room to work. If it does not have enough room, the system has to work overtime trying to find the space.

- Running jobs interactively that are better suited for batch environments. This is especially true if the job in question requires heavy I/O processing. Any job that runs for more than 30 seconds and does not require operator intervention or action is a candidate for batch processing.

- Moving batch jobs to subsystems that were set up to run interactive jobs. These jobs run with the incorrect run-time attributes and adversely affect interactive performance.

- Inadequate memory. You are far better off to have too much than too little. You may remember when 640K (640,000 bytes) was considered to be enough for a personal computer. Just try to run some of today's programs on 640K! These days, all computers require more memory in order to run. We have already shown you how to get more performance out of your system if you have enough main memory.

- Query and SQL. While these are wonderful tools, you need to ensure that they are not regularly run in an interactive environment. You pay a huge performance price if users on your system abuse this privilege.

- Message Logging Levels. How much information is being written to your job logs? This can have an effect on system performance if more information is being recorded than is required. (You learn all about the message logging levels in Chapter 10.)

- Journaling. If you use journaling, you pay a price for the overhead required. You are doubling the amount of the I/O operations required for the files undergoing journaling.

THE BLAME GAME

Numerous articles and publications that focus on the performance of RPG operation codes give the impression that using one operation code over another will have a serious impact on system performance. While we certainly do not deny that the AS/400 performs some operations better than others, we think the dramatic increase in processing power we have seen in the last few years greatly offsets the minimal impact of changing RPG operation codes.

Admittedly, by competitive performance standards, the AS/400 does not perform multiplication and division functions very well. It tends to lag when performing lookups on large arrays or when comparing very large fields to one another. Using file translation or the Translate (XLATE) operation code can cause delays.

But the odds are that you would not be using the function if you did not need it. Your time searching for improved performance would be far better served looking for I/O bottlenecks and memory over-utilization.

PERFORMANCE, PERFORMANCE, PERFORMANCE

Users simply will not be able to get fast enough performance. It is one of the rules in today's computing environment. The faster computers get, the more performance users expect. Who can blame them?

The simple truth is that the AS/400 is competing with lightning-fast, single-user systems that were not designed to run in a multiuser environment. They do not require all of the excess overhead that is considered to be mandatory in the "midrange" market. Of course they can be loaded with comparable layers of software to perform networking, database management, security, print spooling and spool management, and the multitude of other standard operating system functions we have come to expect from our beloved AS/400.

Unfortunately, most comparisons are not and will not be apples to apples. The AS/400 will continue to be considered a dog by some in the computing world, and it probably will never get the industry-wide reputation it so richly deserves.

It is up to the people at our level to get everything out of the system that we possibly can. You should consider your quest for better performance to be your own personal search for the holy grail. It is not whether you arrive at your destination that is important; rather, it is how much you learn along the way.

Chapter 2

Subfiles Belong in Every Programmer's Toolbox

The subfile originally appeared on the IBM System/38 as a simple method of storing data (usually a subset of a collection of database records) in memory for the purposes of presenting them as part of a display file. Like most of the System/38 operating system, the subfile was later migrated to the AS/400 where it has been greatly enhanced since that time.

A subfile is defined similarly to the way you define a database file. In fact, the subfile can be read, chained to, written to, or updated much like a database file. There are some characteristics that differentiate the subfile from the database file, however. You can store data in *hidden* fields—fields that are not displayed, but can be used when you process the file later. You can control which record the cursor is positioned at without having to keep track of a zillion indicators. You can present or process a group of records on the display at the same time with a single command. This list could go on and on, but the primary advantages are speed, performance, ease of coding/maintenance, and the ability to select several records to be processed within a single operation to the workstation.

In this chapter, we cover subfile fundamentals as well as some advanced topics, and code four very different kinds of subfiles. If you are a novice programmer, you should feel comfortable working with subfiles when you complete this chapter. If you are an intermediate- or advanced-level programmer, you may find a few gems within these pages.

THE BASICS

The two principle components of any subfile are the control record and the subfile record. Being true to its name, the control record is used to control the presentation of the subfile through a series of keywords, which generally are controlled with indicators. These keywords are used to indicate how many records are in the subfile, which function keys are allowed, how many records are displayed at one time, etc. The control record can also include input/output fields just as any other record format, and is often used to display the headings of each field in the subfile.

In Figure 2.1, we see a subfile presented in a DDS window. This subfile is used to help an operator select a printer when requesting a printed report or list. The control record (represented by the shaded area) presents the operator with five different options:

- Enter part or all of the printer description and press Enter to advance automatically to the description closest to the characters keyed.

- Enter a 1 in front of the desired printer record and press Enter to indicate the selected choice.

- Press the page keys to scroll forward or back through the printer description records.

- Press F12 to cancel and return to the previous screen.

- Press F3 to exit the application.

Figure 2.1: Subfile Control Record (shaded area)

```
.........................................................
:                                                       :
: Options: 1=Select                                     :
:                                                       :
: OR Key partial description: _____           :
:                                                       :
: Opt  Code          Description                        :
:  _   LASER6    ACCOUNTING - CHECKS                     :
:  _   LASER7    ACCOUNTING - INVOICES                   :
:  _   LASER3    ACCOUNTING - LASER PRINTER              :
:  _   PRT03     COMPUTER ROOM - INVOICE PRINTER         :
:  _   LASER1    COMPUTER ROOM - LASER PRINTER           :
:  _   PRT02     COMPUTER ROOM - LETTER QUALITY          :
:  _   LASER2    FRONT DESK - LASER PRINTER              :
:                                          More... :
: F3=Exit  F12=Previous                                 :
:                                                       :
.........................................................
```

The subfile record is where we define each data field in the subfile. The fields can be specified as input, output, or hidden fields (not displayed). The example in Figure 2.2 shows that the subfile record (represented by the shaded area) has three visible fields:

- An input-capable option field (Opt) to allow the operator to indicate the desired selection.

- The printer ID (Code) that is coded as output only.

- Extended description of the printer (Description), also coded as output only.

Figure 2.2: Subfile Record (shaded area)

```
.........................................................
:                                                       :
: Options: 1=Select                                     :
:                                                       :
: OR Key partial description: _____           :
:                                                       :
: Opt  Code          Description                        :
:  _   LASER6    ACCOUNTING - CHECKS                     :
:  _   LASER7    ACCOUNTING - INVOICES                   :
:  _   LASER3    ACCOUNTING - LASER PRINTER              :
:  _   PRT03     COMPUTER ROOM - INVOICE PRINTER         :
:  _   LASER1    COMPUTER ROOM - LASER PRINTER           :
:  _   PRT02     COMPUTER ROOM - LETTER QUALITY          :
:  _   LASER2    FRONT DESK - LASER PRINTER              :
:                                          More... :
: F3=Exit  F12=Previous                                 :
:                                                       :
.........................................................
```

In the example in Figure 2.2, we easily could have coded the printer ID field (Code) as a hidden field and only displayed the description on the screen. The printer ID field would still be available when we went to process the subfile.

Another thing to notice in the preceding example is that the literal More... is displayed near the bottom of the screen. This indicates that pressing the Page Down key results in the presentation of a new page of subfile records. This feature is discussed in more detail under the heading "The Subfile End (SFLEND) Keyword."

THE SUBFILE RECORD FORMAT (SFL) DDS

When coding a subfile, you must always define the subfile first, and then the control record. The DDS for the subfile record is similar to DDS for a database file, except that you are coding a file that will be presented to the screen and reside only in memory.

A subfile record format must have at least one display field (the exception to this rule is a message subfile, which we talk about later in this chapter). The field locations on the detail records represent the line and position of the fields as they will appear on the first subfile record displayed. The system figures out where the subsequent records belong on the screen based upon the value of the Subfile Page Size (SFLPAG), which is defined in the control record format.

Figure 2.3 shows the definition of a sample subfile record format. Note that the SFACCOUNT# field is defined as a hidden field with a use type of H and there are no line or position entries. This field stores data that we can use later when processing the file, but the data in SFACCOUNT# is not displayed on the screen. The SFLSELECT and SFCUSTDESC fields are displayed beginning on the seventh line in positions 2 and 5, respectively.

Figure 2.3: DDS for a Subfile Record Format

```
.....AAN01N02N03T.Name++++++RLen++TDpBLinPosFunctions+++++++++++++++++++++++++++++
     A           R SFLRCD                       SFL
     A             SFACCOUNT#    10   H
     A             SFLSELECT      1A  B  7  2
     A             SFCUSTDESC    30A  O  7  5
```

THE SUBFILE CONTROL RECORD FORMAT (SFLCTL) DDS

The subfile control record gives you the ability to indicate how the subfile should be presented and should react when various conditions present themselves. There are four record-level keywords that are mandatory for every subfile control record format (see Table 2.1).

Table 2.1: Mandatory DDS Keywords for a Subfile Control Record Format

Keyword	Description
SFLCTL	Subfile Control. Indicates that the record format will control a subfile. It must be coded directly after the subfile record format that it is to control.
SFLDSP	Subfile Display. Indicates to the system that the subfile should be displayed when an output operation is performed on the subfile control record. An option indicator is usually coded with this keyword. If you perform an output operation to the subfile control record while this keyword is active and there are no subfile records to display, your program receives an error message. By indicating an option indicator on the SFLDSP keyword and only turning it on if there happen to be subfile records to display, you avoid the error message.
SFLPAG	Subfile Page. Describes the size of the subfile "page." Generally speaking, this keyword describes how many subfile records appear on the screen at one time. If each subfile record format takes up only one line of the screen, this number matches the number of lines on the screen taken up by the subfile (SFLPAG is 7 for the example in Figure 2.2). On the other hand, if each subfile record format uses two lines, SFLPAG is half of the number of lines required by the display file. Note that not every subfile record must take up the same number of lines (a variable number of lines is allowed if you are using the field selection technique that is discussed later in this chapter).

Keyword	Description
SFLSIZ	Subfile Size. Defines the number of records in the subfile. How this keyword affects the operation of the subfile depends upon whether or not the Subfile Page (SFLPAG) and the Subfile Size (SFLSIZ) are equal (more on this subject later in the chapter). The system may change the value in this field, depending upon conditions that we discuss later in this chapter.

The Subfile Display Control (SFLDSPCTL) keyword (described in the next section) is also required if you are performing any input operation with the subfile control record.

The rest of the keywords that may be used on a subfile control record cover a wide variety of functions. The length of the list may seem a little intimidating, but you will find that many of the keywords are rarely used. In this chapter, we cover the keywords that we feel are most pertinent. The optional subfile control keywords (as of V3R1) are listed in Table 2.2.

Table 2.2: Optional DDS Keywords for a Subfile Control Record Format

Keyword	Description
SFLCLR	Subfile Clear. When you perform an output operation to the subfile control record with this keyword active (conditional indicators are advised), the subfile is cleared of all data. SFLCLR is similar to the Subfile Initialize (SFLINZ) keyword, except that no subfile records exist after execution of this keyword. You need to remember to turn off the conditioning indicator for the Subfile Display (SFLDSP) keyword after performing the SFLCLR operation. Failure to do so causes an error message if you try to perform a subsequent output operation to the subfile control record and you have not written any subfile records first.

Keyword	Description
SFLCSRRRN	Subfile Cursor Relative Record Number. This optional keyword is used to return (to the program) the relative record number of the subfile record where the cursor is currently positioned. The parameter for the keyword is the name of the signed numeric hidden field that you must define in the control record that is used to hold the subfile relative record number.
SFLDLT	Subfile Delete. This conditional keyword is used to delete a subfile. This operation normally is not required with most subfiles because closing the display file accomplishes the same goal. The exception to this rule is if you already have the maximum number of subfiles (12) on the screen, and you need to get rid of one to make room for another.
SFLDROP	Subfile Drop. This conditional keyword is used when the subfile record format requires more than one line on the display. When a subfile record takes more than one line on the display, it is *folded*. When an output operation is performed on the subfile control record with the SFLDROP keyword active, the subfile records are truncated so that they fit on a single display line (the additional information does not appear) and more records will fit on a single page. Execution of the SFLDROP keyword on records that have already been truncated results in the display of the records in a folded state.
SFLDSPCTL	Subfile Display Control. This conditional keyword indicates whether or not the subfile control record format should be displayed when you send an output operation to it. You must use this keyword if you plan to perform any input operations on the subfile control record format (even if no fields are displayed).
SFLEND	Subfile End. Tells the system what action to take when the end of the subfile is encountered. Options on this keyword allow for a plus sign (+), More..., and Bottom, or a graphical scroll bar (on graphical displays only). We discuss SFLEND later in this chapter (see "The Subfile End (SFLEND) Keyword").

Keyword	Description
SFLENTER	Subfile Enter. This optional keyword is used to indicate that the Enter key (or other function key) act as a Page Up key.
SFLFOLD	Subfile Fold. This optional keyword is similar to the SFLDROP keyword, except the multiple-line subfile records initially are brought up in a folded state (instead of truncated). Performing an output operation to the subfile control record format with this keyword active switches the subfile records from a truncated to a folded state and vice versa.
SFLINZ	Subfile Initialize. Used to initialize a subfile to blanks, nulls, and zeros (depending upon the field type). The optional keyword is similar to the SFLCLR keyword, except that the subfile is initialized (records will exist) instead of cleared.
SFLLIN	Subfile Line. Used to describe multiple-column subfiles. This optional keyword can be used when you want to show more than one subfile record on a single display line. The additional parameter is used to specify how many spaces to place between the displayed records. When used, the records are written from top to bottom and then left to right. In other words, the first set of records appears top to bottom in the first column, the next set appears top to bottom in the next column, and so on.
SFLMODE	Subfile Mode. This optional keyword may be used in conjunction with the SFLDROP or SFLFOLD keywords. The required parameter is used to define a hidden field that returns whether or not the subfile is displayed presently in a folded or a truncated mode. You must define the parameter as a hidden, 1-byte alphanumeric field in the subfile control record format.
SFLMSG	Subfile Message. This conditional keyword displays a message when an output operation is performed on the subfile control record format. More on this subject later when we discuss error handling with a message subfile.

Keyword	Description
SFLMSGID	Subfile Message ID. Can be used to conditionally display messages from the specified message file when an output operation is performed on the subfile control record. We cover this in more depth when we discuss error handling with a message subfile.
SFLPGMQ	Subfile Program Queue. This optional keyword can be used in conjunction with the SFLINZ keyword to build a message subfile. The entire message subfile can be built with a single output operation on the subfile control record format. This keyword is unique in that it may appear on the subfile record format or the subfile control record format.
SFLRCDNBR	Subfile Record Number. Allows you to indicate which page of the subfile should be displayed when an output operation is performed on the subfile control record format. If you do not specify this keyword, the system automatically presents the first page of the subfile to the screen. The field associated with this keyword must contain the relative record number of the subfile record you wish to see on the first page. The CURSOR parameter of this keyword can be used to indicate that the cursor is to be positioned automatically at the relative record number in question. The *TOP parameter can be used to indicate that the relative record number specified should represent the record that you wish to position at the top of the screen. If you omit this parameter, the SFLRCDNBR keyword ensures that the record specified appears somewhere on the screen.
SFLRNA	Subfile Records Not Active. Used in conjunction with the Subfile Initialize (SFLINZ) keyword to indicate that, when the subfile is initialized, it is left with no active records.
SFLROLVAL	Subfile Roll Value. Used to describe an input field on the subfile control record. The operator uses the input field to indicate how many subfile records to page up or down. When this keyword is omitted, the system automatically pages the entire value specified in Subfile Page (SFLPAG).

Keyword	Description
SFLSCROLL	Subfile Scroll. This field is used to return the relative record number of the subfile record at the top of the screen back to your program when scroll bars are being used. Scroll bars are an optional feature that can be specified on the Subfile End (SFLEND) keyword if you happen to be using graphical displays.

A sample subfile control record has been coded in Figure 2.4. Note that the SFLCTL, SFLDSP, SFLPAG, and SFLSIZ required keywords are all present. We have added SFLDSPCTL so that our subfile control record is displayed when we write an output operation to the control record. Subfile End (SFLEND) was added so the literal More... or Bottom is displayed on our subfile depending upon how indicator 41 is conditioned when we perform the output operation.

Figure 2.4: DDS for a Subfile Control Record Format

```
.....AAN01N02N03T.Name++++++RLen++TDpBLinPosFunctions+++++++++++++++++++++++++++
     A             R SFLCTL                      SFLCTL(SFLRCD)
     A                                           SFLSIZ(0010)
     A                                           SFLPAG(0010)
     A                                           SFLDSP
     A                                           SFLDSPCTL
     A    41                                     SFLEND(*MORE)
```

You are going to find that writing subfile programs is not that difficult. However, there are more issues that we need to discuss before we begin coding.

LOADING THE SUBFILE

Two methodologies may be employed when loading subfiles. One method is to write enough records to fill a single page of the subfile and then execute the subfile control format. This type of subfile is generally referred to as a *page-at-a-time* subfile. The second method of loading a subfile is to write all database records to the subfile before executing the control format. We refer to this second type as a *load-all* subfile.

The load-all subfile type should *only* be used when there is a fixed, small number of records that ever will be displayed. Remember that these records are being written into main storage memory, and your program is not the only resource contending for that valuable space. If too many programs contend for main memory, the system spends all of its time moving objects in and out of main storage and performance suffers. Second, why perform all of the extra I/O required to fill the subfile? Remember that someone is sitting and waiting at the keyboard while this task is performed. Use the advice that your parents gave you and just take what you need.

If there is a large (or an unknown) number of records to be written to the subfile, you should *always* use the page-at-a-time style of subfiles.

THE RELATIONSHIP BETWEEN SUBFILE SIZE (SFLSIZ) AND SUBFILE PAGE (SFLPAG)

Regardless of whether you are employing page-at-a-time or load-all subfiles, there are two primary categories of subfiles. These types are distinguishable based upon the relationship between the number of records allowed in the subfile (SFLSIZ) and the number of records to be displayed in a single subfile page (SFLPAG).

When SFLSIZ and SFLPAG are the Same

When SFLSIZ and SFLPAG are the same, the maximum number of records allowed in the subfile can never exceed the number of records to be displayed on a single page. The SFLDROP, SFLFOLD, and SFLROLVAL keywords are invalid for this type of subfile because they refer to functions that require more than one page of records to exist in the subfile. Likewise, when an operator presses the Page Up or Page Down keys, control is always returned to the RPG program.

Field selection can be employed on this type of subfile where you use indicators to determine which fields appear in the subfile. Introduction of this type of inconsistency in the data makes the SFLINZ, SFLLIN, SFLRCDNBR, and SFLRNA keywords invalid as well.

When SFLSIZ and SFLPAG are Not Equal

When the values specified for SFLSIZ and SFLPAG are not the same, the system processes the Page Up and Page Down keys without returning control to the RPG program as long as there are records in the subfile to scroll through. When the beginning or end of the subfile is encountered within the scrolling process, control is returned to the RPG program where the decision to write more records or perform some other function can be made.

Typically with this type of subfile, you initially load enough records into the subfile to present a single page and then perform the output operation on the subfile control record format. If the operator presses Page Down, control is returned to the RPG program (there are no more records in the subfile to display) where your program writes an additional page of data to the subfile without clearing the original records and then repeats the process. Using this method, if the operator presses Page Up (after pressing Page Down at least once), the paging is handled entirely by OS/400 without ever having to return control to the RPG program until the beginning of the subfile is encountered.

Another characteristic of this type of subfile is that the subfile automatically extends itself to contain additional records if you write a subfile record with a relative record number greater than the value specified in the SFLSIZ keyword. It continues to extend itself up to 9,999 records, which is the maximum that may be specified for a subfile. It is for this reason that you want to make sure that the field you designate as the subfile relative record number is defined with enough digits to contain the potential end result.

Deciding the initial size of the subfile can be important. If SFLSIZ is too big, memory is wasted, which could hurt overall response time. If the SFLSIZ is too small, the system may be working overtime to extend the size of the subfile continuously. In general, we like to code the SFLSIZ as two or three times the SFLPAG.

THE PAGE KEYS AND THEIR RELATIONSHIP TO THE SUBFILE

As we discussed earlier, the system handles rolling when the page keys are pressed, as long as there are records to display. If you have coded the load-all style of subfile, you do not need to code anything to handle the page keys at all (including the Roll and Page keywords in the subfile control record) because OS/400 performs the task for you.

On the other hand, if you have coded the preferred page-at-a-time subfile, you have a little more work to do. When the subfile hits the end or start of the file (depending upon which page key is pressed), control is passed back to the RPG program so more records can be written.

The Page Down Key for Page-at-a-time Subfiles

When the Page Down key is pressed and the last page of records that have been written to the subfile is displayed, control is returned to the RPG program. A new page of subfile records is added then (without clearing the previous records) and the subfile is displayed. This process continues as long as there is data left to be written to the subfile. Once the condition is reached where no more data exists with which to populate the subfile, the indicator that corresponds with the Subfile End (SFLEND) keyword is set on and the subfile is displayed once again. In Figure 2.4, indicator 41 represents the SFLEND indicator.

The Page Up Key for Page-at-a-time Subfiles

If the user presses the Page Up key and the first page of the subfile is currently displayed, control is returned to the program as well. The database file must first be repositioned so the database file pointer corresponds to the first record in the subfile. To complete the setting of the database file pointer, the program must then read backwards until it has read enough records to fill a subfile page.

Because the program is rolling backwards through the data, the subfile must be cleared before writing a new set of subfile records so that pages won't get out of sequence. This is done by performing an output operation to the subfile control record with the indicators set so that either the Subfile Clear (SFLCLR) or the Subfile Initialize (SFLINZ) keyword is active at the time. You must remember to reset your indicators after clearing the subfile or you will experience problems with subsequent output requests.

After the database file pointer has been reset and the subfile has been cleared, we can loop back up as if the user had pressed the Page Down key.

Controlling Which Page of the Subfile You See First

When the last page of the subfile is not currently displayed and the Page Down key is pressed, the system rolls the screen to the next page in the subfile without ever returning control to the RPG program. On the other hand, if the user presses the Page Down key and the last page of the subfile is displayed, control is returned to the program and we simply continue reading the database records (as long as there are records to read) and writing to the subfile records.

Once we have loaded another page, we redisplay the subfile. The problem with this is that, when a subfile is displayed, the default setting is to display the subfile from the beginning of the subfile. In other words, the first page is always displayed initially. Consequently, if we write additional pages to the subfile and perform an output operation on the subfile control record, the first page of the subfile is displayed again and it looks as if nothing happened. The user must press the Page Down key a second time (where control would not be returned to the RPG program because subfile records already exist) to see the additional pages that were written. Fortunately, there is a solution to this problem. We can control which page of the subfile is displayed by using the Subfile Record Number (SFLRCDNBR) keyword.

To use the SFLRCDNBR keyword, define a four-character, zoned numeric field (with zero decimal positions) within the subfile control record that is used to store a subfile relative record number as we have in Figure 2.5. Generally, we code this field as a hidden field. The program must load this field with the relative record number of a record that is in the page we want displayed. The system then displays that page, but the record corresponding to the relative record number we loaded into the SFLRCDNBR field is not necessarily at the top of the screen.

Figure 2.5: Using the SFLRCDNBR Keyword

```
.....AAN01N02N03T.Name++++++RLen++TDpBLinPosFunctions+++++++++++++++++++++++++++++
     A           R SFLCTL                      SFLCTL(SFLRCD)
     A                                         SFLSIZ(0020)
     A                                         SFLPAG(0010)
     A                                         SFLDSP
     A             SFLRCDNBR     4  0H          SFLRCDNBR
```

Using the example in Figure 2.5, we can use the SFLRCDNBR keyword to control which page of the subfile is to be displayed. To use this option, we load the appropriate subfile relative record number into the SFLRCDNBR field prior to performing an output operation to the subfile control record format. If there are 30 records in the subfile and we want the third page to be displayed, we put any number between 21 and 30 into the SFLRRN field to attain our desired results.

If you want a specific record to appear at the top of the subfile screen, load the appropriate relative record number into the SFLRCDNBR field and use the *TOP parameter in the DDS. This gives you control over which specific record appears at the top of each screen.

You can also use the SFLRCDNBR field to control where the cursor is positioned within the subfile by using the CURSOR parameter. This offers a good alternative to using the position cursor (PC) display attribute within your subfile. The problem with using the display attribute to position the cursor is that the position cursor attribute remains in effect until you update the subfile record with the conditioning indicator off. Subsequent output requests to the subfile control record may have the cursor positioned where you no longer want it.

THE SUBFILE END (SFLEND) KEYWORD

The SFLEND keyword is used to indicate to the program operator whether or not there are more records that may be displayed in the subfile. This keyword is only activated when there are no more records to be written to the subfile.

When we are coding the load-all subfile, we can go ahead and set the conditioning indicator for the SFLEND keyword on from the outset because we know that all the records that ever will be written to the subfile are being written from the start.

But when we are coding page-at-a-time subfiles, we are only going to write records to the subfile as needed, so we do not turn the conditioning indicator on until there are no more records to write. In most cases, this means that we have reached an end-of-file condition on the database file that we happen to be loading into the subfile.

There are three different output options that may be employed when using the SFLEND keyword. The parameter used with the SFLEND keyword indicates to the system which output option you want to use. These optional parameters are *MORE, *PLUS, and *SCRBAR.

Using the SFLEND Keyword with the *MORE Parameter

The *MORE parameter of the SFLEND keyword is probably the most familiar because it is used to display the More... and Bottom literals on the screen much as you see on many output displays throughout the AS/400 operating system. The *MORE keyword tells the system to display More... at the end of every page of the subfile unless the conditioning indicator is on *and* the last page of the subfile currently is displayed, in which case the literal Bottom is displayed. The drawback to using the *MORE parameter on the SFLEND keyword is that you must leave an entire unused line where the More... or Bottom literals appear. This unused line is automatically the line that directly follows the last record of the subfile (output line of the first subfile record + SFLPAG + 1 line).

If you fail to leave the line blank when using the *MORE parameter, your Display File will not compile.

Using the SFLEND Keyword with the *PLUS Parameter

The default option on the SFLEND keyword is *PLUS where a plus sign (+) is displayed in lieu of the More... literal. When the last page of the subfile is displayed and the SFLEND conditioning indicator has been turned on, no plus sign (+) is displayed. This method can be an advantage in that it does not require the extra blank display line that *MORE requires, but its intent is not as clear to some program operators. When present, the plus sign (+) automatically overlays the last three positions of the last subfile record on a page, which may cause a problem if you are not careful when laying out your subfile record on the screen.

Using the SFLEND Keyword with the *SCRBAR Parameter

The final output option parameter for the SFLEND keyword is *SCRBAR, where a graphical scroll bar can be utilized. This option was made available as part of V3R1 and, obviously, only applies to graphical workstations with device descriptions that support a pointer device (generally a mouse). When using the *SCRBAR parameter, you can also specify the *MORE or *PLUS parameter, so the system knows which option to exercise when the application is run from a nongraphical workstation.

The scroll bar works much as it would with other graphical interfaces in that it has a cursor to indicate how big the subfile is and where you are within it. The cursor can be moved with the pointing device and the subfile is repositioned accordingly.

You must leave the three right-most characters in your subfile record blank to leave room for the scroll bar to appear on the screen. This restriction is similar to the extra blank line that must be left when using the *MORE parameter.

By the very nature of the page-at-a-time and load-all subfiles we have discussed, the scroll bar option is a lot more attractive with the latter than it is with the former. If you use the page-at-a-time subfile, the cursor within the scroll bar could be somewhat misleading because it represents the number of records that currently are in the subfile and not those that ultimately could end up there. When used in a load-all subfile, the cursor is obviously a much better representation of where the operator is within the file.

Figure 2.6 shows what a subfile scroll bar looks like. We code the program that presents this display later in this chapter.

Figure 2.6: Example of a Subfile Scroll Bar

```
Options: 1=Select or press ENTER to cancel

Option   State      Description
           AK        ALASKA
           AL        ALABAMA
  _        AR        ARKANSAS
  _        AZ        ARIZONA
  _        CA        CALIFORNIA
  _        CO        COLORADO
  _        DE        DELAWARE
  _
```

CODING THE "CUSTOMER SUBFILE" DISPLAY FILE

Having said all that, writing the code necessary to create and display a subfile is actually fairly simple. The first subfile program we will code is a page-at-a-time subfile used to display a customer file in customer number sequence. This program is not all that functional, but a good example of a variety of the concepts we have been discussing.

As you can see from Figure 2.7, the program operator has the option of pressing the page keys to scroll through the customer file, or pressing Enter to end the program. Every time the Page Down key is pressed, we add a new page of subfile records and perform an output/input operation (EXFMT) to the subfile control record. When the operator presses the Page Up key, our program clears the subfile (so subfile records are not written out of order), resets the database pointers, rebuilds the subfile, and performs the I/O operation.

Figure 2.7: Sample "Customer Subfile" Display

```
                            Customer Subfile


    Press PAGE keys, or Enter to Cancel

    Customer Name              Customer Number
  JEFF'S COMPUTER CABLES           10
  SORRENTO ELECTRICAL SUPPLY       11
  ENCINITAS PAINT                  12
  JOLLYTIME LANDSCAPE              13
  WESTONHILL PROPERTY MANAGEMENT   14
  SOUTH BAY PLUMBING               15
  CHULA VISTA SPRINKLER SUPPLY     16
  SANTEE ELECTRICAL                17
  BAYSIDE REALTY                   18
  ESCONDIDO NURSERY                19
  HOME DEPOT                       20
  WESTERN LUMBER                   21

                                                              More...
```

Let's examine the subfile record and subfile control record as they have been defined in the DDS specifications shown in Figure 2.8. As required, the Subfile Record (SFLRCD) is defined before and directly prior to the Subfile Control Record (SFLCTL). The SFLCTL keyword indicates which subfile record (SFLRCD in this case) is being controlled by the subfile control record format.

Figure 2.8: DDS for "Customer Subfile"

```
     A****************************************************************
     A*   TO COMPILE:
     A*      CRTDSPF FILE(XXXLIB/FIG28DS)
     A****************************************************************

.....AAN01N02N03T.Name+++++RLen++TDpBLinPosFunctions+++++++++++++++++++++++++++
     A          R SFLRCD                    SFL
     A            SFCUSTNAME    30A  O  7  2
     A            SFCUSTNBR     10A  O  7 36
     A          R SFLCTL                    SFLCTL(SFLRCD)
     A                                      SFLSIZ(0024)
     A                                      SFLPAG(0012)
     A 21                                   SFLDSP
     A 22                                   SFLDSPCTL
     A 23                                   SFLCLR
     A 24                                   SFLEND(*MORE)
     A                                      ROLLDOWN(27)
     A                                      ROLLUP(28)
     A            SFLRCDNBR      4   0H     SFLRCDNBR
     A                                    1 29'Customer Subfile'
     A                                      DSPATR(HI UL)
     A                                    4  5'Press PAGE keys, or Enter to-
     A                                         Cancel'
     A                                    6  2'   Customer Name            -
     A                                         Customer Number'
     A                                      DSPATR(HI UL)
```

The subfile control record contains the four mandatory keywords required for every control record format: Subfile Control (SFLCTL), Subfile Display (SFLDSP), Subfile Size (SFLSIZ), and Subfile Page (SFLPAG).

Note that, in our example, SFLSIZ and SFLPAG have different values. SFLPAG has a value of 12 (meaning that up to 12 records appear on the screen at one time) and SFLSIZ contains 24 records (indicating that the subfile will usually consist of about two pages of data). If more than 24 records are written to the subfile, the system automatically extends the size of the subfile to the number of records needed, but users may notice a slight pause in response time while the system performs this task.

We also conditioned the SFLDSP keyword (telling the system when to display the subfile records) with an indicator. If we fail to condition this keyword and an attempt is made to display subfile records when no records have been written to the subfile, the system responds with an error message. We only turn on the conditioning indicator (21) for the SFLDSP keyword if a record is written to the subfile.

The SFLDSPCTL keyword tells the system when to display the control record. This keyword is required on this subfile because we are performing input requests on the subfile control record format, and we have information on the subfile control record format that we wish to display. We have conditioned the SFLDSPCTL on an indicator (22) because we do not want the subfile control record to be displayed when we perform an output operation on the subfile control record to clear the subfile.

An indicator (23) is used to condition the Subfile Clear (SFLCLR) keyword that is only turned on when we want the subfile cleared. For our purposes in this program, this condition is met when the operator presses Page Up. Failure to properly condition this keyword could result in the subfile being cleared on each output operation to the control file record.

The status of the Subfile End (SFLEND) keyword is based upon an indicator (24), which we turn on once we find the end of our customer database file. Turning on this indicator causes the Bottom literal to appear when the last page of the subfile is displayed. When all other pages are displayed, the Page Down key is enabled and the More... literal appears just below the last subfile record.

The ROLLDOWN and ROLLUP keywords are coded to set on indicators 27 and 28 (depending on which key is pressed). Note that the PAGEUP and PAGEDOWN keywords have been added as DDS keywords to be used in lieu of the ROLLUP and ROLLDOWN keywords. They work the exact same way as their counterparts, except that PAGEUP is the equivalent of ROLLDOWN and PAGEDOWN is the equivalent of ROLLUP.

We use the Subfile Record Number (SFLRCDNBR) field to control which page of the subfile is displayed. The subfile relative record number we load into the SFLRCDNBR field determines which page of the subfile is displayed. In this example, we have not specified any parameters for this keyword to indicate where the cursor should be (we have no input fields), and we do not care if the record we specify in the SFLRCDNBR field is at the top of the screen or not.

CODING THE "CUSTOMER SUBFILE" RPG PROGRAM

The RPG program in Figure 2.9 typifies what is involved in writing a page-at-a-time subfile. We read enough database records to fill a page of the subfile and then perform an Execute Format (EXFMT) on the subfile control record so the operator can decide what the next course of action should be. Taking this approach ensures that we have done the minimal number of disk I/O operations on the database file, and that initially there is very little memory required to store our subfile. Because we can not be absolutely certain how many records our customer database file may contain, this is the most logical method to use when designing this subfile.

Figure 2.9: RPG Program for "Customer Subfile"

```
****************************************************************
 *  TO COMPILE:
 *     CRTBNDRPG PGM(XXXLIB/FIG29RG)
 ****************************************************************
FFilename++IPEASF.....L.....A.Device+.Keywords++++++++++++++++++++++++++++++Comments++
FFIG28DS   CF   E                WORKSTN
F                                          SFILE(SFLRCD:SflRcdNbr)
FCUSTOMER  IF   E           K DISK
DName++++++++++ETDsFrom+++To/L+++IDc.Keywords++++++++++++++++++++++++++++++Comments++
D X            S              3 0
CL0N01Factor1+++++++Opcode&ExtFactor2+++++++Result+++++++Len++D+HiLoEq....Comments++
 * Read the first record...
C                   READ      CUSTOMER                          41
C                   MOVEA     '0100'         *IN(21)
 * Stay in the loop until page keys are pressed...   27 = page up, 28 = page down
C                   DOU       (*In27 = *OFF) and (*In28 = *OFF)
C                   DO        12             X
 * Write subfile record if valid record was read...
C                   IF        *In41 = *OFF
C                   EVAL      SfCustName = CustName
C                   EVAL      SfCustNbr  = Customer#
C                   EVAL      SflRcdNbr  = SflRcdNbr + 1
C                   EVAL      *In21 = *ON
C                   WRITE     SFLRCD
C                   READ      CUSTOMER                          41
```

```
C                       ELSE
 * Turn on SFLEND (subfile end) indicator if end of file was encountered
C                       EVAL      *In24 = *ON
C                       ENDIF
C                       ENDDO
 * Fall out of loop and present the subfile to the display...
C                       EXFMT     SFLCTL
 * If Page Up is pressed, go execute RLBACK routine to reset file pointer
C      *IN27            CASEQ     *ON            RLBACK
C                       ENDCS
C                       ENDDO

C                       EVAL      *inLr = *ON

C      RLBACK           BEGSR
 * Reset DataBase File pointer using data from first record in the subfile
C      1                CHAIN     SFLRCD                      41
C      SfCustNbr        SETLL     CUSTOMER
 * Clear the subfile first...
C                       MOVEA     '0010'         *IN(21)
C                       WRITE     SFLCTL
C                       MOVEA     '0100'         *IN(21)
C                       EVAL      SflRcdNbr = *ZEROS
 * Read back through DataBase file to get enough records to fill a page
C                       DO        12
C                       READP     CUSTOMER                    41
C                       IF        *In41 = *ON
 * Reset DataBase file pointer if beginning of file was encountered
C      *LOVAL           SETLL     CUSTOMER
C                       READ      CUSTOMER                    41
C                       LEAVE
C                       ENDIF
C                       ENDDO
C                       ENDSR
```

The first steps performed in our example are to read the first database record and to set the initial conditioning indicators for our subfile control record format. We set on the conditioning indicator (22) to display the subfile control record format so that it appears on our first output operation.

We then enter a loop that populates the subfile with the first 12 records (that is the size of our subfile page). The loop has been coded so that the subfile remains active as long as the page keys are pressed. When the Enter key is pressed, the program exits the loop and the program terminates (indicator LR is set on).

By adding 1 to the SFLRCDNBR field, we ensure that the most recent page of the subfile is always displayed. New pages of the subfile continue to be added to the subfile every time the Page Down key is pressed, until the end of the customer database file is reached. At that point the SFLEND indicator (24) is turned on. This causes the literal Bottom to be displayed.

If the Page Up key is pressed, we execute the RLBACK subroutine, which clears out the subfile and repositions the database file pointer. If the subfile is not cleared, we are adding records to the subfile that are out of sequence.

To reposition the database file pointer, the RLBACK subroutine first chains to the very first record in the subfile that was written to get the record key that will be used to reposition the file. This is more efficient than reading backwards through either the database file or the subfile because we may have accumulated many pages of data in the subfile before rollback was ever pressed. Remember that OS/400 handles the roll back process through the subfile records (without ever returning control to the RPG program) as long as there are subfile records to read.

That was not so difficult, was it? You have taken one of the most widely misunderstood and feared subjects among beginner and intermediate AS/400 programmers and made it look easy. Your confidence with subfiles should be soaring now.

Let's have some fun and move on to that window subfile with the scroll bar we saw back in Figure 2.6. But before we write our next subfile program, we need to cover a few more basic concepts. Because this is a window subfile, we will be dealing with a few DDS window keywords. We are also going to introduce you to a subfile where the operator can perform input.

Writing Subfiles within a DDS Window

Finally! The ability to put subfiles within DDS windows was announced when V2R3 was released. Subfiles have become such a major component of our day-to-day programming that the ability to put them within a window was a very natural progression.

Even though we do not cover the DDS window keywords until the next chapter, do not let that deter you. As you see in Figure 2.10, the code required for the purposes of this example involve only two new DDS keywords, and they are very simple. There are, however, some new issues that we need to cover, before getting into this next example.

Figure 2.10: DDS for State Lookup Window Subfile

```
A*****************************************************************
A*  TO COMPILE:
A*    CRTDSPF FILE(XXXLIB/FIG210DS)
A*****************************************************************
.....AAN01N02N03T.Name+++++RLen++TDpBLinPosFunctions+++++++++++++++++++++++++++++++
A              R WINDOW
A                                          WINDOW(3 4 13 53)
A                                          RMVWDW
A              R SFLRCD                     SFL
A   42                                     SFLNXTCHG
A                SFLRELRCD     4S 0H
A                SFLSELECT     1A B  5  4DSPATR(HI)
A                SFLSTATE      2A O  5 12
A                SFLDESCR     25A O  5 19
A              R SFLCTL                     SFLCTL(SFLRCD)
A                                          OVERLAY
A                                          SFLDSP
A                                          SFLDSPCTL
A   24                                     SFLEND(*SCRBAR *MORE)
A                                          SFLSIZ(0050)
A                                          SFLPAG(0007)
A   42                                     SFLMSG('Invalid Selection Entry')
A                                          WINDOW(WINDOW)
A                SETCSRPOS     4S 0H        SFLRCDNBR(CURSOR)
A                CURCSRPOS     5S 0H        SFLSCROLL
A                                        2  2'Options:'
A                                        2 11'1=Select'
A                                          DSPATR(HI)
A                                        2 20'or press ENTER to cancel'
A                                        4  2'Option   State        Description  -
A                                            '
A                                          DSPATR(UL HI)
A              R DUMMY
A                                          KEEP
A                                          ASSUME
A                                        1  2' '
```

Reading Subfile Records That Have Been Changed

The fact that OS/400 can handle much of the rolling within the subfile without returning control to the RPG program poses a rather unique problem. If our subfile has more than one page of data in it, we do not know which page was displayed at the time input was performed. Nor do we know if input was performed on more than one subfile record.

We could address these potential problems by setting up a loop within our RPG program that chains through the subfile using the subfile relative record number to see if any input was keyed into our input fields. This is not very efficient, however, and does not help us if a record has been updated.

The Read Changed Record (READC) RPG operation code is the answer to this particular problem. When used in conjunction with the Subfile Next Change (SFLNXTCHG) subfile record-level keyword, your program can be coded so that only subfile records that have been modified are read. So, instead of coding a loop to go through all subfile records, you code it so only the records that have been changed are read.

The rub with this particular method of processing is that, if your program detects an error in the entered data and the subfile is redisplayed, you will not read the record in error again unless the operator changes data on the record in error. If you condition this keyword on an indicator, you can beat this problem by setting on the option indicator and performing an UPDAT operation to the subfile record prior to the next EXFMT on the control file record format. This updates the modified data tag and the record is read on the next READC loop whether the operator changes any data in the subfile record or not.

Don't Blank Out That Screen, Dummy!

When using the DDS window keywords, you may have already experienced the frustration of screens inexplicably being blanked out when you try to present your DDS window. If you call an external RPG program that displays a window over a previously displayed screen format, the screen displayed by the preceding program is blanked out before the window is displayed. This seems to defeat the purpose of using a window.

One solution to this problem is to add a dummy format containing the KEEP and ASSUME keywords to the display file that contains the window. Note that there is a DUMMY format in Figure 2.10 that is never called. Removing it, however, results in the problem described above.

Subfile Error Messages

This next example in Figure 2.10 also uses one of the two simplest forms of subfile messages. We use the Subfile Message (SFLMSG) keyword to display error messages on the screen. When the conditioning indicator is turned on and an output operation is performed on the subfile control record format, the message text that is specified along with the SFLMSG keyword is displayed in the message area at the bottom of the screen.

The Subfile Message ID (SFLMSGID) is the other simple subfile message method. This keyword is used like the SFLMSG keyword, except that you specify the message ID and the qualified name and location of the message file.

These methods include conditioning by indicators, so they do not give you a lot of flexibility. When you have programs with a large number of potential errors or you want to pass variable data into the messages, you are better off using message subfiles. We discuss these situations later in this chapter.

I'd Like Scroll Bars with That Subfile, If You Please...

As we discussed earlier when we were describing the Subfile End (SFLEND) keyword, you can now use scroll bars for graphical workstations that have a pointing device. Because our State Lookup subfile is coded as a load-all type of subfile, it was a practical option for this example.

Notice in Figure 2.10 that we are using the *SCRBAR parameter on the SFLEND keyword. We also used the *MORE parameter, so workstations that are incapable of showing the scroll bar use the More... and Bottom literals instead of the less user-friendly plus sign (+).

Because we are using the scroll bar, we were able to demonstrate the field level Subfile Scroll (SFLSCROLL) keyword as well. This keyword returns the relative record number of the subfile record that happens to be at the top of the screen back to your RPG program. The field to hold the returned relative record number must be coded as a five-digit, signed numeric hidden field.

CODING THE STATE LOOKUP WINDOW SUBFILE DISPLAY FILE

Let's examine the DDS in Figure 2.10 that we are using for our State Lookup window subfile program. You are already familiar with most of the keywords we will use.

This program is different from those that we have looked at so far in that our program presents three different record formats (WINDOW, SFLCTL, and SFLRCD) to the screen at the same time.

The DDS for the WINDOW record format is simple. It only tells the system that we are using a DDS window that begins on line 3, in position 4, is 13 lines deep, and is 53 characters across. The RMVWDW keyword has been added so the system will remove existing DDS windows from the screen prior to presenting this one. The WINDOW keyword tells the AS/400 that this format is a DDS window and the system handles the rest of the work for you.

The Subfile Record (SFLRCD) in our example uses the Subfile Next Change (SFLNXTCHG) keyword just discussed. It also has a hidden field (SFLRELRCD) in which we store the subfile relative record number. It comes in handy when we want to control the positioning of our subfile. We then have an input-capable field called SFLSELECT, which a program operator can use to key a selection option. The other two fields are used to store the state code and description.

Our subfile control record has the standard required keywords (SFLSIZ, SFLPAG, SFLDSP, and SFLCTL). This particular subfile is coded as a load-all subfile because we know that we have a small, fixed number of records that can possibly be loaded into the subfile. The fact that there are only 50 states leaves us in a position to know the exact number of records contained in the subfile. By putting all of the records in the subfile up front, we are in a position to let the system handle all of the rolling for us when the page keys are pressed. Note that the Subfile Size (SFLSIZ) is 50, and the Subfile Page (SFLPAG) is 7.

We have also coded the SFLDSPCTL keyword into our control record. This is required because we will be requesting input from our subfile and also because we have information in the control record that we would like displayed on the screen.

We use the SFLRCDNBR field to control which page of the subfile is displayed and where within the subfile the cursor is positioned, by loading the appropriate values into the SETCSRPOS field.

The WINDOW keyword tells the system that this subfile is presented within a window and identifies the name of the window.

CODING THE STATE LOOKUP WINDOW SUBFILE RPG PROGRAM

As you see from the code in Figure 2.11, it does not take very much code to get our window subfile program up and running. This window subfile routine may be called from any program where you want to allow an operator to look up the valid state codes. The selected state code is returned to the calling program in the ReturnCode parameter.

Figure 2.11: RPG for State Lookup Window Subfile Program

```
***************************************************************
*   TO COMPILE:
*      CRTBNDRPG PGM(XXXLIB/FIG211RG)
***************************************************************

FFilename++IPEASF.....L.....A.Device+.Keywords+++++++++++++++++++++++++++++++Comments++
FFIG210DS  CF   E              WORKSTN
F                                        SFILE(SFLRCD:SflRelRcd)
FSTATES    IF   E           K DISK

DName++++++++++ETDsFrom+++To/L+++IDc.Keywords+++++++++++++++++++++++++++++++++Comments++
D ReturnCode      S              2
D GetOut          S              1
D                 SDS
D  PARMS          *PARMS

CL0N01Factor1++++++++Opcode&ExtFactor2+++++++Result+++++++Len++D+HiLoEq....Comments++
C      *ENTRY       PLIST
C                   PARM                      ReturnCode
C                   EVAL      SflSelect = *BLANKS
C                   EVAL      SetCsrPos = 1
C                   WRITE     WINDOW
C                   DO        50
C                   READ      STATES                              24
C                   IF        *In24 = *OFF
C                   EVAL      SflState = State
C                   EVAL      SflDescr = StateDesc
C                   EVAL      SflRelRcd = SflRelRcd + 1
C                   WRITE     SFLRCD
C                   ENDIF
C                   ENDDO

C                   DOU       Getout = *ON
 * Display/Read Subfile
C                   EXFMT     SFLCTL
C                   EVAL      *In42 = *OFF
C                   EVAL      SetCsrPos = CurCsrPos
C                   DOU       *In41 = *ON
 * Look for Record Selection Request
C                   READC     SFLRCD                              41
C                   IF        *In41 = *ON
C                   EVAL      GetOut = *ON
C                   ELSE
 * Enter was pressed without a Request
C                   SELECT
C                   WHEN      SflSelect = '1'
C                   EVAL      ReturnCode = SflState
C                   EVAL      GetOut = *ON
C                   WHEN      SflSelect <> *BLANKS
C                   EVAL      *In42 = *ON
C                   EVAL      SetCsrPos = SflRelRcd
C                   UPDATE    SFLRCD
C                   OTHER
C                   ITER
C                   ENDSL
C                   LEAVE
C                   ENDIF
C                   ENDDO
C                   ENDDO

C                   EVAL      *InLr = *ON
```

The program initially writes the window record format to the screen and then reads through the STATES database file and loads the subfile with each record read from the file. This is typical for a load-all style of subfile.

Once the subfile has been loaded, the program is ready to process and edit input from the operator. An I/O request is made of the subfile control record and the current cursor position is fed back into the SETCSRPOS field that represents our SFLRCDNBR field. This is done because we can not know where the actual cursor position is at the time we read the control record. Remember, the system is controlling our rolling when page keys are pressed, so our current cursor position could be anywhere in the subfile.

Rather than reading all of our subfile records to see if the operator made a selection, we use READC so we may read only the records that have changed. If we find that no records have changed, we can assume that the operator wanted to terminate the program and simply pressed Enter without making a change.

If records have changed, there are only three possibilities:

- The operator made a valid selection by keying a 1 in front of the desired selection.

- An invalid selection was made (a value other than 1 was keyed).

- The selection field contains blanks. Note that, if the operator presses FIELD EXIT through the selection field to get down to the desired record, the selection field is tagged as having been changed but the field has a blank in it. It is for this reason that we have accounted for this possibility by coding the program to ignore records where a blank selection is made.

If the selection made is determined to be in error, we set on the error indicator (42) so the SFLMSG keyword is activated and the error is displayed. We also load the relative record number of the subfile record (stored in the SFLRELRCD hidden field) that is incorrect into the SETCSRPOS (SFLRCDNBR) field. This causes the cursor to be positioned on the error record and ensures that the appropriate page of the subfile is displayed.

Performing an UPDAT operation on the subfile record that is in error is done so the record is flagged as changed the next time the subfile control record is read. If we fail to do this and the operator does not correct or change the record that we found in error, the record is not read the next time the READC operation is performed. The record remains in an error condition and the record is not edited again.

ERROR HANDLING WITH A MESSAGE SUBFILE

The message subfile is unique; it has been designed specifically to present error messages to the screen. It allows us to present multiple error messages in a single output operation and easily lends itself to allowing us to pass variable information into the error messages themselves. And, for those of us who code a lot of subprograms, it also enables us to write an error message in one program and have it sent to the message queue of another.

In this next example, we look at an RPG program that prompts for and edits a customer number. If the customer number is deemed invalid, we use an API to send an error message to our program and output the message to our message subfile.

Figure 2.12 shows the DDS necessary to code an error message subfile. The SFLMSGRCD keyword tells the system on what line to display the error message. The SFLMSGKEY keyword tells the system if it is to display only messages with a certain message ID, or all messages in the message queue. The field identified by the SFLPGMQ keyword indicates which program message queue to display. In our example in Figure 2.13, we load this field with an asterisk (*) to indicate that the current program message queue is to be used.

Figure 2.12: DDS for a Message Subfile

```
     A***********************************************************************
     A*  TO COMPILE:
     A*     CRTDSPF FILE(XXXLIB/FIG212DS)
     A***********************************************************************
.....AAN01N02N03T.Name++++++RLen++TDpBLinPosFunctions+++++++++++++++++++++++++
     A           R MSGSFL                    SFL
     A                                       SFLMSGRCD(24)
     A             MESSAGEKEY                SFLMSGKEY
     A             PROGRAMQUE                SFLPGMQ
     A           R MSGCTL                    SFLCTL(MSGSFL)
     A                                       OVERLAY
     A                                       SFLSIZ(3) SFLPAG(1)
     A                                       SFLDSP SFLINZ
     A 90                                    SFLEND
     A             PROGRAMQUE                SFLPGMQ
     A           R FORMAT1
     A 40                                    OVERLAY
     A                                       CF03(03 'End of job')
     A                             21  3'                          -
     A                                  '                          -
     A                                       DSPATR(UL)
     A                             22  5'F3=Exit'
     A                              9 21'Customer Number:'
     A             CUSTNUMBER  10A B  9 38
     A                              1 27'Customer Inquiry'
     A                                       DSPATR(HI)
     A                                       DSPATR(UL)
```

Figure 2.13: RPG for a Message Subfile

```
     ***********************************************************************
     *   TO COMPILE:
     *      CRTBNDRPG PGM(XXXLIB/FIG213RG)
     ***********************************************************************

FFilename++IPEASF.....L.....A.Device+.Keywords+++++++++++++++++++++++++++++++Comments++
FFIG212DS  CF   E             WORKSTN

DName++++++++++ETDsFrom+++To/L+++IDc.Keywords+++++++++++++++++++++++++++++++Comments++
D ERROR           DS                   INZ
D  BytesProv              1      4B 0  INZ(116)
D  BytesAvail             5      8B 0
D  ErrMsgId               9     15
D  ERR###                16     16
D  ErrMsgData            17    116
D MessageKey      S              4B 0  INZ(0)
D MsgData         S             50
D MsgDataLen      S              4B 0  INZ(50)
D MsgQueNbr       S              4B 0  INZ(0)
D MessageId       S              7      INZ('CPF9898')
D MessageFil      S             20
D MessageTyp      S             10      INZ('*DIAG')
D MessageQue      S             10      INZ('*')
```

```
C                   PARM                    MsgQueNbr
C                   PARM                    MessageKey
 * Error Code
C                   PARM                    Error
C                   ENDSR
```

Like all subfiles, the control record contains the required SFLSIZ, SFLPAG, SFLCTL, and SFLDSP keywords. Our SFLPAG is set to 1, so only one error message line appears at a time, but the user can position the cursor on that line and roll through any other messages that may be in the subfile. A plus sign (+) appears on the message line if there is more than one message.

We chose to use the SFLINZ keyword so that all messages could be written to the message queue in a single output operation. If we had not used the SFLINZ keyword, then only one message at a time could be written to the subfile message record.

The RPG code necessary to write an error message to a message queue and to display that message on the screen is shown in Figure 2.13. The field PROGRAMQUE (which is the field specified on the SFLPGMQ keyword) is loaded with an *. This indicates that the current program message queue is to be used.

Next, the format that contains the customer input field that is to be edited is displayed. If the customer number doesn't pass our edit, the SNDERR subroutine is executed where the API is executed to send an error to our program's message queue.

Substitution Variables in Error Messages

SNDERR uses the global message CPF9898, which is found in every system-supplied QCPFMSG message file. It has only one data field, which is a vacant space where you supply the error to be displayed. Using the Evaluate (EVAL) op code, we construct an error message that contains the variable that we want included in the body of the message.

Our program then uses the QMHSNDPM API (Send Program Message) to send the message to the message queue. The variable MessageQue contains an *, which means send it to this message queue. Message queue number (MsgQueNbr) indicates the number of invocation levels back you want the message sent. A 0 in this field indicates that the message is sent to the current program, a 1 means it should be sent to the previous calling program, and so on.

Once the message is written to the message queue, the write to MSGCTL format displays the error message subfile records. The Execute Format (EXFMT) of FORMAT1 redisplays the screen in error and waits for the correction from the user.

Note that FORMAT1 needs the OVERLAY keyword to be optioned on when an error is being displayed. The normal routine that the system employs when displaying a screen is to first remove everything currently on the screen and then display a new screen. Because this would erase the error message just displayed, we condition the OVERLAY keyword on the FORMAT1 screen, telling the system to leave the screen as it is and write over it with the new screen.

USING SEARCH FIELDS IN THE SUBFILE CONTROL RECORD FORMAT

Most of the time when you want to present a database file in a subfile, you want to allow the program operator the opportunity to search for or *lookup* a specific record. This is particularly true in the case of large database files that you present as page-at-a-time. Obviously it is not productive for somebody to sit and scroll through page after page of data looking for the desired record. You may as well give them a printed list.

It is for this reason that search fields in the subfile control record format are so useful. The search field allows the program operator to key all or part of a search word/field. The keyed entry is used to reposition the database pointer so the subfile can be written with records that more closely match what the operator is looking for.

For our example of this technique (Figure 2.14), we have chosen a printer lookup window subfile program that could be inserted easily into any report or list request program. This window subfile presents the printer description records alphabetically on the screen (by printer description) and allows an end user to look up, or search for, the printer to which the printed output is sent. When a subfile record on the screen is selected (by keying the appropriate option), the printer ID is returned to the calling program in a parameter. If the operator does not see the desired record within the window, they may either press the page keys or key all or part of a printer description and press Enter to reposition the database file (and consequently the subfile) appropriately.

Figure 2.14: Lookup Window to Select a Printer

```
.......................................................
:                                                     :
: Options: 1=Select                                   :
:                                                     :
: OR Key partial description: _____      :
:                                                     :
: Opt  Code           Description                     :
:  _   LASER6    ACCOUNTING - CHECKS                  :
:  _   LASER7    ACCOUNTING - INVOICES                :
:  _   LASER3    ACCOUNTING - LASER PRINTER           :
:  _   PRT03     COMPUTER ROOM - INVOICE PRINTER      :
:  _   LASER1    COMPUTER ROOM - LASER PRINTER        :
:  _   PRT02     COMPUTER ROOM - LETTER QUALITY       :
:  _   LASER2    FRONT DESK - LASER PRINTER           :
:                                         More... :
:                                                     :
: F3=Exit  F12=Previous                               :
:                                                     :
.......................................................
```

For the purposes of our sample program (Figures 2.15 and 2.16), we created DDS for a physical file and a logical file that are used to describe the printers on your system. The physical file is called PRINTER, and the logical file that lets us view the file by description is called PRINTERS.

Figure 2.15: DDS for Physical File PRINTER

```
.....A..........T.Name+++++RLen++TDpB......Functions++++++++++++++++++++++++++++
     A         R PRTREC              TEXT('PRINTER DESCRIPTIONS')
     A           PRINTERID    10A    TEXT('PRINTER I.D.')
     A                               COLHDG('PRINTER' 'I.D.')
     A           PRINTRDESC   35A    TEXT('PRINTER DESCRIPTION')
     A                               COLHDG('PRINTER' 'DESCRIPTION')
```

Figure 2.16: DDS for Logical File PRINTERS

```
.....A..........T.Name+++++.Len++TDpB......Functions++++++++++++++++++++++++++++
     A         R PRTREC              PFILE(PRINTER)
     A         K PRINTRDESC
```

The DDS for this application, seen in Figures 2.17 and 2.18, is very much the same as it would be for any window subfile you are coding. There are three basic ingredients required:

- The DDS window.

- The subfile record.

- The subfile control record.

Figure 2.17: DDS for Printer Lookup Window

```
A*****************************************************************
A*  TO COMPILE:
A*     CRTDSPF FILE(XXXLIB/FIG217DS)
A*****************************************************************

.....AAN01N02N03T.Name++++++RLen++TDpBLinPosFunctions++++++++++++++++++++++++++++
A                                    DSPSIZ(24 80 *DS3)
A                                    PRINT(*LIBL/QSYSPRT)
A            R WINDOW
A                                    WINDOW(3 4 16 56)
A                                    RMVWDW
A                              15   2'F3=Exit  F12=Previous'
A                                    DSPATR(HI)
A            R SFLRC1              SFL
A              HIDDENKEY1   12A  H
A              SFLOPTION     1A  B  7  2DSPATR(HI)
A                                    DSPATR(UL)
A              SFLPRINTID   10A  O  7  5
A              SFLDESCRIP   40A  O  7 16
A            R SFLCT1              SFLCTL(SFLRC1)
A                                    SFLSIZ(0007)
A                                    SFLPAG(0007)
A                                    WINDOW(WINDOW)
A                                    ROLLUP(95)
A                                    ROLLDOWN(96)
A                                    CA03(03 'EOJ')
A                                    CA12(12 'PREVIOUS')
A                                    BLINK
A  40                                ALARM
A                                    OVERLAY
A                                    PUTOVR
A  21                                SFLDSP
A  22                                SFLDSPCTL
A  23                                SFLCLR
A  24                                SFLEND(*MORE)
A                               2  1'Options:'
A                               2 10'1=Select'
A                                    DSPATR(HI)
A                               4  1'OR'
A                                    DSPATR(RI)
A                               4  4'Key partial description:'
A              SEARCHDESC   15A  B  4 29DSPATR(HI)
A  76                                DSPATR(PC)
A                                    OVRATR
```

```
A                         6  1'Opt     Code              Descrip-
A                             tion                    '
A                             DSPATR(UL)
A          R DUMMY
A                             KEEP
A                             ASSUME
A                         1  2' '
```

Figure 2.18: RPG Specifications for Program LOOKUP

```
    *******************************************************************
    *   TO COMPILE:
    *      CRTBNDRPG PGM(XXXLIB/FIG218RG)
    *******************************************************************

    FFilename++IPEASF.....L.....A.Device+.Keywords+++++++++++++++++++++++Comments++
    FFIG217DS CF   E              WORKSTN
    F                                       SFILE(SFLRC1:SflRelRec)
    FPRINTERS  IF   E          K DISK       USROPN

    DName++++++++++ETDsFrom+++To/L+++IDc.Keywords+++++++++++++++++++++++Comments++
    D ReturnCode      S             2
    D Filecode        S             4
    D PasPrintId      S            10
    D NextFormat      S             5
    D Reset           S             1
    D SflRelRec       S             7 0
    D X               S             2 0
    D Y               S             2 0


    * Parameter Descriptions

    * ReturnCode: Code to return after lookup operation is performed. Values:
    *             03 = End of Job Requested
    *             12 = Previous screen requested
    *             50 = Record was selected & record key is in the PASKEY field
    *
    * FileCode:   File to perform lookup operation on

    * PasPrintId: Key Value to return is lookup operation is successful

    CL0N01Factor1++++++Opcode&ExtFactor2+++++++Result++++++++Len++D+HiLoEq.Comments++
    C         *ENTRY    PLIST
    C                   PARM                    ReturnCode
    C                   PARM                    FileCode
    C                   PARM                    PasPrintId

    C                   DOU       ReturnCode <> *BLANKS
 B2 C         NextFormat CASEQ    'FMT1 '       @FMT1
 E2 C                   ENDCS
 E1 C                   ENDDO

    C                   EVAL      *InLr = *ON

    *****    SUBROUTINE: "*INZSR" ***********************************
    ***   PROCESS INITIALIZATION ROUTINE ***************************
    CSR  *INZSR         BEGSR
```

```
B1  C                    IF        FileCode = 'PRT'
    C                    OPEN      PRINTERS
E1  C                    ENDIF

    C                    EVAL      ReturnCode = *BLANKS
    C                    EVAL      Reset = *ON
     * Set DataBase File Pointers
    C                    EXSR      FILSET
     * Populate Subfile
    C                    EXSR      LODSFL
    C                    MOVE      'FMT1 '        NextFormat

CSR                      ENDSR
    *****    SUBROUTINE: "@FMT1"   ************************************
    ***   PROCESS SUBFILE FORMAT   ************************************
CSR  @FMT1               BEGSR

    C                    IF        (*In95 = *OFF) and (*In96 = *OFF)
    C                    WRITE     WINDOW
    C                    ENDIF
    C                    MOVEA     '10'           *IN(22)
    C                    EXFMT     SFLCT1
    C                    MOVEA     '0000'         *IN(38)
     * If Page Up was pressed, page back through the DataBase records
B1  C                    IF        *In96 = *ON
    C                    EXSR      ROLBAK
    C                    GOTO      END1
E1  C                    END
    C                    EVAL      *In97 = *OFF
     * If Page Down was pressed, page forward through the DataBase records
B1  C                    IF        *In95 = *ON
B2  C                    IF        *In24 = *OFF
    C                    EXSR      LODSFL
E2  C                    END
    C                    GOTO      END1
E1  C                    END
     * If a search description was keyed, reposition DataBase file pointer accordingly
B1  C                    IF        SearchDesc <> *BLANKS
    C                    EXSR      FILSET
    C                    EXSR      LODSFL
    C                    GOTO      END1
E1  C                    END
     * If F3 was pressed, Exit program
B1  C                    IF        *In03 = *ON
    C                    EVAL      ReturnCode = '03'
    C                    GOTO      END1
E1  C                    ENDIF
     * If F12 was pressed, return to previous operation
B1  C                    IF        *In12 = *ON
    C                    EVAL      ReturnCode = '12'
    C                    GOTO      END1
E1  C                    ENDIF
     * Read subfile for records changed to see if a record was selected
B1  C                    DOU       *In47 = *ON
    C                    READC     SFLRC1                              47
B1  C                    IF        *In47 = *OFF
     * Sound alarm & position cursor if option keyed is not a "1" or blanks...
B1  C                    IF        (SflOption <> '1') and
    C                              (SflOption <> ' ')
    C                    EVAL      *In40 = *ON
    C                    UPDATE    SFLRC1
X3  C                    ELSE
     * If a "1" was keyed, pass selection back to calling program. If blanks
```

```
                 * were keyed, return to calling program with no selection made.
B1    C                      IF        SflOption = '1'
      C                      EVAL      PasPrintId = HiddenKey1
      C                      EVAL      ReturnCode = '50'
      C                      LEAVE
E4    C                      ENDIF
E3    C                      ENDIF
E2    C                      ENDIF
E1    C   N40                ENDDO
      CSR   END1             ENDSR

      *****    SUBROUTINE: "LODSFL"  **************************************
      ***   BUILD SUBFILE AND DISPLAY WITH SCREEN 1  *********************
      CSR   LODSFL           BEGSR
                 * Clear subfile
      C                      EVAL      SflRelRec = 0
      C                      MOVEA     '0010'         *IN(21)
      C                      WRITE     SFLCT1
                 * Read DataBase records and populate subfile
B1    C       1              DO        7              X
      C                      EXSR      REDFWD
B2    C                      IF        *In24 = *OFF
      C                      EVAL      SflRelRec = (SflRelRec + 1)
      C                      EVAL      *In21 = *ON
      C                      EVAL      SflOption = *BLANKS
                 * FileCode indicates which DataBase file is being processed
      C                      IF        FileCode = 'PRT '
      C                      EVAL      HiddenKey1 = PrinterID
      C                      EVAL      SflPrintId = PrinterID
      C                      EVAL      SflDescrip = PrintrDesc
E3    C                      ENDIF
      C                      WRITE     SFLRC1
E2    C                      END
E1    C   N24                END
      C                      EVAL      SearchDesc = *BLANKS
      CSR                    ENDSR
      *****    SUBROUTINE: "ROLBAK"  **************************************
      ***   ROLL DOWN PROCESSING FOR SUBFILE  ***************************
      CSR   ROLBAK           BEGSR
      C                      EVAL      *In24 = *OFF
      C                      EVAL      Y = (SflRelRec + 8)
B1    C       1              DO        Y              X
      C                      EXSR      REDBAK
B2    C                      IF        *In24 = *ON
      C                      EVAL      Reset = *ON
      C                      EXSR      FILSET
E2    C                      END
E1    C   N24                END
      C                      EXSR      LODSFL
      CSR                    ENDSR
      *****    SUBROUTINE: "FILSET"  **************************************
      ***   SET READ POSITIONING FOR SUBFILE  ***************************
      CSR   FILSET           BEGSR
      C                      IF        FileCode = 'PRT '
                 * If Reset is on, reset DataBase pointer to the beginning of the file
B2    C                      IF        Reset = *ON
      C                      EVAL      SearchDesc = *BLANKS
E2    C                      ENDIF
      C                      EVAL      PrintrDesc = SearchDesc
      C       PrintrDesc     SETLL     PRTREC
E1    C                      ENDIF
      C                      EVAL      Reset = *OFF
      CSR                    ENDSR
```

```
     *****    SUBROUTINE: "REDFWD"  ***************************************
     ***   READ FORWARD THROUGH THE FILE    ****************************
     CSR   REDFWD        BEGSR
     C                   IF          FileCode = 'PRT '
     C                   READ        PRTREC                            24
     * If end-of-file condition encountered, reset DataBase file pointer
     * to reset end-of-file condition
B2   C                   IF          *In24 = *ON
     C     *HIVAL        SETGT       PRTREC
E2   C                   ENDIF
E1   C                   ENDIF
     CSR                 ENDSR
     *****    SUBROUTINE: "REDBAK"  ***************************************
     ***   READ BACKWARDS THROUGH THE FILE    **************************
     CSR   REDBAK        BEGSR
     C                   IF          FileCode = 'PRT '
     C                   READP       PRTREC                            24
     C                   ENDIF
     CSR                 ENDSR
```

Subfiles Over Database Files with Keys That Are Not Unique

Sometimes it is necessary to write a subfile program over a file path where there is no key or where the key is not unique. If you have written a page-at-a-time subfile and you need to reset the database pointer because the Page Up key has been pressed, you have a problem. You can not simply read backwards, because you probably do not know where the file pointer is currently unless you count how many times the Page Down key is pressed.

A file whose path is alphabetical by name is one instance where there may be more than one record with the same key. After all, there are a lot of people named Jones. This can present a problem when paging backwards and one of the duplicate keys is represented by the first record in the subfile, because the first thing the roll back subroutine must do is position the pointer of the database file. The question is, which of the duplicate database records is the correct record at which to position the read/write heads? If you do not position the read/write heads to the correct record, database records are skipped or duplicated when rolling backwards.

The solution to this problem is to keep track of the relative record number of the database record at the time it is written to subfile. We do not want to display this number on the screen, only to use it when rolling. This is accomplished by using a hidden field in the subfile.

The relative record number of the database file can be found in position 397 to 400 of the file information data structure (INFDS). In the example in Figure 2.19, this field is named DBaseRRN in the data structure INFO. (The file information data structure is defined by the INFDS line immediately following the file definition statement.) We then move this field into a hidden field in our subfile.

Figure 2.19: Retrieving the Relative Record Number of a Database File

```
FFilename++IPEASF.....L.....A.Device+.Keywords++++++++++++++++++++++++++++++++++Comments++
FDISPLAY   CF   E               WORKSTN
F                                          SFILE(SFLRCD:RRN)
FFILENAME   IF   E        K   DISK
F                                          INFDS(INFO)


DName++++++++++ETDsFrom+++To/L+++IDc.Keywords++++++++++++++++++++++++++++++++++Comments++
D INFO              DS
D  DBaseRRN              397    400B 0
```

In the roll back subroutine, chain to the first subfile record and then establish a loop to read the database file until the hidden field relative record number equals the relative record number of the database record. The read/write heads are then positioned on the correct record.

HOORAY FOR SUBFILES!

As you read this chapter, you can not have helped but notice that subfiles are one of the most powerful tools in the AS/400 programmer's arsenal. They are both versatile and effective at addressing a variety of needs that we must contend with as programmers. We hope that this chapter has helped you to appreciate and value AS/400 subfiles as much as we do.

Chapter 3

We Do Windows (and Menu Bars Too)!

Surely you have noticed—the world has gone GUI (graphical user interface). You can not pick up a magazine or newspaper without seeing advertisements for personal computers that rely on Windows, OS/2, or Apple Macintosh operating systems. The reason for this, of course, is the overwhelming popularity of the graphical user interface operations that make these systems both intuitive and easy to use.

Let's face it. When it comes to ease of use, the point-and-click interface can not be beat. This does not mean, however, that the green screen is dead and gone. There are millions of green screen interactive programs that work just fine and will be doing the job for many years to come. But the principle reason for this projected longevity is that the cost of rewriting them for a new GUI interface simply can not be justified.

How to Write GUI Applications, without Getting "Gooey" Applications

Newly designed interactive programs can, and probably should, employ a graphical user interface. IBM has begun to offer us a path to get there with the last several releases of the OS/400 operating system. We have seen the announcement of a variety of DDS keywords that support DDS windows, menu bars, scroll bars, radio buttons, and so on. There is every indication that IBM will continue to lead us down the path toward creating programs that use the graphical user interface.

This chapter gives you a head start on this path. We demonstrate how to use a variety of the new DDS functions that have been announced over the last few years. A list of the topics we cover includes the following:

- Hardware Configuration and Its Effect on GUI Applications

  - The equipment you are using will determine what "look" you get.

  - What options work with which equipment?

- Pull-down Menu Bars

  - Radio buttons

  - Choice options

  - Shortcut keys

  - Accelerator keys

  - Choice filters

  - Setting choice defaults

- DDS Windows

  - Borders and colors

  - Window placement

- Message lines

- Restoring the display

- Sample DDS window program

- Scroll Bars

  - Using scroll bars on your subfiles

HARDWARE AND ITS EFFECT ON GUI-ENABLED APPLICATIONS

Before you begin writing GUI-enabled applications, you need to be aware that the actual format of the display presented to the user is dependent upon the hardware configuration. Older workstations and controllers were not designed or manufactured with a graphical user interface in mind.

When IBM began to employ the newer GUI functions in the operating system, they still had to make allowances for the millions of dollars worth of older equipment that was already in place. They were forced to consider the older workstations and workstation controllers attached to the two- or three-hundred thousand AS/400 systems already installed.

Consequently, the look and feel of the new GUI functions vary widely depending upon the equipment you happen to be running. We compiled a table of the equipment possibilities as of V3R1. Table 3.1 shows the possible configurations and how each function appears.

Table 3.1: Hardware Configurations and Workstations

Configuration	Selection Fields	Selection Lists
GUI-programmable Workstations [1]	GUI [2]	Bar selection cursor. Possible check boxes for multiple-choice lists. Possible radio buttons for single-choice lists.
InfoWindow II Display Stations [3] Attached to Enhanced Interface Controller [4]	Character-based GUI [5]	Bar selection cursor. Possible check boxes for multiple-choice lists. Possible radio buttons for single-choice lists.
3477 Display Station Attached to Enhanced Interface Controller [4]	Mnemonics (shortcut keys); bar selection cursor.	Bar selection cursor. Input field to left of list.
5250 Display Station Attached to Enhanced Interface Controller [4]	Bar selection cursor.	Bar selection cursor. Input field to left of list.
ASCII Display Station Attached to ASCII Controller Supporting Enhanced Interface [6]	Bar selection cursor.	Bar selection cursor. Input field to left of list.
Any Display Station Attached to Controller Not Supporting Enhanced Interface [7]	Entry field driven.	Input field to left of list.

Configuration	Selection Fields	Selection Lists
NOTES: [1] For example, RUMBA/400. [2] GUI shows as solid-line window borders. [3] InfoWindow II display stations: 3486, 3487, 3488. [4] Twinaxial controllers: 5494 Release 1.1, features 6050, 2661, 9146, and 9148. [5] Character-based GUI, except lines are created using characters. [6] ASCII controllers that support enhanced interface: features 6041, 6141, 2637, 9145, and 9147. [7] For example, 5250 display stations attached to 5294 and 5394 controllers or features 2638, 6040, and 6140. Another example: Client Access/400—PCs emulating a controller with an attached 5250 display station.		

MY SCREEN STILL DOESN'T LOOK RIGHT

Normally, display files are created with the default for the ENHDSP, which is *YES. This means that, if the display station is capable of enhanced interfaces, they are used automatically. In other words, window borders and menu bar separators are presented graphically on a graphical display. This parameter can be overridden or changed with the OVRDSPF and CHGDSPF commands, respectively. Make sure this parameter is *YES.

If you are showing formats that use ENHDSP *YES and formats that use ENHDSP *NO, all formats display as if ENHDSP *NO is active (no graphics).

If you are using User Interface Manager (UIM) help with a file that has ENHDSP(*YES) specified, the display changes from graphical to character-based.

A window is always displayed as though ENHDSP(*NO) is specified if the window is placed in the first or last column on the screen.

Some PCs ignore the window border and menu bar separator keywords, even if they support the enhanced interface.

Figure 3.2: Example of a Pull-down Menu

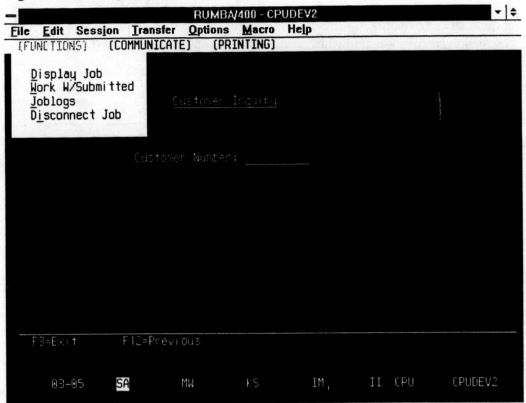

The row of text at the top of the screen with the menu keywords (FUNCTIONS), (COMMUNICATE), and (PRINTING) constitutes the menu bar in Figure 3.1. Positioning the cursor on one of these phrases (using a mouse pointer/mouse button or the F10 function key and pressing the Enter key) displays a pull-down menu of functions you can perform. An example of the result appears in Figure 3.2.

Functions on a pull-down menu usually are executed by positioning the cursor on one of the functions listed and pressing the Enter key or mouse button again (generally referred to as point and click). If you have done any work at all using GUI-enabled personal computer operating systems, you already know all about menu bars. If you haven't, it's time to move into the 20th century.

DDS KEYWORDS FOR CODING THE MENU BAR

Table 3.2 contains DDS keywords that are associated with menu bars. While we have included all of the keywords, only a few are necessary to produce a workable menu bar. The rest provide more functionality, but are not necessarily required.

Table 3.2: Menu Bar DDS Keywords

Keyword	Keyword Text	Description
CHCACCEL	Choice Accelerator Text	Specify text for accelerator function key.
CHCAVAIL	Choice Attribute Available	Specify the color or attribute when displaying choices.
CHCCTL	Choice Control	Control availability of the choices.
CHCSLT	Choice Selected Attribute	Specify the color or display attribute when a choice is selected.
CHCUNACAIL	Choice Unavailable	Specify the color or display attribute for unavailable choices.
CHOICE	Selection Field Choice	Define a field for a selection choice.
MLTCHCFLD	Multiple Choice Selection Field	Define a multiple-choice selection field.
MNUBAR	Menu Bar	Define a menu bar.
MNUBARCHC	Menu Bar Choice	Define a choice for a menu bar field.
MNUBARDSP	Menu Bar Display	Display a menu bar.

Keyword	Keyword Text	Description
MNUBARSEP	Menu Bar Separator	Specify the color, attribute, or character of the menu bar separator character.
MNUBARSW	Menu Bar Switch	Assign a function key to toggle between menu bar and user screen.
MNUCNL	Menu Cancel Key	Assign a function key to cancel the menu bar or pull-down menu.
PULLDOWN	Pull Down Menu	Define a format as a pull-down menu.
SNGCHCFLD	Single Choice Field	Define a single-choice selection field.

The DDS required to code the display file with the menu bar shown in Figures 3.1 and 3.2 is shown in Figure 3.3. We first coded a couple of file-level keywords that control access to the menu bar. MNUBARSW is a keyword that allows you to define a function key that, when pressed, toggles between your format and the menu bar.

Figure 3.3: Sample DDS for Menu Bar in Figures 3.1 and 3.2

```
     *****************************************************************
     *   TO COMPILE:
     *     CRTDSPF FILE(XXXLIB/FIG33DS)
     *****************************************************************

.AAN01N02N03T.Name++++++RLen++TDpBLinPosFunctions++++++++++++++++++++++++++++
     A                                      DSPSIZ(24 80 *DS3)
     A                                      MNUBARSW(CA10)
     A                                      MNUCNL(CA12 12)
     A          R FMTC
     A                                      CF03(03 'End of job')
     A                                      OVERLAY
     A                                      MNUBARDSP(MENUBAR1 &MENUCHOICE +
     A                                        &PULLINPUT)
     A                                 21  3'                              -
     A                                                                     -
     A                                         '
     A                                      DSPATR(UL)
     A                                 22  5'F3=Exit'
     A                                 22 19'F12=Previous'
     A                                  9 21'Customer Number:'
     A            CUSTNUMBER   10A  B   9 38DSPATR(PC)
     A                                  5 27'Customer Inquiry'
     A                                      DSPATR(HI)
     A                                      DSPATR(UL)
     A            MENUCHOICE    2Y  0H
     A            PULLINPUT     2S  0H
     A          R MESSAGESFL               SFL
     A                                      SFLMSGRCD(24)
     A            MESSAGEKEY               SFLMSGKEY
     A            PROGRAMQUE               SFLPGMQ
     A          R MESSAGECTL               SFLCTL(MESSAGESFL)
     A                                      OVERLAY
     A                                      SFLSIZ(3) SFLPAG(1)
     A                                      SFLDSP SFLINZ
     A 90                                   SFLEND
     A            PROGRAMQUE               SFLPGMQ
     A          R MENUBAR1
     A                                      MNUBAR
     A            MENUFIELD     2Y  0B  1  2CHCSLT((*COLOR TRQ))
     A                                      MNUBARCHC(1 SYSREC '(FUNCTIONS)')
     A                                      MNUBARCHC(2 COMREC '(COMMUNICATE)')
     A                                      MNUBARCHC(3 PRTREC '(PRINTING)')
     A          R SYSREC
     A                                      PULLDOWN(*NOSLTIND)
     A                                      WDWBORDER((*COLOR GRN) (*DSPATR RI)-
     A                                        (*CHAR '         '))
     A            SYSTEMFLD     2Y  0B  1  2SNGCHCFLD
     A                                      CHECK(ER)
     A                                      CHOICE(1 '>Display Job')
     A                                      CHOICE(2 '>Work W/Submitted')
     A                                      CHOICE(3 '>Joblogs')
     A                                      CHOICE(4 'D>isconnect Job')
     A          R COMREC
     A                                      PULLDOWN
     A            COMFIELD      2Y  0B  1  3MLTCHCFLD
     A                                      CHOICE(1 '>Passthrough')
     A                                      CHOICE(2 '>Establish Communication')
     A                                      CHOICE(3 '>Send Message')
     A                                      CHOICE(4 '>Delete Communication')
     A                                      CHCCTL(1 &CHOICFLD1)
```

```
A                                         CHCCTL(2 &CHOICFLD2)
A                                         CHCCTL(3 &CHOICFLD3)
A                                         CHCCTL(4 &CHOICFLD4)
A            CHOICFLD1      1Y 0H
A            CHOICFLD2      1Y 0H
A            CHOICFLD3      1Y 0H
A            CHOICFLD4      1Y 0H
A          R PRTREC
A                                         PULLDOWN(*NOSLTIND)
A                                         WDWBORDER((*COLOR GRN)  (*DSPATR RI)-
A                                         (*CHAR '          '))
A            PRINTFIELD     2Y 0B  1  2SNGCHCFLD
A                                         CHECK(ER)
A                                         CHOICE(1 '>Work Writers')
A                                         CHOICE(2 'Work >Spool Files')
A                                         CHOICE(3 'Work >Outqueues')
```

In our example, if the cursor is positioned on the customer number field and F10 is pressed, the cursor automatically moves to the first phrase in the menu bar— (FUNCTIONS). On the other hand, if the cursor is on the menu bar and F10 is pressed, it moves to the customer number field.

The MNUCNL keyword provides a function key that cancels a pull-down menu. In our example, pressing F12 cancels the pull-down menu request.

Next, we need to name the format on which we are going to place the menu bar. The keyword for that is MNUBARDSP. This keyword has two possible formats: one for records that have the MNUBAR keyword and one for records that do not have the MNUBAR keyword. We have chosen to define the menu bar as a separate record with the MNUBAR keyword on another format, so we use the second format of the MNUBARDSP keyword:

MNUBARDSP(Menu bar record &Choice field &Pull down input)

—or—

MNUBARDSP(&Pull down input)

Parameter Definitions:

<u>Menu bar record</u>: The name of the menu bar format to be displayed when this record is written to the screen.

Choice field: Field name that our RPG program can use to determine which option the user selected. This field must be defined on the format as a two-digit hidden field with a Y in position 35 and zero decimal positions.

Pull down input: Optional. If used, must be defined as a two-digit, zoned numeric hidden field. It can be used to retrieve which option was selected on the pull-down menu when the pull-down menu contains only a single-choice selection field.

You designate a format as a menu bar by using the keyword MNUBAR. A format with the MNUBAR keyword specified must also contain a field with at least one MNUBARCHC keyword:

```
MNUBAR(*Separator OR *Noseparator)
```

Parameter Definitions:

*Separator/*Noseparator: An optional parameter is available with this keyword to indicate whether or not a separator line should be placed below the last line of the menu bar choices. *Separator is the default.

The MNUBARCHC keyword does most of the work. The format for this keyword is:

```
MNUBARCHC(choice field, PullDown format name, choice text,
return field)
```

Parameter Definitions:

Choice field: Provides a number that is returned to the program (in the choice field) to indicate which option was selected.

PullDown format name: Names the window format that is presented if the user selects this choice.

Choice text: The phrase that is displayed to represent this choice.

Return field: Optional parameter. Specifies whether or not control is returned to the application when a menu bar choice is selected (instead of automatically presenting the pull-down format). Field must be defined as two-digit, zero-decimal, zoned, and hidden. Possible values are:

- 0 - No selection made.

- n - Choice number in the pull-down menu.

- -1 - Pull-down record contains something other than a single-choice selection field. Read the pull-down format to determine the actual selection made.

The actual pull-down menu that appears is a record format that has been coded with the keyword PULLDOWN.

```
PULLDOWN(*SLTIND OR *NOSLTIND *NORSTCSR OR *RSTCSR)
```

Parameter Definitions:

*SLTIND/*NOSLTIND: Specifies whether or not selection indicators (such as radio buttons) should be displayed. *SLTIND is the default.

*NORSTCSR/*RSTCSR: Specifies whether or not functions should be restricted when the cursor is outside the window. If *NORSTCSR is specified, the window function keys will operate regardless of where the cursor is located. If *RSTCSR is specified and a function key is pressed while the cursor is outside of the window, you hear a beep and the cursor is placed inside the window. Control is not returned to the program at this time.

CODING RPG FOR MENU BARS AND PULL-DOWN MENUS

The RPG for processing a menu bar is straightforward, as you can see in Figure 3.4. The field we named MenuChoice is checked to determine which format to read. Each format has a different choice field that is checked to determine which option was selected.

Figure 3.4: *The RPG Program to Present a Menu Bar*

```
*************************************************************************
*   TO COMPILE:
*     CRTBNDRPG PGM(XXXLIB/FIG34RG)
*************************************************************************

FFilename++IPEASF.....L.....A.Device+.Keywords++++++++++++++++++++++++++Comments++
FFIG33DS   CF   E              WORKSTN

DName+++++++++++ETDsFrom+++To/L+++IDc.Keywords++++++++++++++++++++++++++Comments++
D One           S              1

CL0N01Factor1+++++++Opcode&ExtExtended-factor2+++++++++++++++++++++++++++Comments++
C                   EVAL      ChoicFld1 = 0
C                   EVAL      ChoicFld2 = 0
C                   EVAL      ChoicFld3 = 0
C                   EVAL      ChoicFld4 = 0
C                   EXFMT     FMTC
C                   EXSR      MENUSL
C                   EVAL      *INLR = *ON
C     MENUSL        BEGSR
C                   SELECT
 * System functions
C                   WHEN      MenuChoice = 1
C                   READ      SYSREC                                  68
 * Display Job
C                   IF        SystemFld = 1
C                   CALL      'SYSJOB'
C                   PARM      '1'          One
C                   ENDIF
 * Work with submitted jobs
C                   IF        SystemFld = 2
C                   CALL      'SYSJOB'
C                   PARM      '2'          One
C                   ENDIF
 * Work with job logs
C                   IF        SystemFld = 3
C                   CALL      'SYSJOB'
C                   PARM      '3'          One
C                   ENDIF
 * Disconnect job
C                   IF        SystemFld = 4
C                   CALL      'SYSJOB'
C                   PARM      '4'          One
C                   ENDIF
 * Communications
C                   WHEN      MenuChoice = 2
C                   READ      COMREC                                  68
 * Display station passthrough
C                   IF        ChoicFld1 = 1
C                   CALL      'COMJOB'
C                   PARM      '1'          One
C                   ENDIF
 * Establish communications
C                   IF        ChoicFld2 = 2
C                   CALL      'COMJOB'
C                   PARM      '2'          One
C                   ENDIF
 * Send message
C                   IF        ChoicFld3 = 3
C                   CALL      'COMJOB'
C                   PARM      '3'          One
```

```
C                   ENDIF
 * Delete commuications stuff
C                   IF          ChoicFld4 = 4
C                   CALL        'COMJOB'
C                   PARM        '4'          One
C                   ENDIF
 * Printing
C                   WHEN        MenuChoice = 3
C                   READ        PRTREC                         68
 * Work with writers
C                   IF          PrintField = 1
C                   CALL        'PRTJOB'
C                   PARM        '1'          One
C                   ENDIF
 * Work with spooled files
C                   IF          PrintField = 2
C                   CALL        'PRTJOB'
C                   PARM        '2'          One
C                   ENDIF
 * Work with output queues
C                   IF          PrintField = 3
C                   CALL        'PRTJOB'
C                   PARM        '3'          One
C                   ENDIF
C                   ENDSL
C                   ENDSR
```

This program is presented for example only. The CL programs to actually provide the functions on the pull-down windows are not shown.

SINGLE-CHOICE, PULL-DOWN MENUS

A single-choice selection screen is a screen that contains a fixed number of choices from which only one choice or option is allowed. The choices appear as a vertical list.
You indicate a single-choice field by using the SNGCHCFLD keyword. The format is shown below:

```
SNGCHCFLD((*RSTCST OR *NORSTCSR) (*NOAUTOSLT OR *AUTOSLT OR
*AUTOSLTENH) (*NOSLTIND OR *SLTIND) (*NOAUTOENT OR *AUTOENT
OR *AUTOENTNN) (*NUMCOL NUMBER OF COLUMNS) (*NUMROW NUMBER
OF ROWS) (*GUTTER GUTTER WIDTH))
```

Parameter Definitions:

*RSTCST/*NORSTCSR: Optional parameter that indicates whether or not the arrow keys are allowed to move the cursor outside of the selection field. The default is *NORSTCSR. This parameter is ignored if the display is attached to a controller that does not support an enhanced interface.

An exception to the restrictions imposed by this keyword occurs if the selection field is the only field contained in the pull-down window. If this is true, when the cursor is within the left-most or right-most columns, the respective arrow key closes the current window and opens the pull-down window associated with the menu bar choice to the left or right of the current menu bar choice.

*NOAUTOSLT: Optional parameter indicating whether or not the Enter key is allowed to select the current choice automatically, as determined by the cursor position. *NOAUTOSLT means the users must select the choice. *AUTOSLTENH means that autoselect is only in effect if the display is attached to an enhanced controller.

*NOSLTIND/*SLTIND: Optional parameter indicating whether or not selection indicators (push buttons, check boxes) should be displayed. *SLTIND is the default.

*NOAUTOENT: This parameter indicates to what extent to enable the autoenter feature. The autoenter feature causes the record to be returned to the program as soon as a choice is selected, without the user having to press the Enter key. *Noautoent disables the feature. *AUTOENT enables the feature. *AUTOENTNN enables the feature only if numeric selection of the choices is not required.

*NUMCOL: Optional parameter indicating that the selection field should be displayed in multiple columns sequenced from left to right across the columns as shown below:

choice1   choice2   choice3

choice4   choice5   choice6

*Numrow: Optional parameter indicating that the selection field should be displayed in multiple rows sequenced from top to bottom as shown below:

    choice1   choice3   choice5

    choice2   choice4   choice6

*Gutter: Optional parameter used to control the number of spaces between the columns of multiple-choice selection fields. Must have a minimum value of at least 2; default spacing is three characters.

The choices that appear on the pull-down format are defined with the CHOICE keyword. Similar to the MNUBARCHC keyword, it allows for a choice number to be keyed to select the option and displays the phrase on the pull-down menu. On nongraphical displays, the choice number is displayed next to the choice text.

```
CHOICE(Choice number Choice text *SPACEB)
```

Parameter Definitions:

Choice number: Indicates an identification number representing this choice. Valid values are from 1 to 99. Duplicate values within a selection field are not allowed.

Choice text: Defines the text that appears representing this choice. May be defined as a character string, or as a program-to-system field.

*SPACEB: Optional parameter that inserts a blank line before this choice on the menu bar. Should be used to logically group choices that are numbered consecutively. If the choices are not numbered consecutively and you are using vertical selection fields (single column), a blank line is automatically placed between nonconsecutive choices.

RADIO PUSH BUTTONS

Before the advent of electronic switches and remote-controlled radios for cars, car radios were controlled by pushing a button (we are not making this up). When you wanted to change the station, you pushed a button, which stayed depressed while that station was being selected. The computer industry borrowed this phrase and coupled it with a GUI interface so that, when a user selects an option, it appears as if a button is pushed.

The PULLDOWN keyword accepts a parameter that can be either *SLTIND (which is the default) or *NOSLTIND. If you use the *SLTIND option, when a user selects an option, a box is placed around the option, giving the illusion that a button is being pushed.

MULTIPLE-CHOICE, PULL-DOWN MENUS

Note in Figure 3.3 that format COMREC contained the keyword MLTCHCFLD while the other formats contained the SNGCHCFLD keyword. The single-choice keyword SNGCHCFLD indicates that only one selection at a time is allowed from the pull-down window. The MLTCHCFLD keyword is used to indicate that more than one item can be selected. For example, you may need an application with which to establish communications and pass-through at the same time. The format for the MLTCHFLD keyword is as follows:

```
MLTCHCFLD((*RSTCSR OR *NORSTCSR) (*NOSLTIND OR *SLTIND)
(*NUMCOL NUMBER OF COLUMNS) (*NUMROW NUMBER OF ROWS)
(*GUTTER GUTTER WIDTH))
```

Parameter Definitions:

*RSTCSR/*NORSTCSR: Optional parameter that indicates whether or not the arrow keys are allowed to move the cursor outside of the selection field. The default is *NORSTCSR. This parameter is ignored if the display is attached to a controller that does not support an enhanced interface.

An exception to the restrictions imposed by this keyword occurs if the selection field is the only field contained in the pull-down window. If this is true, when the cursor is within the left-most or right-most columns, the respective arrow key closes the current window and opens the pull-down window associated with the menu bar choice to the left or right of the current menu bar choice.

*NOSLTIND/*SLTIND: Optional parameter indicating whether or not selection indicators (e.g., push buttons, check boxes) should be displayed. *SLTIND is the default.

<u>*NUMCOL</u>: Optional parameter indicating that the selection field should be displayed in multiple columns sequenced from left to right across the columns as shown below:

        choice1   choice2   choice3

        choice4   choice5   choice6

<u>*NUMROW</u>: Optional parameter indicating that the selection field should be displayed in multiple rows sequenced from top to bottom as shown below:

        choice1   choice3   choice5

        choice2   choice4   choice6

<u>*GUTTER</u>: Optional parameter used to control the number of spaces between the columns of multiple-choice selection fields. Must have a minimum value of at least 2, but the default spacing is three characters.

On a multiple-choice format, there must be one CHCCTL keyword for every CHOICE keyword used. The CHCCTL keyword contains the name of the field that the program will use to determine if the choice was selected. As with the single-choice field, a 1 in the field on input indicates it was selected.

On output, you must load the field associated with each CHCCTL field with a 0, 1, or 2. A 0 in the field indicates the selection is available to be selected. A 1 indicates that the selection is available and is also the default selection. A 2 in the corresponding field indicates the selection is not available at this time.

The CHCCTL keyword optionally controls error handling when the user selects an invalid option. You can specify the error message number and the file where it resides. The specified message is displayed if the user selects an invalid option.

You can also hard code the message. A third option is to load the error message into a field in your program and display that field.

```
CHCCTL(Choice number &Control field Msgid Msglib Msgfile)
```

Parameter Definitions:

Choice number: Required parameter that specifies the choice to which this keyword applies.

Control field: Required parameter that is the name of a 1-byte, numeric hidden field. On output, your program outputs the control value to indicate whether or not the field is available. On input, the field indicates if the field was selected. Possible values and their meanings are:

- 0 - Available.

- 1 - Selected.

- 2 - Unavailable; cursor not allowed here unless help is available for choice.

- 3 - Unavailable; placing cursor on choice is allowed.

- 4 - Unavailable; can not place cursor on choice even if help is available.

Msgid: Message number to display if the user selects an unavailable choice. This field is optional and, if not specified, the default message CPD919B is issued. This parameter can also be a program-to-system field, in which case it must be a 7-byte, alphanumeric field with a data type of P and the field must exist in the record format you are defining.

Msglib: Library name containing the message file that contains the message displayed when the user selects an unavailable choice.

Msgfile: Name of the message file containing the message that is displayed when the user selects an unavailable choice.

PULL-DOWN MENU SHORTCUT KEYS

You may have noticed the right angle bracket (>) symbol embedded in the functions displayed in the pull-down menu. This symbol designates a shortcut key that can be used to select the option. The character following the symbol is the shortcut key and is highlighted on the display. Pressing the designated shortcut key while the cursor is positioned on the menu bar also selects the option.

> **Note**: Shortcut keys only work on character-based graphical displays attached to a controller that supports an enhanced interface for nonprogrammable workstations.

PULL-DOWN MENU ACCELERATOR KEYS

An accelerator key is a function key that performs the same function as the selected phrase. It is displayed next to the pull-down menu choice (three spaces after the length of the longest choice text), but the pull-down menu does not have to be displayed for the accelerator key to be active. You define the key just as you define any other function key, at either the file or field level.

After you have defined the function key, you define the text that is displayed with the choice. Use the CHCACCEL keyword to accomplish this. It is up to you to code the program to operate correctly if the function key is pressed, just as you would with any other function key. All the CHCACCEL keyword does is provide a way to enter the text for the accelerator key to be displayed with the choice text.

```
CHCACCEL (Choice number Accelerator text)
```

Parameter Definitions:

Choice number: Specifies the number of the choice to which this keyword applies. Valid values are from 1 to 99.

Accelerator text: Specifies the text displayed to identify the accelerator key. This parameter may be entered in two ways:

- As a quoted character string.

- As a program-to-system field.

This text is placed three columns to the right of the longest choice text. The actual display length of the accelerator text is also determined by the length of the longest choice text in that the combination of the two can not exceed the width of the smallest display size for the file.

CONTROLLING THE ATTRIBUTES OF AVAILABLE/UNAVAILABLE CHOICES

We have already seen that the CHCCTL keyword controls whether or not a field is available when the pull-down menu appears. The CHCAVAIL keyword controls the color or display attribute of available selections in a menu bar or selection field. The CHCUNAVAIL does the same thing for unavailable choices. The CHCSLT keyword specifies the color and display attributes of a selected choice.

```
CHCAVAIL (Color  Display attributes)
```

Parameter Definitions:

Color: Specifies the color of the choice text. It is expressed in the form *COLOR XXX where *XXX* is:

BLU	Blue
GRN	Green
PNK	Pink
RED	Red
TRQ	Turquoise
YLW	Yellow
WHT	White

<u>Display attributes</u>: Specifies the display attribute of the choice text. It is expressed in the form (*DSPATR (value1) (value2)...) where *value* is:

BL	Blink
CS	Column separator
HI	High intensity
ND	Nondisplay
RI	Reverse image
UL	Underline

SETTING PULL-DOWN MENU DEFAULTS

If your program outputs a valid choice in the option field when the format is displayed, that choice becomes the default. If the user simply presses the Enter key without actually making a selection, the choice number in that field is executed. On output, regardless of how the user selects the option (i.e., entering a number, positioning the cursor, or using the shortcut key) this field is filled with the number corresponding to the option selected.

TO MENU BAR OR NOT TO MENU BAR

Using menu bars can give you the look and feel of a graphical user interface if you are on an enhanced controller. If you are not, the look is undesirable and the feel is anything but good. If the software you develop runs on systems with the enhanced controllers (as all newer systems do), menu bars provide a nice and easy interim interface, even for workstations that do not have a mouse.

WE DO WINDOWS

Windows have been with us for a long time. Clever prehistoric programmers (more commonly referred to as System/36 programmers) were able to code pop-up windows in their applications, but it took an extraordinary amount of effort to achieve and maintain these results.

Today's more contemporary programmers (which we of course define as AS/400 RPG programmers) are able to code windows with just a couple of simple DDS keywords. We can put subfiles in windows, move windows around on the fly, control the window border characteristics, put titles on the window, and much more. All of this functionality is achieved simply by using the correct keyword on the file format definition. We've come a long way, baby!

In case you have lived all of your life on the dark side of the moon and still think that a window is a portal you look out of or open for fresh air, let's define terms. Simply put, a *window* is information that overlays an existing screen, with some form of border (or window) around the information to make it stand out. You can view both the information inside the window and the information outside the window so that you do not lose your point of reference. However, only the information inside the window is active; you can not work with the underlying display while the window is active.

WHO NEEDS WINDOWS?

In addition to the dozen reasons any slightly paranoid claustrophobic could come up with, windows can do a lot to enhance the visual appeal and functionality of your programs. One of the most obvious uses for windows is to provide field-level help. Program operators should be able to place the cursor on a field, press the HELP key, and have a pop-up window appear telling them all about the field. You can see this application throughout the OS/400 operating system.

Another good use for a window interface is to provide a *subfile* list of records from which the user can choose. Let's say an operator needs to enter a salesperson's number in a field, but they only know the salesperson's name. You could set up your program so that placing the cursor in the salesperson number field and pressing a function key cause a pop-up window to appear with an alphabetical list of all salespeople. A subfile selection field allows the operator to select the salesperson they want, and the number is entered into the field automatically.

Another good example (demonstrated in this chapter) is to present a subfile of commands that the user can execute by selecting a subfile record from the window. It's a very user-friendly interface to the operating system, similar in function to the assist window, but with the ability to customize the options presented to each user.

These are just a few of the many uses for windows. We are sure you can come up with many more once you see how easy they are to code. The chart shown in Table 3.3 lists the five keywords that allow you to create and work with windows.

Table 3.3: DDS Window Keywords

Keyword	Description
WINDOW	Defines a window, changes the contents of a window, or activates an inactive window.
WDWBORDER	Specifies the color, display attributes, and characters of the border around the window.
WDWTITLE	Specifies the text, color, and display attributes of the title of the window, which is embedded in the top or bottom border.
RMVWDW	Removes other windows from the display.
USRRSTDSP	Prevents the system from automatically saving and restoring the underlying display when a window is written or removed.

THE *WINDOW* KEYWORD

The WINDOW keyword has two different formats, as shown in the following examples. The first format defines a window, while the second format indicates that the system is to place the record format into a window already defined in another record format.

In the first format, you tell the system where to put the window and how big it's going to be. The beginning line number and column fields control where the window is placed on the screen at execution time. For instance, if you are trying to present help text on a particular field, you can retrieve the cursor position and have the window appear one line below it.

But what if the cursor was on the last line, or last column, of the screen? Where would you put the window? What if it was on the second-to-the-last line? You could, with a lot of code, determine the correct placement of the window based upon how close the cursor is to the bottom or edge of the screen. But it would be rather tedious to code and very difficult to maintain if you had to change the screen later.

Wouldn't it be nice if the system could determine the best position of the window? Well, it can! (You knew we were leading up to that, didn't you?) Take a look at the special option *DFT. Instead of the beginning line and column number parameters, you code the keyword *DFT and the system decides where to place the window.

To display a window, the first window record written must contain the window size and location parameters (or you can specify *DFT to let the system do it for you). A window containing the size and location information is called a window definition record. It is the record that actually creates the window and makes it visible. It is all you need to display a window.

It is possible to display the same window on a screen more than once. The second edition of the window becomes the active window and has the same name as the first window. If you want to move the window, write the same window a second time with the RMVWDW keyword active. This keyword removes the first edition of the window from the screen and gives the appearance of moving the window from one location to another.

Here are two different examples of how you may use the WINDOW keyword:

```
WINDOW(Beginning line # OR Field containing beginning line #
Beginning column OR Field containing beginning column Number
of lines Number of columns *MSGLIN OR *NOMSGLIN *RSTCSR OR
*NORSTCSR)
```

—or—

```
WINDOW(*DFT Number of lines Number of columns *MSGLIN OR
*NOMSGLIN *RSTCSR *OR *NORSTCSR)
```

Parameter Definitions:

Beginning line #: The line number at which to place the top of the window, –or– field name containing the line number at which to place the top of the window. If a field name is used, it must exist in the record format as a signed numeric, program-to-system field, with length no greater than 3.

Beginning column: The position of the uppermost left corner of the window, –or– field name containing the position of the uppermost left corner of the window. If a field name is used, it must exist in the record format as a signed numeric, program-to-system field, with length no greater than 3.

<u>*DFT</u>: Let the system decide where the starting line number and column number should be. The system uses a set order of rules when determining where to position the window. See the note following these definitions for the rules.

<u>Number of lines</u>: The total number of lines the window spans. Must be no greater than the number of lines in the display minus 2. The last line in a window is used for messages and can not contain any fields.

<u>Number of columns</u>: The number of columns within the window. Can not exceed four less than the available positions for the display.

<u>*MSGLIN</u>: Message line, indicates that the message line is contained within the window. *MSGLIN is the default. *NOMSGLIN moves the message line out of the window and to the bottom of the screen (or wherever the MSGLOC keyword specifies).

<u>*RSTCSR</u>: Restricted cursor, indicates that the user is limited in functions when the cursor is outside the window. *NORSTCSR indicates that, when the cursor is outside the window, all the function keys are still available as if the cursor is within the window.

SYSTEM RULES FOR AUTOMATIC WINDOW PLACEMENT

If you use the *DFT parameter and let the system decide where to place the window, it uses a set of rules in making that determination. These rules are as follows:

1. If it fits below the cursor, with the top row of the window being one line below the cursor position, place it there. If the window fits on the screen, beginning in the same column as the cursor, place it there. If it does not fit, place it as far to the left of the column as necessary to fit the complete window on the screen.

2. If it does not fit below the cursor, see if it fits above. If it can, place it there. The bottom of the window will be one line above the cursor. Position the window left to right according to the same criteria as rule 1.

3. If the window fits to the right of the cursor, place it there. The right border of the window is placed in the next-to-the-last column of the display. Position the top row of the window on the same line as the cursor, if possible; otherwise position the window only as far above as necessary to fit the window on the screen.

4. If the window fits to the left of the cursor, place it there. Position the right border of the window two columns to the left of the cursor. Position it vertically as described above.

5. Position the window in the lower, right-hand corner of the display if it does not fit anywhere else.

WINDOW BORDER KEYWORD

The Window Border keyword allows you to control the color, attributes, and characters used to create the border of the window. If you specify this keyword, at least one of the parameters also must be specified.

The Window Border keyword has the following format:

```
WDWDORDER((COLOR) (DISPLAY ATTRIBUTE) (CHARACTERS))
```

Parameter Definitions:

<u>COLOR</u>: Specify the color of the border. The default color is blue. The parameter is ignored on a monochrome display.

<u>DISPLAY ATTRIBUTE</u>: Specify the display attribute of the border. Use the form (*DSPATR (value 1 (value 2...))). If more than one attribute is coded, they are combined to form one attribute for the entire border.

<u>CHARACTERS</u>: Specify the characters that make up the border. Use the form (*CHAR 'characters'). This parameter must be an eight-character string, with each character specifying a different position of the window. The order is as follows:

- Position 1 - Top left corner.

- Position 2 - Top border.

- Position 3 - Top right corner.

- Position 4 - Left border.

- Position 5 - Right border.

- Position 6 - Bottom left corner.

- Position 7 - Bottom border.

- Position 8 - Bottom right corner.

WINDOW TITLE KEYWORD

The Window Title (WDWTITLE) keyword is used to assign a title that appears in the header of the window. The Window Title keyword format is as follows:

```
WDWTITLE((Title text) (color) (display attribute) (*CENTER
or *RIGHT or *LEFT or *TOP or *BOTTOM))
```

Parameter Definitions:

Title text: Optional parameter specifying the text to be placed in the border. Use the form (*TEXT value) where value can be either hard coded or a program-to-system field. If the title characters are blanks, a blank title is displayed. If the characters are nulls, then no title is displayed.

Color: Specify the color of the text title. Use the form (*COLOR value). If no color is specified, it defaults to the color of the border. It is ignored on a monochrome display.

*CENTER, *LEFT, *RIGHT: Specify the alignment of the text field.

REMOVE WINDOW KEYWORD

There are no parameters for the RMVWDW keyword. When you write to a format that has this keyword, all other windows currently on the display are removed. If there are no other windows on the display, the keyword is ignored.

If you have multiple windows on the screen and you simply want to ensure that a certain one has the focus (i.e., it is the one most prominently displayed), read or write to the window. This causes the new window to display, and any windows overlaying it to become secondary or to be removed.

User Restore Display Keyword

There are no parameters for the User Restore Display (USRRSTDSP) keyword. Writing to a format with this keyword, in effect, causes the system to bypass the normal window save and restore processing. It shuts off the save operation beginning with the screen prior to the current one with USRRSTDSP specified and all subsequent screens.

Normal window processing by the system creates a situation where, before any window is displayed, the current display is saved (including any windows not being removed). When a window is then removed, the system restores the display from its saved version. Normal window processing is a resource-intensive function and, therefore, use of the USRRSTDSP keyword is greatly encouraged. In fact, under the following conditions, the system actually performs *two* saves of the screen:

- You are displaying only one window at a time.

- The current display file is compiled with RSTDSP(*YES).

- The window record that is to overlay the current display is in a different file.

The first save operation is performed because the display file is compiled with RSTDSP(*YES) and the second save is performed because of normal window processing. Use of USRRSTDSP eliminates the second save operation. Be sure to specify the keyword on the window following the first window you do not want the system to save. The USRRSTDSP keyword is only allowed on records containing the window keyword. It is ignored on the window reference record.

Although option indicators are allowed on the USRRSTDSP keyword, once the keyword is in effect, it remains in effect (even if the option indicator is set off) until you perform I/O on either the initial display screen or the window that is two windows before the window on which the USRRSTDSP is specified.

Although the rules governing USRRSTDSP sound complicated, the reward is worth the effort. The AS/400 sometimes takes an undeserved beating when talking about response time. More often than not, it's programming and operation techniques that cause response problems, not the system itself.

WINDOWS AND RESPONSE TIME

Response time, as it pertains to windows, is dependent upon your communications setup and on the complexity of the window being displayed. For our purposes, complexity is defined as the amount of information that must be saved and restored. The slowest response time occurs when the first window is added to a display and the system must perform the read and save operations.

A window of average size and complexity, on a terminal attached to the AS/400 by twinaxial, local area network (LAN), or other high-speed communications line, should have approximately a 1-second response time. If you are attached to a 9600-baud line, expect about 2.5 seconds to perform the read and save operations and display the window. If you are on a 2400-baud line, well, you're probably not reading this section anyway because you obviously do not care about response time (but figure about 10 seconds to display a window).

THE SYSTEM REQUEST WINDOW PROGRAM

Now let's look at a sample window program that may be used to provide some sizzle to your system. The AS/400 operating system is touted as one of the easiest operating systems to use (not as easy as a graphical user interface, but easy nevertheless). The AS/400 has a consistent command interface: All commands conform to the same naming conventions. Once you learn the convention, it is relatively easy to find commands. But we think that it can be made even easier!

We have put together a System Request Window program that allows you to put all system operation functions at the fingertips of your users. All system operations and special system-wide functions are made available by simply pressing the System Request key (Figure 3.5).

Figure 3.5: System Request Window Program

```
.......................................................
:                                                     :
: Options: 1=Select or press F12 to cancel            :
:                                                     :
: Option    Request                                   :
:   _     DISPLAY JOB                                 :
:   _     WORK WITH SPOOLED FILES                     :
:   _     WORK WITH PRINTERS                          :
:   _     GET COMMAND ENTRY LINE                      :
:   _     WORK WITH SUBMITTED JOBS                    :
:   _     SEND A MESSAGE                              :
:   _     SEND A BREAK MESSAGE                        :
:                                      More...        :
:                                                     :
:.....................................................:
```

This program also allows you to customize the list of options each user should have available. You can establish a default template of options that is available to all users, or you can specify options per User ID for those users you want to make exceptions to the norm.

Figure 3.6 shows the DDS to a physical file that we have named REQUEST. This file holds a display field, a command to be executed, a user name, and a sequence number. A subfile program (shown in Figure 3.7) displays this file in a window. The DDS for the window is shown in Figure 3.8.

Figure 3.6: DDS for File REQUEST

```
     *************************************************************
     *   TO COMPILE:
     *      CRTPF FILE(XXXLIB/REQUEST)
     *************************************************************
     AAN01N02N03T.Name++++++RLen++TDpBLinPosFunctions++++++++++++++++++++++++++++++
     A          R REQREC
     A            USERNAME      10         COLHDG('USER NAME')
     A            DISPLAYFLD    45         COLHDG('DISPLAY FIELD')
     A            SEQUENCE#      5 0       COLHDG('SEQUENCE #')
     A            COMMAND      256         COLHDG('COMMAND')
     A          K USERNAME
     A          K SEQUENCE#
```

Figure 3.7: RPG Attention Window Program

```
     ******************************************************************
     *    TO COMPILE:
     *       CRTBNDRPG PGM(XXXLIB/FIG37RG)
     ******************************************************************

     FFilename++IPEASF.....L.....A.Device+.Keywords+++++++++++++++++++++++Comments++
     FFIG38DS   CF   E             WORKSTN
     F                                      SFILE(SFLRCD:SfRelRec)
     FREQUEST    IF   E             K DISK

     DName+++++++++++ETDsFrom+++To/L+++IDc.Keywords+++++++++++++++++++++++Comments++
     D              SDS
     D  PARMS            *PARMS
     D  UserProfil         254    263
     D  ReturnCode   S             2
     D  CommandLen   S            15  5 INZ(256)

     CL0N01Factor1++++++Opcode&ExtFactor2++++++Result+++++++Len++D+HiLoEq.Comments++
        C       *ENTRY      PLIST
        C                   PARM                      ReturnCode
        C                   EVAL      SfSelect = *BLANKS
        C                   EVAL      SetPosit = 1
        C       UserProfil  SETLL     REQUEST                            24
  B1    C                   IF        *In24 = *OFF
        C                   EVAL      UserProfil = *BLANKS
        C       UserProfil  SETLL     REQUEST
  E1    C                   ENDIF
  B1    C                   DOU       *In24 = *ON
        C       UserProfil  READE     REQUEST                            24
  B1    C                   IF        *In24 = *OFF
        C                   EVAL      SfDesc = DisplayFld
        C                   EVAL      HidSequenc = Sequence#
        C                   EVAL      HidCommand = Command
        C                   EVAL      SfRelRec = (SfRelRec + 1)
        C                   WRITE     SFLRCD
  E2    C                   ENDIF
  E1    C                   ENDDO

        C                   IF        SfRelRec <> *ZEROS
        C                   EVAL      *IN21 = *ON
  E1    C                   ENDIF
  B1    C                   DOU       (*IN12 = *ON) or (*In03 = *ON)
        C                   WRITE     WINDOW
      * Display & Read subfile
        C                   EXFMT     SFLCTL
        C                   IF        (*In12 = *OFF) and (*In03 = *OFF)
        C                   EVAL      *IN42 = *OFF
      * Set cursor position and read changes looking for a selection request
        C                   EVAL      SetPosit = CurrentPos
        C                   DOU       *In41 = *ON
        C                   READC     SFLRCD                             41
        C                   IF        *In41 = *OFF
  B5    C                   SELECT
      * Process record and get out if a record was selected
        C                   WHEN      SfSelect = '1'
        C                   CALL      'QCMDEXC'                          99
        C                   PARM                      HidCommand
        C                   PARM                      CommandLen
      * Reset cursor
        C                   EVAL      SfSelect = *BLANKS
        C                   UPDATE    SFLRCD
```

```
        C                   WHEN       SfSelect <> *BLANKS
        C                   EVAL       *IN42 = *ON
        C                   EVAL       SetPosit = SfRelRec
        C                   UPDATE     SFLRCD
        C                   LEAVE
        C                   OTHER
        C                   ITER
E5      C                   ENDSL
E4      C                   ENDIF
E3      C                   ENDDO
E2      C                   ENDIF
E1      C                   ENDDO

        C                   EVAL       *INLR = *ON
```

Figure 3.8: DDS for the System Request Window

```
     A************************************************************************
     A*   TO COMPILE:
     A*      CRTDSPF FILE(XXXLIB/FIG38DS)
     A************************************************************************

     .AAN01N02N03T.Name++++++RLen++TDpBLinPosFunctions++++++++++++++++++++++++++
     A                                        DSPSIZ(24 80 *DS3)
     A                                        CA12(12)
     A                                        CA03(03)
     A            R WINDOW
     A                                        WINDOW(*DFT 15 53 *NORSTCSR)
     A                                        RMVWDW
     A                                  14  2'F3=Exit'
     A                                        COLOR(BLU)
     A                                  14 11'F12=Cancel'
     A                                        COLOR(BLU)
     A            R SFLRCD               SFL
     A  42                                    SFLNXTCHG
     A              SFSELECT      1A  B   6  4
     A              SFDESC       45A  O   6  8
     A              SFRELREC      4S  0H
     A              HIDSEQUENC    5S  0H
     A              HIDCOMMAND  256A   H
     A            R SFLCTL               SFLCTL(SFLRCD)
     A                                        SFLSIZ(0050)
     A                                        SFLPAG(0007)
     A                                        WINDOW(WINDOW)
     A  21                                    SFLDSP
     A                                        SFLDSPCTL
     A  24                                    SFLEND(*MORE)
     A  42                                    SFLMSG('Invalid Selection Entry')
     A                                        OVERLAY
     A                                        USRRSTDSP
     A              SETPOSIT      4S  0H      SFLRCDNBR(*TOP)
```

```
A            CURRENTPOS      5S 0H        SFLSCROLL
A                                      2  2'Type options, press Enter.'
A                                         COLOR(BLU)
A                                      3  4'1=Select'
A                                         DSPATR(HI)
A                                         COLOR(BLU)
A                                      5  3'Opt  Request'
A                                         DSPATR(HI)
A          R DUMMY
A                                         KEEP
A                                         ASSUME
A                                      1  2' '
```

This program allows a user to run commands by selecting a subfile record from within a window. The command to be run is stored in the REQUEST file, keyed by user name and sequence number. When the user selects a subfile record, the command is executed via QCMDEXC. What could be easier? No commands or parameters to memorize. Just read the screen, select a record based on a description of what the function is, and the command is executed.

To make our program even easier to use, it may be called when the Attention key is pressed. Assuming that you have compiled the program shown in Figure 3.7 as REQ001RG, you change the user profile by entering the following command:

CHGUSRPRF USRPRF(XXX) ATNPGM(REQ001RG)

Thereafter, whenever user XXX presses the Attention key, the window shown in Figure 3.8 appears. The actual functions that appear in the window are dependent upon the records entered into the REQUEST file. We have not provided a file maintenance program for this file. You can either write your own, or use a product like the Data File Utility (DFU). Key the default records you want to make available to all users and leave the User ID field blank. Only specify the User ID for those users whom you want to set up as exceptions.

The code for the RPG subfile program is rather simple. We assume that there will not be many records per user in the REQUEST file, so we use the load-all technique of subfile processing to load the subfile. Because of this, we do not have to code any rolling routines; the system handles rolling for us.

First check to see if this user (taken from the Program Status Data Structure) has any records in the REQUEST file. If not, then we use the default records, which are those with a blank user name. In addition to the fields being displayed in the subfile, we load the command to be run into a hidden field so that we can execute the hidden command when the user makes a selection.

After displaying the subfile, set up a loop and read all changed subfile records looking for a 1 in the selection field. Once one is found, the process subroutine retrieves the correct REQUEST file record and passes the command field to the QCMDEXC API (see Chapter 6) to execute the command. All of the normal prompting characters (e.g., ?? and ?*) can be used in the command field to prompt for the command.

SCROLL BARS AND SUBFILES

The ability to put subfiles into DDS windows was a welcome announcement with the release of V2R3. At long last, we were able to add graphically oriented lookup capabilities to our interactive programs. Subfiles could be presented that would not wipe out the entire displayed screen.

And along with V3R1 came the ability to employ a scroll bar with our subfiles. The AS/400 scroll bar works much as it would with other graphical interfaces in that it has a scroll block to indicate how big the subfile is, and where you are within it. The scroll block can be moved with the pointing device (provided that you are on a graphical workstation) and the subfile is repositioned accordingly.

The scroll bar may be employed by using a keyword option on the Subfile End (SFLEND) DDS keyword. We cover this option in detail in Chapter 2 on subfiles.

GUI THIS, AND GUI THAT

Sizzle, pizzazz, function, and ease of use. That is what the GUI craze is all about. So why shouldn't AS/400 programmers join the fray?

As you have seen, some of the GUI elements are so easy to code that they are actually irresistible! We've been coding windows in programs for more years than we care to admit, and the hoops we had to jump through to do it were numerous—PUTOVR, OVRDTA, OVERLAY, RSTDSP, etc., etc., etc. If you wanted a subfile in a window (and this was a very common request), you had to fake it. If you wanted a pull-down menu, just forget it!

Now, there are just five keywords to control a window and you don't even have to know where the window is going to appear—the system decides for you! Want a subfile in a window? No problem. The system does it. Want a scroll bar displayed on that subfile? Piece of cake!

If you have not added GUI features to your applications yet, **WHAT IN THE WORLD ARE YOU WAITING FOR?**

Chapter 4

Information Data Structures
and Error Handling

While it's true that the AS/400 operating system communicates mainly via messages, it is equally true that it communicates a wealth of information via special data structures. Two such data structures are the File Information Data Structure and the Program Status Data Structure.

In this chapter, we explain the information that is contained in these two very special data structures, and show you how to access them in your RPG programs. We also show you how to handle file and program errors by using the plethora of information that can be found in these data structures.

FILE INFORMATION DATA STRUCTURE

The first thing you should know about the data found in the File Information Data Structure is that it varies depending upon the type of file you are processing. You can get detailed information on every I/O operation you perform in your program—if you know how to get to it.

A File Information Data Structure is maintained for every file that your program uses, regardless of whether or not you code the data structure in your program. It is up to you to decide if you want to access the information. As you will see, it is not difficult to code and can be very advantageous in certain situations. Making the File Information Data Structure available for one of the files in your program is as simple as adding a File Description Specification Keyword to further describe the file in question. You can see two examples of this in Figure 4.1.

Figure 4.1: Specifying the File Information Data Structure

```
FFilename++IPEASF.....L.....A.Device+.Keywords++++++++++++++++++++++++++
FFILE1     IF   E          K DISK      INFDS(File1Ds)
FFILE2     IF   E          K DISK      INFDS(File2Ds)


DName++++++++++ETDsFrom+++To/L+++IDc.Keywords+++++++Comments++++++++++++
D File1Ds         DS
D  F1FileName              1      8
D  F1Status              11     15
D File2Ds         DS
D  F2FileName              1      8
D  F2Status              11     15
```

The File Description Specification Keyword for the Information Data Structure is the INFDS keyword followed by the name of an associated data structure enclosed in parentheses. In Figure 4.1, we see the INFDS keyword directly following the File Description Specification describing the database file named FILE1. You can see that the name of the File Information Data Structure for database file FILE1 is named FILE1DS.

After any I/O operation to FILE1 (including opening the file), the data structure FILE1DS contains the requested information that is coded in the data structure. For our example in Figure 4.1, the file name (F1FileName) and the status code (F1Status) are coded into our data structure. We could name the fields anything because the fields are stored positionally in the data structure. It is the From and To positions of the field that determine what information is in the field.

For the example in Figure 4.1, we also created a File Information Data Structure for the FILE2 database file, named FILE2DS. The naming conventions are totally arbitrary, but you can not have the same field defined in two different data structures, so we named them differently. We believe it is good practice to establish some kind of naming convention to help make the names easy to remember.

The File Information Data Structure is segregated positionally into several primary areas. Note that there is an overlap in positions 367 to 499. Information in this area is dependent upon the type of file being described. Basically, data is segmented into sections (Table 4.1).

Table 4.1: Contents of the File Information Data Structure

Type of Feedback	Positions in the Data Structure
File Feedback Information	1 to 76
Open Feedback	81 to 240
Common I/O Feedback	241 to 366
Device-dependent Feedback—ICF, DSP	367 to 446
Device-dependent Feedback—Printers	367 to 404
Device-dependent Feedback—Database	367 to 499

Special Keywords

IBM has determined that certain fields in the Information Data Structures are more likely to be requested by a program than others. Because of this, these fields have been assigned special keywords that you may use to reference the information. The idea is to free you from the hassle of having to remember the From and To positions in the Information Data Structures. The need for this feature could be ruled as questionable because you still have to remember the special keywords.

Table 4.2 contains a list of the special keywords in the File Information Data Structure. You code the keyword in the Input Specification for the data structure subfield in positions 44 to 51 in lieu of the field positions. Figure 4.2 shows an example of how to code a File Information Data Structure using one of the special keywords.

Table 4.2: Special Keywords

Keyword	From Position	To Position	Decimal Positions	Description
*FILE	1	8	—	The first eight characters of the file name used by the RPG program associated with this data structure.
*INP	71	72	0	For workstation device files, this is the national language input capability.
*OUT	73	74	0	For workstation device files, this is the national language output capability.
*OPCODE	16	21	—	RPG operation code last used to access the file. Note that op codes with six-letter names will be shortened to the five characters formerly used in the OPM version of RPG III. These include DELETE (DELET), EXCEPT (EXCPT), READPE (REDPE), UNLOCK (UNLCK), and UPDATE (UPDAT).
*SIZE	67	70	0	Total number of characters that can fit on the workstation device.
*STATUS	11	15	0	Status codes (defined later in this chapter).
*RECORD	38	45	—	Format name being processed.

Keyword	From Position	To Position	Decimal Positions	Description
*ROUTINE	22	29	—	RPG routine that was processing the file.

Figure 4.2: Coding Special Keywords

```
FFilename++IPEASF.....L......A.Device+.Keywords+++++++++++++++++++++++++
FFILE1     IF   E        K DISK     INFDS(File1Ds)


DName++++++++++ETDsFrom+++To/L+++IDc.Keywords++++++Comments+++++++++++
D File1Ds          DS
D  F1FileName              1     8
D  F1Status             *STATUS
```

FIELD DEFINITIONS

Now that you have seen two ways to code a File Information Data Structure, let's take a look at all of the common fields in the File Information Data. Figure 4.3 shows a sample data structure for all of the common fields that may be accessed, and field definitions. These fields are in the same positions, regardless of the file type. (Remember, some other portions of the data structure change based upon the type of file being described.)

Figure 4.3: Common Fields in File Information Data Structure

```
DName++++++++++ETDsFrom+++To/L+++IDc.Keywords++++++Comments+++++++++++
D File1Ds          DS
D  F1FileName              1     8
D  F1OpenInd               9     9
D  F1EndofFil             10    10
D  F1Status               11    15
D  F1OperCode             16    21
D  F1Routine              22    29
D  F1StmtNbr              30    37
D  F1SpeclRtn             38    42  0
D  F1RecordCd             38    45
D  F1MesageId             46    52
D  F1Unused               53    66
D  F1WkstnSiz             67    70  0
D  F1LangInp              71    72  0
D  F1LangOut              73    74  0
D  F1LangMode             75    76  0
```

Field Definitions of the Common Fields in the File Information Data Structure:

Field Name	Description
F1FileName	First eight characters of the file name (as used by the RPG program).
F1OpenInd	File open indicator (1 = Open).
F1EndOfFil	File at end of file indicator (1 = End of File).
F1Status	Status codes. Very useful for error determination and handling (see Table 4.3 for complete list).
F1OperCode	RPG operation code last used to access the file. The first five characters specify the code while the sixth position is itself a code, where: F = Op code specified on a file name. R = Op code specified on a record format name. I = Last operation was implicit.
F1Routine	Name of the RPG routine that was processing the file. Possible values are: *INIT - Program initialization. *GETIN - Read a record. *DETC - Detail calculations. *DETL - Detail output. *TOTC - Total calculation time (Level Break). *TOTL - Total time output. *OFL - Overflow output. *TERM - Program termination. PGMNAME - Name of a called program (for SPECIAL files).
F1StmtNbr	RPG source statement number.
F1SpeclRtn	User-specified return code for SPECIAL files.

Field Name	Description
F1RecordCd	For an externally described file, the first eight characters of the name of the record format being processed when the error occurred. For internally described files, the record format indicator is left-justified into the field.
F1MesageId	System message ID of the error, i.e., CPF9801.
F1WkstnSiz	Total number of characters that fit on the workstation display.
F1LangInp	National language input capability.
F1LangOut	National language output capability.
F1LangMode	National language preferred mode.

In Table 4.3, we list the possible status codes that may be contained in positions 11 to 15 of the File Information Data Structure. As previously noted, the *STATUS keyword may be used to access the status codes too.

Table 4.3: File Information Data Structure Status Codes

Code	Condition
00000	No exception/error occurred.
00002	Function key used to end display.
00011	Read to end of file.
00012	No record found on a CHAIN, SETLL, or SETGT operation.
00013	Subfile is full; trying to write another record.
01011	Undefined record type.

Code	Condition
01021	Attempted to write duplicate record (either database or subfile).
01022	Referential constraint error detected on file member.
01031	Matching records out of sequence.
01041	Array or table load sequence error.
01042	Alternate collating sequence for table error
01051	Too many entries in table or array.
01071	Numeric sequence error.
01121	Print key pressed, but no indicator specified in DDS for print.
01122	Rollup pressed, but no indicator specified in DDS.
01123	Rolldown pressed, but no indicator specified in DDS.
01124	Clear key pressed, but no indicator specified in DDS.
01125	Help key pressed, but no indicator specified in DDS.
01126	Home key pressed, but no indicator specified in DDS.
01201	Record mismatch detected on input.
01211	I/O operation to a closed file.
01215	Open issued to a file already opened.
01216	Error on an implicit OPEN/CLOSE operation.
01217	Error on an explicit OPEN/CLOSE operation.

Code	Condition
01218	Record locked; unable to allocate.
01221	Update without prior read or chain.
01222	Record cannot be allocated due to referential constraint error.
01231	Error on SPECIAL file.
01235	Error in PRTCTL space or skip entries.
01241	Record number not found in ADDROUT file.
01251	Permanent I/O error.
01255	Session or device error. Recovery may be possible.
01261	Attempted to exceed maximum number of acquired devices.
01271	Attempted to acquire unavailable device.
01281	Operation to device not yet acquired.
01282	Job ending with controlled option.
01284	Unable to acquire second device for single device file.
01285	Attempted to acquire a previously acquired device.
01286	Attempted to open shared file with SAVDS or IND file options.
01287	Response indicators overlap IND indicators.
01299	Other I/O error detected.
01331	Wait time exceeded for READ from WORKSTN file.

Open Feedback Information

By now you may be feeling overwhelmed by the sheer volume of information available to you that is stored in the File Information Data Structure. But wait! There's more! Remember, the data structure varies, depending upon the file type.

The open feedback area resides in positions 81 to 240. RPG copies the contents of the file Open Feedback area to the Information Data Structure whenever the associated file is opened (hence the name). Members in a multimembered file opened as a result of a read operation to a member are copied into this area as well.

The Data Management Guide contains a layout of all these fields, but if you go there, be prepared to do a little math. The fields are laid out in this book by giving you the length, data type, and offset of each. You must calculate the actual From and To positions. To do so, you will need to use the following formula:

$$\text{From} = 81 + \text{Offset}$$

$$\text{To} = \text{From} - 1 + \text{Character Length (in bytes)}$$

We have done the math for you, and you can see the results in Figure 4.4.

Figure 4.4: Open Feedback Area

```
    DName++++++++++ETDsFrom+++To/L+++IDc.Keywords++++++Comments++++++++++++
    D OpenFeedBk       DS
    D  F1OdpType               81     82
    D  F1FileName              83     92
    D  F1FileLib               93    102
    D  F1SpoolNam             103    112
    D  F1SpoolLib             113    122
    D  F1SpoolNbr             123    124B 0
    D  F1RecordLn             125    126B 0
    D  F1MaxKeyLn             127    128B 0
    D  F1MbrName              129    138
    D  F1FilTypCd             147    148B 0
    D  F1NbrLines             152    153B 0
    D  F1NbrColum             154    155B 0
    D  F1RcdCnt               156    159B 0
    D  F1AccesTyp             160    161
    D  F1DupeKeys             162    162
    D  F1Source               163    163
    D  F1CntlBlck             164    173
    D  F1CBlkOvr              174    183
    D  F1VolIdOff             184    185B 0
    D  F1BlockLmt             186    187B 0
    D  F1OvrFlowL             188    189B 0
    D  F1BlockOff             190    191B 0
    D  F1ReqrName             197    206
    D  F1OpenCnt              207    208B 0
```

```
D   FlNbrBased              211   212B 0
D   FlOpenId                214   215
D   FlMaxFmtLn              216   217B 0
D   FlCCSID                 218   219B 0
D   FlNbrDefnd              227   230B 0
```

Field Definitions of the Open Feedback Area:

Field Name	Description
FlOdpType	Open data path type. Possible values are: DB = Database. DS = Display device. SP = Spooled file.
FlFileName	File name as it is known to the system (which may be different from the way the RPG program knows it).
FlFileLib	Library name in which the file resides.
FlSpoolNam	Spooled file name.
FlSpoolLib	Library name in which the spooled file resides.
FlSpoolNbr	Spooled file number.
FlRecordLn	Record length of the file associated with this data structure.
FlMaxKeyLen	Maximum key length.
FlMbrName	Member name.
FlFileTypCd	Type of file subtype code.
FlNbrLines	Number of lines on the workstation display.
FlNbrColum	Number of columns on the workstation display.
FlRcdCnt	Number of records in the file when the file was opened.

Field Name	Description
F1AccesTyp	Type of data-file access. Possible values are: AR = Arrival sequence. KF = Keyed FIFO; duplicate keys allowed. KL = Keyed LIFO; duplicate keys allowed. KU = Keyed unique.
F1DupeKeys	Duplicate keys indicator. Possible values are: D = Duplicate keys are valid. U = Unique keys only.
F1Source	Source file indicator (Y = This is a source file).
F1CntlBlck	User-file control block parameters.
F1CBlkOvr	User-file control block parameter overrides.
F1VolIdOff	Offset to the location of the volume ID on the tape.
F1BlockLmt	Blocked input/output limit.
F1OvrFlowL	Overflow line number.
F1BlockOff	Blocked input/output offset. The offset from this record to the next record.
F1ReqrName	Requester name.
F1OpenCnt	Open count.
F1NbrBased	Number of members based on file.
F1OpenId	Open identifier.
F1MaxFmtLn	Maximum record format length.

Field Name	Description
F1CCSID	Database CCSID.
F1NbrDefnd	Number of devices defined.

I/O Feedback Area

Positions 241 through 366 are used for the I/O feedback information area. The content of this area is copied by RPG to the File Information Data Structure:

- On every I/O operation if a POST operation for the file is not specified anywhere in your program.

- Only after a POST for the file, if a POST operation for the file is specified anywhere in your program.

Again, you must go to the Data Management Guide to get a breakdown of the information in the data structure. Use the same calculations to figure From and To positions for this area of the File Information Data Structure as you do for the open feedback area (using an offset position of 241 instead of 81), or refer to Figure 4.5 where we have, once again, done the math for you.

Figure 4.5: I/O Feedback Area

```
    DName++++++++++ETDsFrom+++To/L+++IDc.Keywords+++++++Comments+++++++++++
D   IOFeedBack      DS
D    F1NbrWrite            243    246B 0
D    F1NbrReads            247    250B 0
D    F1NbrBoth             251    254B 0
D    F1NbrOther            255    258B 0
D    F1CurOper             260    260
D    F1FmtName             261    270
D    F1DevClass            271    272
D    F1DevName             273    282
D    F1RcdLen              283    286B 0
```

Field Definitions of the I/O Feedback Area:

Field Name	Description
F1NbrWrite	Number of writes performed.
F1NbrReads	Number of reads performed.
F1NbrBoth	Number of writes and reads performed.
F1NbrOther	Number of other I/Os performed.
F1CurOper	Current operation.
F1FmtName	Record format name.
F1DevClass	Device class.
F1DevName	Device name.
F1IRcdLen	Record length.

Device-specific Feedback Area

The device-specific feedback area begins in position 367 and its length is dependent on two factors: The device type and whether or not DISK files are keyed. The minimum length of the data area when device-specific feedback is used is 528 bytes:

- On every I/O operation, if a POST operation for the file is not specified anywhere in your program.

- Only after a POST for the file, if a POST operation for the file is specified anywhere in your program.

For the device-specific feedback areas, the offset position begins in 367 (if you want to go to the Data Management Guide). We went ahead and did the math for you in Figures 4.6, 4.7, and 4.8. Figure 4.6 shows this portion of the data structure for a printer file, Figure 4.7 reflects the data structure for a database file, and Figure 4.8 shows a breakdown of this part of the data structure for a workstation file.

Figure 4.6: Device-specific Feedback Area—Printers

```
     DName++++++++++ETDsFrom+++To/L+++IDc.Keywords++++++Comments+++++++++++
D PrintFeedB        DS
D   F1CurLine#              367    368B 0
D   F1CurPage#              369    372B 0
D   F1MajorCod              401    402
D   F1MinorCod              403    404
```

Field Definitions of the Printer Device-specific Feedback Area:

Field Name	Description
F1CurLine#	Current line number.
F1CurPage#	Current page number.
F1MajorCod	Major return code.
F1MinorCod	Minor return code.

Figure 4.7: Device-specific Feedback Area—Database File

```
     DName++++++++++ETDsFrom+++To/L+++IDc.Keywords++++++Comments+++++++++++
D DBFilFeedB        DS
D   F1FeedBSiz              367    370B 0
D   F1JoinFile              371    374
D   F1NbrLockd              377    378B 0
D   F1MaxField              379    380B 0
D   F1BitMapOf              381    384B 0
D   F1FPosBits              385    385  0
D   F1CurRecDl              386    386  0
D   F1NbrKeys               387    388B 0
D   F1LenKeys               393    394B 0
D   F1MbrNbr                395    396B 0
D   F1RelRec#               397    400B 0
D   F1KeyValue              401    2400
```

Field Definitions of the Database File Device-specific Feedback Area:

Field Name	Description
FlFeedBSiz	Size of database feedback area.
FlJoinFile	Joined file indicator.
FlNbrLockd	Number of locked records.
FlMaxField	Maximum number of fields.
FlBitMapOf	Offset to error bit map.
FlFPosBits	File position bits.
FlCurRecDl	Current record deleted indicator.
FlNbrKeys	Number of keys.
FlLenKeys	Length of keys
FlMbrNbr	Member number.
FlRelRec#	Relative record number.
FlKeyValue	Key value (maximum length 2,000 characters).

Figure 4.8: Device-specific Feedback Area—Workstation File

```
       DName+++++++++++ETDsFrom+++To/L+++IDc.Keywords++++++Comments++++++++++++
       D WkStnFeedB       DS
       D   F1DspFlags            367     368
       D   F1AidKey              369     369
       D   F1CursrLoc            370     371
       D   F1DataLen             372     375B 0
       D   F1SfRelRec            376     377B 0
       D   F1SfMinRrn            378     379B 0
       D   F1SfNbrRec            380     381B 0
       D   F1WinCsrLc            382     383
       D   F1MajorCod            401     402
       D   F1MinorCod            403     404
```

Field Definitions of the Workstation File Device-specific Feedback Area:

Field Name	Description
FlDspFlags	Display flags.
FlAidKey	AID byte.
FlCursrLoc	Cursor location.
FlDataLen	Actual data length.
FlSfRelRec	Subfile relative record number.
FlSfMinRrn	Subfile minimum relative record number.
FlSfNbrRec	Number of records in the subfile.
FlWinCsrLoc	Active window cursor location.
FlMajorCod	Major return code.
FlMinorCod	Minor return code.

In Figure 4.9, we show the fields required to get device-specific attribute feedback information. Attribute information may be retrieved for a display device or ICF communication session. The actual operation to retrieve the device-specific attributes will be performed when a POST operation is performed with a program device specified for Factor 1.

Figure 4.9: Device-specific Attribute Feedback Area—Workstation File

```
.....DName++++++++++ETDsFrom+++To/L+++IDc.Keywords++++++++++++++++++++++++++++++++Comments++
    D WkStnAtrFB       DS
    D   ProgramDev           241    250
    D   DeviceDesc           251    260
    D   UserId               261    270
    D   DeviceCls            271    271
    D   DeviceType           272    277
    D   Requester            278    278
    D   AcquireSts           279    279
    D   InviteSts            280    280
    D   DataAvail            281    281
```

```
D   NbrRows           282   283B 0
D   NbrCols           284   285B 0
D   Blink             286   286
D   LineSts           287   287
D   DisplayLoc        288   288
D   DisplayTyp        289   289
D   KeybdType         290   290
D   CntrlrInfo        342   342
D   ColorCapbl        343   343
D   GridCapbl         344   344
```

Field Definitions of the Workstation File Device-specific Attribute Feedback Area:

Field Name	Description
ProgramDev	Workstation device.
DeviceDesc	Workstation description.
UserId	User Profile ID signed on to workstation.
DeviceCls	Workstation device Class.
DeviceType	Workstation device Type.
Requester	Requesting workstation?
AcquireSts	Workstation acquire status.
InviteSts	Workstation invite status.
DataAvail	Data available.
NbrRows	Number of rows on workstation.
NbrCols	Number of columns on workstation.
Blink	Workstation capable of using blink attribute?
LineSts	Workstation on-line or off-line?
DisplayLoc	Display location.

Field Name	Description
DisplayTyp	Display type.
KeybdType	Type of keyboard on workstation.
CntrlrInfo	Workstation Controller information.
ColorCapbl	Workstation color enabled?
GridCapbl	Workstation capable of displaying a grid?

Figure 4.9 shows this portion of the data structure for a workstation file, and Figure 4.10 reflects the data structure for an ICF ISDN communication session.

Figure 4.10: Device-specific Attribute Feedback Area—ISDN ICF Communication Session

```
.....DName++++++++++ETDsFrom+++To/L+++IDc.Keywords++++++++++++++++++++++++++++++Comments++
     D ISDNFeedBk     DS
     D   ISDNLength        385    386B 0
     D   ISDNType          387    388
     D   ISDNPlan          389    390
     D   ISDNNbr           391    430
     D   ISDNSubLen        435    436B 0
     D   ISDNSubTyp        437    438
     D   ISDNSubAdr        439    478
     D   ISDNConect        480    480
     D   ISDNRmtLen        481    482B 0
     D   ISDNRmtAdr        483    514
     D   ISDNExtLen        519    520
     D   ISDNExtTyp        521    521
     D   ISDNExtNum        522    561
     D   ISDNX25           566    566
```

Field Definitions of the ISDN ICF Communication Session Device-specific Attribute Feedback Area:

Field Name	Description
ISDNLength	Remote number length.
ISDNType	Remote number type.
ISDNPlan	Remote number plan.
ISDNNbr	Remote number.
ISDNSubLen	Remote sub-address length.
ISDNSubTyp	Remote sub-address type.
ISDNSubAdr	Remote sub-address.
ISDNConect	Connection.
ISDNRmtLen	Remote address length.
ISDNRmtAdr	Remote address.
ISDNExtLen	Extension length.
ISDNExtTyp	Extension type.
ISDNExtNum	Extension number.
ISDNX25	X.25 call type.

PROGRAM STATUS DATA STRUCTURE

The Program Status Data Structure is similar to the File Information Data Structure, except that its purpose is to provide exception/error information about an RPG program. While a File Information Data Structure can be defined for each file, a Program Status Data Structure is defined once per program. Even though we show all of the fields in our example, you only need to code the elements that you need for your purposes. As you can see in Figure 4.11, the data structure is extremely easy to define.

Figure 4.11: Defining a Program Status Data Structure

```
      DName++++++++++ETDsFrom+++To/L+++IDc.Keywords++++++Comments++++++++++++
      D                 SDS
      D   ProcName          1     10
      D   StatusCode       11     15
      D   PrevStatus       16     20
      D   SourcStmt#       21     28
      D   ErrRoutine       29     36
      D   NbrParms         37     39  0
      D   ExcType          40     42
      D   ExcNumber        43     46
      D   MIObjDefTm       47     50
      D   MsgWrkArea       51     80
      D   PgmLibName       81     90
      D   MessageDta       91    170
      D   PrevMsgId       171    174
      D   Century         199    200  0
      D   ErrFilName      201    208
      D   ErrFileSts      209    243
      D   JobName         244    253
      D   UserProfil      254    263
      D   JobNumber       264    269  0
      D   RunDate         270    275  0
      D   SystemDate      276    281  0
      D   RunTime         282    287  0
      D   CompilDate      288    293  0
      D   CompilTime      294    299  0
      D   CompilLevl      300    303
      D   SourceFile      304    313
      D   SourceLib       314    323
      D   SourceMbr       324    333
      D   ProgramNam      334    343
      D   ModuleName      344    353
      D   Unused2         354    429
```

Field Definitions:

Field Name	Description
ProcName	Procedure name.
StatusCode	Status codes. See Figure 4.12 and Table 4.5.
PrevStatus	Previous status code.
SourceStmt#	RPG IV Source statement sequence number.

Field Name	Description
ErrRoutine	RPG routine in which the exception/error occurred.
NbrParms	Number of parms passed to this program.
ExcType	Exception type (CPF or MCH).
ExcNumber	Exception number.
MIObjDefTm	Machine instruction object definition template number.
MsgWrkArea	Work area for messages. Used internally by the compiler.
PgmLibName	Library name in which the program resides.
MessageDta	Error message data. CPF messages are placed here when status contains 09999.
PrevMsgId	Previous message ID. Identifies the exception that caused RPG9001 (the called program failed) to be signaled.
Century	First two digits of four-digit year.
ErrFilName	File name on which the last file operation occurred. Updated only when error occurs.
ErrFileSts	File status on the last file used. Includes status code, routine name, statement number, and record name. Updated only when error occurs.
JobName	Job name.
UserProfil	User profile name.
JobNumber	Job number.
RunDate	Date program started running in the system. UDATE is derived from this date.
SystemDate	System date.

Field Name	Description
RunTime	Time of program running.
CompilDate	Date program was compiled.
CompilTime	Time program was compiled.
CompilLevl	Level of the compiler.
SourceFile	Source file name used to compile the program.
SourceLib	Source library name.
SourceMbr	Source file member name used to compile the program.
ProgramNam	Name of program containing procedure.
ModuleName	Name of module containing procedure.

All you need to do to define the Program Status Data Structure is code an S in position 23 followed by DS in positions 24 and 25, then define the subfields you want to make accessible to your program. The Program Status Data Structure and all of the possible subfields are shown in Figure 4.11.

Just as the File Information Data Structure has predefined keywords for frequently used fields, the Program Status Data Structure does also. You can access these fields either by providing the From and To positions in the data structure, or by coding the special keyword in the From and To positions.

Figure 4.12 shows examples of both methods. Table 4.4 shows all of the special keywords in the Program Status Data Structure.

Figure 4.12: Defining Subfields with Special Keywords

```
DName++++++++++ETDsFrom+++To/L+++IDc.Keywords++++++Comments++++++++++++
D               SDS
D   ProgramNam           1    10
D   StatusCode         *STATUS
D   PrevStatus          16    20
```

Table 4.4: Special Keywords

Keyword	From Position	To Position	Decimal Positions	Description
*PROC	1	10	—	Name of this procedure. [1]
*STATUS	11	15	—	Status codes. See Table 4.5.
*ROUTINE	29	36	—	Error routine. [2]
*PARMS	37	39	—	Number of parameters passed to this program. [3]

Notes:

[1] If the module is running and someone compiles it, the module is renamed and put in library QRPLLIB. This parameter maintains the original name of the program.

[2] Possible error routines:

*INIT Program initialization
*DETL   Detail lines
*GETIN   Get an input record
*TOTC   Total calculations
*DETC   Detail calculations
*OFL Overflow lines
*TERM   Program ending

[3] Parameters expected by the program, but not passed by the calling program, do not cause a problem until the program attempts to access the field. If you first check the number of parameters passed to the program and do not use the field if it was not passed, you can have a variable number of parameters.

In Table 4.5, we list the possible status codes that may be contained in positions 11 to 15 of the Program Status Data Structure. Remember that the *STATUS keyword may be used to access the status codes too.

Table 4.5: Program Status Data Structure Status Codes

Code	Condition
00000	No exception/error occurred.
00001	Called program returned with the last record (LR) indicator on.
00100	Out-of-range condition occurred on a string operation.
00101	A negative square root was encountered on a mathematic operation.
00102	Divide-by-zero condition detected.
00103	Intermediate result field is not large enough to contain the result (occurs in freeform arithmetic operations).
00112	Invalid Date, Time, or Timestamp value has been detected.
00113	Invalid date calculation resulting in a date less than *LOVAL or greater than *HIVAL encountered.
00114	Date mapping error from a four-digit year to a two-digit year where the mapped date does not fall between 1940 and 2039.
00120	Array or table load sequence error.
00121	Array index is not valid.
00122	OCCUR operation is being performed on element outside of the data structure boundaries.
00123	Reset was attempted during program initialization.

Code	Condition
00202	Called program or procedure failed and the halt indicators (H1 through H9) are not on.
00211	Error encountered trying to call a program or procedure.
00221	Called program tried to use a parameter that was not passed to it.
00222	Pointer or parameter error.
00231	Called program or procedure returned with one of the halt indicators (H1 through H9) on.
00232	Halt indicator is on.
00233	Halt indicator is on when the RETURN operation is run.
00299	RPG IV formatted dump failed.
00333	Error encountered on DSPLY operation.
00401	Data area that is specified on IN or OUT operation could not be found.
00402	The Program Data Area (*PDA) not valid for a non-prestart job.
00411	Data area type or length does not match definition.
00412	Data area was not locked for an output operation.
00413	Error encountered on a data area IN or OUT operation.
00414	User is not currently authorized to use data area.
00415	User is not currently authorized to update data area.
00421	Error encountered on an UNLOCK operation.

Code	Condition
00431	Data area was previously locked by another program.
00432	Data area was previously locked by the current program.
00450	Character field is not entirely enclosed by shift-out and shift-in characters.
00501	Failure to retrieve the sort sequence.
00502	Failure to convert the sort sequence.
00802	Commitment control is not active.
00803	Commitment control roll back operation failed.
00804	Error occurred on the COMMIT (commitment control) operation.
00805	Error occurred on the ROLBAK (commitment control) operation.
00907	Data decimal error was encountered. The sign or digit was not valid.
00970	The RPG IV compiler used to create the program does not match the level number of the run-time subroutines encountered.
09998	Internal failure encountered in RPG IV compiler or internal subroutines.
09999	Program exception encountered in system routine.

Error Handling

If you have been programming on the AS/400 for longer than, say, a day, then you undoubtedly have experienced the frustration of having a program blow up. It's bad enough that some user has figured out a way to use a perfectly good program that you wrote in some totally weird and unexpected fashion that causes it to crash. And then, the system takes over and issues a totally useless and confusing message that only means something to someone buried deep within the halls of IBM.

Adding insult to injury, the user is sometimes given options to continue! Now when was the last time you met a user who, when presented with a choice of options, would choose the correct one? (Does option C mean Continue or Cancel?)

Wouldn't it be nice if you could tell the system what to do anytime it encounters an error, even if you hadn't thought of the error when you wrote the program? Well, this method of error prevention is called a *PSSR subroutine.

IMPLEMENTING THE *PSSR SUBROUTINE

A *PSSR subroutine is a user-written subroutine that receives control when the system detects an error in a program. You identify the subroutine by coding (surprise!) *PSSR in factor one of the BEGSR statement.

You can access a *PSSR subroutine in three different ways:

- When you code a file access statement, such as CHAIN, and you do not specify an error indicator in positions 56 and 57, control is transferred by the system to this subroutine when an error occurs.

- You can code an error indicator in positions 56 and 57 and when this error indicator comes on, execute the subroutine by coding *PSSR in Factor 2 of the EXSR statement.

- Name it (*PSSR) in positions 60 through 64 on the File Definition Specification continuation line, with INFSR in positions 54 through 59.

The first thing you should be aware of when coding this type of subroutine is the possibility of creating an endless loop, which tends to slow other users' response time and totally destroy yours.

This subroutine is called by the system whenever an error occurs, so if an error occurs while you are in the subroutine, the subroutine gets called again, which could cause the error again, which again calls the subroutine, which again causes the error... Well, you get the picture.

So, to make sure this does not occur, the first thing to do in the *PSSR subroutine is to check and make sure that you have not come from an error inside the subroutine itself. This is done very simply by checking a field for blanks. If it's not blank, let the system take over and display its own error messages. If it is blank, continue with the subroutine and make the field nonblank. This flagging routine is very basic coding that must be done in every *PSSR subroutine that you write. The program compiles and runs without this code, but if you leave it out you pay the price.

So, now you are down inside the *PSSR subroutine, past the endless loop check so you know an error has occurred in your program. But, *what* happened? You can interrogate the *STATUS field of the File Information Data Structure or the MSGDTA field of the Program Status Data Structure to find out.

Another thing you could do at this point is call a generic error-handling program and pass it the File Information Data Structure and the Program Status Data Structure. This program could then log the error information to a database file and present an error screen with a message like "An error has occurred - CALL Ron or Doug at 123-4567." This is a very nice technique that eliminates IBM's cryptic messages and also provides a log of all errors that occur.

Return Points

Regardless of what you do inside the subroutine, you have some options as to where to return control of the program. Factor 2 of the ENDSR statement of a *PSSR subroutine can be a field name that contains the control return point. Table 4.6 lists the valid values and their meanings. If the field contains an invalid entry, no error is indicated and the system acts as if the field is blank.

Table 4.6: Error Return Points

Value	Description
*CANCL	Cancel program.
*DETC	Detail calculations.
*DETL	Detail lines.
*GETIN	Get an input record.
*OFL	Overflow lines.
*TOTC	Continue at beginning of total calculations.
*TOTL	Continue at beginning of total lines.
Blanks	Return control to the system. This is true if field is blanks or not specified, or if field contains an invalid entry. If routine was called explicitly, control returns to the next sequential statement.

If the *PSSR subroutine is called explicitly via the EXSR statement and no return point is indicated, control returns to the next sequential statement after the EXSR statement.

If the subroutine is called implicitly (via INFSR on an F-Specification or no indicator on a CHAIN op code), a system error message is probably issued. An error message is not issued if the status code is from 1121 to 1126 because these error codes indicate that some invalid key was pressed on the keyboard (e.g., print or rollup). In this case, control returns to the next sequential statement.

Points to Remember

After the *PSSR subroutine is run, the system resets the field specified in Factor 2 of the ENDSR statement to blanks. This means that your program should set the value of the field each time the subroutine is executed. If an error occurs during the start or end of the program, control passes to the system and not to the *PSSR subroutine.

Record Locks

Every good programmer knows the proper way to code the functions of accessing a file so that the system does not maintain a lock on the record until you actually need the record (and every programmer has a different "proper" way to do it). But what about all those other "bad guys" who access the record and keep it locked so your program can't get at it?

Wouldn't it be nice if, when you chained to a file to get a record and some other program had that record locked, you could send a message to your user giving them the name of the bonehead who is keeping your program from running? The File Information Data Structure can tell you that you had a record lock on the file and the Program Status Data Structure can tell you the name of the job that has the lock! The sample programs in Figures 4.13 and 4.14 demonstrate this technique.

Figure 4.13: DDS for Sample Record Lock Program

```
A********************************************************************
A*   TO COMPILE:
A*      CRTDSPF FILE(XXXLIB/FIG413DS)
A********************************************************************

.....AAN01N02N03T.Name++++++RLen++TDpBLinPosFunctions++++++++++++++++++++++++++++
A                                      DSPSIZ(24 80 *DS3)
A              R FMTC
A                                      CF03(03 'End of job')
A                                      CF12(12 'Return to Previous')
A                                      OVERLAY
A                                  21  3'                             -
A                                           '
A                                      DSPATR(UL)
A                                  22  5'F3=Exit'
A                                  22 19'F12=Previous'
A                                   9 21'Customer Number:'
A              CUSTNUMBER    10A  B  9 38
A  99                                  ERRMSGID(CPF9898 QSYS/QCPFMSG 99 &M-
A                                      ESSAGEHLD)
A                                   1 27'Customer Update'
A                                      DSPATR(HI)
A                                      DSPATR(UL)
A              MESSAGEHLD    80A  P
```

Figure 4.14: Sample RPG Program for Record Locks

```
*************************************************************
*   TO COMPILE:
*     CRTBNDRPG PGM(XXXLIB/FIG414RG)
*************************************************************

FFilename++IPEASF.....L.....A.Device+.Keywords++++++++++++++++++++++++Comments++++++++++
+
FRCDLCKDS  CF    E             WORKSTN
FCUSTOMER  UF    E          K DISK
F                                    INFDS(Info)


DName++++++++++ETDsFrom+++To/L+++IDc.Keywords++++++++++++++++++++++++Comments++++++++++
+
D Info            DS
D  Status              *STATUS
D                SDS
D  MessageDta         91    170
D InB4          S            1
D MessageHld    S           80


CL0N01Factor1+++++++Opcode&ExtExtendedFactor2+++++++++++++++++++++++Comments++++++++++
C                   DOU       *In99 = *OFF
C                   EXFMT     FMTC
C     CustNumber    CHAIN     CUSTOMER                              6899
C     *IN99         IFEQ      *ON
C                   EXSR      *PSSR
C                   ENDIF
C                   ENDDO
C                   EVAL      *INLR  = *ON
CSR   *PSSR         BEGSR
C     InB4          IFEQ      *ON
C                   EVAL      *INLR  = *ON
C                   RETURN
C                   ELSE
C                   EVAL      InB4   = *ON
 * Record Lock
C     Status        IFEQ      01218
C                   EVAL      MessageHld = MessageDta
C                   ENDIF
C                   ENDIF
C                   EVAL      InB4   = *OFF
CSR                 ENDSR
```

The program in our example first brings up a screen asking for a customer number. It then attempts to get the record via the CHAIN op code. Because the file is coded as an update file in the File Specification, the system checks to see that the record is not being held for update elsewhere. If some other job (or even a previous job step within your job) has a lock on the record, indicator 99 comes on. Be aware that the amount of time the system waits for a record is determined by the RCDWAIT parameter on the CRTPF or CHGPF commands. The normal default is 60 seconds, but, if this is changed to *NOMAX, you could be waiting until you are old and gray.

When indicator 99 comes on, the *PSSR subroutine is called explicitly. The first thing it does is make sure that it is not taking part in an endless loop by checking the INB4 field. If it is, it terminates. If it's not, it interrogates the status field for code 1218—record locked, unable to allocate.

If a record lock problem exists, it moves the message data field from the Program Status Data Structure into the program-to-system field MessageHld. This field is defined on an ERRMSGID keyword, so the message data from the Program Status Data Structure is displayed as an error message at the bottom of the screen when the record format is output.

We then fall out of the *PSSR subroutine (after blanking out our endless loop protection field). We have not coded a return point in Factor 2 of the ENDSR statement and the subroutine was called explicitly, so control returns to the next sequential statement after the EXSR statement. Because indicator 99 is still on, we loop back up and redisplay the format with the error message indicating which job has the record locked.

INFORMATION IS POWER

The File Information Data Structure and the Program Status Data Structure can provide a wealth of information to your programs. The special keywords provided in each structure make accessing the essential information a very easy task.

You can use the information, such as program name, rather than hard coding the data in your program. The obvious advantage is that, when the information changes (such as the program being renamed or cloned), the program does not have to be changed.

When combined with the *PSSR subroutine, these information data structures provide your program with a great deal of flexibility when handling errors. You can elect to present your own global error screen whenever an unexpected error occurs. You can monitor for particular errors, take appropriate action on them, and let the system handle any other unexpected errors.

The bottom line is: The choice is yours. Information is power!

Chapter 5

Tips and Techniques for the RPG/400 Programmer

The fact that you bought this book and are reading this chapter indicates one of three things:

A. You are an experienced programmer who is always looking for ways to improve.

B. You are a beginning programmer who is always looking for ways to improve.

C. You are a family member or close friend.

If you are reading this book for reasons A or B, we trust you will find something to add to your toolbox. If you are reading this for reason C, thank you. Your obligation has been met and you may stop reading now.

In this chapter, we cover a little something for everyone. We start off by reviewing some basic RPG operation codes to perform routine tasks. For instance, did you know you can left-justify a field with only two statements of code? CHECK it out! There are a couple of ways we know of to translate lowercase to uppercase. We demonstrate how to do it using the Translate (XLATE) operation code.

The BITON/BITOFF operation codes have been around for a long time and still make a very useful tool to have around, although they can be a "bit" cumbersome to use. Our example shows how they are used to control the display attributes of embedded fields. This can be a useful technique if you need to highlight or reverse image a key word or phrase within a line of text.

We follow this information with some techniques to make routine file maintenance tasks a little easier. Did you know that, with the proper use of the RTNDTA keyword, you can eliminate all of the tedious MOVE statements that are usually coded to move fields from a database file to a display file? We not only demonstrate this technique, we cover how to use multiple views of the same file in a program.

Parameters. To pass or not to pass, that is the question (please forgive us William Shakespeare). And the answer is... Who cares? If you code the receiving program correctly, it will not blow up, even if the calling program does not pass the parameters it expects.

REMOVING LEADING BLANKS (LEFT JUSTIFY)

The CHECK op code is very useful for removing leading blanks. When used in conjunction with the Substring (SUBST) op code, leading blanks can be removed from a field with two simple statements (Figure 5.1).

Figure 5.1: Using CHECK to Remove Leading Blanks

```
CL0N01Factor1+++++++Opcode&ExtFactor2+++++++Result++++++++Len++D+HiLoEq....Comments+
C           ' '           CHECK     NAME           X                 2 0
C                         SUBST(P)  NAME:X         NAME
```

The example in Figure 5.1 uses the CHECK op code to find the first nonblank character in the NAME field and stores the address of that field in a numeric variable called X. The Substring (SUBST) function is then used to move the nonblank characters of NAME into the left-most characters of the NAME field, and then pad the remaining positions of the NAME field with blanks.

For example, let's apply the code in Figure 5.1 to the following NAME field:

```
...+... 1 ...+... 2 ...+... 3
       SMITH
```

The results after the operation in Figure 5.1 look like this:

```
...+... 1 ...+... 2 ...+... 3
SMITH
```

TRANSLATE (XLATE) PERFORMS SINGLE-CHARACTER SUBSTITUTION WITHIN CHARACTER STRINGS

The XLATE op code is a handy tool when you need to perform character substitution within a character string. You can specify From and To characters to be translated, or entire strings of characters that need to be translated.

One of the more popular uses for this op code is to translate a lowercase character string to uppercase. This is a frequent requirement when you are importing data from an external source. Figure 5.2 is an example of how to address this issue.

Figure 5.2: Using XLATE to Translate Lowercase Character Strings to Uppercase

```
DName++++++++++ETDsFrom+++To/L+++IDc.Keywords++++++++++++++++++++++++Comments++++++
DLower            C                    'abcdefghijklmnopqrstuvwxyz'
DUpper            C                    'ABCDEFGHIJKLMNOPQRSTUVWXYZ'

CL0N01Factor1+++++++Opcode&ExtFactor2+++++++Result+++++++Len++D+HiLoEq....Comments+
C     Lower:Upper   XLATE     LowerField     UpperField
```

USING *BITON/BITOFF* OPERATION CODES

BITON and the converse op code BITOFF allow you to change the status of the bits in a single-byte field. The BITON op code changes the specified bits from a 0 (off) to a 1 (on) (Figure 5.3). Conversely, the BITOFF op code does just the opposite.

Figure 5.3: Example of the BITON RPG Op Code

Factor 1	Op Code	Factor 2	Result Field	Ext	HI	LO	EQ
—	**BITON**	'bit pattern'	1 byte field	—	N/A	N/A	N/A

In both of the operation codes, Factor 1 is left blank. Factor 2 can contain either a single-byte character field or a named constant containing a bit pattern. If a field is used in Factor 2, then the bits that are on in that field are set off in the results field. The bits that are off in the field in Factor 2 are ignored in the results field.

You should be aware of the horizontal method of addressing bits used in RPG. There are eight bits in a byte. The bits are numbered from left to right, beginning with 0.

One of our favorite uses of these operation codes is to change a display attribute of some portion of a text field. The DSPATR keyword is easy to use, but works on the complete field. You can not use it to highlight a single word inside a text field. But you can use the BITON/BITOFF operation codes to accomplish this. Let's take at look a the code in Figure 5.4.

Figure 5.4: Using BITON/BITOFF to Change Display Attributes

```
CL0N01Factor1+++++++Opcode&ExtFactor2+++++++Result++++++++Len++D+HiLoEq....Comments+
C                   BITOFF    '01234567'    HighLight        1
C                   BITON     '26'          HighLight        1
C                   BITOFF    '01234567'    Normal           1
C                   BITON     '2'           Normal           1
C                   BITOFF    '01234567'    ReversImag       1
C                   BITON     '27'          ReversImag       1
C                   MOVEL     HighLight     Field
C                   MOVE      Normal        Field
```

We first use the BITOFF op code to set off all of the bits in our field named HighLight. This is similar in function to initializing a field. We then use the BITON op code to set on bits 2 and 6. This combination of bits, when sent to a display device, translates into a command character that tells the system to turn on highlighting.

Again we use the BITON/BITOFF op codes to set on bit 2 in a field called Normal. (You might notice that we have included the bit pattern for the field named ReversImag, which is short for Reverse Image. We are not using it in this example, but we thought you might find it useful.) We use the Normal field to turn off the highlighting function. Next we move the field HighLight to the beginning of the field we want highlighted and move the field Normal to the end of the field we want highlighted. When this field, named (cleverly enough) FIELD, is displayed on a device, it is highlighted. This field can then be embedded in an array or "substringed" (you will not find this word in your Webster's Dictionary, but consider it to be a derivative of the Substring op code) together with other text that would be displayed normally.

When using this technique, be sure to use the normal pattern to shut off the display attribute that you set. If you do not, the attribute remains in effect until the end of the displayed line.

Using RTNDTA in File Maintenance

A file maintenance program is like a sewer; it performs a very necessary function, but nobody likes to work there. Let's face it, file maintenance programs are boring and tedious. Every one of them performs pretty much the same routines—read a record, move the fields from the record to the screen, display the screen, edit the fields, move the fields back to the record, update the record. This a standard, low-tech, boring job that must be done.

There is a DDS keyword, RTNDTA, that can eliminate a lot of code. While it can't actually make you *like* doing file maintenance programs, it simplifies the task by eliminating a lot of tedious move statements.

Figure 5.5 shows a typical file maintenance task. It reads a record, moves the fields in the record to the screen, and waits for the user to enter some data. The record is not locked at this point because we don't know how long this user will be at lunch while this record is on the screen. When the user comes back from their break and presses the Enter key, we get the database record (this time locking the record for update), move the fields from the screen to the record, and update the database record.

Figure 5.5: Routine File Maintenance Task

```
CL0N01Factor1+++++++Opcode&ExtFactor2+++++++Result++++++++Len++D+HiLoEq....Comments+
C         CustKey       CHAIN(N)   Customer                           68
C                       EVAL       DispName = CustName
C                       EVAL       DispAddr1 = CustAddr1
C                       EVAL       DispAddr2 = CustAddr2
C                       EVAL       DispCity = CustCity
C                       EVAL       DispState = CustState
C                       EVAL       DispZip = CustZip
C                       EXFMT      Format1
C         CustKey       CHAIN      Customer                           68
C                       EVAL       CustName = DispName
C                       EVAL       CustAddr1 = DispAddr1
C                       EVAL       CustAddr2 = DispAddr2
C                       EVAL       CustCity = DispCity
C                       EVAL       CustState = DispState
C                       EVAL       CustZip = DispZip
C                       UPDATE     CustRec
```

Figure 5.6 shows the same function as Figure 5.5, but uses the RTNDTA DDS keyword in the display file. All of the fields in the display file are named the same as the fields in the database file. This eliminates the need to code all of the move statements to get them from the database record to the display file record format.

Figure 5.6: Maintenance Function with RTNDTA Keyword

```
CL0N01Factor1+++++++Opcode&ExtFactor2+++++++Result++++++++Len++D+HiLoEq....Comments+
C         CustKey       CHAIN(N)   Customer                           68
C                       EXFMT      Format1
C         CustKey       CHAIN      Customer                           68
C                       READ       Format1                                68
C                       UPDATE     CustRec
```

But wait, you say, when it chains back out to the database record to get it for update, it will lose any of the data keyed into the fields in the display format. This is true, and so we have coded another read to the display file record format (Format1). The RTNDTA keyword is coded on this record format and this was the last record format written to the screen, so the system gets the fields from the screen again, as the user keyed them. But wait another minute, you say, the READ Format1 statement will cause the program to wait for input from the user. Normally true, but the RTNDTA keyword also prevents this from happening.

This is a very powerful technique that potentially can eliminate tons of code and reduce the amount of maintenance that must be performed later. In this very simple example, we eliminated a lot of extraneous code. And, remember our motto—Less code, fewer errors.

PROCESSING MULTIPLE VIEWS OF THE SAME DATABASE FILE

Options, options, and more options. We are really in the business of providing people with options. The more the merrier. One of the options that every user seems to demand is the ability to display the records from a database file in a sequence other than the database designer intended. With DB/400's support of logical files, this does not present much of a problem. Remember the performance considerations when utilizing this technique (see Chapter 1, "Performance Starts with Program Design").

In Figure 5.7, we present our usual method of handling multiple views of the same file in a single program. The first step is to define the files in the File Description Specifications. The compiler frowns upon using two file definitions with the same record format, so we must rename one of the record formats. This is accomplished using the RENAME keyword. We name the actual record format and then give it an alias with which to refer to it inside the RPG program.

Figure 5.7: Multiple Views of the Same File in a Single Program

```
FFilename++IPEASFRlen+LKlen+AIDevice+.Keywords++++++++++++++++++++++++Comments++++++
FFile1      IF   E         K DISK
FFile1LogicIF   E         K DISK       Rename(FileRec:LogicRec)


CL0N01Factor1+++++++Opcode&ExtFactor2+++++++Result++++++++Len++D+HiLoEq....Comments+
C                   SELECT
C                   WHEN      *IN71 = *ON
C                   READ      File1                              68
C                   WHEN      *IN72 = *ON
C                   READ      File1Logic                         68
C                   ENDSL
```

Now that the compiler is happy, we can continue on our merry way and read whichever view of the database file the user is happy with. The system keeps two independent file pointers for each "view" of your data. You do, however, need to be careful in handling the contents of individual fields.

One of our complaints with RPG is that the file access operation codes (e.g., READ and CHAIN) do not allow a field name in Factor 2. When dealing with multiple views of the same database file, this would greatly simplify the amount of code necessary to accomplish the task. So, the next time someone at a users' conference asks you to fill out a REQUIREMENTS form, you know what to ask for, right?

PASS THE PARAMETER, IF YOU PLEASE

As with everything else on the AS/400, there are numerous ways to handle passing information between programs. You can use files, data queues, message queues, data areas, parameters, and so on.

Parameters are defined in a program using a Parameter List (PLIST) statement, with *ENTRY defined in Factor 1. A PLIST statement must be followed by at least one Parameter (PARM) statement. This PARM statement defines the data being received by the program.

We see an example of this in Figure 5.8. Two parameters are being passed to this program: A two-character, alphanumeric return code and a two-digit, numeric location code.

Figure 5.8: Passing a Variable Number of Parameters between Programs

```
DName++++++++++ETDsFrom+++To/L+++IDc.Keywords++++++++++++++++++++++++Comments++++++
D               SDS
DParms           *PARMS

CL0N01Factor1+++++++Opcode&ExtFactor2+++++++Result++++++++Len++D+HiLoEq....Comments+
C     *ENTRY        PLIST
C                   PARM                      ReturnCode      2
C                   PARM                      PasLocCode      2 0
C                   IF        Parms >= 1
C                   EVAL      ReturnCode = *blanks
C                   ENDIF
C                   IF        Parms >= 2
C                   EVAL      WrkLocCode = PasLocCode
C                   ENDIF
```

The thing to remember about parameter passing is that the program neither checks, nor cares, about any of the parameters until it actually tries to use them. This means that, if a program calls another program and does not pass all of the parameters that the called program is expecting, nothing happens until—and if—the called program tries to access one of the passed parameters. If the called program does try to use a parameter and the program that initiated the call did not pass the field, you get introduced to one of the nifty little error handling routines of the operating system.

There is a simple method of avoiding this error. Code the Program Status Data Structure and use the keyword *PARMS as we did in Figure 5.8. The field PARMS contains the number of parameters that the calling program passed to the called program.

If the field PARMS tells us that a parameter was passed to this program, we move it to a work field. Thereafter, the program only works with the work fields, unless it is passing data back to the calling program, in which case it must check the PARMS field again. At no time does the program attempt to access a parameter without first checking the PARMS field to see if the field was passed to it.

USING A RTNCOD PARAMETER BETWEEN PROGRAMS

We all know the problems associated with using one big program to do many different functions. The program is slow to load into memory, difficult to follow, and hard for others to maintain. In large and complex applications, it is far better to design many small programs controlled by one *driver* program. These smaller programs are generally referred to as *subprograms*. The subprograms only get loaded into memory when they are needed. Maintenance can usually be isolated to one small, easy-to-follow subprogram.

This technique can present something of a problem in that the calling program often needs to know what happened in the called program. If the driver program calls a subprogram that presents the user with a screen and the user presses F3 to Exit, the driver program must know this in order to end the job step. As usual, there are many ways to accomplish this—one of which is to use a parameter to pass the function key that was pressed. Figure 5.9 illustrates this technique.

Figure 5.9: Using a RTNCOD Parameter between Programs

```
CL0N01Factor1+++++++Opcode&ExtFactor2+++++++Result+++++++Len++D+HiLoEq....Comments+
C       *ENTRY      PLIST
C                   PARM                      ReturnCode        2
C                   EXFMT    Format1
C                   IF       *INKC = *On
C                   EVAL     ReturnCode = '03'
C                   EVAL     *InLr = *On
C                   ENDIF
C                   IF       *INKL = *On
C                   EVAL     ReturnCode = '12'
C                   ENDIF
```

USING THE INDICATOR ARRAY

One technique that we often take for granted is one that new programmers might not yet be aware of. You can use the array handling operation code Move Array (MOVEA) to set on and off many indicators at once. We use this technique quite often at the beginning of edit routines to set off all of the error indicators. Figure 5.10 demonstrates this technique.

Figure 5.10: Using the Indicator Array

```
DName++++++++++ETDsFrom+++To/L+++IDc.Keywords++++++++++++++++++++++++++Comments++++++
DIndicatSet        C                    '0011001111100001111-
D                                       00000000'

CL0N01Factor1++++++++Opcode&ExtFactor2+++++++Result++++++++Len++D+HiLoEq....Comments+
C                 EXFMT     Format1
C                 MOVEA     *ALL'0'        *IN(40)
C                 EXFMT     Format2
C                 MOVEA     '000000'       *IN(32)
C                 EXFMT     Format3
C                 MOVEA     IndicatSet     *IN(50)
```

In our example, after displaying FORMAT1, the MOVEA operation code is used to set off indicators 40 through 99. The reserved word *ALL is used to indicate the settings of the indicators. We could just as easily specify *ALL(1) to set all of the indicators on.

In the second example in Figure 5.10, after displaying FORMAT2, the MOVEA operation code is used to set off indicators 32 through 37. The length of Factor 2 is only eight characters, so this version of the technique is limited in the number of indicators affected by the operation code.

The third example in Figure 5.10 uses a named constant to set the status of 26 indicators, namely 50 through 75. This version of the technique can handle as many indicators as you want, and set them to any status required.

When you use this technique, be aware that the indicators that are affected by the MOVEA statement do not show up in the RPG compile listing as having been used. This is because they are individual elements in an array.

USING INDICATORS AS FIELD NAMES

You can also refer to an indicator as a named field. Every indicator has its own name using the format *INXX, where *XX* is the indicator number. The first two statements shown in Figure 5.11 basically are equal. You can, and should, test the status of indicators by using the indicator name, either in Factor 1 on an IFEQ statement, or anywhere in an EVAL statement.

Figure 5.11: Indicators as Named Fields

```
CLON01Factor1+++++++Opcode&ExtFactor2+++++++Result++++++++Len++D+HiLoEq....Comments+
C                   SETON                                                01
C                   EVAL      *IN01 = *ON
C                   IF        *IN01 = *ON
C                   MOVE      *ON             *INLR
C                   ENDIF
```

We have a strong aversion to using indicators to condition Calculation Specifications. While it's easier to code, it's harder to read, follow, and, especially, maintain.

RETRIEVING THE PROGRAM NAME

One very useful bit of information that you can extract from the Program Status Data Structure is the name of the program that is running. Why is this useful, you ask? After all, you wrote the program so you know its name. Why do you need the Program Status Data Structure to tell you this?

The obvious answer is maintenance. After you have been programming for some time, you should find that you almost never write programs from scratch anymore. You find something from your toolbox that is similar to the task at hand and you start there. So, the less hard coding you have in any program, the easier it is to clone and use for the basis of something else.

But there is another, less obvious, answer. The system sometimes changes the name of the program! If a program is executing and some inattentive programmer compiles that same program, the system moves the program that is executing into the QRPLLIB library. As it does this, it renames the object. The net result is that the program that is running still runs the old code, while any new instances of the program run the newly compiled version.

While that program is running in QRPLLIB, it has a different name. If you have hard coded the name of the program into any fields (such as message queue name), you might experience the system-handling error routine. This is kind of like meeting the Master Control Program (for all you TRON fans)—a very nasty experience.

So, the best way to code the name of the program is to retrieve it from the Program Status Data Structure. An example of this is shown in Figure 5.12. The program name is retrieved by using the keyword *PROC and assigns it a field name of *ProgramNam*.

(You should note that RPG III used the keyword *PROGRAM while RPG IV uses *PROC.)

Figure 5.12: Extracting the Program Name

```
DName++++++++++ETDsFrom+++To/L+++IDc.Keywords++++++++++++++++++++++++Comments++++++
D                SDS
DProgramNam          *PROC
```

USING MULTIPLE FORMAT FILES

The AS/400 uses a very strong relational database file manager. File definitions are external to the programs processing the data, thus ensuring consistency and relieving the programmer of the necessity of defining the data.

But some people believe that this file management system can not handle multiple format files. While it is true that a single file can only contain one format, it is also true that a logical file can be built over multiple files (each file having a different format). The net result appears to be a multiple format file. This is especially useful in a header/detail type file relationship.

If you perform a read on the logical file, you get a record from either database file (either the header record or the detail record), depending upon which was next in sequence. From a programming perspective, the problem becomes how to determine which record format was just read. This information can be obtained from the File Information Data Structure. Figure 5.13 shows the RPG code that demonstrates this technique.

Figure 5.13: Processing a Multiple-format Logical File

```
FFilename++IPEASFRlen+LKlen+AIDevice+.Keywords++++++++++++++++++++++++Comments++++++
FLogical   IF   E          K DISK    INFDS(InfoDs)


DName++++++++++ETDsFrom+++To/L+++IDc.Keywords++++++++++++++++++++++++Comments++++++
DInfoDs          DS
DFormatName          *RECORD

CL0N01Factor1++++++Opcode&ExtFactor2++++++Result++++++++Len++D+HiLoEq....Comments+
C                  READ      Logical                              68
C                  SELECT
C                  WHEN      FormatName = 'HEADER'
C                  EXSR      Header
C                  WHEN      FormatName = 'DETAIL'
C                  EXSR      Detail
C                  ENDSL
```

You must be sure to read the file and not the record format. If you specify the file name on the read statement, then you read either the header record or the detail record. On the other hand, if you specify a record format name on the read statement, then you only read records that are in that format. Once we have read the file, the field we named FORMAT, which has been named with the special keyword *RECORD, contains the name of the record format that we just read. We use this field to determine if we have read a header record or a detail record.

LOCALIZED INDICATORS

It's unfortunate, but true—indicators are still a fact of life in RPG. We still need them to communicate to I/O devices. Complex programs can still use quite a few indicators. One way to hold down the number of indicators used in a program is to use the concept of localized indicators.

A localized indicator is an indicator whose value is only seen within the subroutine in which they are being used. It's kind of like each subroutine having its own indicator array. While RPG IV does not support this concept, you can fake it.

Simply put, when we enter a subroutine, we save the contents of the indicator array. We then clear the array. This allows the subroutine to use any indicator it needs without disturbing the normal flow of the program. At the end of the subroutine, we restore the indicator array to its original state.

The net effect of this technique is to make the entire subroutine "indicatorless." This can prove very useful if this subroutine will be used in many places. Figure 5.14 shows an example of this technique.

Figure 5.14: Code Sample for Localized Indicators

```
CL0N01Factor1++++++Opcode&ExtFactor2++++++Result++++++++Len++D+HiLoEq....Comments+
C                   EXSR      Example
C     Example       BEGSR
C                   MOVEA     *IN(1)        SaveIndic        99
C                   MOVEA     *OFF          *IN(1)
 ** Processing stuff goes here
C                   MOVEA     SaveIndic     *IN(1)
C                   ENDSR
```

USING THE *CLEAR* OP CODE

We have already seen how the use of the RTNDTA keyword can eliminate a bunch of tedious move statements to update fields. The CLEAR op code can do the same thing when you want to blank out all of the fields on a screen.

Normally, before you present an input screen, you blank out the input fields so that, whatever the user entered into those fields the last time the screen was displayed, it will not show up this time around. If there are 10 fields on the screen, 10 move statements are required to clear them. You can clear all 10 fields with one CLEAR statement. And best of all, if someone comes along later and adds a new field to the screen, it too is cleared with the same CLEAR statement without any additional coding changes.

Figure 5.15 shows the Clear op code. If you specify a format name in Factor 2, all fields in the format are cleared. You can also use the Clear op code to clear a field or all fields in a database file record format. Fields that are numeric are set to all zeros; alphanumeric fields are set to all blanks. While this, in itself, does nothing to help future maintenance (after all, it's not likely that the field will change from alphanumeric to numeric), it does relieve you from having to know what type of field you are clearing.

Figure 5.15: Clear Op Code

Factor 1	Op Code	Factor 2	Result Field
—	CLEAR	Format Name	—

SOFT CODING FUNCTION KEYS

Soft coding function keys refers to a technique of determining what function key the user presses without the use of indicators. In place of indicators, you assign meaningful field names to the function key that was pressed.

The main advantage to using this technique is ease of maintenance. It is much easier to read and understand the intention of the programmer. You be the judge. Which of the following lines of code makes the most sense?

```
If (*IN13 = *ON)

If (*INKM = *ON)

If (WhatKey = F13)
```

The *WhatKey=F13* line is the only line that immediately tells you that what follows is to be executed if the user presses the F13 function key. The *IF *INKM* line comes close, but then you have to translate the KM into the correct function key.

Figure 5.16 shows how to soft code function keys. The File Information Data Structure (see Chapter 4, "Information Data Structures and Error Handling") has what function key was pressed by the user in position 369. We then set up named constants for each key that could be pressed using the hexadecimal code generated by each key. We assign meaningful names to each key and then all we have to do is compare byte 369 of the file information data structure with the each of the named constants. The result? Clear, concise, colorful, captivating code. (Sounds like a soft drink commercial, doesn't it?)

Figure 5.16: Soft Coding Function Keys

```
FFilename++IPEASFRlen+LKlen+AIDevice+.Keywords+++++++++++++++++++++++++Comments++++++
FDsplayFileCF   E             WORKSTN INFDS(InfoDs)

DName+++++++++++ETDsFrom+++To/L+++IDc.Keywords+++++++++++++++++++++++++Comments++++++
DInfoDs         DS
DWhatKey                369     369
DF01            C                       CONST(X'31')
DF02            C                       CONST(X'32')
DF03            C                       CONST(X'33')
DF04            C                       CONST(X'34')
DF05            C                       CONST(X'35')
DF06            C                       CONST(X'36')
DF07            C                       CONST(X'37')
DF08            C                       CONST(X'38')
DF09            C                       CONST(X'39')
DF10            C                       CONST(X'3A')
DF11            C                       CONST(X'3B')
DF12            C                       CONST(X'3C')
DF13            C                       CONST(X'B1')
DF14            C                       CONST(X'B2')
DF15            C                       CONST(X'B3')
DF16            C                       CONST(X'B4')
DF17            C                       CONST(X'B5')
DF18            C                       CONST(X'B6')
```

```
DF19               C                     CONST(X'B7')
DF20               C                     CONST(X'B8')
DF21               C                     CONST(X'B9')
DF22               C                     CONST(X'BA')
DF23               C                     CONST(X'BB')
DF24               C                     CONST(X'BC')
DClearKey          C                     CONST(X'BD')
DEnterKey          C                     CONST(X'F1')
DHelpKey           C                     CONST(X'F3')
DPageDown          C                     CONST(X'F5')
DPageUp            C                     CONST(X'F4')
DPrintKey          C                     CONST(X'F6')


CL0N01Factor1++++++++Opcode&ExtFactor2+++++++Result++++++++Len++D+HiLoEq....Comments+
C                  EXFMT     Format1
C                  SELECT
C                  WHEN      WhatKey = F01
 *   Function key F1 pressed
C                  WHEN      WhatKey = F02
 *   Function key F2 pressed
C                  WHEN      WhatKey = EnterKey
 *   Enter key pressed
C                  ENDSL
C                  ENDSR
```

A Diverse Arsenal is Your Best Defense

Regardless of how long you remain in this business, you can never have too many tools in your toolbox. Knowing where to get the tool to get the job done is usually the most important step in programming.

Chapter 6

The Power of Command Processing APIs

This chapter is dedicated to covering two very special API programs. The *Command Execute (QCMDEXC)* and *QCAPCMD* APIs can be used to reduce the amount of code you use and greatly increase the flexibility of your RPG programs.

The Command Execute (QCMDEXC) API is used to call AS/400 commands from within your RPG or CL programs. It is a powerful tool and should certainly be in every RPG programmer's arsenal. Almost anything you would ever want to do with a single command can be done right from within your program!

The second API we will cover in this chapter is the Process Commands (QCAPCMD) API. It allows you to edit a command string for validity, allows prompting, and returns the command parameters to your RPG program.

THE WHAT, THE WHY, AND THE HOW OF COMMAND EXECUTE (QCMDEXC)

Think about the possibilities. You can submit jobs, manipulate library lists, override printer parameters, sort database files, plus a veritable plethora of other tasks, all from within your RPG program.

In this chapter, we give you three sample ways to use the Command Execute (QCMDEXC) API to get more flexibility from your RPG programs.

- Running the Open Query File (OPNQRYF) command from within a print program to sequence a file into the order you want before listing it.

- Overriding printer parameters within the RPG program to allow you to send the printed output to a specific printer and change the number of copies.

- Submitting a job from within an RPG program.

The Command Execute (QCMDEXC) API is not only versatile, it is also very easy to use. All you need to do is call the program and pass it two parameters: The command you want to run, and the length of the command (you can even fudge a little on this one because the system does not seem to mind if you pad the back end of your command with blanks). The length of the second parameter, which specifies the command length, must be a 15-digit field with 5 decimal positions. It is that easy!

The example in Figure 6.1 shows how to embed the Work with Spool Files (WRKSPLF) command into an RPG program. Let's get into some more practical examples of the Command Execute (QCMDEXC) API.

Figure 6.1: Using QCMDEXC to Run WRKSPLF from within an RPG Program

```
DName+++++++++++ETDsFrom+++To/L+++IDc.Keywords+++++++++++++++++++++++++++++++Comments++
D Command        S              7
D CmdLength      S             15  5 INZ(7)

CL0N01Factor1+++++++Opcode&ExtFactor2+++++++Result++++++++Len++D+HiLoEq....Comments++
C                   CALL      'QCMDEXC'
C                   PARM      'WRKSPLF'     Command
C                   PARM                    CmdLength
```

RUNNING OPNQRYF TO SORT A DATABASE FILE FROM WITHIN AN RPG PROGRAM

If your system has multiple report programs that produce the same output, the odds are pretty good that the reason they are different programs is because they have different sequence or selection criteria. When output change requests are made, you may be asked to make the same changes to all of them. By sequencing and selecting your data dynamically, you could add a great deal of flexibility to your programs and reduce the amount of maintenance performed.

The first sample program in this chapter gives you the ability to accomplish just that. The RPG program is a simple file listing program that prints our Customer File in customer name or customer number order. When the program is called, a parameter is passed that determines the sequence in which the records are printed. If a 1 is passed to the program, the list is printed in customer name sequence. Otherwise, the list prints in customer number order.

Note the User Controlled Open (USROPN) keyword specified on the File Description Specification for the CUST file. This tells the system that the file open and close to our CUST file is user-controlled within the program (see Chapter 1 for more information on user-controlled file opens). Before we can open the file, we must perform the file overrides on the file. The override we use tells the system that we want our RPG program and the OPNQRYF command to share the same data path of our CUST file. We do this by using the Override Data Base File (OVRDBF) command.

Also note that the program uses Command Execute (QCMDEXC) to call the commands specifying that the program use a shared access path for the CUST file and then again to perform the OPNQRYF operation to sequence the data. The option ALLWCPYDTA(*OPTIMIZE) is specified to enhance the performance of the OPNQRYF function (this option allows OPNQRYF to make the decision as to whether or not the file should be sorted). An Evaluate (EVAL) expression operation is used to concatenate the primary element of the OPNQRYF command to the appropriate KEYFLD parameter. The KEYFLD parameter chosen is dependent upon the value within the parameter passed to the program. Once the OPNQRYF command has been performed, the CUST file can be opened for use within our RPG program.

The QCMDEXC program is called upon three different times in the example in Figure 6.2. First it is used to run the Override Data Base File (OVRDBF) command so the system knows to share the open data path between the OPNQRYF command and the RPG program. Second, QCMDEXC is used to perform the OPNQRYF command where the data is then sequenced. And third, the Command Execute (QCMDEXC) command is used to close the CUST file once we are finished with the list. Failure to close the file could cause some interesting and unintended results in subsequent programs that use the CUST file.

Figure 6.2: Using QCMDEXC to Run OPNQRYF from within an RPG Program

```
 ***********************************************************************
 *   TO COMPILE:
 *      CRTBNDRPG PGM(XXXLIB/FIG62RG)
 ***********************************************************************
FFilename++IPEASF.....L.....A.Device+.Keywords++++++++++++++++++++++++++++Comments++
FCUSTOMER  IF   E            DISK     USROPN
FQSYSPRT   O    F  132       PRINTER  OFLIND(*INOF)


DName++++++++++ETDsFrom+++To/L+++IDc.Keywords++++++++++++++++++++++++++++Comments++
D CmdAry         S            80     DIM(5) CTDATA PERRCD(1)
D Sequence#      S             1
D Command        S            80
D CmdLength      S            15  5 INZ(80)

CL0N01Factor1+++++++Opcode&ExtFactor2+++++++Result++++++++Len++D+HiLoEq....Comments++
C      *ENTRY      PLIST
C                  PARM                      Sequence#
 * Over-ride the Open Data Path of the CUSTOMER file
C                  MOVEL     CmdAry(1)       Command
C                  CALL      'QCMDEXC'
C                  PARM                      Command
C                  PARM                      CmdLength
C       Sequence#  IFEQ      '1'
 * Perform OPNQRYF to sequence records into customer name order
C                  EVAL      Command = %TRIMR(CmdAry(2))
C                             + ' ' + CmdAry(3)
C                  ELSE
 * Perform OPNQRYF to sequence records into customer number order
C                  EVAL      Command = %TRIMR(CmdAry(2))
C                             + ' ' + CmdAry(4)
C                  ENDIF
C                  CALL      'QCMDEXC'
C                  PARM                      Command
C                  PARM                      CmdLength
 * Now that OPNQRYF has been performed, the file may be opened
C                  OPEN      CUSTOMER
C                  EXCEPT    HEDING
 * Read and print records
C                  DOU       *In50 = *ON
C                  READ      CUSREC                              50
C      *IN50       IFEQ      *OFF
C                  EXCEPT    DETAIL
C                  ENDIF
C                  ENDDO
 * Close the CUSTOMER file
C                  EVAL      Command = CmdAry(5)
C                  CALL      'QCMDEXC'
C                  PARM                      Command
C                  PARM                      CmdLength
C                  EVAL      *InLr = *ON
```

```
OFilename++DF..N01N02N03Excnam++++B++A++Sb+Sa+.........................Comments++
OQSYSPRT    E             HEDING        2 02
O           OR   OF
O                                         72 'CUSTOMER LIST'
O           E             HEDING        1
O           OR   OF
O                                         15 'CUSTOMER NUMBER'
O                                         45 'CUSTOMER NAME'
O           EF            DETAIL        1
O                         Customer#        15
O                         Custname         65

** CmdAry compile time array
OVRDBF FILE(CUSTOMER) SHARE(*YES)
OPNQRYF FILE((CUSTOMER)) ALWCPYDTA(*OPTIMIZE)
KEYFLD((CUSTNAME))
KEYFLD((CUSTOMER#))
CLOF CUSTOMER
```

Employing this methodology, we create a listing program to sequence the data
dynamically. This may eliminate the need to code and maintain additional programs with
similar output. It also allows us to process the data in the CUST file in arrival sequence,
rather than the less-efficient method of reading the file by key (see Chapter 1).

OVERRIDING PRINTER PARAMETERS FROM WITHIN AN RPG PROGRAM

Allowing users to decide where they want a report printed is pretty standard stuff. The
odds are good that you already have found a way to handle this request. But, if you are
not familiar with the QCMDEXC program, you may want to check out this next example.

In Figure 6.3, we use the QCMDEXC program to change printers and the number of
copies printed, from within our RPG print program. Parameter one of our program is
the number of copies to print, and parameter two is the printer device to which to
direct the output.

Figure 6.3: Using QCMDEXC to Override Printer Attributes

```
********************************************************************
*   TO COMPILE:
*      CRTBNDRPG PGM(XXXLIB/FIG63RG)
********************************************************************
FFilename++IPEASF.....L.....A.Device+.Keywords+++++++++++++++++++++++++++++Comments++
FCUSTOMER  IF   E              DISK
FQSYSPRT   O    F  132         PRINTER OFLIND(*INOF)
F                                      USROPN

DName+++++++++++ETDsFrom+++To/L+++IDc.Keywords+++++++++++++++++++++++++++++Comments++
D CmdAry          S             70     DIM(1) CTDATA PERRCD(1)
D INbrCopies      S              2
D IPrinter        S             10
D CmdLength       S             15  5  INZ(70)
D TotRecords      S              5  0
 *
D                 DS
D Command                       70
D  NbrCopies                     2     OVERLAY(Command:30)
D  Printer                      10     OVERLAY(Command:38)
 *
D                 SDS
D  Parameters      *PARMS

CL0N01Factor1+++++++Opcode&ExtFactor2+++++++Result+++++++Len++D+HiLoEq....Comments++
C     *ENTRY      PLIST
C                 PARM                    INbrCopies
C                 PARM                    IPrinter
 * Perform the printer over-rides
C     Parameters  IFGT      *ZEROS
C                 MOVEA     CmdAry(1)     Command
C                 EVAL      NbrCopies = INbrCopies
C                 EVAL      Printer = IPrinter
C                 CALL      'QCMDEXC'
C                 PARM                    Command
C                 PARM                    CmdLength
C                 ENDIF
 * Open printer file and begin output operations
C                 OPEN      QSYSPRT
C                 EXCEPT    HEDING
 * Read and print customer file records
C                 DOU       *In50 = *ON
C                 READ      CUSREC                              50
C     *IN50       IFEQ      *OFF
C                 EVAL      TotRecords = (TotRecords + 1)
C                 EXCEPT    DETAIL
C                 ENDIF
C                 ENDDO
C                 EXCEPT    TOTALS
C                 CLOSE     QSYSPRT
C                 EVAL      *InLr = *ON

OFilename++DF..N01N02N03Excnam++++B++A++Sb+Sa+...........................Comments++
OQSYSPRT   E              HEDING          3 02
O          OR  OF
O                                             5 'DATE:'
O                         UDATE        Y     14
O                                            70 'CUSTOMER LIST'
O                                           121 'PAGE:'
O                         PAGE         Z    127
O          E              HEDING          1
```

```
O           OR     OF
O                                               20  'CUSTOMER NUMBER'
O                                               46  'CUSTOMER NAME'
O           EF         DETAIL        1
O                      Customer#              20
O                      CustName               66
O           E          TOTALS        2  1
O                      TotRecords    1       14
O                                               35  'TOTAL RECORDS LISTED'

** Cmdary compile time array
OVRPRTF FILE(QSYSPRT) COPIES(   ) DEV(            ) OUTQ(*DEV)
```

As in our previous example, the file we are overriding must remain closed while we perform the file overrides. Notice the USROPN keyword specified on the File Description Specification of the printer file (QSYSPRT), which tells the system this file is a user-controlled file. We code the open and close of QSYSPRT ourselves, once we have performed our desired file overrides.

We choose to use the PARMS field in the Program Status Data Structure to indicate to the program whether or not parameters are passed to the program (the Program Status Data Structure is discussed in Chapter 4). If the customer file listing program is called with parameters 1 and 2 specified (the PARMS field is greater than zero), we perform printer file overrides to specify our desired printer and number of copies. If no parameters are passed to the program, the override is not performed.

The only element of the CMDARY compile time array (which is defined in the Definition Specification in Figure 6.3) holds the shell of the Override Printer File (OVRPRTF) command. We choose to use a data structure as a tool to load the parameters of the OVRPRTF command because it is generally easier to follow than using the CAT command to concatenate the various components. We begin by loading the CMDARY compile time array element into our data structure and then overlaying it with the values passed into the program as parameters 1 and 2. The net result is a complete OVRPRTF command that is ready to be executed. This is done by calling the Command Execute (QCMDEXC) API. Once the override to the printer file is performed, the printer file is opened and the rest of the simple list program is completed.

SUBMITTING A JOB TO THE JOB QUEUE FROM WITHIN AN RPG PROGRAM

As an RPG programmer on the AS/400, you may have wondered why there is no SMBJOB op code that allows you to submit jobs from within your RPG program. We have too. But the good news is that, by using the Command Execute (QCMDEXC) API, you can do just that.

For our next example, we use a little RPG prompt program, which prompts for a printer ID and the number of copies, validates the values entered, and then submits a program to the job queue. The program we are submitting is the customer list program, which we wrote in our previous example (Figure 6.3). The display file coded in Figure 6.4 is used to present the prompt screen as it is seen in Figure 6.5.

Figure 6.4: Customer List Prompt Screen Display File

```
     A********************************************************************
     A*   TO COMPILE:
     A*      CRTDSPF FILE(XXXLIB/FIG64DS)
     A********************************************************************

.....AAN01N02N03T.Name++++++RLen++TDpBLinPosFunctions++++++++++++++++++++++++++
     A             R FORMAT1
     A                                         CHGINPDFT
     A                                         CF03
     A                                       1 26'List Customer File'
     A                                         DSPATR(UL HI)
     A                                       8  7'Printer to send report to.........-
     A                                         ................'
     A               PRINTER       10   B  8 58DSPATR(HI UL)
     A  41                                     ERRMSG('Invalid Printer Id Entered')
     A  43                                     ERRMSG('Your list was submitted...')
     A                                      10  7'Number of copies to print.........-
     A                                         ................'
     A               NBRCOPIES     2D 0B 10 58DSPATR(HI)
     A                                         CHECK(RZ)
     A  42                                     ERRMSG('Invalid Number of Copies')
     A                                      21  3'                                  -
     A                                                                             -
     A                                                '
     A                                         DSPATR(UL)
     A                                      23  4'F3=Exit'
```

Figure 6.5: Customer List Prompt Screen

```
                              List Customer File



     Printer to send report to........................ _____

     Number of copies to print........................ 01




    _____

      F3=Exit
```

In the RPG program in Figure 6.6, we first establish the default values for the number-of-copies field and then present our prompt screen. The program has been coded to continue presenting the prompt screen until F3 is pressed. If the entries keyed pass the edits, the print job is submitted to the job queue and a confirmation message is sent to the screen.

Figure 6.6: Using QCMDEXC to Submit Jobs from within an RPG Program

```
****************************************************************************
 *   TO COMPILE:
 *      CRTBNDRPG PGM(XXXLIB/FIG66RG)
****************************************************************************


FFilename++IPEASF.....L.....A.Device+.Keywords++++++++++++++++++++++++++++++Comments++
FLCUSTDSP  CF  E              WORKSTN


DName++++++++++ETDsFrom+++To/L+++IDc.Keywords++++++++++++++++++++++++++++++++Comments++
D CmdAry          S             80    DIM(1) CTDATA PERRCD(1)
D Library         S             10    INZ('*LIBL')
D ObjectType      S             10    INZ('*DEVD')
D ObjIsValid      S              1
D CmdLength       S             15  5 INZ(80)
 *
D                 DS                  INZ
D Command                       80
D   PassCopies                   2    OVERLAY(Command:35)
D   PassPrintr                  10    OVERLAY(Command:40)


CL0N01Factor1+++++++Opcode&ExtFactor2+++++++Result++++++++Len++D+HiLoEq....Comments++
 *   Establish defaults
C                   MOVEA     Cmdary(1)      Command
C                   Eval      NbrCopies = 1
 *  Do until an EOJ request is encountered
C                   DOU       *InKC = *ON
C                   EXFMT     FORMAT1
C                   MOVEA     '000'          *IN(41)
 *  Validate printer ID
C     *INKC         IFEQ      *OFF
C                   CALL      'FIG67RG'
```

```
C                       PARM                    Printer
C                       PARM                    Library
C                       PARM                    ObjectType
C                       PARM                    ObjIsValid
*   Send error message if entry is not valid
C       ObjIsValid      IFNE        'Y'
C                       Eval        *In41 = *ON
C                       ITER
C                       ENDIF
*   Must specify the number of copies
C       NbrCopies       IFEQ        *ZEROS
C                       Eval        *In42 = *ON
C                       ITER
C                       ENDIF
*   Submit Customer List
C                       Eval        *In43 = *ON
C                       MOVE        NbrCopies       PassCopies
C                       Eval        PassPrintr = Printer
C                       CALL        'QCMDEXC'
C                       PARM                        Command
C                       PARM                        CmdLength
C                       ENDIF
C                       ENDDO
 **
C                       Eval        *InLr = *ON

** Cmdary compile time array
SBMJOB CMD(CALL PGM(LSTCUS) PARM('99' 'Printer ID')) JOB(LISTCUST)
```

The next step is to edit the printer ID that is keyed by the program operator. We use the FIG67RG API program (shown in Figure 6.7), which is explained in further detail when we cover system APIs in Chapter 9. The purpose of the API program is to make sure the device description of the printer ID keyed does, in fact, exist on the system.

Figure 6.7: RPG API Program to Validate Printer Existence

```
*****************************************************************
*   TO COMPILE:
*      CRTBNDRPG PGM(XXXLIB/FIG67RG)
*****************************************************************

DName++++++++++++ETDsFrom+++To/L+++IDc.Keywords+++++++++++++++++++++++++++++++Comments++
D ErrorDs          DS                    INZ
D  BytesProvd               1      4B 0
D  BytesAvail               5      8B 0
D  MessageId                9     15
D  ERR###                  16     16
D  MessageDta              17    116
D Receiver         S             100
D ReceivrLen       S               4B 0 INZ(100)
D Object           S              10
D ObjLibrary       S              10
D ObjType          S               8
D ExistYesNo       S               1
D FileLib          S              20
D FileFormat       S               8        INZ('OBJD0100')

CL0N01Factor1+++++++Opcode&ExtFactor2+++++++Result++++++++Len++D+HiLoEq....Comments++
C     *ENTRY      PLIST
C                 PARM                         Object
C                 PARM                         ObjLibrary
C                 PARM                         ObjType
C                 PARM                         ExistYesNo
C     ObjLibrary  IFEQ     *BLANKS
C                 EVAL     ObjLibrary = 'LIBL'
C                 ENDIF
C                 EVAL     FileLib = Object + ObjLibrary
* Attempt to retrieve object description
C                 CALL     'QUSROBJD'
C                 PARM                         Receiver
C                 PARM                         ReceivrLen
C                 PARM                         FileFormat
C                 PARM                         FileLib
C                 PARM                         ObjType
C                 PARM                         ErrorDs
C                 EVAL     ExistYesNo = 'Y'
C     MessageId   IFNE     *BLANKS
C                 EVAL     ExistYesNo = 'N'
C                 ENDIF
C                 EVAL     *InLr = *ON
```

If either the printer ID or the number-of-copies fields are deemed invalid, the prompt screen is redisplayed with the appropriate error message indicator on. The operator may then press Error Reset, correct the value in error, and press Enter; or press F3 to terminate the program.

If the field entries keyed pass the edits, the Command Execute (QCMDEXC) API is called and the program is submitted to the job queue passing along the printer ID and number of copies keyed as parameters. The confirmation indicator (*IN43) is then turned on and the screen is redisplayed. A message is displayed indicating that the requested job was submitted to the job queue.

QCMDEXC: AN API FOR ALL SEASONS

As you have seen in the preceding examples, the Command Execute (QCMDEXC) API is a very powerful and easy-to-use tool. Once you have the hang of it, you may be surprised at how many different uses you can find for it.

THE COMMAND PROCESSING API

You now have a pretty good understanding of the Command Execute (QCMDEXC) API. You know that this API can be used to execute almost any command from within your program. But what if you simply wanted the operator to press a function key to get a window where a command could be keyed? You would probably want to edit that command for validity, rather than presenting one of those nasty CPF errors if an invalid command happened to be keyed. And would you ever want to trap the information that the user keyed in response to that prompt?

The way to accomplish these goals is via the QCAPCMD API. It will allow you to edit a command string for validity, allow prompting, and return the command parameters to your program.

The first step would be to prompt the user with an entry line where a command could be keyed. You would then pass that field (filled with whatever the user had entered) to the QCAPCMD API which would verify that a proper command was entered, prompt for that command (if requested to do so), and return to your program the changed command string (updated with whatever the user had entered into the prompted fields). The QCAPCMD API can either process the keyed command or simply verify that the command is valid and let you pass the changed command on to the Command Execute (QCMDEXC) API to run it.

Let's take a closer look at the QCAPCMD API. You first give it the command string to be processed (trailing blanks are allowed), followed by the length of the command string field. The next three parameters (option control block, block length, and block format) are used to control the various functions that the API can perform (run the command, or just verify that it's a valid command, prompt, etc.). Parameter number 6 will return the updated command string with any variable information that the user may have entered. Parameter 7 is the length of the changed command string, and the last parameter is the standard error code data structure that is described in detail in Chapter 9. Table 6.1 shows the required input parameters to use this API.

Table 6.1: Required Input Parameters for the Command Processing (QCAPCMD) API

Parameter	Description	Type	Size
1	Source command string	Input	Char(*)
2	Command string length	Input	Binary(4)
3	Option control block	Input	Char(*)
4	Option control block length	Input	Char(20)
5	Option control block format	Input	Char(8)
6	Changed command string	Output	Char(*)
7	Length available for changed command string	Input	Binary(4)
8	Error code data structure	Both	Char(*)

Parameter Definitions:

Source command string: The command string that is to be processed, either prompted for or run.

Command string length: The length of the source command string. Valid values are between 1 and 6000. Trailing blanks in the command string can count in the length.

Option control block: Currently there is only one format allowed. See Table 6.2 for the format of this structure.

Control block length: The length of the option control block parameter. Must be a minimum of 20 bytes.

<u>Control block format name</u>: The name of the data structure defining the data in the control block. Currently, the only valid entry is CPOP0100.

<u>Changed command string</u>: The updated command string. This may be considerably longer than the source command string as it contains the keywords. No padding is performed on this field; you must use the length of changed command string field to determine the number of characters returned. This field will not be changed if an error occurred during the execution of the QCAPCMD API.

<u>Length available to changed command string</u>: Total number of bytes the QCAPCMD API has to return the changed command string. If the string is larger than this number, the returned command string will be truncated to fit.

<u>Error Data Structure</u>: The standard error code data structure as described in Chapter 9.

Table 6.2: Format of the Option Control Block (CPOP0100)

Offset	Type	Description
0	Binary(4)	Type of command processing
4	Char(1)	DBCS handling
5	Char(1)	Prompter action
6	Char(1)	Command string syntax
7	Char(4)	Message retrieve key
11	Char(9)	Reserved

Parameter Definitions:

<u>Source command string</u>: The command string that is to be processed.

<u>Type of processing</u>: Type of command processing to be performed. Valid values and their meaning are as follows:

0 - Command running. Processes in the same way as QCMDEXC.

1 - Command syntax check. Processes in the same way as QCMDCHK.

2 - Command line running. Processes in the same way as QCMDEXC except limited user checking and prompting for missing required parameters are performed.

3 - Command line syntax checking. Complement of type 2.

4 - CL program statement. Checked according to the same rules as SEU for CL. Variable names are allowed.

5 - CL input stream. Checked according to the same rules as input batch stream.

6 - Command definition statements.

7 - Binder definition statements. Checked according to the same rules as SEU for BND.

8 - User-defined option. Allows user to create commands similar to those used in PDM.

9 - ILE CL programs source. Checked according to the rules of SEU for ILE CL.

<u>DBCS data handling</u>: Determines whether or not the command analyzer should handle the SO/SI characters as DBCS.

0 - Ignore DBCS.

1 - Handle DBCS.

Prompter action: Should the prompter be called for the command string? Valid values are:

0 - Never call the prompter, even if prompting characters (?, *?, etc.) are embedded in the command string.

1 - Always call the prompter, even if there are no prompting characters embedded in the string.

2 - Prompt only if prompting characters are present. Error code CPF3CF1 is issued if this code is used with command processing type 4 through 8.

3 - Show help. Provide help display for the command.

Command string syntax: Specifies whether the command is in the AS/400 syntax (library/object) or the System 38 syntax (object.library).

Message retrieve key: The message retrieve key of the request message that contains the source command statements to process.

COMMAND PERFORMANCE

The QCAPCMD API is much more flexible than the Command Execute (QCMDEXC) API. But as usual, with flexibility comes complexity. However, this API performs a very useful function. It allows you to provide a command entry line in your programs where you can both validate and execute the requested user action. As an added bonus, you have the capability of "trapping" what the user entered.

Take the time to learn how to use these two very special APIs. You may surprise yourself with how much power is at your command.

Chapter 7

Array and String Handling

Webster's Dictionary defines an array as "an orderly grouping." While that definition does describe an array in RPG, perhaps a better description for our purposes is found in the IBM *RPG/400 Reference Guide*. The guide refers to an array as "a systematic program-internal arrangement of data fields (array elements) with the same field length, data type (character or numeric), and number of decimal positions (if numeric)."

WHAT IS AN ARRAY?

As the description indicates, an array consists of a consecutive set of like data elements that are stored in main memory while your RPG program is running. Prior to V3R1 and RPG IV, arrays required a fixed amount of main storage that was defined to the system when your program was compiled. Arrays always had a fixed number of elements, and each element had to (and still must) be the same size and data type.

New functions and features were introduced with V3R1 that removed most of the inflexibility that used to be associated with using arrays. Even though the role of arrays has changed, you will see that arrays still have their place on the AS/400. We begin by defining the different types of arrays and giving you a couple of examples so you will see that they are quite useful.

WHAT WOULD YOU USE AN ARRAY FOR?

Up until the introduction of the string handling op codes and built-in functions (also known as built-in functions), arrays were a major component of every RPG programmer's toolbox. Whether you needed to pack a name into *Last name, First* or pack city, state, and zip code together, arrays were the best tool available for the job.

Introduction of the string handling op codes and built-in functions in RPG/400 changed all that. Arrays were instantly outdated for this purpose because they required too much code compared to their successors. What used to take 10 or more lines of code could now be done in 1 or 2. Less code meant fewer opportunities for error.

But as you will see, arrays are still a valuable tool. They are great for accumulating totals when printing a report. They are useful for validating data in your interactive programs. They can be used to pull like data elements together so they can be processed from within a loop. They are often without peer when it comes to formatting data that is to appear on reports and screens.

ARRAY BASICS

Within your RPG program, you define the field size, the data type, and the maximum number of data elements that will exist within the array. Also within your program, you manage the sequence and content of the data elements with techniques that we demonstrate within this chapter.

Prior to ILE RPG and V3R1, the only way to define an array was with an Extension Specification. The Extension Specification has now been replaced with the Definition Specification. The Definition Specification tells the system the name of your array and how many elements it has, as well as the size and type of the elements. If your array happens to be numeric, this specification also tells the system the number of decimal positions that belong to each element.

RPG IV allows you to address arrays wholly or as individual array elements. When you use the array name followed by a numeric field or value enclosed in parentheses, you are addressing an individual array element. This field or value is commonly referred to as an *array index*.

Array indices must contain valid array address values when used. If a statement is encountered where an array index is zero or it is greater than the maximum number of array elements allowed, the result is an *array index error*, which causes the program to be interrupted. You need to use care when coding arrays to make sure these conditions can not possibly exist. We will show you some tips that you may employ that will help you make sure this error condition does not occur.

RPG IV allows you to specify *compile-time*, *run-time*, and *dynamic arrays*. As the name implies, the data for a compile-time array is loaded when the program is compiled. The run-time array is loaded and managed from within the RPG program while it is running. The dynamic array allows you to utilize dynamic memory allocation to control the amount of memory required from within your program.

It is the run-time array that we will initially focus our attention on. But before we get too carried away with run-time arrays, we need to mention that there is a fourth type of array, which we like to call the *two-dimensional* array. The two-dimensional array is not just an array. It is a hybrid combination of a Multiple-occurrence Data Structure and multiple arrays. It differs from arrays in that each element is itself a data structure with fields of varying size and data type. Refer to the chapter on data structures (Chapter 8) for a more detailed description of this special type of array.

THE RUN-TIME ARRAY

In Figure 7.1, we define two run-time arrays. The first array is called StateCode. It has 50 array elements and each element is two characters long. This array is used to hold the two-character abbreviation for each of the 50 United States. Because there are only 50 states, we are able to set the size of the array at a maximum size of 50. We also know that the size of the field we use as an index only needs to be two digits because it is highly unlikely there will ever be more than 99 states (which is the maximum number that will fit in a two-digit field).

Figure 7.1: Defining Run-time Arrays with a Definition Specification

```
DName++++++++++ETDsFrom+++To/L+++IDc.Keywords+++++++++++++++++++++++++++++++Comments
D StateCode       S             2    DIM(50)
D StateTot        S             5  0 DIM(50)
```

Setting the size of your array can be something of a science. The idea is to set a size that is at least as large as the maximum number of elements you could possibly encounter, but at the same time keep the number of elements to a minimum because main storage (memory) is being allocated every time your program is run. The number of elements multiplied by the size of each element translates into how much main storage is being allocated each time your program is run.

Prior to V3R1, the number of array elements in memory could not be increased from within your program. We will show you later in this chapter how to use *dynamic arrays* where you will tell your program the maximum number of array elements it could possibly encounter, but only allocate the storage in memory for the elements that you use.

The second array in Figure 7.1 is called StateTot and is used to store the total number of customers that reside in each state. Each StateTot array element is five digits with zero decimal positions.

In Figure 7.2, we use the arrays defined in the previous example to accumulate and store the total number of customers we have in each state. This method to accumulate totals is especially valuable if you can not control the sequence of the records being read.

Figure 7.2: Accumulating Totals in Run-time Arrays

```
CL0N01Factor1+++++++Opcode&ExtFactor2+++++++Result+++++++Len++D+HiLoEq....Comments
* Read all customer records and accumulate totals by state
C                   DOU       *IN50
C                   READ      CUSREC                             50
C                   IF        *IN50 = *OFF
C                   EVAL      X = 1
C       State       LOOKUP    StateCode(X)                       68
 * If current state is not already in the array, find a spot for it
C                   IF        *IN68 = *OFF
C       ' '         LOOKUP    StateCode(X)                       68
C                   ENDIF
 * Increment total for current state
C                   EVAL      StateCode(X) = State
C                   EVAL      StateTot(X) = StateTot(X) + 1
C                   ENDIF
C                   ENDDO
```

For example, let's say you need to write a Customer List RPG program that is to be printed alphabetically by customer name, but you also need to print summary totals at the bottom of the report showing how many customers are in each state. The totals will be printed twice. First in the sequence of the two-character abbreviation for each state, and a second time by the number of customers in each state.

This poses a potential problem. Reading the customer records in a sequence that presents the records alphabetically by customer name will, in all likelihood, result in totals that are recorded in a sequence that does not match our desired output for the summary by state. And what about when we print the totals by the number of customers in each state?

Do you resequence the file into state order and read all of the records a second time just to print the totals in the desired sequence? Probably not. As we talked about in Chapter 1, reducing I/O can have a big impact on overall system performance.

Do you create a totals-output field for each of the 50 states? This would be very tedious and the repetition creates a situation that leaves room for error. Would this solution even be viable if we were talking about 500 totals-output fields? Probably not.

Figure 7.2 demonstrates a technique that allows us to accumulate totals into array elements that may be processed for output later. By accumulating the totals as you read the records, you are prepared to output a summary later without making another pass through the data. In Figure 7.2, we read and print the customer file records as we process them in alphabetical order, and at the same time store our totals in the StateTot array. We use the StateCode array to keep track of which state the corresponding StateTot array element represents.

After the totals have been accumulated, the final result looks something like this:

StateCode Array:

CA	NV	AZ	OR	ID	NY

StateTot Array:

451	103	55	28	12	1033

A quick glance at the arrays tell us that we have 451 customers in California, 55 in Arizona, 12 in Idaho, and so on. Each data element in the StateTot array directly corresponds to the element in the StateCode array.

Using Run-time Arrays to Store and Accumulate Totals

Let's analyze the code in Figure 7.2 to see how our totals are accumulated. If the first customer record read is from California, the program uses the LOOKUP op code to perform a *lookup* in the StateCode array to see if we have already processed a customer record from California.

The LOOKUP op code is unique to tables and arrays. Its name aptly describes its function. The LOOKUP op code performs a lookup operation to see if the search argument specified in Factor 1 already exists somewhere within the array. If the search argument does, in fact, exist, the indicator *IN68 specified in position 75 (the = column) is turned on and the number of the element where the search argument was found is returned to the index field (X in this case). The index field is enclosed in parentheses directly after the name of the array specified in Factor 2 (positions 36 through 49). The index field is a numeric field that is enclosed in parentheses following the name of the array in the LOOKUP statement. Note that, prior to the lookup operation, the index was reset to 1. This must be done because the search begins from where the index happens to be set.

Back to our example. Let's assume that this was the first record read. The lookup failed to find an array element of CA and needs to add it. We have coded the program to look for the first available array element in the StateCode array by performing another lookup using the LOOKUP op code to find the first array element filled with blanks.

Once the first available blank element is found, the CA state code is moved into the StateCode array and a count of 1 is added to the corresponding array element in the StateTot array. After reading our first customer record and processing the record, our arrays look like this:

StateCode Array:

CA					

StateTot Array:

	1				

If the next customer record read is from Nevada, the StateCode array lookup is performed with the NV state code, and, as before, the NV code is added when NV is not found initially. After reading and processing our second customer record from Nevada, our arrays look like this:

StateCode Array:

CA	NV				

StateTot Array:

	1	1			

Let's assume that the third customer record read is again from California. In this case, the lookup in the StateCode array for CA is successful (as indicated when indicator 68 comes on) and the appropriate array index is returned and stored in the field X.

This time, we simply add 1 to the StateTot array element that directly corresponds to the StateCode array element that was found in the lookup operation. After reading and processing the third customer record, our arrays look like this:

StateCode Array:

CA	NV				

StateTot Array:

2	1				

When all of the customer records have been read and processed, we end up with a StateCode array that contains state codes for each and every customer record in our file. The StateTot array contains a count representing the number of customers we have in each state.

Sequencing Run-time Arrays for Output Operations

We now have the data we need to print our summary totals at the bottom of our report. But there is a problem. How are we going to get the totals to print out in state or customer count order? Our arrays have been built based upon the customer name arrival sequence of the records because our report specifications called for printing the detail in that order. The solution to this problem lies in a technique that is demonstrated in Figure 7.3.

Figure 7.3: Using Sort Array (SORTA) to Resequence Array Elements

```
     FFilename++IPEASF.....L.....A.Device+.Keywords++++++++++++++++++++++++++++++Comments
     FCUSTOMER  IF   E              DISK
     FSTATES    IF   E          K DISK
     FQSYSPRT   O    F   132        PRINTER OFLIND(*INOF)


     DName++++++++++ETDsFrom++To/L+++IDc.Keywords++++++++++++++++++++++++++++++++Comments
     D                   DS
     D State_Info                7    DIM(50)
     D  StateCode                2    OVERLAY(State_Info)
     D  StateTot                 5  0 OVERLAY(State_Info:3) INZ
      *
     D Total           S         7  0
     D X               S         3  0


     CL0N01Factor1+++++++Opcode&ExtFactor2+++++++Result+++++++Len++D+HiLoEq....Comments
      * Print report heading
     C                   EXCEPT    HEDING

      * Read customer file and accumulate totals by state
B1   C                   DOU       *IN50
     C                   READ      CUSREC                           50
B2   C                   IF        *IN50 = *OFF
     C                   EVAL      X = 1
     C         State     LOOKUP    StateCode(X)                     68
B3   C                   IF        *IN68 = *OFF
     C         '  '      LOOKUP    StateCode(X)                     68
E3   C                   ENDIF
      * Increment total for current state
     C                   EVAL      StateCode(X) = State
```

```
        C                 EVAL       StateTot(X) = (StateTot(X) + 1)
E2      C                 ENDIF
E1      C                 ENDDO

        * Sort the entire State_Info array alphabetically into state sequence
        C                 SORTA      StateCode

        * Run through the State_Info array and print totals
B1      C                 DO         50          X
B2      C                 IF         StateCode(X) <> *BLANKS
        C     StateCode(X) CHAIN     STATES                        68
        C                 EVAL       Total = (Total + StateTot(X))
        C                 EXCEPT     DETAIL
E2      C                 ENDIF
E1      C                 ENDDO
        * Print array totals
        C                 EXCEPT     TOTALS

        * Print report heading again
        C                 EXCEPT     HEDING

        * Sort the State_Info array numerically by the number of customers per state
        C                 SORTA      StateTot

        * Repeat the process of printing the State_Info array
B1      C                 DO         50          X
B2      C                 IF         StateCode(X) <> *BLANKS
        C     StateCode(X) CHAIN     STATES                        68
        C                 EXCEPT     DETAIL
E2      C                 ENDIF
E1      C                 ENDDO

        * Print array totals
        C                 EXCEPT     TOTALS
        C                 EVAL       *INLR = *ON

        OFilename++DF..N01N02N03Excnam++++B++A++Sb+Sa+..........................Comments
        OQSYSPRT   E                 HEDING        3 02
        O          OR       OF
        O                                            70 'Summary by State'

        O          E                 HEDING        1
        O          OR       OF
        O                                            16 'State'
        O                                            42 'Total'

        O          EF                DETAIL        1
        O                             StateCode(X)      4
        O                             StateDesc        31
        O                             StateTot(X)   1  40

        O          E                 TOTALS      2 1
        O                             TOTAL         1  14
        O                                            30 'Total Customers'
```

In Figure 7.3, we code a print program that simply prints the customer-summary-by-state report, similar to the summary we have been talking about. We employ a loop to load the arrays, much as we did in the previous example.

Take a look at the Definition Specifications for the State_Info array. By defining the State_Info array within a data structure, we are able to use the OVERLAY keyword to embed the StateCode and StateTot arrays within the State_Info array. By defining the arrays this way, each element of the State_Info array is actually seven characters. The first two characters of each State_Info array element compose the state code and the last five digits are the customer totals for each state. Coding it this way allows us to use both the StateCode and StateTot arrays independently as if they were defined as standalone arrays.

In order to print our totals in state code order, we need to sort the State_Info array. The Sort Array (SORTA) op code is perfect for this purpose, except that sorting the State_Info array would result in totals sequenced by state code only (because the first two characters of the State_Info array are the state code). But RPG IV allows us to use the data structure subfields to sort the array. (Note: This is *way* cool!)

In Figure 7.3, we used our loop to compile our totals first. We the used the SORTA op code to sort our array into state code sequence and then used a loop to print the array contents. We then printed a new heading, used the SORTA op code again to sort our array into our totals sequence, and used a loop to print the contents again.

The resulting output looked something like this:

```
                    Summary by State

            State                    Total
   AZ    ARIZONA                        2
   CA    CALIFORNIA                     9
   ID    IDAHO                          3
   NV    NEVADA                         1
   OR    OREGON                         1
   WA    WASHINGTON                     2

             18 Total Customers

                    Summary by State

            State                    Total
   NV    NEVADA                         1
   OR    OREGON                         1
   WA    WASHINGTON                     2
   AZ    ARIZONA                        2
   ID    IDAHO                          3
   CA    CALIFORNIA                     9

             18 Total Customers
```

Using Run-time Arrays to Format Data for Output

In our next example, we are going to use arrays to solve a common output problem. We want to print a customer phone list, but it needs to be a three-column alphabetical list, much like a phone book. This output is desirable on multicolumn, alphabetical reports because the format makes it easier to look up entries.

Our customer phone list program in Figure 7.4 uses a compile-time array (which we will explain later in this chapter) and two arrays to store data that will be printed. The program uses OPNQRYF to sequence the customer file first. The file is then read and the fields we are going to print are saved in the Names and Numbers arrays. The Names array holds the customer name, and the Numbers array holds the phone number. Storing the data in the arrays gives us the flexibility to produce the list in the desired format.

Figure 7.4: Multicolumn Customer Phone List Using Arrays to Format Output

```
FFilename++IPEASF.....L......A.Device+.Keywords+++++++++++++++++++++++++++++Comments
FCUSTOMER   IF   E              DISK     USROPN
FQSYSPRT    O    F   132        PRINTER  OFLIND(*INOF)
*
DName+++++++++++ETDsFrom+++To/L+++IDc.Keywords+++++++++++++++++++++++++++++++Comments
D Commands       S            80     DIM(3) CTDATA PERRCD(1)
D Names          S            29     DIM(120)
D Numbers        S            10   0 DIM(120)
*
D Command        S            80A
D Length         S            15   5
D X              S             3   0
D Y              S             3   0
D Z              S             3   0

CL0N01Factor1++++++Opcode&ExtFactor2+++++++Result++++++++Len++D+HiLoEq....Comments
* Over-ride the customer file so the data path will be shared
C                   CALL      'QCMDEXC'
C                   PARM      Commands(1)    Command
C                   PARM      80             Length

 * Perform the OPNQRYF function to sequence the file
C                   CALL      'QCMDEXC'
C                   PARM      Commands(2)    Command
C                   PARM      80             Length

C                   OPEN      CUSTOMER
C                   DOU       *IN50
C                   READ      CUSREC                                 50
 * If end of file is encountered, print array contents and get out of loop
C                   IF        *IN50
C      X            CASGT     *ZEROS         OUTPUT
C                   ENDCS
C                   LEAVE
C                   ENDIF
 * Put names in arrays until there are enough entries for a page
C                   EVAL      X = (X + 1)
C                   MOVEL     CUSTNAME       Names(X)
```

```
C                       MOVE        PHONENBR        Numbers(X)
C       X               CASEQ       120             OUTPUT
C                       ENDCS
C                       ENDDO
 * Close the file
C                       CALL        'QCMDEXC'
C                       PARM        Commands(3)     Command
C                       PARM        80              Length
C                       EVAL        *INLR = *ON

CSR     OUTPUT          BEGSR
C                       EXCEPT      HEDING
C       1               DO          40              X
C                       EVAL        Y = (X + 40)
C                       EVAL        Z = (X + 80)
C                       EXCEPT      DETAIL
C                       ENDDO
C                       EVAL        X = 0
C                       CLEAR                       Names
C                       CLEAR                       Numbers
CSR                     ENDSR

OQSYSPRT    E           HEDING          2 02
O           OR      OF
O                                       78 'CUSTOMER PHONE LIST'

O           E           HEDING          1
O           OR      OF
O                                       15 'CUSTOMER'
O                                       40 'PHONE#'
O                                       59 'CUSTOMER'
O                                       84 'PHONE#'
O                                      103 'CUSTOMER'
O                                      128 'PHONE#'

O           EF          DETAIL          1
O                       Names(X)        29
O                       Numbers(X)      42 '   /   -   0'
O                       Names(Y)        73
O                       Numbers(Y)      86 '   /   -   0'
O                       Names(Z)       117
O                       Numbers(Z)     130 '   /   -   0'
**
OVRDBF FILE(CUSTOMER) SHARE(*YES)
OPNQRYF FILE((CUSTOMER)) ALWCPYDTA(*OPTIMIZE) KEYFLD((CUSTNAME))
CLOF CUSTOMER
```

The program first runs OPNQRYF from within the RPG program to sequence the customer file into customer name order. We use the QCMDEXC API program in conjunction with the Commands compile-time array to perform the OPNQRYF operation (we first examined this technique in Chapter 6).

Once our file is in the desired sequence, we load our output arrays accordingly. The Names array is loaded alphabetically by customer name because that is the sequence in which we are reading the file. The customer phone numbers are loaded into the corresponding Numbers array elements.

Our program specifications call for a phone list that prints 3 columns across and 40 records deep. To be able to output the data in our desired sequence, we fill all 120 array elements (3 columns multiplied by 40 records deep) and then use a print loop to dump the array contents. Because we also need to print the partially filled arrays when our end-of-file is reached, we have separated the output operation into a subroutine called OUTPUT (seems appropriate enough, does it not?).

In the output subroutine, we use three separate array indices to stagger the output to meet our desired format. In other words, we want the 1st array element to print on the same line as the 41st and the 81st array elements. The end result is a list designed so that you can look for a customer name alphabetically down the first column and, if not found, look down the second column, and so on.

The X index is used to print array elements 1 through 40, which are listed in the first column. The Y index is used to print elements 41 through 80 (the second column), and Z is used to print elements 81 through 120 (column three).

By using this technique, our list prints alphabetically top to bottom and then left to right. This phone-book style of output is made easy thanks to the use of arrays.

THE %ELEM BUILT-IN FUNCTION PREVENTS ARRAY INDEX ERRORS

In the example in Figure 7.4, the "do loop" to print our array elements was hard coded to perform 40 iterations of the loop. Prior to the announcement of built-in functions (which we will discuss later in this chapter) this was about the only way you could tell the system how many times a loop should be performed.

But there is a new built-in function called %ELEM which returns the number of elements in a table, array, or Multiple-occurrence Data Structure. So instead of code that looks like this:

```
CL0N01Factor1+++++++Opcode&ExtFactor2+++++++Result++++++++Len++D+HiLoEq....Comments
C     1          DO        100       X
```

You would want to code it something like this:

```
CL0N01Factor1+++++++Opcode&ExtFactor2+++++++Result++++++++Len++D+HiLoEq....Comments
C     1          DO        %ELEM(Array) X
```

By coding the program in this fashion, you prevent errors when writing and performing maintenance on your programs. If the number of array elements should need to be increased or decreased, the code processing the array may not need to be modified. By using the %ELEM built-in function to limit the number of iterations, the loop will automatically be performed for each array element, regardless of the number of elements in the array.

It should be noted that the %ELEM function may be used in the Definition Specifications as well. If you have several arrays with the same number of elements, you only need to indicate the number of elements once, and then use the %ELEM function to define the rest.

RUN-TIME ARRAY HANDLING RPG OP CODES

Now that we have defined and discussed the value of run-time arrays, we need to look at how the various RPG op codes affect arrays. Some of these op codes only apply to arrays and others work differently than you might expect.

Most of the arithmetic op codes work with numeric arrays. You specify that you are performing the operations on the entire array or just on a specific array element through the use of an array index. If you specify the index (by following the array reference with a number or numeric field enclosed in parentheses), the operation is performed on the specified array element. If you do not specify an index, the operation is performed on the entire array.

Using the MOVE and Move Left (MOVEL) op codes on single-array elements (by specifying the array index) works in the same fashion as if you had specified individual fields. Using these operations on whole arrays may not produce the kind of results you expect. Performing a MOVE or MOVEL from a field, constant, or data structure into an entire array performs the move as if it is being performed with a single field, but the same results are recorded into all elements of the array.

For example, let's say we wanted to move the lieral SMITH into an array of single, one-character elements. We call our array Name. If we simply perform a MOVEL:

```
CL0N01Factor1+++++++Opcode&ExtFactor2+++++++Result++++++++Len++D+HiLoEq....Comments
C                    MOVEL     'SMITH'       Name
```

the results in the Name array look like this:

S	S	S	S	S

While this may, in fact, be our intended result, it is more likely that we wanted to put each character of our constant into an element of the array.

That is where the Move Array (MOVEA) op code comes in. MOVEA was introduced to allow you to perform moves that cross the boundaries of the array. Let's see what the results are when we perform the same operation using MOVEA in place of MOVEL.

```
CL0N01Factor1+++++++Opcode&ExtFactor2+++++++Result++++++++Len++D+HiLoEq....Comments
C                   MOVEA       'SMITH'     Name
```

the results in the Name array look like this:

S	M	I	T	H

Table 7.1 outlines the op codes that are used specifically with arrays (with the exception of the LOOKUP op code that may be used for tables as well).

Table 7.1: Op Codes That are Used Specifically with Arrays

Op Code	Description
LOOKUP	The Lookup (LOOKUP) op code can actually be used for tables or arrays. It is used to perform a "seek and find" operation to determine if the search argument specified in Factor 1 exists in the table or array. If the search argument is found, the EQ indicator (in position 75) is turned on and the address of the array element found is returned to the index field of Factor 2 (position 36) if the index field was specified. When an index is specified, the lookup begins at the array element initially specified in the index.

Op Code	Description
	If you want the search to begin at the start of the array, you must make sure the index is set to 1. You may also use the LOOKUP operation to perform high or low lookups that seek out the array elements that are closest to the search argument specified, but still satisfy the search conditions. The high or low lookups are done by utilizing the indicators in positions 71 and 72 (HI) or 73 and 74 (LO), depending upon the desired search criteria.
MOVEA	Move Array (MOVEA) is used to move values to and from arrays. This op code may be used to move an array to a field, a field to an array, or an array to another array. In this case, a data structure or any constant qualifies as a field too. MOVEA may be used for alphanumeric or numeric arrays and fields, but the Factor 2 and Result field types must match. An index may be specified in Factor 2 or the Result field, and the move operation begins at the point of the index. The move that is performed is similar to a Move Left (MOVEL) in that the move begins with the left-most point of Factor 2 and begins loading the value into the left-most portion of the Result field. If Factor 2 and the Result fields are not equal in length, the move is performed for the length that matches the shorter of the two.
SORTA	Sort Array (SORTA) performs the function that the name of the op code implies. The name of the array you want to sort goes into Factor 2. The array elements are automatically resequenced into an order that coincides with the value of the array elements. If array elements include blanks or zeros, these entries appear first after SORTA is executed. If the SORTA is performed on a field that happens to be a subfield in a data structure, the entire array is sequenced in the order of the subfield specified as Factor 2 of the SORTA statement (see Figure 7.3).
XFOOT	Cross Foot (XFOOT) sums all of the values of a numeric array in a single command. The Result field must contain a valid numeric field or array element where the total is placed when the operation is performed.

THE COMPILE-TIME ARRAY

Another type of array is the compile-time array. Like the name implies, data is loaded into this type of array when a program is compiled. The data used to load the array is coded right into the source of your RPG program.

This type of array can be useful when you need to work with a small number of data elements that always remain constant and are not subject to change. An example of this type of data is days of the week. There are a limited number of days in a week and they are not likely to change. Rather than store them in a file or data area, it is easier to simply store them in a compile-time array at the end of a program.

Compile-time array data is actually stored *after* the source to your program and there are two ways it may be stored. The first way is to use one of three special keywords that are used to tell the compiler that compile-time array data is about to follow. These keywords are **CTDATA (compile-time data), **ALTSEQ (compile-time data follows with an alternating collating sequence), and **FTRANS (compile-time file translation data follows).

If you choose to use these three new keywords, your compile-time array data can be placed in any order following your program source (as long as the array data directly follows the keyword describing said array). If you do not use these new keywords, your compile-time array data needs to directly follow the last source statement (generally an Output or Calculation Specification) and must match the same sequence with which the arrays were defined. In other words, if your program has multiple compile-time arrays and you do not choose to use the keywords, the array data must be defined in the program in the same sequence as the Definition Specifications describing them.

The data of each compile-time array will be designated and separated beginning with two asterisks (**) keyed into positions 1 and 2 of the source statement directly following your program source. The two asterisks act as a trigger record to tell the compiler that table or compile-time-array data follows.

The source records that follow the trigger record represent the data for the compile-time array. Figure 7.5 shows two examples of what compile-time-array data looks like. In the first example, the compile-time array is designated without any keyword. In the second example, the **CTDATA keyword was used to designate that compile-time data follows.

Figure 7.5: Examples of Compile-time-array Data

```
...+... 1 ...+... 2 ...+... 3 ...+... 4 ...+... 5 ...+... 6 ...+... 7
**
AL
AK
AZ


...+... 1 ...+... 2 ...+... 3 ...+... 4 ...+... 5 ...+... 6 ...+... 7
**CTDATA States
AL
AK
AZ
```

In Figure 7.6, we have defined a compile-time array with a Definition Specification. Our array is named States, has 50 total elements that are each two characters in length (representing each of the 50 United States), and there is one entry per source record. The CTDATA keyword tells the compiler that this array represents compile-time data. The PERRCD keyword tells the compiler that there is only one array entry per source record. Figure 7.5 shows the trigger record and the first few array entry source records.

Figure 7.6: Defining a Compile-time Array with a Definition Specification

```
DName++++++++++ETDsFrom+++To/L+++IDc.Keywords+++++++++++++++++++++++++++++Comments
D States          S              2      DIM(50) CTDATA PERRCD(1)
```

This array can be used to validate the state entered on a data entry screen. You can use the Lookup (LOOKUP) op code with the value entered on the screen against the States array to see if the value keyed exists in the array. If the value keyed is not found, you can issue an error message so the program operator can correct the field before the data keyed is accepted.

ALTERNATIVE DEFINITION OF ARRAYS

The most common way to load an array is with some form of logic loop as in our previous examples. But, there are some other very useful ways to load data into arrays that will help you at input, output, and calculation time.

You can use File Input Specifications to redefine data fields into array elements. The specifications can be used to take entire fields from a file and split them up into array elements. They can also be used to take individual fields and redefine them so the system considers them to be part of an array.

In Figure 7.7, we define an array called AGE. The array is used to store and process aged accounts receivable amounts that are stored in our customer file. We could load each aging field stored in the customer file into our array, perform the necessary processing, and then move the fields back prior to output. But this would be time-consuming and tedious.

Figure 7.7: Redefining Run-time Arrays Using Input Specifications

```
DName++++++++++ETDsFrom+++To/L+++IDc.Keywords+++++++++++++++++++++++++++++Comments
D AGE             S               9  2 DIM(6)
I..............Ext-field+..................Field++++++++L1M1..PlMnZr......Comments
ICUSREC
I                 CUS000                   AGE(1)
I                 CUS030                   AGE(2)
I                 CUS060                   AGE(3)
I                 CUS090                   AGE(4)
I                 CUS120                   AGE(5)
I                 CUS150                   AGE(6)
```

A better way is to tell the system at file-definition time that each of the aging fields in our customer file represents a specific array element. The example in Figure 7.7 does exactly that. Even though our customer file is externally described, we use an internal definition of the CUSREC record format to tell the system that field CUS000 is the first array element in the AGE array, CUS030 is the second element, and so on.

Another example of redefining input file data fields into array elements is shown in Figure 7.8. While our first example uses field names from our externally described customer file, this second example uses the field positions within the file to tell the system which fields in our customer file to use as array elements. In lieu of the field names that exist in the external description of the file, we place the array name along with the index that is used to describe which element within the array represents the specified field positions. This method is less desirable than the method demonstrated in Figure 7.7 because changes in the size and type of data can cause a lot of extra, tedious work.

Figure 7.8: Redefining Run-time Arrays with Multiple Input Specifications

```
DName++++++++++ETDsFrom+++To/L+++IDc.Keywords++++++++++++++++++++++++++++Comments
D AGE             S              9 2 DIM(6)
I.....................Fmt+SPFrom+To+++DcField++++++++L1M1FrPlMnZr......Comments+
ICUSREC
I                              P  101  105  AGE(1)
I                              P  106  110  AGE(2)
I                              P  111  115  AGE(3)
I                              P  116  120  AGE(4)
I                              P  121  125  AGE(5)
I                              P  126  130  AGE(6)
```

Notice that there are no decimal positions specified on the Input Specifications, even though the array definition reflects the array elements as being nine digits with two decimal places. The compiler will not allow you to specify decimal positions at the input level when you are redefining array elements. Instead, it takes the definition from the Definition Specification describing the array.

Interestingly enough, the compiler insists that you handle the data type in the opposite manner. Our example in Figure 7.8 shows that the data in our customer file is in a packed format, as specified in column 36 of the Input Specifications, but the compiler will not let you specify that the array is packed on the Definition Specification. The compiler takes the data type definition from the Input Specification describing the input file.

The aging fields from the customer file shown in the example in Figure 7.8 are contiguous fields (stored consecutively in the file). It is easier to redefine the array elements with a single Input Specification, as shown in Figure 7.9.

Figure 7.9: Redefining Multiple Run-time Array Elements with a Single Input Specification

```
DName++++++++++ETDsFrom+++To/L+++IDc.Keywords++++++++++++++++++++++++++++Comments
D AGE             S              9 2 DIM(6)
I.....................Fmt+SPFrom+To+++DcField++++++++L1M1FrPlMnZr......Comments+
ICUSREC
I                              P  101  130  AGE
```

You can also use data structures to redefine arrays just like you do with file input specifications. If you choose to use this method, however, you must be careful to initialize your numeric data structures before your program tries to use them. As we will discuss in the next chapter, numeric data structures are considered to have blanks in them until you initialize or load data into them. Failure to perform one of these options will likely result in a Data Decimal Error, which occurs when the system encounters non-numeric data in a numeric field.

ARRAYS CAN BE VERY DYNAMIC

A new type of array was introduced when V3R1 was rolled out. This new array has the ability to dynamically allocate storage and is logically referred to as a *dynamic* array. The idea is that you define the array to take very little main memory initially, and then size your array on the fly, taking only the memory that you need.

To code a dynamic array, you need to utilize three new system APIs: CEEGTST (get heap storage), CEECZST (reallocate storage), and CEEFRST (free storage).

Coding this type of array can get kind of involved. Because there is a very good example of how to code a program using this type of array in IBM's *ILE RPG/400 Programmers Guide*, we decided not to duplicate their efforts here. But if you have a situation where you need to code a run-time array where you cannot predict the ultimate number of elements, you may want to look this one up.

STRING HANDLING IS NOT JUST FOR PEOPLE WITH YO-YOS ANYMORE

String handling op codes were a significant (and long-awaited) announcement as part of the Version 2 operating system. When Version 3 was announced, string handling was further enhanced with the new built-in functions. These new tools allow us to concatenate, scan, and parse results from data fields without having to load them into arrays first.

Built-in functions can be readily identified because they begin with a percent (%) sign. Unlike the other string handling op codes we will cover in this chapter, built-in functions may be placed in Definition Specifications as well as Calculation Specifications. Unlike op codes, however, built-in functions return a value rather than place function results in a Result field. Only the string handling built-in functions and the aforementioned %ELEM built-in function are covered in this chapter.

The op codes and built-in functions listed in Table 7.2 make the process of string manipulation a far more palatable task.

Table 7.2: String Handling Op Codes and Built-in Functions

Op Code	Description
CAT	Concatenates (joins) two character or constant fields into a single Result field. You can specify how many (if any) blanks you want to exist between the two fields once they have been concatenated.
CHECK	Used primarily to validate data in one string of data, and checks to see if all of the characters from the string being checked happen to exist in another string. If invalid characters exist in the string being searched, the address position(s) of illegal characters can be returned to a field or array.
CHECKR	Functions similarly to the CHECK op code, except the check for character validity is performed from the right-most character to the left. Just like the CHECK op code, checking is discontinued once an illegal character is found unless the Result field specified happens to be a numeric array.
SCAN	Scans (searches) a data field or array for a specific search argument and returns the positional address(es) of where within the searched field or array the search argument is found. No positional address is returned if the search argument is not found. If the Result field of this op code is a numeric array, multiple positional addresses may be returned if there are multiple occurrences of the search argument within the field or array being searched.
SUBST	Substrings (extracts) a portion of a character field, array element, or data structure element and places it into another. You specify the start position of the extract and the size of the Result field is used to determine how many characters are moved. This op code generally is used in conjunction with the SCAN or CHECK op codes.
XLATE	Translates characters of a field, array element, or data structure from one value (or set of values) to another. An example of how to use this op code is the translation of fields from lowercase to uppercase.

Op Code	Description
%SIZE	Returns the number of bytes occupied by a constant or field. %SIZE can be used on arrays, tables, fields, literals, data structures, or variables. An optional second parameter of *ALL may be used with an array name, data structure name, or table name where the number of bytes occupied by the entire structure will be returned.
%SUBST	Serves essentially the same function as the SUBST (substring) op code. Because %SUBST is a built-in function, it may be used in Definition Specifications as well as Calculation Specifications.
%TRIM	Used to trim leading and trailing blanks for any character string.
%TRIML	Used to trim leading blanks from any character string.
%TRIMR	Used to trim trailing blanks from any character string.

EVERYBODY WANTS TO BE A CAT

For many years, arrays were the only tool RPG programmers could use for string handling and manipulation. As you can see from the example in Figure 7.10, array handling was not always terribly efficient.

Figure 7.10: Using RPG III Arrays to Pack City, State, and Zip Code

```
.....E....FromfileTofile++Name++N/rN/tbLenPDSArrnamLenPDSComments+++++++++......
     E               WRK         40 1                   WORKING ARRAY
     *
.....CL0N01N02N03Factor1+++OpcdeFactor2+++ResultLenDHHiLoEqComments+++++++......
     C               MOVE *BLANKS   WRK
     C               MOVEACITY      WRK
     C          WRK,X DOWEQ*BLANKS                       FIND LAST NON-BLANK
     C               SUB  1         X            68      CHARACTER
     C    68         END
     C               ADD  1         X
     C               MOVEA','       WRK,X               ADD A COMMA
     C               ADD  2         X
     C               MOVEASTATE     WRK,X               ADD THE STATE
     C               ADD  3         X
     C               MOVEAZIPCOD    WRK,X               ADD THE ZIP
     C               ADD  5         X
     C               MOVE '-'       WRK,X
     C               ADD  1         X
     C               MOVEAZIP4      WRK,X               ADD ZIP + 4
     C               MOVEAWRK       CSZ      40         MOVE RESULT TO FIELD
     *
```

The objective of this routine is to take the contents of the following fields and pack them together into one field:

Field	Size and Attributes	Contents
CITY	15A	San Diego
STATE	2A	CA
ZIPCOD	5A	92126
ZIP4	4A	4440

The result after the routine is run looks something like this:

```
San Diego, CA 92126-4440
```

As you can see from the example in Figure 7.11, it requires significantly less code to use the CAT op code to perform the same operation shown in Figure 7.10. As you already know, less code means less maintenance and fewer chances for error.

Figure 7.11: Using the CAT Op Code to Pack City, State, and Zip Code

```
DName+++++++++++ETDsFrom+++To/L+++IDc.Keywords+++++++++++++++++++++++++++++++++++Comments
D CSZ             S          40A


CL0N01Factor1++++++++Opcode&ExtFactor2++++++++Result++++++++Len++D+HiLoEq....Comments
C     CITY         CAT(P)     ',':0           CSZ
C                  CAT        STATE:1         CSZ
C                  CAT        ZIPCOD:1        CSZ
C                  CAT        '-':0           CSZ
C                  CAT        ZIP4:0          CSZ
```

The first statement of the example in Figure 7.11 uses the CAT op code to concatenate the contents of the field CITY in Factor 1 to a constant comma (,) found in Factor 2. Because the P extender is specified directly after the CAT op code, our Result field (CSZ) is *padded,* or filled with blanks, prior to placing the results of our CAT operation there. After filling the CSZ field with blanks, the results of the concatenation are placed into the Result field:

Factor 1	Op Code	Factor 2	Result Field
[1st character string]	**CAT[P]**	2nd string[:# of blanks]	concatenation result

Placing a colon (:) and a numeric value or field after the constant or field specified in Factor 2 tells the system how many blanks to use between the Factor 1 and Factor 2 values once the concatenation is complete. On the first line of the example in Figure 7.11, we tell the system that we want a comma (represented by the constant specified in Factor 2) to directly follow the field value of Factor 1 with no spaces between them. The results recorded in the CSZ field after the first line of the example in Figure 7.11 looks like this:

```
San Diego,
```

The second line of our example is used to concatenate the STATE field to the current value of the CSZ field, leaving a single space between the two values. Factor 1 is left blank here because the system automatically assumes that Factor 1 is the same as the Result field unless you specify otherwise.

The remaining statements concatenate the ZIPCOD, a dash (-), and the ZIP4 field to the end of the CSZ field to attain the desired results. We are able to accomplish our goal with approximately one quarter the number of statements. Another advantage is that we did not need to worry about array index errors because arrays are no longer part of the equation.

Note that this operation was made simpler because the zip code is stored as an alphanumeric field. If it were stored as numeric, we would have to move the code to an alphanumeric field before performing the CAT operation.

The new freeform expressions announced in V3R1 make this task even easier, as you can see in Figure 7.12.

Figure 7.12: Using Freeform Expressions to Pack City, State, and Zip Code

```
DName++++++++++ETDsFrom+++To/L+++IDc.Keywords++++++++++++++++++++++++++++++++Comments
D CSZ             S           40A

CLON01Factor1+++++++Opcode&ExtExtended-factor2+++++++++++++++++++++++++++++++Comments
C                   EVAL      CSZ = %TRIM(CITY) + ', ' +
C                             STATE + ' ' + ZIPCOD + '-' + ZIP4
```

In Figure 7.12, we used the EVAL op code to pull our city, state, and zip code fields together. We first specified the %TRIM function on the CITY field to trim off the leading and trailing blanks (we could have used the %TRIMR as only trailing blanks are likely to be present in this field). We then used the plus sign (+) to concatenate the result of our %TRIM function to the literal that includes a comma (,) and a trailing blank that will appear after the city, but before the state.

The first line of our EVAL statement ended with a plus sign (indicating a pending concatenation), so the next line serves as a continuation of our EVAL statement. We then used the plus sign to concatenate the state and zip code fields to our CSZ field.

The net result of the code in Figure 7.12 was the same as the code in Figures 7.10 and 7.11 but, as you can see, they were performed with substantially less code.

In Figure 7.13, you can see how much code was required when we used RPG III arrays to pack a first name, middle initial, and last name into a single field. This operation was made much simpler when the CAT op code was announced, as you can see in Figure 7.14, and even easier with built-in functions, as shown in Figure 7.15.

Figure 7.13: Using Arrays to Pack First Name, Middle Initial, and Last Name

```
.....E....FromfileTofile++Name++N/rN/tbLenPDSArrnamLenPDSComments+++++++++......
     E                    WRK          30 1               WORKING ARRAY
     E*
.....CL0N01N02N03Factor1+++OpcdeFactor2+++ResultLenDHHiLoEqComments+++++++......
     C                    MOVE *BLANKS  WRK
     C                    MOVE *BLANKS  NAME
     C                    MOVEAFIRST    WRK
     C                    Z-ADD10       X         20        FIND LAST NON-BLANK
B1   C          WRK,X     DOWEQ*BLANKS                      CHARACTER
     C                    SUB  1        X            68
E1   C    68             ENDDO
     C                    ADD  2        X
B1   C          INIT      IFNE *BLANKS                       ADD MIDDLE INITIAL
     C                    MOVE INIT     WRK,X
     C                    ADD  2        X
E1   C                    ENDIF
     C                    MOVEALAST     WRK,X               ADD LAST NAME
     C                    MOVEAWRK      NAME
```

Figure 7.14: Using CAT to Pack First Name, Middle Initial, and Last Name

```
CL0N01Factor1+++++++Opcode&ExtFactor2+++++++Result++++++++Len++D+HiLoEq....Comments
C    FIRST     CAT(P)    INIT:1     NAME
C              CAT       LAST:1     NAME
```

Figure 7.15: Using Freeform Expressions to Pack First Name, Middle Initial, and Last Name (incorrectly)

```
CL0N01Factor1+++++++Opcode&ExtExtended-factor2+++++++++++++++++++++++++++++++Comments
C              EVAL       NAME = %TRIM(FIRST) + ' ' + INIT + ' ' LAST
```

Notice that in Figure 7.15, we used the %TRIM built-in function to strip leading and trailing blanks from the first name, but not the other two elements to be concatenated. This is because the INIT field is only one character and therefore cannot have leading or trailing blanks. We did not care if the last name had trailing blanks because it had no consequences in our results.

The code in Figure 7.15 would not return our desired results, however, if the INIT field could have blanks. This is because our code concatenated one blank before the INIT field, then the blank INIT field, and then another blank after the INIT field. This would result in a NAME field with three blanks in the middle of it when no middle initial was specified. To get our desired result, we need to trim the trailing blanks off the result of our first set of concatenations, in a manner something like that used in Figure 7.16.

Figure 7.16: Using Freeform Expressions to Pack First Name, Middle Initial, and Last Name (correctly)

```
CL0N01Factor1+++++++Opcode&ExtExtended-factor2++++++++++++++++++++++++++++++Comments
C                   EVAL      NAME = %TRIM(FIRST) + ' ' + INIT
C                   EVAL      NAME = %TRIMR(NAME) + ' ' LAST
```

CHECK, Please

The CHECK op code is a useful tool for validating data in a string. Figure 7.17 uses the CHECK op code to validate data in the alphanumeric field called Tstamt to make sure the data is entirely numeric. If the test determines that all characters in the field are numeric, it moves the value in Tstamt to the field called Amount. Otherwise, the Amount field is filled with zeros.

Figure 7.17: Using CHECK to Validate a Numeric Field

```
DName++++++++++++ETDsFrom+++To/L+++IDc.Keywords++++++++++++++++++++++++++++++++Comments
D Number          C                   CONST('0123456789')
D Amount          S              9  2
CL0N01Factor1+++++++Opcode&ExtFactor2+++++++Result++++++++Len++D+HiLoEq....Comments
C     Number      CHECK     Tstamt                                     68
C                 IF        *IN68
C                 EVAL      Amount = 0
C                 ELSE
C                 EVAL      Amount = Tstamt
C                 ENDIF
```

You may have occasion to perform this test to avoid Data Decimal Errors. As you are aware, the AS/400 is very particular about data types. If a field is defined as being numeric, the AS/400 tends to get a little upset if it finds data other than numbers. Unfortunately, data imported into the AS/400 often comes from other systems (including some of the AS/400's predecessors) that are not nearly as vigilant in checking the validity of their data.

You can also specify a Result field with the CHECK op code that will be used to store the address(es) of the digits that were found to be invalid. The Result field can be a numeric field or array.

Factor 1	Op Code	Factor 2	Result Field	HI	LO	EQ
validation string	**CHECK**	string to check[:start position]	[position(s)]	----	[Err]	[Found]

If the Result field specified happens to be a numeric array, the CHECK operation checks the entire contents of the string specified in Factor 2, and returns the address of the fields found to be invalid to the Result field array.

USING THE %TRIML BUILT-IN FUNCTION TO REMOVE LEADING BLANKS

The %TRIML built-in function was designed for the purpose of removing leading blanks. The example in Figure 7.18 shows how to use the %TRIML built-in function to ensure that any leading blanks in the NAME field are removed. Another way to describe this particular function would be to say that we are using the %TRIML built-in function to left-justify the NAME field.

Figure 7.18: Using %TRIML to Remove Leading Blanks

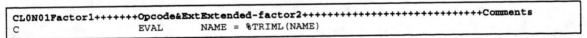

```
CL0N01Factor1++++++Opcode&ExtExtended-factor2+++++++++++++++++++++++++++++Comments
C                   EVAL      NAME = %TRIML(NAME)
```

For example, let's apply the code in Figure 7.18 to the following NAME field:

```
...+... 1 ...+... 2 ...+... 3
      SMITH
```

The results after the operation look like this:

```
...+... 1 ...+... 2 ...+... 3
SMITH
```

USING THE %TRIMR BUILT-IN FUNCTION TO REMOVE TRAILING BLANKS

Sometimes you need to right-justify a field by removing trailing blanks from it. The %TRIMR built-in function is used to perform this function. The example in Figure 7.19 shows how to use the %TRIMR built-in function to remove trailing blanks in the NAME field.

Figure 7.19: Using %TRIMR to Remove Trailing Blanks

```
CLON01Factor1+++++++Opcode&ExtExtended-factor2+++++++++++++++++++++++++++++Comments
C                   EVAL      NAME = %TRIMR(NAME)
```

For example, let's apply the code in Figure 7.19 to the following NAME field:

```
...+... 1 ...+... 2 ...+... 3
      SMITH
```

The results after the operation look like this:

```
...+... 1 ...+... 2 ...+... 3
                        SMITH
```

USING THE %TRIM BUILT-IN FUNCTION TO REMOVE LEADING AND TRAILING BLANKS

You may also find yourself with a need to remove both leading and trailing blanks from a field to strip out the pertinent data. The %TRIM built-in function will perform this service. The example in Figure 7.20 shows how to use the %TRIM built-in function to remove both leading and trailing blanks in the NAME field and put the results in a field called LAST.

Figure 7.20: Using %TRIM to Remove Leading and Trailing Blanks

```
CLON01Factor1+++++++Opcode&ExtExtended-factor2+++++++++++++++++++++++++++++Comments
C                   EVAL      LAST = %TRIM(NAME)
```

For example, let's apply the code in Figure 7.20 to the following NAME field:

```
...+... 1 ...+... 2 ...+... 3
        SMITH
```

After the operation, the results in the field called LAST look like this:

```
...+... 1
SMITH
```

CHECKR Validates Character Strings from Right to Left

The CHECKR op code serves basically the same function as the CHECK op code, except that the string is validated from the right-most characters of the string being validated back to the left-most character.

Factor 1	Op Code	Factor 2	Result Field	HI	LO	EQ
validation string	**CHECKR**	string to check[:start position]	[position(s)]	----	[Err]	[Found]

If you choose to use indexing on Factor 2 (the string being searched), the CHECKR operation begins at the character address specified by the index field and searches from right to left, back to the beginning character of the string.

Seek and Ye Shall Find—with SCAN

SCAN allows you to search a character string for a specific search argument, and then return a character address if the search argument is found. Figure 7.21 is an example of how to use the SCAN op code to find the address of the comma that is embedded into a name field that was keyed as Last, First. The objective of the routine is to look for the comma and then extract the first and last names if the comma is found. If no comma is found, the first name field is blanked out and the rest of the characters are put in the last name field.

Figure 7.21: Using SCAN to Extract First and Last Names from a Field Keyed as Last, First

```
DName++++++++++ETDsFrom+++To/L+++IDc.Keywords+++++++++++++++++++++++++++++Comments
D Left             S              2 0
D Pos              S              2 0
CL0N01Factor1++++++Opcode&ExtFactor2++++++Result++++++++Len++D+HiLoEq....Comments
C      ','         SCAN      Name:1        Pos                   68
 * If a comma was found, separate the fields...
C      *IN68       IFEQ      *ON
C      Pos         ANDGT     1
C                  SUB       1             Pos
C      Pos         SUBST(P)  Name:1        Last
C      Pos         IFLT      26
C                  ADD       3             Pos
C      28          SUB       Pos           Left
C      Left        SUBST(P)  Name:Pos      First
C                  ENDIF
C                  ELSE
 * If no comma was found, put entire field in Last...
C                  MOVE      *BLANKS       First
C                  MOVEL(P)  Name          Last
C                  ENDIF
```

In our example in Figure 7.21, the length of the search argument happened to be a single character (we could have used the CHECK op code to perform this same function). But the SCAN op code can look for entire strings of data too.

For example, let's say we want to know how many of the customers in our customer file are corporations. We could search the customer names for the characters INC and get a pretty good idea. The code looks something like Figure 7.22.

Figure 7.22: Using SCAN to Find Customers with INC in the Customer Name Field

```
CL0N01Factor1++++++Opcode&ExtFactor2++++++Result++++++++Len++D+HiLoEq....Comments
C      'INC':3     SCAN      CUSNAM                              68
 * If a corporation was found, go print the record...
C      *IN68       CASEQ     *ON           PRINT
C                  ENDCS
```

The search argument of the SCAN op code is always specified in Factor 1. The argument can be a constant, all or part of a field, an array element, or a table name. You can specify that you only want to use the first portion of a field by indicating the field length in Factor 1. The field length is specified by following the value in Factor 1 with a colon (:) and a numeric field or constant.

Factor 1	Op Code	Factor 2	Result Field	HI	LO	EQ
search argument[:length]	**SCAN**	string to scan[:start position]	[position(s)]	----	[Err]	[Found]

Factor 2 contains the string that you want searched. The string must be a character, but it can be a field, constant, array element, or table.

If you choose to specify the optional Result field, it is loaded with the positional address of the search argument if it happens to be found. If you choose to omit the Result field, you must specify an indicator in position 75. The indicator is turned on if the search argument is found and turned off if it is not.

Note that the SCAN op code is case sensitive. Using SCAN to detect an uppercase character string does not detect the same string in lowercase, and vice versa. If you want to perform a search that crosses the case boundaries, you can do so if you utilize the SCAN op code in conjunction with the Translate (XLATE) op code, discussed later in this chapter.

SUBSTRING (SUBST) TIES THE WHOLE STRING-HANDLING THING TOGETHER

You can use Substring (SUBST) to extract a value or values from a character string and move the results to the desired target character string, all from within a single operation. The character strings involved must be alphanumeric data. These elements may be arrays, array elements, and data structures, to name a few possibilities.

Factor 1	Op Code	Factor 2	Result Field	HI	LO	EQ
[Length to be extracted]	**SUBST[P]**	Base string[:start]	Target string	----	[Err]	--

The Substring (SUBST) function really performs two or three functions at the same time. It extracts the data you desire and then performs a "move left" function into the Result field. If you specify a P in the extender field (directly following the op code), the remainder of the Result field is padded with blanks.

The character string from which you want to extract data is specified in Factor 2. Optionally, you may indicate the position within the string where you want the extraction to begin by following the string specified in Factor 2 with a colon (:) and a number or numeric field that contains the character address where the search should begin.

You tell the system how many characters to extract by the numeric value or numeric field that you specify in Factor 1. If Factor 1 is omitted, the system calculates the length of the extraction based upon the start position and the length of the string that was specified in Factor 2.

The example in Figure 7.23 shows how to take an alphabetical date field that is stored as YYMMDD (year, month, day) and parse it out (split it up) into three distinct fields.

Figure 7.23: Using SUBST to Parse Out an Alpha DATE Field into Three 2-character Fields Called Month, Day, and Year

```
CL0N01Factor1+++++++Opcode&ExtFactor2+++++++Result++++++++Len++D+HiLoEq....Comments
C     2          SUBST     Date:1        Year
C     2          SUBST     Date:3        Month
C     2          SUBST     Date:5        Day
```

Factor 1 is specified to indicate the number of characters we want to extract. Factor 2 contains the name of the original field Date followed by a colon (:) and a number that represents the position within the string where the extraction should begin.

In this simple example of the use of SUBST, numeric values are specified for the length to extract and the beginning positions. More advanced examples of this tool are shown in Figure 7.24 where both the starting position and the length to extract are specified as variables.

Figure 7.24: Using SUBST to Separate a Name Field That is Last, First into Separate First and Last Name Fields

```
DName+++++++++++ETDsFrom+++To/L+++IDc.Keywords+++++++++++++++++++++++++++++++Comments
D X               S                  2 0
D First           S                 10
D Last            S                 15
CL0N01Factor1++++++++Opcode&ExtFactor2+++++++Result++++++++Len++D+HiLoEq....Comments
C        ',':1         SCAN       Name          X                    68
C        *IN68         IFEQ       *ON
C                      SUB        1             X
C        X            SUBST(P)    Name:1        Last
C                      ADD        2             X
C                     SUBST(P)    Name:X        First
C                      EVAL       First = %TRIML(First)
C                      ELSE
C                     MOVEL(P)    Name          Last
C                      MOVE       *BLANKS       First
C                      ENDIF
```

In Figure 7.24, we have a name field that is stored as Last Name, First Name, and we want to separate the data into two separate fields. We first use the SCAN op code to determine if the names are stored as Last, First. If a comma is found, we use SUBST to parse the data into distinctly different fields.

The SCAN operation returns the character address of the comma within the Name character string, so we are able to ascertain that all characters prior to the comma belong in the last name field Last. We subtract 1 from X (so the comma is not included in the data we extract) and perform the SUBST operation on the Name field beginning in position 1 for a length of X (which now stores the length of the last name field). We use the P extender to pad the rest of the Last name field with blanks in case there are characters in the field from a prior operation.

The next step is to add 2 to X to move the character address past the comma in the Name string. We assume that all characters beyond the comma belong in the first name field, so we perform the SUBST operation beginning at the character address, which places us a single character beyond the comma. We do not indicate the number of characters to extract in the SUBST operation because we want all characters through the end of the string to be moved into our target field. Again, we use the P extender to clear undesired characters from the First field.

At this point, we have performed our desired function of separating the first and last names. We put an additional step into the code to ensure that leading blanks are stripped from the first name field. If the initial Name character string came from a data entry process somewhere, you are likely to have inconsistencies in the way the field is keyed.

Some operators may be inclined to key the name with a blank after the comma where others would not. By using the %TRIML built-in function, we are able to suppress the leading blanks in this field.

In Figure 7.25, we used the %SUBST built-in function to perform the same function as we performed in Figure 7.24. But as you can see, using the built-in functions and freeform expressions is more efficient because we are able to perform several functions in a single step.

Figure 7.25: Using %SUBST to Separate a Name Field That is Last, First into Separate First and Last Name Fields

```
DName+++++++++++ETDsFrom+++To/L+++IDc.Keywords+++++++++++++++++++++++++++++++Comments
D X               S             2 0
D First           S            10
D Last            S            15
CL0N01Factor1+++++++Opcode&ExtFactor2+++++++Result++++++++Len++D+HiLoEq....Comments
C       ',':1        SCAN       Name            X                        68
C       *IN68        IFEQ       *ON
C                    EVAL       First = %SUBST(Name:X+1)
C                    EVAL       First = %TRIML(First)
C                    EVAL       Last = %SUBST(Name:X-1)
C                    ELSE
C                    MOVEL(P)   Name            Last
C                    MOVE       *BLANKS         First
C                    ENDIF
```

TRANSLATE (XLATE) PERFORMS SINGLE-CHARACTER SUBSTITUTION WITHIN CHARACTER STRINGS

The XLATE op code is a handy tool when you need to perform character substitution within a character string. You can specify From and To characters to translate, or entire strings of characters that need to be translated.

Factor 1	Op Code	Factor 2	Result Field	HI	LO	EQ
From value:To value	**XLATE[P]**	Base string[:start]	Target string	----	[Err]	--

One of the more popular uses for this op code is to translate a lowercase character string to uppercase. This is a frequent requirement when you are importing data from an external source. Figure 7.26 is an example of how to address this issue.

Figure 7.26: Using XLATE to Translate Lowercase Character Strings to Uppercase

```
DName+++++++++++ETDsFrom+++To/L+++IDc.Keywords++++++++++++++++++++++++++++++++Comments
D Lower           C                        CONST('abcdefghijklmnopqrst-
D                                          uvwxyz')
D Upper           C                        CONST('ABCDEFGHIJKLMNOPQRST-
D                                          UVWXYZ')
CL0N01Factor1++++++++Opcode&ExtFactor2+++++++Result++++++++Len++D+HiLoEq....Comments
C       Lower:Upper    XLATE(P)   InName        OutName
```

In Figure 7.26, we take an input field named InName, that may or may not contain lowercase characters, and translate the characters to uppercase, placing the end results in a field called OutName. To do this, we use a named constant field Lower that contains all the lowercase characters that we want to translate. We use another named constant Upper that holds the corresponding uppercase characters.

The XLATE operation looks for characters in the InName field that happen to exist in the Lower named constant and replaces them with the corresponding character found within the Upper named constant.

In Figure 7.27, we use the XLATE op code to translate brackets in the field called InField to parentheses.

Figure 7.27: Using XLATE to Translate Brackets to Parentheses

```
CL0N01Factor1++++++++Opcode&ExtFactor2+++++++Result++++++++Len++D+HiLoEq....Comments
C       '{':'('      XLATE(P)   InField       InField
C       '}':')'      XLATE(P)   InField       InField
```

FINAL WORDS ABOUT ARRAY AND STRING HANDLING

As you have seen while reading this chapter, array and string handling are a vital part of RPG programming. Array handling is invaluable for performing data validation, formatting output, and storing totals that will be output later in a program. The string handling op codes make difficult character manipulation chores much easier to perform.

Take the time to become familiar with the tools discussed in this chapter. You will find that it is time well spent.

Chapter 8

Data Structures, Data Areas, and the Local Data Area

In this chapter, we discuss three valuable components that are used for definition, composition, and transportation of data elements both to and from your RPG programs. As the AS/400 has continued its logical evolution, these three components have become a bigger part of the overall scheme of things. We have seen a myriad of APIs announced, which use data structures to pass system data back and forth to our programs. Multiple-occurrence Data Structures have been added to reduce the number of fields and arrays required as well as to give us a method for creating *two-dimensional* arrays. And the local data area (LDA) is still one of the best ways to pass localized data from one program to the next.

You will find that a thorough knowledge of these tools can give you a distinct competitive advantage over your programming counterparts. Once you have mastered these techniques, you will be able to write more efficient code that also performs better. Let's continue on our path of education by example to discuss the merit and functions of each of these methods.

THE DATA STRUCTURE

Data structures are used primarily to define and redefine data elements. In its simplest form, you can consider a data structure to be a sum of all of its parts. It is used to subdivide larger fields into smaller subfields, or compose smaller fields into larger ones.

By allowing you to create subdivisions in the data, a unique condition is created where data in the lesser subfields is dynamically bound to the larger fields that are being divided. If data in the subfield is changed, the value of the larger field is changed as well. Consequently, if values in the larger field are changed, the subdivided data is changed at the same time. This can eliminate an awful lot of code that would otherwise be needed to move data back and forth.

Let's begin by looking at a hypothetical point-of-sale transaction. In the following example, we look at a stock-keeping unit (SKU) number that might be used in a retail application. SKU numbers are used to identify a particular product or service.

The SKU number usually can be parsed out into codes that represent the department, manufacturer, vendor, model number, and stock number. As a general rule, the SKU number is used to record and track sales as well as to help manage the inventory.

When we read an SKU number from our hypothetical point-of-sale transaction, we could perform a series of MOVE and MOVEL operations to parse, or separate out, our department, manufacturer, vendor, model, and stock numbers. But it is time-consuming to code and involves setting up a series of work fields. Another option is to use the new string handling op codes that we covered in Chapter 7. But these methods involve several steps, which leaves more room for error.

A much simpler way to perform this same task is to use a data structure to subdivide the number for you. Every time the SKU number changes, the subfields that make up the data structure defining the SKU number change as well.

In the following example, our sample SKU number is 22502807224089123491A405. Whew! While this number appears to be large and unwieldy, it is not nearly as overwhelming if you break it down as follows:

Sample SKU number:

Department	Manufacturer	Vendor	Model	Stock Number
22	502	80722	4089123491A	405

Figure 8.1 shows two different data structures that break down the SKU number for us. Note that the subfields (Department, Manufactur, Vendor, ModelNbr, and StockNbr) are all subsets of the field positions that make up the SKUNumber field.

Figure 8.1: Using Data Structure Definition Specifications to Break Down an SKU Number

```
* Example of a data structure using "from" and "to" field positions

DName++++++++++ETDsFrom+++To/L+++IDc.Keywords+++++++++++++++++++Comments++++++++++++
D                 DS
DSKUNumber             1    24
D   Department         1     2  0
D   Manufactur         3     5  0
D   Vendor             6    10  0
D   ModelNbr          11    21
D   StockNbr          22    24

 * Example of a data structure using field lengths and the OVERLAY keyword

DName++++++++++ETDsFrom+++To/L+++IDc.Keywords+++++++++++++++++++Comments++++++++++++
D                 DS
DSKUNumber                  24
D   Department              2  0 OVERLAY(SKUNumber)
D   Manufactur              3  0 OVERLAY(SKUNumber:3)
D   Vendor                  5  0 OVERLAY(SKUNumber:6)
D   ModelNbr               11    OVERLAY(SKUNumber:11)
D   StockNbr                3    OVERLAY(SKUNumber:22)
```

The first example in Figure 8.1 shows a data structure that is defined using From and To field positions, much like it was defined in the Input Specifications when we worked with RPG III.

The second example in Figure 8.1 shows how RPG IV allows us to simply code the length of the field(s); the compiler will calculate the From and To lengths for us. Note that the OVERLAY keyword was specified on the subfields that make up the SKU number, so the system would know that the subfields are subsets of the SKUNumber field. The OVERLAY keyword did not require a starting position for Department because the overlay began in position 1 of the SKU number. The OVERLAY keyword for the manufacturer number did require a start position, however, because the manufacturer number represents the third, fourth, and fifth characters of the SKU number field.

Either of these data structures, in effect, redefines the SKU number field into the various subfields we desire. Notice that we have told the system that the first three fields (Department, Manufactur, and Vendor) are all numeric fields, even though they are sub-elements of a larger alphanumeric field (SKUNumber).

If our retail point-of-sale application reads a database or display file record that contains the field called SKUNumber, our program could address and use the various subfields without having to worry about any additional overhead or work to extract the subfields. In this particular case, the SKUNumber field in the database or display file needs to be 24 alphanumeric characters, just like it is defined in the data structure. The compiler gives you a hard time if you try to define it otherwise.

In the next example, we do not define the length of the SKUNumber field in our data structures. Instead, we simply name the data structure and define just the subfields.

The data structures in Figure 8.2 serve essentially the same function as the data structures in Figure 8.1. The difference is that, instead of defining the field SKUNumber down in the Definition Specifications with the subfields, SKUNumber has been used as the name of the data structure.

Figure 8.2: Alternate Data Structure Definitions to Break Down an SKU Number

```
 * Example of a data structure using "from" and "to" field positions

DName++++++++++++ETDsFrom+++To/L+++IDc.Keywords+++++++++++++++++++++Comments++++++++++++
D SKUNumber       DS
D   Department            1      2  0
D   Manufactur            3      5  0
D   Vendor                6     10  0
D   ModelNbr             11     21
D   StockNbr             22     24

 * Example of a data structure using field lengths

DName++++++++++++ETDsFrom+++To/L+++IDc.Keywords+++++++++++++++++++++Comments++++++++++++
D                 DS
DSKUNumber
D   Department                   2  0
D   Manufactur                   3  0
D   Vendor                       5  0
D   ModelNbr                    11
D   StockNbr                     3
```

In the examples in Figure 8.2, we do not need to specify the size of the SKUNumber field. In this instance, it is assumed that the size of the data structure is merely a sum of all of its parts. As a general rule, if you do not specify the size of a data structure, the compiler defines the length of it by computing the length of all of the subfields within the structure. However, if the name of the data structure also happens to be an input field from a file, the definition comes from the file instead.

For the first example in Figure 8.2, we defined the buffer positions within the SKUNumber data structure that represent the various subfields. In the second example, we merely specified the lengths of the subfields and let the system calculate the buffer positions for us.

Rules Regarding Data Structures

Data structures can be externally described or program-described (as shown in Figures 8.1 and 8.2) and are defined in the Definition Specifications of your RPG program. They support character, graphic, date, time, timestamp, basing-pointer, procedure-pointer, zoned-decimal, packed, and binary data types. Data types are defined in the same manner, and generally follow the same rules, as you adhere to when coding data files.

The definition of a data structure begins with the characters DS in positions 24 and 25 of a Definition Specification. If your data structure is internally described, you may optionally name your data structure in columns 7 through 21 of the same Definition Specification. When a data structure is externally described (we discuss more on that later in the chapter when we cover "Externally Defined Data Structures"), you must either specify the name in positions 7 through 21 or use the EXTNAME keyword.

The fields for a data structure and its subfields must all appear together within the Definition Specifications (they may not be mixed in with file definitions or other data structures). The compiler does not allow field names within a data structure to exist in any other data structures within the program. As shown in the previous example, however, they may exist in database or display file definitions.

A data structure can go all the way up to 32,767 characters in size, which happens to be the same as the maximum size of an alphanumeric field in RPG IV.

Special Data Structures

There are four very unique data structures on the AS/400 that are used for special purposes:

- **File Information Data Structure.** A special data structure that serves as a feedback area used to retrieve additional information about a file from the system. This data structure is initiated by the use of a special keyword that is specified in the File Description Specifications. This data structure is used primarily for error detection and prevention (i.e., record lock conditions or errors trying to open a database file). Chapter 4 offers a detailed explanation of the File Information Data Structure and its potential uses.

- **Program Status Data Structure.** Used to retrieve information about the program that is running. This information includes procedure name, job number, user ID, library name where the program resides, and a variety of other job information that may be pertinent to the task at run time. Chapter 4 illustrates examples of what information can be retrieved and where you may want to use it within your programs.

- **Data Area Data Structure.** Used to describe the information inside a data area. A data area is kind of like a single-record data file that happens to come in two flavors: Local and global. The local data area (LDA) is unique to each program session and is used primarily to pass information from one job stream component to the next. On the other hand, global data areas can reside in any library and can be accessed by programs and CL alike. Data Area Data Structures may be used to describe and define both types of data areas. Examples of this type of data structure are covered later in this chapter.

- **Multiple-occurrence Data Structure.** Offers a way to define multiple like-data structures at once within your RPG program. The Multiple-occurrence Data Structure introduces flexibility into your RPG programs that may be used to eliminate arrays, fields, and work files from your RPG programs. If you eliminate work files, you are also eliminating unnecessary I/O processing. We visit the topic of Multiple-occurrence Data Structures a little later in the chapter.

There are also other special data structures like the Program Initialization (PIP) Data Structure and those involving system APIs (covered in detail in Chapter 9).

Dynamics of Data Structures

As stated, one of the advantages of using data structures is that, when you change data in one of the components, it can dynamically change the data fields or subfields being used to redefine the component. In Figure 8.1, we saw how reading a database or display file record with the SKUNumber field in it dynamically changed the values of the data structure subfields to redefine the SKUNumber field.

What happens when the situation is reversed? Let's calculate a follow-up date that might be used in an Accounts Receivable application. The objective of this routine is to create a follow-up date that is the 15th of the following month. To perform this function, begin by using the data structure shown in Figures 8.3.

Figure 8.3: Using Data Structure Input Specifications to Break Down a Date Field

```
DName+++++++++++ETDsFrom+++To/L+++IDc.Keywords+++++++++++++++++++++++++++++++Comments
D                          DS
D  MonDayYear                       D   DATFMT(*MDY) INZ
D  Month                        2       OVERLAY(MonDayYear:1)
D  Day                          2       OVERLAY(MonDayYear:4)
D  Year                         2       OVERLAY(MonDayYear:7)
```

Although there are a number of ways to perform this type of operation, we are going to use a data structure to help us perform this simple calculation. The first step is to load today's date into our data structure field.

You will note that the MonDayYear field has a data type (specified on column 40) of D, indicating that the field is a date data type. The DATFMT keyword is used to further describe the date field to the system. In this case, the *MDY indicates that the date is stored in a Month-Day-Year format. The date data type includes separator characters, so the date of December 31, 1996, would be stored as 12/31/96. Also note that we did not need to specify the size of the field. The system knows that a field with a date data type in conjunction with a date format of *MDY will appear as eight characters to your RPG IV program.

The Month, Day, and Year fields have been specified in the data structure using the aforementioned OVERLAY keyword. The month is in the first two positions of the field, a separator character in the third position, the day in the fourth and fifth positions, and so on.

The task of retrieving the current date could easily be performed in a variety of ways. Our options include using the TIME op code; loading UYEAR, UMONTH, and UDAY into the appropriate subfields (Year, Month, and Day); or moving UDATE into the MonDayYear data structure field (if your system date format is Month/Day/Year). The method chosen to load our date field is unimportant for our example.

Let's say that our current date is December 31, 1996.

After loading our MonDayYear data structure field, the value of the MonDayYear field is 12/31/96. The values of the various subfields are:

Month	Day	Year
12	31	96

Applying the code shown in Figure 8.4 results in a date field in the MonDayYear data structure that represents the 15th of the month following the original date.

Figure 8.4: RPG Code Using the Data Structure in Figure 8.3 to Add a Month to a Date Field

```
CLON01Factor1+++++++Opcode(E)+Factor2+++++++Result+++++++Len++D+HiLoEq....Comments
C                   MOVE      UDATE          MonDayYear
C                   ADDDUR    1:*M           MonDayYear
C                   MOVE      '15'           Day
```

In Figure 8.4, we moved UDATE (the system date) into our MonDayYear date field and then used the ADDDUR (Add duration) op code to increase the date by one month. We could have accomplished the same thing by incrementing the Month field, but then we would have had to worry about whether the month had rolled over to an invalid month (in this case it would have been 13) and write code to increment the Year field and restore the Month field to a valid value. The ADDDUR op code is a much cleaner way to deal with a date field.

We then moved 15 into the Day field, replacing whatever happened to be there.

After applying the code in Figure 8.4, the MonDayYear data structure field contains a value of 01/15/97, and the subfield values are:

Month	Day	Year
01	15	97

There are other ways we could have found our desired follow-up date but, as you can see, the data structure gives us an easy way to use data structure subfields to dynamically change data.

The Data Structure and the Data Decimal Error

As you are no doubt aware, your AS/400 is terribly picky about data types. If you define a field as signed numeric, then that is exactly what the AS/400 expects to see. If it encounters blanks or alphanumeric data where it expects to see numeric data, the system complains very loudly in the form of a Data Decimal Error.

Data structures are one area of RPG where it is very easy to create a condition for Data Decimal Errors occur. This is because data structures are initially assumed to be alphanumeric data, regardless of the data type of the subfields defined within.

This potential error condition exists because data structures are not automatically initialized at program initiation unless you instruct your program to do so. If the data defined in your data structure is defined as signed numeric, and your program tries to refer to the numeric field prior to initializing or loading numeric data into the field, your program experiences a Data Decimal Error condition.

For example, let's say your program contains the data structure shown in Figure 8.5. If your program refers to the Amount, Dollars, or Cents numeric fields prior to loading data or moving zeros into them, you have a Data Decimal Error on your hands when the program is run.

Figure 8.5: Example of a Data Decimal Error Waiting to Happen

```
DName+++++++++++ETDsFrom+++To/L+++IDc.Keywords++++++++++++++++++++Comments++++++++++++
D                       DS
D   Amount                         9  2
D     Dollars                      7  0 OVERLAY(Amount)
D     Cents                        2  0 OVERLAY(Amount:8)
```

One way to address this potential problem is to always load data into the field(s) prior to using the field(s). An even safer way to address this problem is to instruct the system to automatically initialize the data structure at program initiation time.

To initialize a data structure at program initiation time, simply use the INZ keyword in the Definition Specification that defines the data structure. The INZ keyword should appear with other keywords beginning in position 44 of the Definition Specification.

Figure 8.6 provides an example of the same data structure shown in Figure 8.5, except that this one is initialized automatically at program run time just prior to running the optional Initialize (*INZSR) subroutine. When this subroutine is present in your RPG program, it runs before the execution of all other Calculation Specifications.

Figure 8.6: Performing Data Structure Initialization

```
DName+++++++++++ETDsFrom+++To/L+++IDc.Keywords++++++++++++++++++++Comments++++++++++++
D                       DS
D    Amount                      9  2 INZ
D      Dollars                   7  0 OVERLAY(Amount)
D      Cents                     2  0 OVERLAY(Amount:8)
```

The data structure in Figure 8.6 has the INZ keyword in position 44 of the Definition Specification of the Amount field, so there are no Data Decimal Errors associated with the Amount, Dollars, or Cents fields unless the same fields happen to be defined in a database file with invalid numeric data. It should be noted that this initialization could have been accomplished by using the INZ keyword on the Definition Specification defining the data structure as well. The subfields would automatically have been dynamically initialized either way.

Because we did not specify otherwise, the three numeric fields in our example are initialized as zeros. Data structure initialization is performed based upon data type. In other words, alphanumeric fields are initialized to blanks and numeric fields are initialized to zeros, unless you specify otherwise. Date fields would be initialized with a month of 01, a day of 01, and a year of 0001, because zeros are invalid in a field designated as a date data type. The next section deals with situations where we want fields initialized to values other than the data type default values.

Default Values and Data Subfield Initialization

As we saw in the previous example, data structure initialization is a handy way to clear the fields in an entire data structure. But subfields within a data structure may be initialized as well, and not necessarily to values dictated by the data type.

To initialize subfields in a data structure, simply put an INZ keyword in the Definition Specification describing the data structure subfield. Figure 8.7 shows the same data structure as the previous two examples, except the initialization is performed on a subfield level instead of the entire data structure.

Figure 8.7: Data Structure Subfield Initialization

```
DName++++++++++ETDsFrom+++To/L+++IDc.Keywords++++++++++++++++++++Comments++++++++++++
D  Amount                          9 2
D   Dollars                        7 0 INZ OVERLAY(Amount)
D   Cents                          2 0 INZ OVERLAY(Amount:8)
```

This example serves essentially the same purpose as the example in Figure 8.6. The Dollars, and Cents fields are initialized to zeros because their data types are signed numeric and an INZ has been specified as a keyword in the Definition Specifications. The subfields make up the entire Amount field, so initializing the subfields initialized the Amount field as well.

What sets subfield initialization apart from data structure initialization is that default values may be established for each subfield. The default values are placed in parentheses following the INZ keyword when using the Definition Specification to define the subfield. Just like Calculation Specifications, defaults for alphanumeric fields are placed in quotes, while numeric values are not.

In Figure 8.8, we choose to use both forms of data structure initialization at the same time. We specify an INZ keyword in the data structure Definition Specification telling the system to initialize the entire data structure based upon data type. We then place a default value in parentheses following the INZ keyword when defining the Dollars subfield with a default value of 5.

Figure 8.8: Data Structure Subfield Initialization with Default Values

```
DName++++++++++ETDsFrom+++To/L+++IDc.Keywords++++++++++++++++++++Comments++++++++++++
D              DS                      INZ
D  Amount                          9 2
D   Dollars                        7 0 INZ(5) OVERLAY(Amount)
D   Cents                          2 0 OVERLAY(Amount:8)
```

In this example, the entire data structure is initialized according to data type (in this case zeros) and then the default value of 5 is placed in the Dollars subfield. Consequently, the value of the Amount field after initialization is 5.00.

This same technique can be applied to alphanumeric fields. For instance, let's say that we could initialize a description field with the value of Not on File, with the assumption that we probably will replace the initial value with a valid description later.

The example in Figure 8.9 establishes the definition of the field called Descriptn and initializes the original value of the field as Not on File (by placing the literal in parentheses following the INZ keyword).

Figure 8.9: Alphanumeric Subfield Initialization with Default Values

```
DName++++++++++ETDsFrom+++To/L+++IDc.Keywords++++++++++++++++++++Comments++++++++++++
D   Descriptn                   35      INZ('Not on File')
```

In lieu of the literal default value in parentheses, we could have specified the name of a named constant, figurative constant, or built-in function. The value in the named constant, figurative constant (i.e., *ALL 'a'), or built-in function would then serve as the default entry.

Note: Default values may be re-established by using the RESET op code.

In Figure 8.9, we established the initial value of the field called Descriptn as Not on File with the idea that we would replace the value once a valid entry was made. If the RESET op code is specified later in the program, the default values are re-established at that time. The RESET op code may be specified for a single field, or for an entire data structure like that shown in Figure 8.10.

Figure 8.10: Data Structure Subfield Initialization with Default Values

```
DName++++++++++ETDsFrom+++To/L+++IDc.Keywords++++++++++++++++++++Comments++++++++++++
D   ResetData       DS                  INZ
D   Amount                       9 2
D     Dollars                    7 0 INZ(5) OVERLAY(Amount)
D     Cents                      2 0 OVERLAY(Amount:8)
D   Descriptn                   35    INZ('Not on File')
```

If RESET is applied to the ResetData data structure, all of the subfields in the data structure are reinitialized to their original values. The Dollars and Descriptn fields are reset to include the default values specified, and the Cents field is reinitialized to zeros because of its numeric data type.

The Amount field in this example is simply a redefinition of the Dollars and Cents fields, so the value of the Amount field is reset to 5.00 and the Descriptn field is reset to Not on File.

Externally Described Data Structures

Externally Described Data Structures can be used to define LDAs, data areas, program-described files, and parameter lists. We will discuss these topics more as this chapter progresses.

Many of the same attributes that make externally described data files such a powerful tool on the AS/400 also apply to Externally Described Data Structures. Because they are defined in a single place, there is consistency in definition. Programs using the data structure are easier to maintain because they do not necessarily need to be modified when the data structure changes, unless the program happens to use the fields within the data structure that were changed.

If an external data structure does change, programs using the data structure only need to be recompiled, with two notable exceptions. The first exception is if the program uses one or more of the fields in the data structure that was changed, as mentioned. The second exception is if new fields were added to the end of the data structure. In this case, only the programs using the newly added field(s) need to be modified or compiled.

External data structure definitions are coded with DDS just like you would code any other data file. In fact, an external definition really is just a physical file, and you can use other physical file specifications as external data structures. This technique can come in handy when your program uses a work file that exactly matches another physical file.

Basically, it does not matter whether the external definition you refer to in your Definition Specifications ever has data or not. The physical file specifications are simply being used as a data structure that is being used to describe and define your data.

Figure 8.11 shows the DDS for a simple externally defined data structure. Figure 8.12 shows the RPG Input Specifications for the external definition called ExternlDef.

Figure 8.11: DDS for an Externally Described Data Structure

```
A..........T.Name++++++RLen++TDpB......Functions++++++++++++++++++++++++++++++
A           R ExternlDef               TEXT('External Data Structure')
A             CompanyNum    3S 0       COLHDG('Company Number')
A             CompanyNam   40A         COLHDG('Company Name')
```

Figure 8.12: RPG Input Specifications for an Externally Described Data Structure

```
DName+++++++++++ETDsFrom+++To/L+++IDc.Keywords++++++++++++++++++++Comments++++++++++++
D Definition     E DS                     EXTNAME(ExternlDef)
```

The name of the data structure defined by the RPG IV Definition Specifications in Figure 8.12 is Definition. The data structure subfields called CompanyNum and CompanyNam are defined and ready for use from within the RPG IV program, just as if you had defined the data structure from within the program.

To get a full appreciation for the value of the Externally Described Data Structure, we really need to see how this methodology applies when used in conjunction with data areas, LDAs, program-described files, and parameter lists.

DATA AREAS

As the name implies, data areas are areas on disk that are used to store data. They are similar to data files in that they reside in a library, are used to store data, and may be externally or program-described. They are unlike files in that they may not have multiple record formats or multiple records.

As we mentioned earlier in this chapter, data areas come in two flavors: Local and global. Data kept in the LDA is temporary in nature and is pertinent only to the session with which it is associated. In other words, the LDA is unique to each program session and is used primarily to pass information from one job stream component to the next. Consequently, workstation sessions may not share the LDA, and the information is unique to each workstation session. The information in the LDA is only available until the session is terminated.

Data kept in a global data area is permanent in nature and is available to all. This type of data area can reside in any library and can be accessed by RPG IV programs (other languages too) and CL alike. Data areas can be accessed by any job and may be shared throughout the system.

You may have your RPG IV program open, close, and lock global data areas automatically for you, or you may perform these functions yourself. Similar to record-level locks for data files, you can lock a data area to prevent another program from updating it while you need it.

Global Data Areas

Global data areas are generally created on demand by keying the Create Data Area (CRTDTAARA) command, or from within a CL program. We discuss three ways your RPG IV programs can define data areas. These three ways consist of using a Data Area Data Structure, using an externally described data area, or simply using a program-described data area.

Data Area Data Structures

Data Area Data Structures are the easiest of the three to code, but are less flexible than the other two methods mentioned. Defining a Data Area Data Structure instructs your RPG IV program to read and lock the data area at program initialization and then perform an update to the data area and release the lock at last record time.

Unless you use the Unlock (UNLOCK) or Write Data Out to a Data Area (OUT) operation codes within your RPG IV program, the initial lock on the data area remains in effect until your program ends. This is not always practical when your data area is shared by other programs throughout the system.

Data Area Data Structures are defined by placing a U in position 23 of the Definition Specification that defines the data structure. We see an example of this in Figures 8.13 and 8.14. In Figure 8.13, we define a Data Area Data Structure named DataDef. As you can see, the DDS resembles specifications that you would use for any physical file.

Figure 8.13: Data Definition Specifications for a Data Area Data Structure

```
A..........T.Name+++++RLen++TDpB......Functions++++++++++++++++++++++++++
A           R DATADEF
A             DEVICE        10A         COLHDG('Tape Device')
A             PRINTER       10A         COLHDG('Printer Name)
A             OUTQUEUE      10A         COLHDG('OutQueue')
```

Figure 8.14: Input Specifications for a Data Area Data Structure

```
DName++++++++++ETDsFrom+++To/L+++IDc.Keywords++++++++++++++++++++Comments++++++++++++
D             EUDS            EXTNAME(DATADEF)
```

By specifying a U in position 23 of the Definition Specification (as seen in Figure 8.14), we are telling the system to read in and lock the DATADEF data area when the program is initialized, and then write out and unlock the data area when the program ends. The data stored in the data area is available throughout the program, and the field values may be updated as needed. The results of the update are recorded when the program ends.

Externally Described Data Areas

Externally described data areas are very similar in nature to the Data Area Data Structure. The principle difference is that they offer a little more flexibility with regard to lock state conditions and when data is retrieved or written to the data area. You will find this to be true of the program-described data areas as well, but you lose the rigidity and standardization with regard to data area definition.

Externally described and program-described data areas offer more control of when the data area is read, locked, written to, and released. Unlike Data Area Data Structures, data areas are not automatically read and locked during program initiation and written to at Last Record (LR) time.

Instead, there are four specific operation codes that you use in your RPG IV program when working with data areas. These are Define (DEFINE), Read IN Data from a Data Area (IN), Write Data OUT to a Data Area (OUT), and UNLOCK a Data Area or Other Object (UNLOCK).

The DEFINE op code is useful for a variety of definition functions, but we want to discuss how it relates to data areas.

Factor 1	Op Code	Factor 2	Result Field
*DTAARA	**DEFINE**	[Data Area Name]	Data Structure Name

Specifying *DTAARA in Factor 1 of the DEFINE statement tells the system that we are defining a data structure to represent the data area. We may optionally put the name of the data area in Factor 2, but for the examples here we use the Definition Specifications to indicate the name of our data area. The Result field contains the field or data structure name that is used to represent the data area.

The IN operation code is used to perform a controlled read of a single data area or all data areas defined in the program. If you specify *LOCK as Factor 1 of the IN operation code, the data areas in Factor 2 are locked until they are unlocked using the UNLOCK or OUT operation codes, or the job is terminated.

Factor 1	Op Code	Factor 2
[*LOCK]	IN	Data Area or *DTAARA

Factor 2 of the IN operation code is either the name of the data area in question or the literal *DTAARA. Choosing the *DTAARA option causes all data areas defined in the program to be read. Also, the data areas are all locked if specified to do so in Factor 1.

The OUT operation code is used to perform a controlled update of a data area.

Factor 1	Op Code	Factor 2
[*LOCK]	OUT	Data Area or *DTAARA

If you specify *LOCK as Factor 1 of the OUT op code, the locks on the data areas in Factor 2 remain in effect after data has been written to them. The locks remain in effect until the data areas are unlocked using the UNLOCK op code, using a subsequent OUT operation code that does not have *LOCK specified, or when the job is terminated.

Factor 2 of the OUT op code is either the name of a data area or the literal *DTAARA. Just like the IN operation code, the *DTAARA option specified in Factor 2 causes all data areas defined in the program to be written to and the locks either remain in effect or are released depending upon the contents of Factor 1.

The UNLOCK operation code is used to release a data area or record of a file that has been opened for update.

Op Code	Factor 2
UNLOCK	Data Area or File Name

Note: When used with data areas, the IN, OUT, and UNLOCK op codes may only refer to data areas that have been defined with the DEFINE statement.

In our next example (Figure 8.15), we look at the same data structure we looked at in Figures 8.13 and 8.14. However, this time we use the definition for an Externally Described Data Structure.

Figure 8.15: Input Specifications for an Externally Described Data Area

```
DName++++++++++ETDsFrom+++To/L+++IDc.Keywords++++++++++++++++++++Comments++++++++++++
D DataArea       E DS                  EXTNAME(DATADEF)
```

In the following example, we define a data structure named DataArea. By specifying an E in column 22 of our Definition Specification, we tell the compiler that this data structure is externally defined and the name of the external definition can be found in parentheses following the EXTNAME keyword (DATADEF in this case). The name identified in the parentheses refer to a physical file found somewhere in the library list at the time the RPG IV program is compiled. Figure 8.16 shows the Calculation Specifications that define, lock, read, write, and unlock the DTADEF data area.

Figure 8. 16: Calculation Specifications for Opening, Locking, and Updating an Externally Described Data Area

```
CL0N01Factor1+++++++Opcode(E)+Factor2+++++++Result++++++++Len++D+HiLoEq....Comments
* Read and Lock Data Area
C      *DTAARA     DEFINE                    DataArea        30
C      *LOCK       IN         DataArea
C                  MOVE       Print          Printer
C                  MOVE       Tape           Device
 * Write changes out to the data area
C                  OUT        DataArea
```

By using *DTAARA in the DEFINE statement, we tell the system that we are defining a data area. In this case, we did not put the name of the data area in Factor 2, but instead put the name of a data structure in the Result field (DataArea). This definition (in conjunction with the Definition Specifications) tells the system that we are using the DataArea data structure to redefine the DATADEF data area. The process of redefining the data area is similar to when we redefined the SKUNumber earlier in this chapter.

In the next step, we read the data from the DATADEF data area using the IN op code, placing a lock on the data area at that time. Remember that the IN operation is a destructive read, and whatever was in the fields defined by the DATADEF data structure is replaced with the data from the data area. Consequently, as long as the IN operation is performed prior to any reference to the fields specified in the data structure, we do not need to worry about data structure initialization.

After performing our IN operation, we move data into the externally described fields that we want to change, and write the data back out to the data area. We did not specify otherwise on the OUT statement, so the lock we previously placed on the data area when performing the IN operation is released.

Program-described Data Areas

The last category of global data areas to cover is program-described data areas. In the following example, we use a data area that has no external definition. We have decided, instead, to define the data area and then move it to an internal Program-described Data Structure for processing. Once we are done manipulating the data, we move data defined by our Program-described Data Structure back into the data area.

In Figure 8.17, we define a data area variable named DataArea using the DEFINE statement. The fact that we used *DTAARA in Factor 1 of this statement tells the system that we are defining a variable that is to be supported by a data area.

Figure 8.17: RPG Calculation Specifications to Lock and Read a Data Area

```
CLON01Factor1+++++++Opcode(E)+Factor2+++++++Result+++++++Len++D+HiLoEq....Comments
 * Read the data area and put the data in a data structure
C     *DTAARA     DEFINE                    DataArea          30
C     *LOCK       IN        DataArea
C                 MOVE      DataArea         DataDs
```

We then read and lock our data area and move the data area contents to a data structure named DataDS, as seen in Figure 8.18. It should be noted here that a lock remains in effect on DataArea until we perform an OUT or an UNLOCK operation (on the data area), or until our job terminates. Just like file record locks, no other job is able to obtain a lock on the data area until we have released our lock.

Figure 8.18: Program-described Data Structure Used to Define a Data Area

```
DName++++++++++ETDsFrom+++To/L+++IDc.Keywords+++++++++++++++++++++++++++++++Comments
D DataDS           DS
D   Device                        10
D   Printer                       10
D   OutQueue                      10
```

In Figure 8.19, we move the contents of our DataDS data structure back into our variable (DataArea) and then write the contents back out to the data area. The lock is released automatically at this time, because we did not specify *LOCK in Factor 1 of our OUT statement. If we had used *LOCK as Factor 1 of our OUT statement, the data area would have been updated and the lock would have remained in effect.

Figure 8.19: RPG Calculation Specifications to Write to and Unlock a Data Area

```
CL0N01Factor1+++++++Opcode(E)+Factor2+++++++Result++++++++Len++D+HiLoEq....Comments
* Put the contents of the data structure back into the data area
C                   MOVE      DataDS        DataArea
C                   OUT       DataArea
```

THE LOCAL DATA AREA

For those of you who were around for the IBM System/34 and System/36, you will recognize the local data area as one of the most powerful tools that could be used for passing limited amounts of data from one program to the next. The data in the LDA is special in that it is "local" and only available for the current job. Submitted jobs, jobs in other workstation sessions, and jobs running on other workstations each have their own unique LDAs.

In the case of the AS/400, the size of the LDA has been expanded to 1K, or 1024 bytes. You can use any or all of the LDA from any of your programs.

LDA on the AS/400 is still a powerful tool for program-to-program communications. It can be externally described with a data structure and is useful in reducing the number of parameters that must be passed from one program to the next. This is especially true if the data only needs to be accessible to a few links within a chain of programs. Instead of using the same parameters from one program to the next, you can place the data in LDA and only access or update it in the programs that need it.

In the case of submitted jobs, the LDA originally consists of the same contents as the LDA of the workstation that submitted the job. Once the submitted job is running, however, the LDA takes on a life of its own. Changes occurring to the data in the LDA are isolated within the submitted job only, and the data is only held in the system as long as the submitted job is still running.

Program-described Local Data Area

The designation of LDA is very similar to the data area definitions we just studied. In Figure 8.20, we show the simplest form of LDA. In this case, we used a Data Area Data Structure to describe LDA.

Figure 8.20: Program-described Input Specifications Defining the LDA

```
DName++++++++++ETDsFrom+++To/L+++IDc.Keywords+++++++++++++++++++++++++++++++++Comments
D                       UDS
D   Device                  10
D   Printer                 10
D   OutQueue                10
```

The U in position 23 of the data structure Definition Specification tells the system we are defining a Data Area Data Structure. The system knows we are defining the LDA (as opposed to a global data area) because positions 7 through 21 of that same statement are blank.

In Figure 8.20, we define the first 30 bytes of LDA. The total size of LDA is 1024 bytes of character data, but your program only needs to define the portion of the LDA that it will use. Notice that we only specified the length of the subfields and let the system calculate the From and To positions for us.

Using a Program-described Data Structure to Define the LDA

In Figures 8.21, 8.22, and 8.23, we read the LDA in our Calcultion Specifications and then move the data into our LoclDtaAra data structure. We write that data back out to the LDA using our Program-described Data Structure (LoclDtaAra).

Figure 8.21: Program-described Data Structure Used to Redefine the LDA

```
DName++++++++++++ETDsFrom+++To/L+++IDc.Keywords+++++++++++++++++++++++++++++++++Comments
D LoclDtaAra      DS
D  Device                       10
D  Printer                      10
D  Outqueue                     10
```

Figure 8.22: RPG Calculation Specifications Used to Read the LDA and Move It to a Program-described Data Structure

```
CLON01Factor1+++++++Opcode(E)+Factor2+++++++Result++++++++Len++D+HiLoEq....Comments
* Read data from LDA and place it in a data structure
C     *DTAARA       DEFINE    *LDA          LoclDtaAra
C                   IN        LoclDtaAra
```

Figure 8.23: RPG Calculation Specifications Used to Write Data to the LDA via a Program-described Data Structure

```
CLON01Factor1+++++++Opcode(E)+Factor2+++++++Result++++++++Len++D+HiLoEq....Comments
* Read data from LDA and place it in a data structure
C                   OUT       LoclDtaAra
```

In Figure 8.22, we define LDA to our program using the special keyword *LDA in Factor 2 of the DEFINE statement. At the same time, we tell the system that we are using the LoclDtaAra data structure to redefine LDA within our program. Note that we did not use the *LOCK parameter of the IN op code in our example because the LDA is unique to the current session and may not be accessed by any other job. On the subsequent statement, we read in LDA and consequently move the data into our data structure.

Later in our program we write the contents of our data structure back out to the LDA by performing the code in Figure 8.23. The changed data in the LDA is then available to any subsequent programs in the job stream.

Using Externally Described Data Structures to Define the LDA

External data structures can be useful to define your LDA too. By using an external definition, you assure consistent definitions from program to program, and also reduce the amount of maintenance required when the definition of LDA must change. This is especially true when you have many programs that use the same definitions of LDA. In

Figures 8.24 through 8.27, you can see an example of using an external data structure (LOCALDEF) to define the LDA.

Figure 8.24: *Data Description Specifications for an External Data Structure Used to Define the LDA*

```
A..........T.Name++++++RLen++TDpB......Functions+++++++++++++++++++++++++++++
A           R LOCALDEF
A             CUSTNBR      10A         COLHDG('CUSTOMER NUMBER')
A             CUSTNAME     40A         COLHDG('CUSTOMER NAME')
A             CUSTADDRS    30A         COLHDG('CUSTOMER ADDRESS')
A             CUSTCITY     30A         COLHDG('CUSTOMER CITY')
A             CUSTSTATE     2A         COLHDG('CUSTOMER STATE')
A             CUSTZIPCOD    9A         COLHDG('CUSTOMER ZIP CODE')
A             SALESMAN      5A         COLHDG('CUSTOMER SALESMAN')
A             CUSTPHONE    10S 0       COLHDG('CUSTOMER PHONE#')
```

Figure 8.25: *Input Specifications Designating an External Data Structure Used to Define the LDA*

```
DName+++++++++++ETDsFrom+++To/L+++IDc.Keywords+++++++++++++++++++++++++++++++++Comments
D LoclDtaAra      EUDS                 EXTNAME(LOCALDEF)
```

Figure 8.26: *Calculation Specifications Defining and Reading the LDA via an External Data Structure*

```
CL0N01Factor1+++++++Opcode(E)+Factor2+++++++Result++++++++Len++D+HiLoEq....Comments
 * Read and initialize local data area
C     *DTAARA      DEFINE    *LDA       LoclDtaAra
C                  IN        LoclDtaAra
C                  CLEAR                LoclDtaAra
```

Figure 8.27: *Calculation Specifications Writing Data to the LDA via an External Data Structure*

```
CL0N01Factor1+++++++Opcode(E)+Factor2+++++++Result++++++++Len++D+HiLoEq....Comment
 * Update Local Data Area
C                  OUT       LoclDtaAra
```

USING EXTERNALLY DESCRIBED DATA STRUCTURES TO DEFINE PROGRAM-DESCRIBED DATA FILES

Externally Described Data Structures also offer a viable alternative to program-described files. This is of particular interest to those programmers working on legacy systems that happen to be running under the System/36 environment.

Instead of internally describing all of the fields in a file within the RPG program, you can use an Externally Described Data Structure to define the data fields within the file. This allows you to define the file in a single place and simply call on that definition each time you use the file. Changes in the file definition are made once, and programs requiring that change only need to be recompiled.

This method is particularly useful when you wish to store multiple formats of data in the same file. You can use a record-type code to determine which data structure to move the data to, and create your own multiple-format data file.

The biggest benefit to this method must be field name and size consistency. You do not have to worry about a field being named something different in every program. Consistency helps eliminate errors.

This method is certainly not a substitute for externally described files, but it is definitely a step up from leaving all of the file definitions as program-described. You are unable to use any of the database tools like query or Display File Field Description (DSPFFD) because the system file definition still does not have that level of detail.

In Figure 8.28, we see a conventional program-described file. Figures 8.29 and 8.30 represent the same file, but with an external data structure used for file definition.

Figure 8.28: Program-described Customer File

```
IFilename++SqNORiPos1+NCCPos2+NCCPos3+NCC...............................Comments
ICustomer   NS
I..............Ext_field+Fmt+SPFrom+To+++DcField+++++++++L1M1FrP1MnZr......Comments
I                              1   10   CustNbr
I                             11   50   CustName
I                             51   80   CustAddrs
I                             81  110   CustCity
I                            111  112   CustState
I                            113  121   CustZipCod
I                            122  126   Salesman
I                            127  136   0CustPhone
```

Figure 8.29: Data Description Specifications for an External Data Structure Describing the Customer File

```
A..........T.Name++++++RLen++TDpB......Functions++++++++++++++++++++++++++
A          R CUSTREC
A            CUSTNBR      10A         COLHDG('CUSTOMER NUMBER')
A            CUSTNAME     40A         COLHDG('CUSTOMER NAME')
A            CUSTADDRS    30A         COLHDG('CUSTOMER ADDRESS')
A            CUSTCITY     30A         COLHDG('CUSTOMER CITY')
A            CUSTSTATE     2A         COLHDG('CUSTOMER STATE')
A            CUSTZIPCOD    9A         COLHDG('CUSTOMER ZIP CODE')
A            SALESMAN      5A         COLHDG('CUSTOMER SALESMAN')
A            CUSTPHONE    10S 0       COLHDG('CUSTOMER PHONE#')
```

Figure 8.30: Input Specifications Designating an External Data Structure Used to Describe the Customer File

```
DName+++++++++++ETDsFrom+++To/L+++IDc.Keywords++++++++++++++++++++++++++++++++Comments
D CustData       E DS                EXTNAME(CUSTREC)
```

By using the data structure in Figure 8.29 to redefine the data in the customer file, all of the fields defined by the Externally Described Data Structure become available.

USING DATA STRUCTURES TO REDUCE PROGRAM PARAMETERS

Programs that pass too many parameters are a common problem in many AS/400 systems. Programs that are initially written with 2 or 3 parameters end up with 10, 12, or even more.

When you have that many parameters being passed back and forth between programs, you have plenty of room for error. The programs being called, and those doing the calling, must be in constant synchronization. When a subprogram is called by multiple calling programs, the room for error gets multiplied. Program maintenance can become a nightmare.

A simple solution to this problem that is just waiting to happen is to use an external data structure as a parameter in lieu of a parameter list. The data structure can hold many fields and, because the definition is external, you have consistency between the various programs.

In the example in Figure 8.31, we define a data structure for use as a parameter in Figure 8.32. The data description specifications in Figure 8.31 are compiled as a physical file, even though the "file" will not contain data.

Figure 8.31: Data Definition Specifications for a Parameter Data Structure

```
A..........T.Name++++++RLen++TDpB......Functions++++++++++++++++++++++++++
A           R DATADEF
A             DEVICE       10A          COLHDG('Tape Device')
A             PRINTER      10A          COLHDG('Printer Name')
A             OUTQUEUE     10A          COLHDG('OutQueue')
```

Figure 8.32: Calculation Specifications Defining a Parameter Data Structure

```
CL0N01Factor1+++++++Opcode(E)+Factor2+++++++Result++++++++Len++D+HiLoEq....Comments
C     *ENTRY       PLIST
C                  PARM                     ParmDtaStr
```

Figure 8.33 shows the Definition Specifications necessary to define the external data structure to our program. The PLIST in Figure 8.32 refers the program to the ParmDtaStr data structure for a list of the parameters that are passed between the programs.

Figure 8.33: Input Specifications for a Parameter Data Structure

```
DName++++++++++++ETDsFrom+++To/L+++IDc.Keywords++++++++++++++++++++++++++++++++++Comments
D ParmDtaStr      E DS                   EXTNAME(DATADEF)
```

In the example here, we only have a few fields in our DATADEF external data structure, but you can use your imagination. Instead of using extensive parameter lists, your programs could simply reference the ParmDtaStr Externally Defined Data Structure. The length of the parameter does not need to be specified because the Externally Defined Data Structure length is used instead.

Maintenance could be made considerably easier. No matter how many fields in the Externally Defined Data Structure get changed, the program does not require additional maintenance (unless the program in question uses the fields that have changed; see "Externally Described Data Structures" in this chapter).

MULTIPLE-OCCURRENCE DATA STRUCTURES AND THE TWO-DIMENSIONAL ARRAY

A Multiple-occurrence Data Structure is a data structure like any other, except it has multiple copies (referred to as *occurrences*), each containing different data. Each occurrence or copy is actually treated as a separate, self-contained data structure, except that you do not have to define each occurrence separately. The occurrences are accessed with an index, much as you would access an array.

Figure 8.34 shows an example of the Definition Specification necessary to define a multiple-occurring data structure. The name of the data structure (DtaStrName) is specified in positions 7 through 21, and the *OCCURS* keyword is used to indicate how many occurrences of the data structure exist. Columns 33 through 39 are used for the length of the data structure, but as with all data structures, this field is optional. If you do not specify the length, the system automatically assigns the data structure the length of the accumulated subfields within it.

Figure 8.34: Input Specifications Defining a Multiple-occurrence Data Structure

```
DName++++++++++ETDsFrom+++To/L+++IDc.Keywords+++++++++++++++++++Comments++++++++++++
D DtaStrName      DS                        OCCURS(5)
D  TotalAmt                 1      7 2
D  TotalCount               8     13 0
D  LocCode                 14     15 0
D  LocName                 16     45
```

In our example, we have indicated that our data structure has five occurrences. Because we did not specify the length of the data structure in columns 33 through 39, the length assigned to this data structure is 45 characters (that is where the last subfield ends).

Table 8.1 represents the DtaStrName Multiple-occurrence Data Structure defined in Figure 8.34 after data has been loaded into it. As you can see in the example, it is almost as if we had defined five separate data structures with the same four fields defined for each.

Table 8.1: Example of Data Stored in a Multiple-occurrence Data Structure

Occurrence	TotalAmt	TotalCount	LocCode	LocName
1	50.00	1	01	Store number 1
2	150.00	3	05	Store number 5
3	250.00	5	19	Store number 19
4	150.00	3	14	Store number 14
5	50.00	1	12	Store number 12

The data structure index is either set or retrieved using the OCCUR op code. When setting the data structure index, the OCCUR statement tells the system which copy of the structure to use. The OCCUR statement can also be used to retrieve the current index and return it to a variable.

Factor 1	Op Code	Factor 2	Result Field
[index pointer]	**OCCUR**	Data Structure Name	[Occurrence Value]

If you want to set the occurrence (i.e., index) of a Multiple-occurrence Data Structure named DtaStrName to 1, do so by employing the following code:

```
CL0N01Factor1+++++++Opcode(E)+Factor2+++++++Result++++++++Len++D+HiLoEq....Comments
     C    1               OCCUR     DtaStrName
```

In effect, you are telling the system that you want to work with the first occurrence of the Multiple-occurrence data structure. Using the previous example, all references to subfields within the data structure refer to the first occurrence of the data structure. This remains the case until the OCCUR operation is performed again with a different index specified.

The index you use for the OCCUR operation could be a numeric literal as specified in the previous example, or it could be any other numeric field. You need to make sure, however, that the index specified falls within the range of the number of elements (occurrences) that are defined for the Multiple-occurrence Data Structure.

The OCCUR operation allows you to retrieve the index value of where the index pointer is set currently. If your goal is to find the occurrence to which the data structure is pointing, use code somewhat like the following:

```
CLON01Factor1+++++++Opcode(E)+Factor2+++++++Result++++++++Len++D+HiLoEq....Comments
     C                   OCCUR     DtaStrName    X
```

In this example, the current occurrence pointer value is retrieved from the system and written to the variable X.

Initializing the Multiple-occurrence Data Structure

As we have previously stated, data structures are considered to be alphanumeric, regardless of the data type specified in the subfields within. If you attempt to access a numeric subfield within a data structure prior to initializing it or loading it with numeric data, you find yourself with a Data Decimal Error. Multiple-occurrence Data Structures are no exception to this rule.

Utilizing the INZ keyword on the Definition Specification used to define the Multiple-occurrence Data Structure causes all occurrences within the data structure to be initialized for you when the program is run. If you specify default subfield values (by using the INZ keyword on the subfield Definition Specification), the default is copied automatically to all occurrences.

If you need to reinitialize the Multiple-occurrence Data Structure (to be reused, for example), you find that the system does not automatically initialize each copy of the structure for you. Using the CLEAR or RESET operations simply clears or resets the occurrence where the index happens to be set.

If you want to clear the entire data structure, you need to establish a loop. In Figure 8.35, we have coded a loop to step through the occurrences of the data structure and reset the subfields within all of the occurrences of the Multiple-occurrence Data Structure.

Figure 8.35: Resetting a Multiple-occurrence Data Structure to Its Original Values

```
DName++++++++++ETDsFrom+++To/L+++IDc.Keywords++++++++++++++++++++++++++++Comments+++++++++++
D DtaStrName      DS                     OCCURS(5)
D  TotalAmt               1      7 2
D  TotalCount             8     13 0
D  LocCode               14     15 0
D  LocName               16     45      INZ('Not on File')

CL0N01Factor1+++++++Opcode(E)+Factor2+++++++Result++++++++Len++D+HiLoEq....Comments++++++
C                   DO        5                 X                 1 0
C       X           OCCUR     DtaStrName
C                   RESET                       DtaStrName
C                   ENDDO
```

The numeric fields are cleared and reset to zero because there are no default values coded for them. The LocName field, however, is initialized to Not on File in each occurrence of the data structure. The INZ keyword on the Definition Specification defining the LocName subfield tells the system to initialize the field with the constant specified in the parentheses following the INZ keyword. We could have used a named constant for this purpose instead of the literal.

The Two-dimensional Array

Reproducing the function of the Multiple-occurrence Data Structure coded in Figure 8.35 could be accomplished easily by replacing each field in the structure with its own array. But this would require four arrays, each with five elements, instead of the Multiple-occurrence Data Structure. Both methods work, but the data structure is probably easier to manage. The power of multiple-occurring data structures, however, is unmatched when you combine the power of arrays and Multiple-occurrence Data Structures together to create the two-dimensional array. By defining an array within the Multiple-occurrence Data Structure, you are, in effect, creating a two-dimensional array.

For an example of the two-dimensional array in action, let's establish a scenario that we might encounter when asked to write a sales analysis report. Say we want to create a 31-element array, called AR$, that holds the total dollar amount of goods sold for each day of the month. Further, let's create another 31-element array called AR#, to hold the number of sales transactions performed for each day of the month. On top of that, we want to keep each month's totals separate within the fiscal year.

To code this without multiple-occurring data structures requires 24 arrays! You need one array to represent the total dollar amount sold for each month of the year as well as an array to represent the number of sales for each month. That is quite a bit of code to write and maintain.

By using a simple multiple-occurring data structure with 12 occurrences (1 for each month), we are able to trim down the amount of code required for this operation considerably. In the following example, we code two arrays called ARAmount (dollar amount sold per month) and ARCount (number of sales per month). These arrays exist as separate copies within each occurrence of the Multiple-occurrence Data Structure. As you can see from the code in Figure 8.36, it is not difficult to code this two-dimensional structure.

Figure 8.36: *Creating Two-dimensional Arrays Using Multiple-occurrence Data Structures*

```
DName++++++++++++ETDsFrom+++To/L+++IDc.Keywords++++++++++++++++++++++++++++Comments++++++++++++
D DtaStrName      DS                        OCCURS(12) INZ
D  ARAmount              1     217  2
D                                           DIM(31)
D  ARCount              218    372  0
D                                           DIM(31)

CL0N01Factor1++++++++Opcode(E)+Factor2++++++Result++++++++Len++D+HiLoEq....Comments++++++++
C      Month          OCCUR     DtaStrName
* Amount sold
C                     ADD       AMOUNT        ARAmount(Day)
 * Count sold
C                     ADD       1             ARCount(Day)
```

The first dimension of our structure is indexed using the month of the sales transaction, and is used to set the occurrence of the structure. The second dimension is indexed by the day of the sale, and is used as the index for each of the arrays.

In Figure 8.36, the Month field represents the month of the sale. In our example, we use this field to set the occurrence of the data structure prior to adding any data to the arrays. This, in effect, tells the system which copy of the arrays to use. The Day field was used as the index to the arrays that were selected as a result of the OCCUR op code.

If the code specified in the Calculation Specifications of our example is run against all sales transactions that met our report criteria, the net result is that we effectively have 24 arrays potentially filled with data. We can then establish a loop to step through the data structure occurrences and print the data from each.

YOUR *RPG* TREASURE CHEST

By now, you realize all of the power that can be at your disposal by simply being well-versed on the components covered in this chapter. Scenarios in which you can exhibit this new-found power are only limited by your imagination.

Using these tools properly results in far more efficient code (and far less of it). Ultimately, this results in less program maintenance and more time to work on those projects that you like.

Chapter 9

System APIs

You are about to embark upon a brave new world. It is the wonderful world of APIs. You will find that it is a world of speed, efficiency, and information—*lots* of information.

In this chapter, we unravel some of the mystery and confusion surrounding APIs. We cover Retrieve, Message, Spool Files, Document Handling, ILE, and List APIs. We explain the whys and hows of user spaces. And last, but not least, we show you how APIs are used in one of our favorite programming utilities.

If you do not know how to use APIs, if they are not part of your toolbox, a whole world of information remains behind closed doors. The good news is that opening those doors is not very difficult once you have the key. We are confident that you will have found that key after you have finished reading this chapter.

WHAT IS AN API?

Let us begin by defining an API. API stands for application program interface. The interface referred to here is the missing link between your programs and the IBM operating system.

An API is an IBM program that you can call from within your RPG programs to perform work. This work includes, but is not limited to, retrieving system information. Your program passes parameters to indicate the work you want performed, and the API returns the data you requested in the form of a parameter or data structures placed into a user space (which we discuss in detail later in this chapter). Understanding these parameters and data structures serves as your master key and opens many doors inside your system.

The information provided for and returned from APIs usually is defined in a data structure or series of data structures. One of the principle advantages of using APIs is that IBM will not change the data structure in future releases. If they decide to alter an API in order to show more information, they will add another data structure and leave the existing data structures intact. We define these data structures in detail as we go along.

You can find a complete listing of all APIs in the *System Programmer's Interface Reference Manual* (QBKA8402, SC41-8223). IBM insiders refer to this manual as the SPI (pronounced *spy*) manual. The SPI manual defines each parameter for every API, and is extremely helpful when getting started with most of the APIs. Another great place for information on APIs is QUSRTOOL (which came free with your operating system prior to V3R1).

Many APIs return information into a variable data structure (or structures), which can be quite complex and tedious to code. However, many of these structures are defined in various members in the QUSRTOOL library. If you happen to have QUSRTOOL, you can copy the code that defines these data structures right into your programs.

Many APIs are not all that complex. In fact, some APIs are very simple. The Command Execute (QCMDEXC) program, covered in Chapter 6, is probably the most powerful, but at the same time it's one of the most basic. It allows you to run any command from within your RPG program. The QCMDEXC program is simple in that it has only two parameters. The first parameter consists of the command to be executed and the second parameter defines the length of the command within the first parameter.

Even easier to use than QCMDEXC is the Command Line API (QUSCMDLN). This API has no parameters, you simply call it and a command entry window appears on your screen.

After reading this chapter, you should feel comfortable navigating through any of the APIs that you will need to perform your job. Although Table 9.1 lists the many APIs that we cover, there are hundreds more.

Table 9.1: Application Program Interfaces Covered in Chapter 9

API Name	Description
QBNLPGMI	List ILE program information
QCLRPGMI	Retrieve program information
QCMDEXC	Command execute
QDBLDBR	List database relations
QDBRTVFD	Retrieve file description
QHFCLSDR	Close directory
QHFOPNDR	Open directory
QHFRDDR	Read directory
QMHRMVPM	Remove program message
QMHSNDPM	Send program message
QOCCTLOF	Control office services
QSPMOVSP	Move spooled file
QUSCMDLN	Command entry line
QUSCRTUS	Create user space

API Name	Description
QUSLFLD	List fields
QUSLSPL	List spooled file
QUSROBJD	Retrieve object description
QUSRTVUS	Retrieve user space

RETRIEVE APIs

As the name implies, Retrieve APIs are used to extract information from the system. These APIs have both input and output parameters. You pass information to tell the APIs what kind of information you are trying to retrieve, and the APIs retrieves the requested information into a variable for you.

Before the advent of APIs, this type of programming was performed with a CLP command that directed its output to an OUTFILE (usually with all the speed of a fast turtle). You then had to process the OUTFILE to get the information you wanted.

With APIs, you can execute one quick call within an RPG program and the information you seek is loaded into a data structure for you. Another advantage to APIs is that you have some measure of control over the speed of the API. As you would expect, the more information you ask for, the longer it takes to retrieve. Asking for just the information you need speeds up the process.

When using the Retrieve APIs, the format name parameter is where you indicate the type of information you want returned. In general, APIs where the lower-numbered format names are specified run faster than those where the higher-numbered formats are specified. The variation in speed is due primarily to the amount of information involved. The Retrieve Job Information (QUSRJOBI) API is one notable exception to this rule—its formats have nothing to do with performance.

One of the more complex Retrieve APIs is the Retrieve File Description (QDBRTVFD) API. It has 10 parameters and, like many APIs, directs its output to a user space. Prior to using the QDBRTVFD API, the user space must be created. We can perform this function using the Create User Space (QUSCRTUS) API.

PUTTING THE POWER OF RETRIEVE APIS TO USE

Suppose we want to issue a warning error message to the system operator reminding them to back up their files. If we simply send the message every day, it becomes familiar and tends to get ignored. The warning message is more effective if it is sent only when the files have not been backed up within a prescribed time frame. In order to do this effectively, we need to know the last time the files were saved.

To find the date a file was last saved, use the Retrieve Object Description (QUSROBJD) API. The chart in Table 9.2 shows the parameters for this specific API. You can find a similar chart for every API in the aforementioned *System Programmer's Interface Reference Manual* (QBKA8402, SC41-8223).

Table 9.2: Required Parameter Group for the Retrieve Object Description (QUSROBJD) API

Parameter	Parameter Description	Type	Size
1	Receiver variable	Output	Char(*)
2	Length of receiver variable	Input	Binary(4)
3	Format name	Input	Char(8)
4	Object and library name	Input	Char(20)
5	Object type	Input	Char(10)

Optional Error Data Structure Parameter:

Parameter	Parameter Description	Type	Size
6	Error	Output	Char(*)

Parameter Definitions:

Receiver variable: This parameter represents the variable, or data structure, into which the system returns the requested information. Notice that the field is output in nature and the size column has CHAR(*), indicating that the field is a variable-length field.

Length of receiver variable: The second parameter of the API is the receiver variable length, which defines the length of the preceding parameter. This field is an input type and it is here that we tell the system the length of the receiver variable parameter that we want returned.

Format name: The third parameter of this API is the format name. The format parameter is where we indicate to the system exactly what information we are looking for. The format name we enter here tells the system how to format the data returned in the receiver variable parameter.

Object and library name: Here is where we specify the name and library of the object about which we are requesting information.

Object type: Defines the object type.

Error structure: The sixth parameter of this API is the optional error data structure we are about to discuss.

THE OPTIONAL API ERROR CODE PARAMETER

Most APIs include an optional error code parameter. It is a variable-length data structure, but do not let that deter you. The fact that it is variable in length simply means that, the larger you define the data structure, the more information there is to return to you. The required components of the Optional API Error Code Parameter are shown in Table 9.3.

Table 9.3: Required Parameter Group for the Optional API Error Code Data Structure

Parameter	Description	Type	Size
1	Bytes provided	Input	Binary(4)
2	Bytes available	Output	Binary(4)
3	Message identification code	Output	Char(7)
4	Error number	Output	Char(1)
5	Message data	Output	Char(*)

Parameter Definitions:

Bytes provided: A field whereby we tell the API the length of the message data we want returned in the Message Data field.

Bytes available: The actual length of the data returned if an error occurs. If this field is 0, you can safely assume the API executed properly. If its value is greater than 0, an error occurred and the parameter returns the number of bytes returned to your program.

Message ID: If an error was detected, and the Bytes Available field is greater than zero, the Message Identification field contains the message identifier of the detected error.

Error number: The fourth parameter, Error Number, is reserved by the system and should be ignored.

Message data: If an error occurs, this parameter contains the substitution variables for the system message ID.

If the error code parameter is available to the API and you do *not* include it in the call, the API returns both diagnostic and escape messages. This means you get the normally cryptic system error message screen.

On the other hand, if you do code the program to use the error code parameter, only escape messages are returned to the program and the system does not present an error message screen. In general, if the error code parameter is available, use it. Once you have performed the error routine's initial deployment, the structure is easily cloned from program to program.

USING APIs TO RETRIEVE OBJECT DESCRIPTIONS

Output from the OBJD0300 format of the Retrieve Object Description (QUSROBJD) API is depicted in Table 9.4. Data is returned in this format if the format name in parameter 3 of the input parameters is specified as OBJD0300.

Table 9.4: Retrieve Object Description (USROBJD) API
Output Descriptions for Format OBJD0300

Dec	Hex	Type	Description
—	—	—	Everything from OBJD0100/OBJD0200 formats
180	B4	Char(13)	Source file updated date and time
193	C1	Char(13)	Object saved date and time
206	CE	Char(13)	Object restored date and time
219	DB	Char(10)	Creator's user profile
229	E5	Char(8)	System where object was created
237	ED	Char(7)	Reset date
244	F4	Binary(4)	Save size
248	F8	Binary(4)	Save sequence number
252	FC	Char(10)	Storage
262	106	Char(10)	Save command

Dec	Hex	Type	Description
272	110	Char(71)	Save volume ID
343	157	Char(10)	Save device
353	161	Char(10)	Save file name
363	16B	Char(10)	Save file library name
373	175	Char(17)	Save label
390	186	Char(9)	System level
399	18F	Char(16)	Compiler
415	19F	Char(8)	Object level
423	1A7	Char(1)	User changed
424	1A8	Char(16)	Licensed program
440	1B8	Char(10)	Program temporary fix (PTF)
450	1C2	Char(10)	Authorized program analysis report (APAR)

The QUSROBJD API returns data in one of the four possible formats seen in Table 9.5. We chose the OBJD0300 format for the following example because it contains the date and time an object was last saved.

Table 9.5: Formats for Retrieve Object Description (QUSROBJD) API

QUSROBJD API Format	Description
OBJD0100	Basic information
OBJD0200	Information similar to PDM
OBJD0300	Service information
OBJD0400	Full information

As is the case for the input parameters, the output parameters are also defined in the SPI manual. Note that the offsets in the table begin at 0, so you must add 1 to the given decimal position when you define it in an RPG Input Specification.

For example, suppose we want to know the volume ID of the tape that holds the last copy of this file. The chart in Table 9.4 shows that the save volume ID resides in position 272 for a length of 71 bytes. The RPG Input Specifications to access that field are shown in Figure 9.1 and begin in 273.

Figure 9.1: Sample Input Specifications Representing an API Data Structure Offset

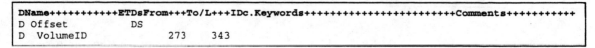

```
DName+++++++++++ETDsFrom+++To/L+++IDc.Keywords++++++++++++++++++++++++++Comments++++++++++++
D Offset          DS
D  VolumeID              273   343
```

Figure 9.2 shows the FIG92RG RPG program, which has all the necessary code to use the Retrieve Object Description (QUSROBJD) API. The FIG92RG program has the file and library names as input parameters, and date/time last saved as an output parameter.

Figure 9.2: Sample of the Retrieve Object Description (QUSROBJD) API

```
****************************************************************
*   TO COMPILE:
*     CRTBNDRPG PGM(XXXLIB/FIG92RG)
****************************************************************

DName++++++++++ETDsFrom+++To/L+++IDc.Keywords++++++++++++++++++++++++++Comments++++++++++
D ErrorDs          DS                     INZ
D  BytesProvd               1      4B 0   INZ(116)
D  BytesAvail               5      8B 0
D  MessageId                9     15
D  ERR###                  16     16
D  MessageDta              17    116
D                  DS
D Receiver                       206
D  DateSaved                     13       OVERLAY(Receiver:194)
D ReceiveLen       S             4B 0     INZ(206)
D FileLib          S            20
D PassInFile       S            10
D PassInLib        S            10
D PassDateSv       S            13
D FormatName       S             8        INZ('OBJD0300')
D ObjectType       S            10        INZ('*FILE')

CL0N01Factor1++++++Opcode&ExtFactor2++++++Result++++++++Len++D+HiLoEq....Comments++++++
C     *ENTRY       PLIST
C                  PARM                          PassInFile
C                  PARM                          PassInLib
C                  PARM                          PassDateSv
C                  EVAL     FileLib = PassInFile + PassInLib
C                  CALL     'QUSROBJD'
C                  PARM                          Receiver
C                  PARM                          ReceiveLen
C                  PARM                          FormatName
C                  PARM                          FileLib
C                  PARM                          ObjectType
C                  PARM                          ErrorDs
C                  IF       DateSaved <> *BLANKS
C                  EVAL     PassDateSv = DateSaved
C                  ENDIF
C                  EVAL     *InLr = *ON
```

When reviewing the FIG92RG program, you see that, if the Error Message ID field is blanks after the call to QUSROBJD, the DateSaved field contains the date and time the file was last saved. The FIG92RG program, in turn, returns the date last saved to the calling program in the PassDateSv parameter. The calling program can then use the returned parameter information to determine how many days have elapsed since the file was last saved. If the number of days that have elapsed is considered to be too many, the warning message is sent to the program operator.

CHECKING FOR OBJECTS USING THE RETRIEVE OBJECT DESCRIPTION (QUSROBJD) API

With slight variations to the previous program used in Figure 9.2, we could use the same API to create a program that checks for the existence of any object. And that's exactly what we've done in the FIG93RG RPG program shown in Figure 9.3.

Figure 9.3: Sample RPG Program to Validate Object Existence

```
******************************************************************
*   TO COMPILE:
*      CRTBNDRPG PGM(XXXLIB/FIG93RG)
******************************************************************

DName+++++++++++ETDsFrom+++To/L+++IDc.Keywords+++++++++++++++++++++++++++Comments++++++++++++
D ErrorDs          DS                    INZ
D  BytesProvd              1      4B 0 INZ(116)
D  BytesAvail              5      8B 0
D  MessageId               9     15
D  ERR###                 16     16
D  MessageDta             17    116
D Receiver         S            100
D ReceivrLen       S              4B 0 INZ(100)
D Object           S             10
D ObjLibrary       S             10
D ObjType          S              8
D ExistYesNo       S              1
D FileLib          S             20
D FileFormat       S              8      INZ('OBJD0100')

CL0N01Factor1++++++++Opcode&ExtFactor2+++++++Result++++++++Len++D+HiLoEq....Comments++++++
C     *ENTRY        PLIST
C                   PARM                          Object
C                   PARM                          ObjLibrary
C                   PARM                          ObjType
C                   PARM                          ExistYesNo
C                   IF        ObjLibrary = *BLANKS
C                   EVAL      ObjLibrary = 'LIBL'
C                   ENDIF
C                   EVAL      FileLib = Object + ObjLibrary
 * Attempt to retrieve object description
C                   CALL      'QUSROBJD'
C                   PARM                          Receiver
C                   PARM                          ReceivrLen
C                   PARM                          FileFormat
C                   PARM                          FileLib
C                   PARM                          ObjType
C                   PARM                          ErrorDs
C                   EVAL      ExistYesNo = 'Y'
C                   IF        MessageId <> *BLANKS
C                   EVAL      ExistYesNo = 'N'
C                   ENDIF
C                   EVAL      *InLr = *ON
```

An example of where you might want to use the FIG93RG program is when prompting for a report or list. If you ask the operator which printer to direct the output to, you should check the device to see if it exists as well as if it is the correct device type. Checking the response at time of entry prevents potential errors down the line.

When running the program in Figure 9.3, you pass it the object name, library, and object type. The program, in turn, passes back a Yes/No parameter indicating whether or not an object with the specified name, type, and library exists. If you choose not to specify a library name for the object being validated, the program uses the library list.

In the example, we modify the FileFormat parameter so the QUSROBJD API returns the data defined by format OBJD0100. The objective in this case is simply to know if the object exists, so we don't really care what information is returned. Therefore, we choose to use the format with the smallest number of fields for maximum API performance.

The FIG93RG RPG program in Figure 9.3 may be called from other application programs to verify the existence, type, and library of an object.

MESSAGE APIS

Let's continue our lessons by example and demonstrate how to send a message to a program message queue using the Send Program Message (QMHSNDPM) API. Message APIs provide a method for you to design your programs to work with AS/400 messages.

Examine the RPG program shown in Figure 9.4 to see how to use the QMHSNDPM API. The DDS for the program in Figure 9.5 is shown so you can compile and run this utility.

Figure 9.4: Sample RPG Program Using the Send Program Message (QMHSNDPM) API

```
****************************************************************
*   TO COMPILE:
*      CRTBNDRPG PGM(XXXLIB/FIG94RG)
****************************************************************

HKeywords++++++++++++++++++++++++++++++++++++++++++++++++++++++++++++Comments++++++++++++
H DATFMT(*YMD)

FFilename++IPEASFRlen+LKlen+AIDevice+.Keywords++++++++++++++++++++++++Comments++++++++++++
FFIG95DS   CF  E           WORKSTN

DName+++++++++++ETDsFrom+++To/L+++IDc.Keywords+++++++++++++++++++++++++Comments++++++++++++
D ErrorDs        DS                    INZ
D  BytesProvd           1      4B 0 INZ(116)
D  BytesAvail           5      8B 0
D  MessageId            9     15
D  Err###              16     16
D  MessageDta          17    116

D StartPosit     S              8B 0
D StartLen       S              8B 0
D SpaceLen       S              8B 0
D ReceiveLen     S              8B 0
D MsgDtaLen      S              8B 0 INZ(60)
D MsgQueNbr      S              8B 0 INZ(0)
D MessageQue     S             10    INZ('*')
D MessageKey     S              4
D MessageFil     S             20
D MsgRemove      S             10    INZ('*ALL')
D ProgramQue     S             10    INZ('*')
D FileName       S             10    INZ('CUSTOMER')
D Library        S             10    INZ('QBOOK')
D MessageTyp     S             10    INZ('*DIAG')

D               DS
D PassDate             13
D  PassYMDA             6    OVERLAY(PassDate:2)

D PassYMD        S              6  0
D DateSaved      S              D    DATFMT(*YMD) INZ(D'40/01/01')
D Today          S              D    DATFMT(*YMD)
D MessageDat     S             10A
D CompareMDY     S              D    DATFMT(*MDY)

D DateErrCon     C                   'WARNING - Customer file last backed+
D                                    up on '

CL0N01Factor1+++++++Opcode&ExtFactor2+++++++Result+++++++Len++D+HiLoEq....Comments++++++
C                   EVAL      *In90 = *ON
C                   CALL      'FIG92RG'
C                   PARM                    FileName
C                   PARM                    Library
C                   PARM                    PassDate

C                   MOVE      PassYMDA      PassYMD
C       *YMD        TEST(D)                 PassYMD              01
C                   MOVE      UDATE         CompareMDY
C                   SUBDUR    2:*D          CompareMDY
C                   IF        *In01 <> *ON
```

```
C       *YMD            MOVEL       PassYMD         DateSaved
C                       ENDIF
 * If file was not saved in the last two days, send a warning message
C                       IF          DateSaved < CompareMDY
C                       EXSR        SNDMSG
C                       WRITE       MSGCTL
C                       ENDIF
C                       EXFMT       FMTC
C                       EXSR        CLRMSG
C                       EVAL        *InLr = *ON
CSR     CLRMSG          BEGSR
 * Remove message API
C                       CALL        'QMHRMVPM'
C                       PARM                        MessageQue
C                       PARM                        MsgQueNbr
C                       PARM                        MessageKey
C                       PARM                        MsgRemove
C                       PARM                        ErrorDs
C                       ENDSR
C       SNDMSG          BEGSR
C                       EVAL        MessageFil = ('QCPFMSG   ' + 'QSYS')
C                       EVAL        MessageID  = 'CPF9898'
C                       IF          *In01 <> *ON
C                       MOVE        DateSaved       MessageDat
C                       ELSE
C                       EVAL        MessageDat = '000000     '
C                       ENDIF
C                       EVAL        MessageDta  = DateErrCon + MessageDat
 * Send error message
C                       CALL        'QMHSNDPM'
C                       PARM                        MessageId
C                       PARM                        MessageFil
C                       PARM                        MessageDta
C                       PARM                        MsgDtaLen
C                       PARM                        MessageTyp
C                       PARM                        MessageQue
C                       PARM                        MsgQueNbr
C                       PARM                        MessageKey
C                       PARM                        ErrorDs
C                       ENDSR
```

Figure 9.5: DDS for the FIG94RG RPG Program Using the Send Program Message (QMHSNDPM) API

```
A*************************************************************************
A*   TO COMPILE:
A*      CRTDSPF FILE(XXXLIB/FIG95DS)
A*************************************************************************

AAN01N02N03T.Name+++++RLen++TDpBLinPosFunctions++++++++++++++++++++++++++++
A                                          DSPSIZ(24 80 *DS3)
A            R FMTC
A                                          CF03(03 'End of job')
A                                          CF12(12 'Return to Previous')
A                                          OVERLAY
A                                     21  3'                              -
A                                                                         -
A                                                       .
A                                          DSPATR(UL)
A                                     22  5'F3=Exit'
A                                     22 19'F12=Previous'
A                                      9 21'Customer Number:'
A              CUSTOMER#    10A  B     9 38
A                                      1 27'Customer Inquiry'
A                                          DSPATR(HI)
A                                          DSPATR(UL)
A            R MSGSFL                       SFL
A                                          SFLMSGRCD(24)
A              SFLMSGKEY                    SFLMSGKEY
A              PROGRAMQUE                   SFLPGMQ
A            R MSGCTL                       SFLCTL(MSGSFL)
A                                          OVERLAY
A                                          SFLSIZ(3) SFLPAG(1)
A                                          SFLDSP SFLINZ
A    90                                     SFLEND
A              PROGRAMQUE                   SFLPGMQ
```

In the example in Figure 9.4, the FIG92RG program is called to find the date the customer file was last saved. This function is performed prior to bringing up a screen format. (See Figure 9.2 for the code to the FIG92RG program.)

If the current date happens to be greater than the date last saved, it can be safely assumed that the customer file has not been saved today. When this happens to be the case, our warning is sent to the program operator via the FIG94RG program we just examined. It is in the FIG94RG program that the SNDMSG subroutine is then executed. The SNDMSG subroutine uses the QMHSNDPM API to send the message. The required parameter group for the QMHSNDPM API is shown in Table 9.6.

Table 9.6: Required Parameter Group for theSend Program Message (QMHSNDPM) API

Parameter	Description	Type	Size
1	Message ID	Input	Char(7)
2	Message file name and library	Input	Char(20)
3	Message data	Input	Char(*)
4	Message data length	Input	Binary(4)
5	Message type	Input	Char(10)
6	Message queue name	Input	Char(10)
7	Job invocation number	Input	Binary(4)
8	Message key	Input	Char(4)
9	Error data structure	Both	Char(*)

Parameter Definitions:

Message ID: The message identification code of the message to be sent, or blanks for an immediate message. If you specify a message ID code, you must also specify the message file name and library in parameter 2.

Message file name and library: The name of the file and library that contain the message ID specified in parameter 1. The first 10 characters of the parameter are file name, and the last 10 characters are the library name. You may also specify the following special values: *CURLIB (Current Library) or *LIBL (Library List).

Message data: If using a predefined Message ID in parameter 1, this parameter is used to pass the data to insert into the message substitution variables. If sending an immediate message (indicated by sending blanks in parameter 1), this parameter field is the complete text of the immediate message.

Message data length: The number of bytes occupied by the message data field in the preceding parameter.

Message type: One of the following values: Completion (*COMP), Diagnostic (*DIAG), Escape (*ESCAPE), Informational (*INFO), Inquiry (*INQ), Notify (*NOTIFY), Request (*RQS), or Status (*STATUS). The Inquiry (*INQ) message type is only valid if the message is sent to the external message queue.

Message queue name: The name of the external message queue, the call stack entry to which to send the message, or the name of the entry to start counting from if job invocation number is 0.

Job invocation number: The location (invocation number) in the call stack that identifies the target entry of the message queue to which the message is sent. The number is relative to the message queue name parameter, indicating how many calls up the stack the target entry is from the message queue name entry.

Message key: The key to the message being sent. This parameter is ignored if the message type is specified as *STATUS.

Error data structure: The standard Optional Error Code Data Structure.

For the program in Figure 9.4, we choose to use the system-provided Message ID CPF9898 in message file QCPFMSG in library QSYS. This is a useful general purpose message and can be used to format any message on the fly, including any variable you want displayed with the message.

The CPF9898 message has no incoming text associated with it, and only one data field. We create our message using the free format EVAL op code to embed the date the file was last saved into our message and put it in the message data field for the system to display.

We have loaded an asterisk (*) in the message queue parameter indicating that the message is to be sent to the current job's message queue. The job invocation stack is 0, so the message is sent to the current program's message queue. Any other number put in this field causes the message to be sent back up the invocation stack. The number placed in the job invocation number parameter determines how far back in the stack the message is sent.

Our FIG94RG program issues a warning message to the program operator. It is displayed via the write to the MSGCTL format, and then followed by a general input screen (FMTC in this case).

To prevent the error from reappearing after entering data on the screen (this is only an informational warning message), the program executes the clear message subroutine. This subroutine uses another useful API—the Remove Program Messages (QMHRMVPM) API.

In this particular example, it is really not necessary to remove the messages from the program message queue because the program is going to set on the last record indicator and terminate. But in a working application, you would probably edit the data entered on the screen and loop back up to issue any error messages. You want to clear the message queue before issuing new messages so the old ones do not redisplay.

The Remove Program Messages API accepts five input parameters and two sets of optional parameters. For our purposes, we only cover the required entries and they are shown in Table 9.7.

Table 9.7: Required Parameter Group for the Remove Program Messages (QMHRMVPM) API

Parameter	Description	Type	Size
1	Message queue.	Input	Char(10)
2	Call stack counter relative to parameter 1. Indicates how many entries up the stack to go to find the message queue to remove.	Input	Binary(4)
3	Message key.	Input	Binary(4)
4	Messages to remove.	Input	Char(10)
5	Error.	Both	Char(*)

Parameter Definitions:

Message queue: The name of the call stack entry to which to send the message, or the name of the entry to start counting from if the job invocation number is 0. You can also specify the external message queue, or *, for the current job's message queue.

Call stack counter: The location in the call stack identifying the entry to whose message queue the message is to be sent. The number is relative to the message queue name parameter, indicating how many calls up the stack the target entry is from the message queue name entry. Special values are:

*	The message queue of the current call stack.
* ALLINACT	All message queues for inactive call stack entries.
* EXT	The external message queue.

Message key: The message file key to the message being removed.

Messages to remove: The message or group of messages being removed. Valid values are:

*ALL	All messages in the message queue.
*BYKEY	Only the message specified by the key parameter.
*KEEPRQS	All messages except request messages.
*NEW	All new messages in the queue.
*OLD	All old messages in the queue.

Error: The standard Optional Error Code Data Structure.

We code an asterisk (*) in the Message Queue field (MSGQ) indicating that we want to clear this job's message queue. We also place a 0 in the call stack counter indicating that we want to clear the message queue of the program in which this command is coded. The Message Key (MSGKY) field is left blank. The Message Type to Remove (MSGRMV) is coded with *ALL to indicate that all messages are to be removed from the message queue.

USER SPACES

A user space is an area created and defined by the user, and used for storing any kind of information that you want to put in it. All of the list APIs direct their output to a user space that must exist at the time the API runs. Consequently, you must be able to use the Create User Space (QUSCRTUS) API if you intend to use any of the list APIs.

The maximum size of a user space is 16 megabytes (as opposed to 2000 bytes for a data area). If you create a space that is too small to hold the complete list from the API, it is extended to the nearest memory page boundary. If the space is still too small to hold the list, the API puts as much data as possible in the space and returns an error message in the Optional Error Code parameter.

Creating User Spaces

An example of how to create a user space is shown in Figure 9.6. After this code is executed, library QTEMP contains an object called SPACENAM (of type *USRSPC) that is 1024 bytes long. The user space is initialized to value X'00', which allows the creation of the user space to execute faster than the default of *BLANKS.

Figure 9.6: Sample RPG Code to Create a User Space

```
*******************************************************************
*   TO COMPILE:
*       CRTBNDRPG PGM(XXXLIB/FIG96RG)
*******************************************************************

DName++++++++++++ETDsFrom+++To/L+++IDc.Keywords++++++++++++++++++++++++Comments++++++++++++
D ErrorDs          DS                       INZ
D  BytesProvd                 1      4B 0   INZ(116)
D  BytesAvail                 5      8B 0
D  MessageId                  9     15
D  ERR###                    16     16
D  MessageDta                17    116
D InputDs          DS                       INZ
D  UserSpace                        20
D   SpaceName                       10      OVERLAY(UserSpace:1)
D                                           INZ('SPACENAME')
D   SpaceLib                        10      OVERLAY(UserSpace:11)
D                                           INZ('QTEMP')
D  SpaceLen        S                8B 0    INZ(1024)
D  SpaceAttr       S               10
D  SpaceValue      S                1
D  SpaceAuth       S               10       INZ('*CHANGE')
D  SpaceText       S               50
D  SpaceReplc      S               10       INZ('*YES')

CL0N01Factor1+++++++Opcode&ExtFactor2+++++++Result+++++++Len++D+HiLoEq....Comments++++++
*   Create a user space named SPACENAM in library QTEMP
C                   CALL      'QUSCRTUS'
C                   PARM                    UserSpace
C                   PARM      *BLANKS       SpaceAttr
C                   PARM      1024          SpaceLen
C                   PARM      *BLANKS       SpaceValue
C                   PARM      '*CHANGE'     SpaceAuth
C                   PARM      *BLANKS       SpaceText
C                   PARM      '*YES'        SpaceReplc
C                   PARM                    ErrorDs
C                   EVAL      *InLr = *ON
```

Retrieving Data from a User Space

You extract data from a user space by using the Retrieve User Space (QUSRTVUS) API. This API gets information from the user space and puts it in a data area. It is relatively easy to use.

The Retrieve User Space (QUSRTVUS) API accepts four parameters: The name and the library that contain the user space, the starting position, the length of the data to extract, and the name of the data structure for the retrieved data.

Figure 9.7 shows an example of the code necessary to use this API. After the call to the Retrieve User Space (QUSRTVUS) API, the data structure GeneralDS contains whatever was in the user space beginning at location 1 for 140 bytes.

Figure 9.7: Example of the Retrieve User Space (QUSRTVUS) API

```
**********************************************************************
*    TO COMPILE:
*      CRTBNDRPG PGM(XXXLIB/FIG97RG)
**********************************************************************

DName+++++++++++ETDsFrom+++To/L+++IDc.Keywords++++++++++++++++++++++++++Comments+++++++++++
D GeneralDs       DS            140    INZ
D   StartPosit    S             4B 0
D   StartLen      S             4B 0
D                 DS             20    INZ
D   UserSpace                    20
D     SpaceName                  10    OVERLAY(UserSpace:1)
D                                      INZ('SPACENAME')
D     SpaceLib                   10    OVERLAY(UserSpace:11)
D                                      INZ('QTEMP')

CL0N01Factor1+++++++Opcode&ExtFactor2+++++++Result++++++++Len++D+HiLoEq....Comments++++++
C                   EVAL      StartPosit = 1
C                   EVAL      StartLen = 140
 * Retrieve user space information beginnning in position 1
C                   CALL      'QUSRTVUS'
C                   PARM                    UserSpace
C                   PARM                    StartPosit
C                   PARM                    StartLen
C                   PARM                    GeneralDs
C                   EVAL      *InLr = *ON
```

LIST APIS

The List APIs generate list information and output into a user space. You must create and maintain the user space yourself (see "User Spaces" in this chapter). The challenge when using List APIs lies in extracting the generated list from the user space because it sometimes requires several steps to retrieve the correct fields and data structures you need to get the list. It is not uncommon to have to step through several data structures to get to the information retrieved with the List APIs.

Each List API follows the same general format when putting data into a user space. For each of the List APIs, there is an input section, a general header section, and a list section.

General Header Section

The general header section is the same for each List API. It contains general information about the objective of the API, but more importantly, it contains pointers to information about the list data within the user space. In other words, the header section serves as the information directory for the information you request.

The data structure in Figure 9.8 shows the field definitions required to find the data in the user space. Table 9.8 shows all of the fields included in the general header section.

Figure 9.8: Data Structure Including Primary Fields for the General Header of the List APIs

```
DName++++++++++ETDsFrom+++To/L+++IDc.Keywords++++++++++++++++++++++++++Comments+++++++++++
D GenHeadDs       DS             140    INZ
D  InputSize             113     116B 0
D  ListOffset            125     128B 0
D  NumberList            133     136B 0
D  EntrySize             137     140B 0
```

Table 9.8: General Header of the List APIs—All Fields

Dec	Type	Field
0	Char(64)	User area
64	Binary(4)	Size of generic header
68	Char(4)	Structure's release and level
72	Char(8)	Format name
80	Char(10)	API used
90	Char(13)	Date and time used
103	Char(1)	Information status
104	Binary(4)	Size of user space used
108	Binary(4)	Offset to input parameter section

Dec	Type	Field
112	Binary(4)	Size of input parameter section
116	Binary(4)	Offset to header section
120	Binary(4)	Size of header section
124	Binary(4)	Offset to list data section
128	Binary(4)	Size of list data section
132	Binary(4)	Number of list entries
136	Binary(4)	Size of each entry

As you can see, the RPG Input Specifications in Figure 9.8 differ from the chart definition in Table 9.8 by one character. This is because the chart starts at offset 0 while the Input Specifications must start at position 1. This is very common in most of the API charts in the SPI manual, so be aware. Also notice that the data type is specified as a B, indicating that the data is stored in a binary format.

List Section

The list section begins in the user space at the position indicated by the field ListOffSet in Figure 9.8. The number of entries in the list is indicated in NumberList and the size of each entry is in EntrySize. Generally speaking, when using these fields, you set up a Do Loop to step through the user space extracting an item on the list for each step.

The data residing in the list section varies, depending on the API used. Its structure is defined in the aforementioned SPI manual for each API. In general, the lists are extracted with the Retrieve User Space (QUSRTVUS) API and moved to the data structure describing the information retrieved.

Handles—Internal Identification

Some APIs require (as input) information that can only be gotten from other APIs. This type of parameter information is usually referred to as a *handle*. A handle is a temporary, system-generated identification number used to decrease the time it takes to locate information. You can think of a handle as an address that the system places in its own temporary system address book.

DISPLAY ACCESS PATH COMMAND

Now let's examine one of our favorite utilities that uses many of the different types of APIs, including a List API—the List Database Relations (QDBLDBR) API. This utility is an enhanced form of the Display Database Relations command.

To find the existing data paths that are available over a physical file on the AS/400, you generally perform the following steps:

1. Run the Display Database Relations (DSPDBR) command over the physical file in question.

2. Write down the file and library names of each logical file found on the DSPDBR display.

3. Run the Display File Description (DSPFD) command over each logical file to see if the data path you need already exists.

These steps are time-consuming and cut into your productivity as a programmer. We have written the DSPPATH command to combine those steps for you.

The DSPPATH command output looks like the example in Figure 9.9 (the code for the command is in Figure 9.12). The path for the physical file is listed first. Key fields and sequence (ascending or descending) are shown, followed by any select omit statements used. Then the path information is listed for each logical file built over the physical (even if the logical file is built in a different library than where the physical file resides).

Figure 9.9: Output from the DSPPATH Command

```
                         Display Access Paths

Physical File . . . . . . . .:  CUSTOMER   Number of logicals. . . . .:  0013
Library . . . . . . . . . . .:  *LIBL

Library    File       Format      Key Field Seq Select/Omit Values
FILES      CUSTOMER   CUSREC      CUSTNO    A   CUSTOMER NUMBER

FILES      CLACT3     JBYCLS      FMCLAS    A   FINANCIAL CLASS

FILES      CUSTL      CSTREC      CUSNAM    A   CUSTOMER NAME
                                  CUSDLT        O  EQ  '*'

FILES      CUSTLA     CSTREC      CUSNAM    A   CUSTOMER NAME
                                  CUSNUM    A   CUSTOMER NUMBER
                                  CUSDLT        O  EQ  '*'

FILES      CUSTLO     CSTREC      CULPMT    A   DATE OF LAST PAYMENT
                                                               More...



   F3=Exit        F12=Previous
```

Breaking Down the Code in the DSPPATH Program

Examine the code in Figures 9.10, 9.11, and 9.12. After creating some work fields, including a user space, the program calls the GETFIL subroutine to retrieve the key field information for the physical file.

Figure 9.10: FIG910RG RPG Program

```
 ************************************************************************
 *   TO COMPILE:
 *      CRTRPGPGM PGM(XXXLIB/FIG910RG)
 ************************************************************************
FFilename++IPEASFRlen+LKlen+AIDevice+.Keywords+++++++++++++++++++++++++Comments+++++
FFig911Ds  CF   E             WORKSTN
F                                        SFILE(SFLRCD:RelRecNbr)

DName++++++++++++ETDsFrom+++To/L+++IDc.Keywords+++++++++++++++++++++++++Comments+++++
D AR              S              1     DIM(4096)
D A2              S              1     DIM(28)
D ARYF            S             10     DIM(1000)
D ARYT            S             40     DIM(1000)
D SaveStart       S              9B 0
D SaveLen         S              9B 0
D OutFile         S             10
D OutLibrary      S             10
D First           S              1
D ObjFileFmt      S              8
D ObjectType      S             10
D LstOutFmt       S              8
D Ignore          S             10
D MessageFil      S             20
D MessageTyp      S             10
D MessageQue      S             10
D FileFmt         S              8
D RecordFmt       S             10
D OverRide        S              1
D System          S             10
D FmtType         S             10
D ListFormat      S             10
D TestType        S              1
D SpaceAttr       S             10
D SpaceValue      S              1
D SpaceText       S             50
D SpaceAuth       S             10     INZ('*CHANGE')
D SpaceReplc      S             10     INZ('*YES')
D C               S              4  0
D S               S              4  0
D I               S              4  0
D I1              S              4  0
D I2              S              4  0
D B               S              4  0
D RelRecNbr       S              4  0
D SfCompare       S              2
D SfRule          S              1
D SfValue         S             28
D SFileLib        S             20
D RFileLib        S             20
D ObjReceivr      S            100
D StartPosit      S              9B 0
D StartLen        S              9B 0
D ReceiveLen      S              9B 0
D MessageKey      S              9B 0
D MsgDtaLen       S              9B 0
D MsgQueNbr       S              9B 0
D FilStartP       S              9B 0
D FilStartL       S              9B 0
D SpaceLen        S              9B 0  INZ(1024)
D InFileLib       S             20
D InputDs         DS
```

```
D  UserSpace                    1    20
D   SpaceName                        10        OVERLAY(UserSpace:1)
D   SpaceLib                         10        OVERLAY(UserSpace:11)
D  OutFormat                   21    28
D  FileLib                     29    48
D   FileName                         10        OVERLAY(FileLib:1)
D   FileLibr                         10        OVERLAY(FileLib:11)
D ListDs          DS
D  MainFileLb                   1    20
D  MainFile                         10        OVERLAY(MainFileLb:1)
D  MainLib                          10        OVERLAY(MainFileLb:11)
D  DependFil                   21    30
D  DependLib                   31    40
D                 DS
D  FieldSpace                   1    20
D  FSpaceName                       10        OVERLAY(FieldSpace:1)
D  FSpaceLib                        10        OVERLAY(FieldSpace:11)
D ErrorDs         DS                           INZ
D  BytesProvd                   1     4B 0
D  BytesAvail                   5     8B 0
D  MessageId                    9    15
D  Err###                      16    16
D  MessageDta                  17   116
D KeyData         DS
D  DependKey                    1    10
D  AscendDes                   14    14
D FindSelect      DS                150        INZ
D  FindFormat                  70    79
D  NbrKeys                    117   118B 0
D  NbrSelOmit                 130   131B 0
D  OffSelOmit                 132   135B 0
D  OffSet                     136   139B 0
D KeySelect       DS                150        INZ
D  Rule                         3     3
D  Compare                      4     5
D  CompName                     6    15
D  NbrSO                       16    17B 0
D  OffsetSO                    29    32B 0
D KeySOS          DS                150        INZ
D  POffset                      1     4B 0
D  NL                           5     6B 0
D  SelectVar                   21    48
D                 DS
D  FFileLib                     1    20
D  FFileLibr                        10        OVERLAY(FFileLib:1)
D  FFileName                        10        OVERLAY(FFileLib:11)
D FGeneralDs      DS                           INZ
D  FSizeInput                 113   116B 0
D  FOffsetHed                 117   120B 0
D  FSizeHead                  121   124B 0
D  FOfftoList                 125   128B 0
D  FNbrInList                 133   136B 0
D  FSizeEntry                 137   140B 0
D FListDs         DS
D  FFieldName                   1    10
D  FFieldText                  33    82
D GenHeadDs       DS                           INZ
D  InputSize                  113   116B 0
D  ListOffset                 125   128B 0
D  NumberList                 133   136B 0
D  EntrySize                  137   140B 0
D Receiver        DS               4096        INZ
D  NbrFormats                  62    63B 0
```

```
D  DBFileOffS                317     320B 0
D  AccessType                337     338
D  Requester       C                        CONST('*REQUESTER*LIBL')

CL0N01Factor1++++++Opcode&ExtFactor2++++++Result+++++++Len++D+HiLoEq....Comments+
C         *ENTRY      PLIST
C                     PARM                          InFileLib
C                     EVAL      OutFile = %SUBST(InFileLib:1:10)
C                     EVAL      OutLibrary = %SUBST(InFileLib:11:10)
C                     EVAL      SpaceName = 'USRSPC'
C                     EVAL      SpaceLib = 'QTEMP'
C                     EVAL      FileName = OutFile
C                     EVAL      FileLibr = OutLibrary
C                     EVAL      BytesProvd = 116
C                     EVAL      MessageFil = ('QCPFMSG   ' + 'QSYS')
C                     EVAL      *IN53 = *ON
 *   Create user space
C                     CALL      'QUSCRTUS'
C                     PARM                          UserSpace
C                     PARM                          SpaceAttr
C                     PARM      1024                SpaceLen
C                     PARM                          SpaceValue
C                     PARM                          SpaceAuth
C                     PARM                          SpaceText
C                     PARM                          SpaceReplc
C                     PARM                          ErrorDs
 *   Attempt to retrieve object description
C                     CALL      'QUSROBJD'
C                     PARM                          ObjReceivr
C                     PARM      100                 ReceiveLen
C                     PARM      'OBJD0100'          ObjFileFmt
C                     PARM                          InFileLib
C                     PARM      '*FILE'             ObjectType
C                     PARM                          ErrorDs
 *   If file doesn't exist, send message and get out
C                     IF        MessageId <> *BLANKS
C                     EXSR      SNDMSG
C                     GOTO      END
C                     ENDIF
 *   Create user space for fields
C                     EXSR      SPACE1
 *
C                     EVAL      SFileLib = InFileLib
C                     EVAL      First = *ON
 *   Write access path
C                     EXSR      GETFIL
C         MessageId   CABEQ     'CPF5715'           NORECS
C         MessageId   CABEQ     'CPF3210'           END
C                     EVAL      First = *OFF
C                     EVAL      SpaceName = 'USRSPC'
C                     EVAL      SpaceLib = 'QTEMP'
 * List database relations to user space
C                     CALL      'QDBLDBR'
C                     PARM                          UserSpace
C                     PARM      'DBRL0100'          LstOutFmt
C                     PARM                          SFileLib
C                     PARM      '*FIRST'            RecordFmt
C                     PARM      *BLANKS             Ignore
C                     PARM                          ErrorDs
C         MessageId   CABEQ     'CPF5715'           NORECS
C                     EVAL      StartPosit = 1
C                     EVAL      StartLen = 140
C                     EVAL      SpaceName = 'USRSPC'
```

```
        C                   EVAL      SpaceLib = 'QTEMP'
        * Retrieve user space general information
        C                   CALL      'QUSRTVUS'
        C                   PARM                    UserSpace
        C                   PARM                    StartPosit
        C                   PARM                    StartLen
        C                   PARM                    GenHeadDs
        C                   EVAL      StartPosit = 1
        C                   EVAL      StartLen = InputSize
        C                   EVAL      SpaceName = 'USRSPC'
        C                   EVAL      SpaceLib = 'QTEMP'
        *  Retrieve user space detail information
        C                   CALL      'QUSRTVUS'
        C                   PARM                    UserSpace
        C                   PARM                    StartPosit
        C                   PARM                    StartLen
        C                   PARM                    InputDs
        C                   EVAL      StartPosit = (ListOffset + 1)
        C                   EVAL      StartLen = EntrySize
        C                   EVAL      SaveLen = EntrySize
        C                   EVAL      NbrLogics = NumberList
        *  Retrieve the list by walking through the user space
   B1   C                   DO        Nbrlogics
        C                   EVAL      SpaceName = 'USRSPC'
        C                   EVAL      SpaceLib = 'QTEMP'
        C                   EVAL      SaveStart = StartPosit
        C                   CALL      'QUSRTVUS'
        C                   PARM                    UserSpace
        C                   PARM                    StartPosit
        C                   PARM                    StartLen
        C                   PARM                    ListDs
        C       DependFil   CABEQ     '*NONE'       NORECS
        C                   EVAL      SpaceName = 'USRSPC'
        C                   EVAL      SpaceLib = 'QTEMP'
        C                   EVAL      SFileLib = DependFil
        C                   EVAL      %SUBST(SFileLib:11:10) = DependLib
        C                   EXSR      GETFIL
        C                   EXSR      CLEAR
        C                   EVAL      StartPosit = (SaveStart + SaveLen)
   E1   C                   ENDDO
        C       NORECS      TAG
        C                   IF        RelRecNbr > 0
        C                   EVAL      *In21 = *ON
   E1   C                   ENDIF
        C                   WRITE     FORMAT1
        C                   EXFMT     SFLCTL
        C       END         TAG
        C                   EVAL      *InLr = *ON
        *
        C       SNDMSG      BEGSR
        * Send error message
        C                   CALL      'QMHSNDPM'
        C                   PARM                    MessageId
        C                   PARM                    MessageFil
        C                   PARM                    InFileLib
        C                   PARM      20            MsgDtaLen
        C                   PARM      '*STATUS'     MessageTyp
        C                   PARM      '*EXT'        MessageQue
        C                   PARM      1             MsgQueNbr
        C                   PARM                    MessageKey
        C                   PARM                    ErrorDs
        C                   ENDSR
```

```
      C       GETFIL          BEGSR
      *       Retrieve key field information for each logical file
      C                       CALL      'QDBRTVFD'
      C                       PARM                    Receiver
      C                       PARM      4096          ReceiveLen
      C                       PARM                    RFileLib
      C                       PARM      'FILD0100'    FileFmt
      C                       PARM                    SFileLib
      C                       PARM                    RecordFmt
      C                       PARM      '0'           OverRide
      C                       PARM      '*LCL'        System
      C                       PARM      '*EXT'        FmtType
      C                       PARM                    ErrorDs
      C       MessageId       CABEQ     'CPF5715'     ENDGET
      C                       MOVEA     Receiver      AR(1)
      C                       IF        First = *ON
      *       File must be a physical file
      C                       MOVE      AR(9)         TestType
      C                       TESTB     '2'           TestType              01
      C                       IF        *In01 = *ON
      C                       EVAL      MessageId = 'CPF3210'
      C                       EXSR      SNDMSG
      C                       GOTO      ENDGET
E2    C                       ENDIF
E1    C                       ENDIF

      C                       EVAL      I = DbFileOffs
B1    C                       DO        NbrFormats
      C                       MOVEA     AR(I)         FindSelect
      C                       EVAL      S = (Offset + 1)
      C                       IF        First = *OFF
      *       Write blank line for clarity
      C                       EXSR      CLEAR
      C                       EVAL      RelRecNbr = RelRecNbr + 1
      C                       WRITE     SFLRCD
E2    C                       ENDIF
      C                       EVAL      SfLibrary = %SUBST(RFileLib:1:10)
      C                       EVAL      SfFileName = %SUBST(RFileLib:11:10)
      C                       EVAL      SfFormat = FindFormat
      C                       EXSR      GETTXT
B2    C                       DO        NbrKeys
      C                       MOVEA     AR(S)         KeyData
      C                       TESTB     '0'           AscendDes             79
B3    C                       SELECT
      C                       WHEN      *In79 = *OFF
      C                       EVAL      SfAsendDec = 'A'
      C                       WHEN      *In79 = *ON
      C                       EVAL      SfAsendDec = 'D'
E3    C                       ENDSL
      C                       EVAL      SfKeyField = DependKey
      C                       DO        B             C
      C                       IF        ARYF(C) = DependKey
      C                       EVAL      SfValue = Aryt(C)
      C                       LEAVE
      C                       ENDIF
E3    C                       ENDDO
      C                       EVAL      SfText = SfValue
      C                       EVAL      RelRecNbr = RelRecNbr + 1
      C                       WRITE     SFLRCD
      C                       EVAL      SfLibrary = *BLANKS
      C                       EVAL      SfFileName = *BLANKS
      C                       EVAL      SfFormat = *BLANKS
      C                       EVAL      SfValue = *BLANKS
```

```
   C                    EVAL      S = S + 32
E2 C                    ENDDO
   *   If select/omit statements exist
   C                    IF        NbrSelOmit <> *ZEROS
   C                    EXSR      SELOMT
E2 C                    ENDIF
   C                    EVAL      SfCompare = *BLANKS
   C                    EVAL      SfRule = *BLANKS
   C                    EVAL      I = I + 160
E1 C                    ENDDO
   C        ENDGET      TAG
   C                    ENDSR

   C        SELOMT      BEGSR
   C                    EVAL      I1 = (OffSelOmit + 1)
   C                    DO        NbrSelOmit
B1 C                    MOVEA     AR(I1)          KeySelect
   C                    IF        Compare = 'AL'
   C                    ITER
E2 C                    ENDIF
   C                    EVAL      SfCompare = Compare
   C                    EVAL      SfRule = Rule
   C                    EVAL      I2 = OffsetSo + 1
   C                    DO        NbrSO
   C                    MOVEA     AR(I2)          KeySOS
   C                    MOVEA     SelectVar       A2
   C                    EVAL      NL = NL - 19
   C                    IF        NL > *ZEROS
   C                    MOVEA     *BLANKS         A2(NL)
   C                    ENDIF
   C                    MOVEA     A2(1)           SfValue
   C                    EVAL      SfKeyField = CompName
   C                    EVAL      RelRecNbr = RelRecNbr + 1
   C                    EVAL      SfAsendDec = *BLANKS
   C                    EVAL      SfText = (SfRule + ' ' + SfCompare +
   C                                        ' ' + SfValue)
   C                    EVAL      *In59 = *ON
   C                    WRITE     SFLRCD
   C                    EVAL      *In59 = *OFF
   C                    EVAL      I2 = POffset + 1
   C                    ENDDO
   C                    EVAL      I1 = (I1 + 32)
E1 C                    ENDDO
   C                    ENDSR

   C        CLEAR       BEGSR
   C                    EVAL      SfLibrary = *BLANKS
   C                    EVAL      SfFileName = *BLANKS
   C                    EVAL      SfFormat = *BLANKS
   C                    EVAL      SfKeyField = *BLANKS
   C                    EVAL      SfText = *BLANKS
   C                    EVAL      SfCompare = *BLANKS
   C                    EVAL      SfRule = *BLANKS
   C                    EVAL      SfAsendDec = *BLANKS
   C                    ENDSR
   *  Get text for each field
   C        GETTXT      BEGSR
   C                    EVAL      FFileName = SfFileName
   C                    EVAL      FFileLibr = SfLibrary
   C                    EVAL      FSpaceName = 'FLDSPC'
   C                    EVAL      FSpaceLib = 'QTEMP'
   *  List fields to user space
   C                    CALL      'QUSLFLD'
```

```
       C                    PARM                      FieldSpace
       C                    PARM      'FLDL0100'      ListFormat
       C                    PARM                      FFileLib
       C                    PARM      SfFormat        RecordFmt
       C                    PARM      '1'             OverRide
       C                    Z-ADD     1               FilStartP
       C                    Z-ADD     140             FilStartL
       C                    EVAL      FSpaceName = 'FLDSPC'
       C                    EVAL      FSpaceLib = 'QTEMP'
        *  Retrieve user space general information
       C                    CALL      'QUSRTVUS'
       C                    PARM                      FieldSpace
       C                    PARM                      FilStartP
       C                    PARM                      FilStartL
       C                    PARM                      FGeneralDs
       C                    EVAL      FilStartP = FOffsetHed + 1
       C                    EVAL      FilStartL = FSizeHead
       C                    EVAL      FSpaceName = 'FLDSPC'
       C                    EVAL      FSpaceLib = 'QTEMP'
       C                    EVAL      FilStartP = FOfftoList + 1
       C                    EVAL      FilStartL = FSizeEntry
        *  Retrieve the list by walking through the user space
   B1  C                    DO        FNbrInList
       C                    EVAL      FSpaceName = 'FLDSPC'
       C                    EVAL      FSpaceLib = 'QTEMP'
       C                    CALL      'QUSRTVUS'
       C                    PARM                      FieldSpace
       C                    PARM                      FilStartP
       C                    PARM                      FilStartL
       C                    PARM                      FListDs
       C                    EVAL      B = B + 1
       C                    EVAL      ARYF(B) = FFieldName
       C                    EVAL      ARYT(B) = FFieldText
       C                    EVAL      FilStartP = FilStartP + FSizeEntry
   E1  C                    ENDDO
       C                    ENDSR
        * Create user space for listing fields
       C         SPACE1     BEGSR
       C                    EVAL      FSpaceName = 'FLDSPC'
       C                    EVAL      FSpaceLib = 'QTEMP'
       C                    CALL      'QUSCRTUS'
       C                    PARM                      FieldSpace
       C                    PARM      *BLANKS         SpaceAttr
       C                    PARM      1024            SpaceLen
       C                    PARM      *BLANKS         SpaceValue
       C                    PARM      '*CHANGE'       SpaceAuth
       C                    PARM      *BLANKS         SpaceText
       C                    PARM      '*YES'          SpaceReplc
       C                    PARM                      ErrorDs
       C                    ENDSR
```

Figure 9.11: FIG911DS Display File

```
A*******************************************************************
A*  TO COMPILE:
A*     CRTDSPF FILE(XXXLIB/FIG911DS)
A*******************************************************************
AAN01N02N03T.Name+++++RLen++TDpBLinPosFunctions++++++++++++++++++++++
A                                      CF03    CF12
A          R SFLRCD                    SFL
A            SFLIBRARY   10A  O  7  2
A            SFFILENAME  10A  O  7 13
A            SFKEYFIELD  10A  O  7 35
A            SFFORMAT    10A  O  7 24
A            SFASENDDEC   1   O  7 46
A            SFTEXT      32   O  7 48
A  59                                  DSPATR(HI)
A          R SFLCTL                    SFLCTL(SFLRCD)
A                                      SFLSIZ(0024)  SFLPAG(0012)
A                                      OVERLAY
A  21                                  SFLDSP
A                                      SFLDSPCTL
A  53                                  SFLEND(*MORE)
A                                    1 29'Display Access Paths' DSPATR(HI)
A                                    3  2'Physical File . . . . . . . . . :'
A            OUTFILE     10A  O  3 35DSPATR(HI)
A                                    4  2'Library . . . . . . . . . . . :'
A            OUTLIBRARY  10A  O  4 35DSPATR(HI)
A                                    6  2'Library   '   DSPATR(HI)
A                                    6 13'File      '   DSPATR(HI)
A                                    6 35'Key Field'   DSPATR(HI)
A                                    6 49'Select/Omit Values'  DSPATR(HI)
A                                    6 24'Format'      DSPATR(HI)
A                                    6 45'Seq'         DSPATR(HI)
A                                    3 47'Number of logicals. . . . . :'
A            NBRLOGICS    4  00  3 77DSPATR(HI)
A          R FORMAT1
A                                   23  4'F3=Exit'     COLOR(BLU)
A                                   23 18'F12=Previous'  COLOR(BLU)
```

Figure 9.12: The Display Access Path (DSPPATH) Command

```
/*===============================================================*/
/* To compile:                                                   */
/*                                                               */
/*        CRTCMD     CMD(XXX/DSPPATH)   PGM(XXX/FIG910RG)        */
/*                   SRCMBR(FIG912CM)                            */
/*                                                               */
/*===============================================================*/
        CMD        PROMPT('DISPLAY ACCESS PATH')
        PARM       KWD(FILE) TYPE(NAME1) MIN(1) PROMPT('File +
                   Name:')
NAME1:  QUAL       TYPE(*NAME) LEN(10)
        QUAL       TYPE(*CHAR) LEN(10) DFT(*LIBL) SPCVAL((' ' +
                   *LIBL)) CHOICE('Name, *LIBL') +
                   PROMPT('Library Name:')
```

The GETFIL subroutine calls the Retrieve File Description (QDBRTVFD) API to return all of the needed information in one variable, called Receiver. This variable contains different data structures, which can be in a different offset each time you run the command. The variable also contains offset pointers to indicate where each data structure is located. The Receiver field data is loaded into one long, generic array and then (using the offset pointer fields) parts of the array are moved into the correct data structure.

Two loops are established to get all the key field information. The first loop uses NbrFormats, which is the number of formats in the file (logical files can have more than one format). The field DBFileOffs contains the offset location to key field information defined in the FindSelect data structure.

Before we use the information in the FindSelect data structure, we need to get the text description of each field in the file. This is not included in any API we have yet used, but the List Fields (QUSLFLD) API does allow us to get at this information. So, we call subroutine GETTXT, which lists the fields in the file into another user space. We walk through and load the file names and descriptions into two arrays. When it's time to write the subfile record, these arrays are used to retrieve the field descriptions. Then we use the FindSelect structure information.

The FindSelect structure contains the Offset field, which points to an array of key field names. The field NbrKeys indicates how many key fields exist, and is used as the index for the second loop. One subfile record is written for each key field in the array.

The next step is to determine whether or not there are any select or omit statements used in the path. The FindSelect structure also contains pointers to get at this information. NbrSelOmit is the number of select/omit statements while OffSelOmit is the offset to the array.

To get a list of all of the logicals over the physical file, the program uses the List Database Relations (QDBLDBR) API. This API produces its list in the user space that was created earlier. The Retrieve User Space (QUSRTVUS) API is then used to extract the file information for each of the logical files. This is done by first retrieving a generic header structure, which contains pointers to the space that has the file information, and then walking through the list stored in the user space until each file has been processed. For each file in the list, the GETFIL subroutine is called to perform the same functions as those performed on the physical file. Once the entire list has been processed, the information is written to the screen.

As you see when you run this command, you now have in instant road map of all of the paths that exist over any physical file on your system. This tool can be a real time saver when you are designing new programs.

OFFICEVISION/400 APIs

IBM Office programs put a great deal of functionality at your fingertips. You can send E-mail, maintain calendars, send notes, do word processing—in short, you can do almost anything a small office needs to do. And, with the wealth of APIs available, you can integrate these functions into your application seamlessly.

Controlling OfficeVision/400 Services

If you have integrated any of the office functions into your applications, you need to know about the Control Office Services (QOCCTLOF) API. This API makes requests of the office services and indicates that several office tasks will be performed. This means that, when you complete an office function (such as displaying a document), all of the office files and work spaces can be left open, thereby providing a significant performance improvement.

Table 9.9 shows the required input parameter group for this API. QOCCTLOF is a very simple API. You provide the request type, which can be *START, *END, or *CHECK. You also can specify the standard Optional Error Code Data Structure.

Table 9.9: QOCCTLOF—Control Office Services Input Parameters

Parameter	Description	Type	Size
1	Request type	Input	Char(10)
2	Error code	Both	Char(*)

Parameter Definitions:

<u>Request type</u>: Indicate the type of control you are requesting. Valid values are *START, *END, and *CHECK:

*START Start a service block. This indicates that more office commands will be used. Office services leaves the job in such a state as to maximize the performance of subsequent office service functions. This includes leaving office files open (and you know the performance impact of opening and closing files—see Chapter 1) and leaving work spaces created and already initialized. It is your responsibility to end the service block when you are finished.

*END End a service block. This indicates that no more office functions will be used, the office files will be closed, and the work space deleted.

*CHECK Check to see if a service block is active. An error will be returned if a service block is not active.

<u>Error code</u>: The standard Optional Error Code Data Structure.

Your application should call the Control Office Services API when the application starts up, telling Office Services to power up and stay up. When your application finishes, it should call the Office Services API again, telling it to clean up and go home. These two simple calls can cut down significantly on the system overhead required to initiate OfficeVision/400.

Hierarchical File System

The first question that comes to your mind about a *hierarchical file system* is probably, "What is it?" In basic terms, it is the operating system's method of controlling the format of information that it processes.

In a relational database, information is stored in data files. These files contain records, each of which is formatted in exactly the same way. In a hierarchical file system, these files are called *stream files* because they consist of a stream of bytes with no consistent record structure.

Instead of fixed-length records, each record contains pointers that point to where information is stored in the file. In OfficeVision/400, these stream files are called *documents* because they are used to hold text. A stream file is basically a series of data structures that can be accessed using a series of pointers.

These stream files are then arranged in a multilevel structure. Data is grouped into files and files are grouped into larger units, called *directories*. In OfficeVision/400, a directory is called a *folder*. A directory does not contain data, it is simply a named grouping of files. This combination of directories and files in OfficeVision/400 is a good example of a hierarchical file system.

Processing OfficeVision/400 Documents

Let's look at how to read an OfficeVision/400 directory of all documents in a folder, read the document, and then clean up the environment when you are finished. The programming example provided (Figure 9.13) reads all of the documents in a given folder and returns the accumulated collective size.

Figure 9.13: Program to Retrieve and Accumulate the Size of All Documents in a Folder

```
    *************************************************************************
    *   TO COMPILE:
    *       CRTBNDRPG PGM(XXXLIB/FIG913RG)
    *************************************************************************

DName++++++++++ETDsFrom+++To/L+++IDc.Keywords++++++++++++++++++++++++++Comments+++++
D AB              S              1     DIM(2000)
D                 DS
D  TableLen              1      4B 0
D  DirBLen               5      8B 0
D  NbrDir                9     12B 0
D  NbrDirRead           13     16B 0
D  DirLen               17     20B 0
D  DirPathLen           21     24B 0
D DirBuffer       DS          2000
D Binary          DS            40
D  O                     1      4B 0
D Binary1         DS            40
D  AO                    1      4B 0
D Attributes      DS            40
D  Aname                13     20
D ErrorDs         DS                   INZ
D  BytesAvail            1      4B 0
D  BytesProvd            5      8B 0
D  MessageId             9     15
D  Err###               16     16
D  MessageDta           17    116
D DirOpnCon       C                    CONST('10      ')
D DirPath         S             16
D DirOIF          S              6
D DirHandle       S             16
D FolderName      S             16
D SizeAlpha       S             12
D TableSpace      S            200
D Size            S              9 0
D TotalSize       S             12 0
D At#             S              4 0
D P               S              4 0
D I               S              4 0
D X               S              1 0
D NbrEntry        S              4 0

CL0N01Factor1++++++++Opcode&ExtFactor2++++++Result++++++++Len++D+HiLoEq....Comments+
C     *ENTRY        PLIST
C                   PARM                      FolderName
C                   PARM                      SizeAlpha
C                   EVAL      DirPath = '/QDLS/' + FolderName
C                   EVAL      DirOIF = DirOpnCon
C                   EVAL      BytesProvd = 116
C                   EVAL      TableLen = -1
  * Open directory and retrieve directory handle
C                   CALL      'QHFOPNDR'
C                   PARM                      DirHandle
C                   PARM                      DirPath
C                   PARM      16              DirPathLen
C                   PARM                      DirOIF
C                   PARM      ' '             TableSpace
C                   PARM                      TableLen
C                   PARM                      ErrorDs
```

```
B1   C                     DOU          NbrDirRead = 0
      * Read directory entries, 10 at a time
     C                     CALL         'QHFRDDR'
     C                     PARM                       DirHandle
     C                     PARM                       DirBuffer
     C                     PARM         2000          DirBLen
     C                     PARM         10            NbrDir
     C                     PARM                       NbrDirRead
     C                     PARM                       DirLen
     C                     PARM                       ErrorDs
     C                     MOVEA        DirBuffer     AB(1)
     C                     MOVEA        AB(1)         Binary
     C                     EVAL         NbrEntry = 0
     C                     EVAL         X = 1
      * Do for number of entries received
B2   C                     DO           NbrEntry
     C                     EVAL         X = X + 4
     C                     MOVEA        AB(X)         Binary
     C                     EVAL         O = O + 1
     C                     EVAL         P = O
     C                     EVAL         I = P + 4
     C                     MOVEA        AB(O)         Binary
     C                     EVAL         At# = O
      * Get attributes (document name, size, etc.)
B3   C                     DO           At#
     C                     MOVEA        AB(I)         Binary1
     C                     EVAL         Ao = Ao + P
     C                     MOVEA        AB(AO)        Attributes
B4   C                     IF           Aname <> 'QALCSIZE'
     C                     EVAL         I = I + 4
     C                     ITER
E4   C                     ENDIF
     C                     EVAL         Ao = Ao + 20
     C                     MOVEA        AB(AO)        Binary
     C                     EVAL         Size = O
     C                     EVAL         TotalSize = TotalSize + Size
     C                     LEAVE
E3   C                     ENDDO
E2   C                     ENDDO
E1   C                     ENDDO
      * Close Directory
     C                     CALL         'QHFCLODR'
     C                     PARM                       DirHandle
     C                     PARM                       ErrorDs
     C                     MOVE         TotalSize     SizeAlpha
     C                     EVAL         *InLr = *ON
```

The first thing this program does is create a path to get at the requested folder. While a path can serve basically the same function as a library list (after all, it does the same function of listing search objects), it must follow the format /QDLS/Folder name. The program then uses the path retrieved in the QHFOPNDR API to open the directory (folder).

Table 9.10 shows the required parameter group for the Open Directory (QHFOPNDR) API. One of the parameters is the attribute table, followed by a parameter defining the table length. This parameter is where you describe the information that you receive when you read the directory.

Table 9.10: Required Input Parameters for Open Directory (QHFOPNDR)

Parameter	Description	Type	Size
1	Directory handle	Output	Char(16)
2	Path name	Input	Char(*)
3	Length of path	Input	Binary(4)
4	Open information	Input	Char(6)
5	Attribute selection table (Table 9.11)	Input	Char(*)
6	Length of attribute selection table	Input	Binary(4)
7	Error code	Both	Char(*)

Parameter Definitions

Directory handle: Handle returned by the API, to be used in other APIs. An example of this is opening and closing the directory.

Path name: Tells the system which objects to open. If the last name in the path is a specific name, then that folder is opened and all documents in that folder are read (using other APIs). If the last name in the path is a generic name, then the next-to-the-last entry in the path is presumed to be the folder name. Only documents that meet the generic entry in that folder are read.

Length of path: Tells the system the length of the path name.

Open information: A 6-byte field where each byte tells the system something about how to perform the open. Character positions and their meanings are:

Position 1 - Lock mode indicating how other jobs can access the directory.

0 - No lock. Other jobs can do whatever they are authorized to do.

1 - Deny none. Other jobs can read or change but not rer.ame/delete.

2 - Deny write. Read only; no change, rename, or delete.

Position 2 - Type of open to perform.

0 - Normal open.

1 - Permanent open. End Request and Reclaim Resources do not close the directory. Directory is closed when job ends or close API in run.

Position 3 - Reserved; must be blank.

Position 4 - Reserved; must be blank.

Position 5 - Reserved; must be blank.

Position 6 - Reserved; must be blank.

Attribute selection table: This is where you indicate what information should be returned when reading the directory. See Table 9.4 for a complete listing of the standard attributes that you can request with this parameter.

Length of attribute selection table: Indicate the length of attribute selection table. If length is -1, then all attributes are returned and the attribute selection table can be blank.

Error code: Optional Error Code Data Structure.

Table 9.11: Attribute Selection Table

Attribute Name	Size	Description
QNAME	CHAR(*)	Current name of file or directory. Not needed with the QHFRDDR API and not allowed with the QHFCHGAT API.
QFILSIZE	BINARY(4)	The number of bytes of a file's data. This entry is ignored for directories; it is only used for files.
QALCSIZE	BINARY(4)	The number of bytes allocated for a file. It is ignored for directories.
QCRTDTM	CHAR(13)	Date and time the file or directory was created, in CYYMMDDHHMMSS format. Not allowed when creating a directory or file, only when retrieving or changing.
QACCDTTM	CHAR(13)	Date and time last accessed, in CYYMMDDHHMMSS format.
QWRTDTTM	CHAR(13)	Date and time file or directory was last written to, in CYYMMDDHHMMSS format.

Attribute Name	Size	Description
QFILATR	CHAR(10)	The type of item the directory entry is for. Positions 6 to 10 must be blank and positions 1 to 5 must be 0 (no) or 1 (yes). Positions: 1 = Read-only file. File can not be accessed in write mode and can not be deleted. 2 = Hidden file or directory 3 = System file or directory. 4 = Entry is a directory (not a file). 5 = Changed file.
QERROR	CHAR(7)	An attribute returned by the Read Directory (QHFRDDR) API when an error is encountered in retrieving the attributes of a directory entry. It contains a CPF error message ID.

In our example, we are specifying a blank table with a length of negative 1. This is a rather dubious method of telling the API to return every possible attribute (field) that is defined for the directory. While this method is, admittedly, less efficient than specifying only the attributes in which you are interested, it does save quite a few headaches when trying to format the attribute table. This method, in turn, makes maintenance of the program far easier.

Now that the directory is open, our program needs to read it. Our example uses the Read Directory (QHFRDDR) API to accomplish this task. With this API, you give it the handle of the directory that was opened with the Open Directory (QHFOPNDR) API. As we stated in the previous section, a handle is simply a temporary internal name given to an object. Some APIs (such as this one) require the use of handles.

The next step in our example is to tell the API how many directory entries to read at one time and then to return information on how many it actually read. When that number is 0, all of the entries in the directory have been read. Table 9.12 shows the required parameter group for the Read Directory (QHFRDDR) API.

Table 9.12: Required Parameter Group for Read Directory (QHFRDDR) API

Parameter	Description	Type	Size
1	Open directory handle	Input	Char(16)
2	Data buffer	Output	Char(*)
3	Length of data buffer	Input	Binary(4)
4	Number of directory entries to read	Input	Binary(4)
5	Number of directory entries read	Output	Binary(4)
6	Length of data returned	Output	Binary(4)
7	Error code	Both	Char(*)

Parameter Definitions

Open directory handle: The field returned from the Open Directory (QHFOPNDR) API.

Data buffer: The name of the field where the API puts the requested information. See Figure 9.2 for the format of this data. What information gets returned in this field is dependent upon the attributes selected in the attribute selection table when the directory was opened. The QNAME attribute is always returned, but never specified, in the table thereby ensuring that there is always at least one attribute returned for every directory entry found.

<u>Length of data buffer</u>: The length of the field in parameter 2. It must be large enough to hold at least one directory entry. If it is not, an error is returned. However, the Length of Data Returned parameter (parameter 6) contains the size of the data the system tried to return. You can use this field to try and correct any problem.

<u>Number of directory entries to read</u>: The number of directory entries to place in the data buffer.

<u>Number of directory entries read</u>: The actual number of directory entries placed in the data buffer. This field is 0 when there are no more entries to read.

<u>Length of data returned</u>: The total number of bytes returned in the buffer if the read was successful. If it was not successful because the field was not large enough to contain at least one directory entry, then this field contains the number of bytes required to hold the next directory entry.

<u>Error code</u>: The standard Optional Error Code Data Structure.

The field DirBuffer is loaded with as many directory entries as it can handle, within the limits of the number of buffers we requested. We ask that 10 directory entries be returned (NbrDir = 10) with each call to the API. However, the length of the data buffer (2000) can only hold three directory entries, so that is actually how many directory entries are returned with each call to the API. If you need to improve the performance of this utility, this is the place to do it. Increasing the length of the data buffer decreases the number of calls to the API to read all of the directory entries. However, the Catch 22 is that doing this requires more memory for the program to run.

The actual number of directory entries returned from the API is stored in binary form in the first 4 bytes of the buffer. We get that number and use it to establish another loop to read the buffer. The format of the buffer is shown in Tables 9.13, 9.14, and 9.15. We then search through the buffer, looking for the attribute name QALCSIZE (Allocated Size). When we find it, we accumulate the value retrieved to calculate the size of the folder.

Table 9.13: Format of Data Buffer from the Read Directory (QHFRDDR) API

Type	Field
BINARY(4)	Number of directory entries returned.
BINARY(4)	Offset to directory entry. This field is repeated for each directory entry that is returned.
Directory entry	Attribute information table for this directory entry. See Figure 9.3 for layout of attribute information table. (**Note**: Any offsets given within this table are from the beginning of the directory entry, not from the beginning of the data buffer.)

Table 9.14: Attribute Information Table

Type	Field
BINARY(4)	Number of attributes defined in the table.
BINARY(4)	Offset to the attributes. This field repeats for every attribute being defined or retrieved.

Table 9.15: Attribute Description Table

Type	Description
BINARY(4)	Length of attribute name
BINARY(4)	Length of the data returned for this attribute
BINARY(4)	Reserved
CHAR(*)	Attribute name
CHAR(*)	Attribute value
Note: The attribute descriptions repeat for every attribute in the table, as does the offset to the attribute descriptions.	

The last thing the program does is close the directory using the Close Directory (QHFCLODR) API. You simply supply this API with the handle that was returned in the Open Directory (QHFOPNDR) API and also provide it with the standard Optional Error Code Data Structure.

SPOOL FILE APIS

The Spool File APIs allow you to manipulate spool files. Use them to generate a list of spool files based on a given selection criteria. You can access a specific spooled file and get the attribute or data within it.

A chart of all spool files and descriptions of their functions are shown in Table 9.16. We use some of the Spool File APIs in a utility that moves all spool file entries from one spool file to another.

Table 9.16: Spool File APIs and Their Functions

Name	Title	Description
QSPCLOSP	Close Spooled File	Close an open spool file.
QSPCRTSP	Create Spooled File	Create a spool file. When it is created, it does not contain any data.
QSPGETSP	Get Spooled File	Get data from an existing spool file, previously opened by the Open Spooled File (QSPOPNSP) API.
QUSLSPL	List Spooled File	Generate a list of spooled files into a user space. Selection criteria can be specified to filter the list.
QSPMOVSP	Move Spooled File	Move the spooled file to a different position within the output queue, or move it to another output queue.
QSPOPNSP	Open Spooled File	Open an existing spooled file for the Get Spooled File (QSPGETSP) API, which puts the data in a user space.
QSPPUTSP	Put Spooled File	Put the data into a spooled file that was created using the Create Spooled File (QSPCRTSP) API.
QUSRSPLA	Retrieve Spooled File Attributes	Put specific information about a spooled file into a field. The bigger the field, the greater the amount of information returned.

Moving Spool Files

Why would you want to move spool files? Because you can. But, aside from that, such spool file manipulation can be used to help ensure that all spool files for a particular job are kept together. This is a feature (Figure 9.14) that you may find handy.

Figure 9.14: Move Spool File Utility

```
    ****************************************************************************
    *    TO COMPILE:
    *      CRTBNDRPG PGM(XXXLIB/FIG914RG)
    ****************************************************************************

    DName++++++++++ETDsFrom+++To/L+++IDc.Keywords++++++++++++++++++++++++++Comments+++++
    D ARY             S                     1    DIM(200)
    D GeneralHed      DS
    D  Offset                        1      4B 0
    D  NumberList                    9     12B 0
    D  EntrySize                    13     16B 0
    D                 DS
    D  UserSpace                     1     20
    D  SpaceName                     1     10
    D  SpaceLib                     11     20
    D  OutSpool                     21     40
    D  OutputQue                           10    OVERLAY(OutSpool:1)
    D  QueLibrary                          10    OVERLAY(OutSpool:11)
    D  StartPosit                   41     44B 0
    D  SpaceLen                     45     48B 0
    D  NbrOfKeys                    49     52B 0
    D  MoveLen                      53     56B 0
    D Receiver        DS
    D  NbrReturnd                    1      4B 0
    D  Retrieved                     5    204
    D KeyData         DS
    D  FldRtnLen                     1      4B 0
    D  KeyReturn                     5      8B 0
    D  KeyField                     17     26
    D                 DS
    D  KeyField1                     1     10
    D  SflNbr                        1      4B 0
    D ErrorDs         DS                          INZ
    D  BytesAvail                    1      4B 0
    D  BytesProvd                    5      8B 0
    D  MessageId                     9     15
    D  Err###                       16     16
    D  MessageDta                   17    116
    D Keys            DS
    D  Key1                          1      4B 0
    D  Key2                          5      8B 0
    D  Key3                          9     12B 0
    D  Key4                         13     16B 0
    D  Key5                         17     20B 0
    D MoveDS          DS
    D  MsJobName                     1     10
    D  MsJobUsr                     11     20
    D  MsJobNbr                     21     26
    D  MsJHandle                    27     42
    D  MsSplHndle                   43     58
    D  MsSpoolNam                   59     68
    D  MsSplNbr                     69     72B 0
    D  MsOutQue                     73     82
    D  MsQueLib                     83     92
    D FromQue         S                    10
    D FromLib         S                    10
    D FromUser        S                    10
    D ToQue           S                    10
    D ToLibrary       S                    10
    D FormatName      S                     8
    D UserName        S                    10
```

```
     D FormType        S             10
     D UserData        S             10
     D JobName         S             26
     D I               S              3 0
     D DoNbr           S              8B 0 INZ
     D SpaceValue      S              1
     D Storage         S              1
     D SpaceAttr       S             10
     D SpaceAuth       S             10
     D SpaceText       S             50
     D SpaceReplc      S             10
     D MovFormat       S              8

     CL0N01Factor1+++++++Opcode&ExtFactor2+++++++Result+++++++++Len++D+HiLoEq....Comments+
     C     *ENTRY      PLIST
     C                 PARM                       FromQue
     C                 PARM                       FromLib
     C                 PARM                       FromUser
     C                 PARM                       ToQue
     C                 PARM                       ToLibrary
     C                 EVAL      SpaceName = 'SPLSPACE'
     C                 EVAL      SpaceLib = 'QTEMP'
     C                 EVAL      BytesProvd = 116
B1   C                 IF        (FromUser = *BLANKS)
     C                 EVAL      FromUser = '*ALL'
E1   C                 ENDIF
     C                 EXSR      SPACE
     C                 EVAL      OutputQue = FromQue
     C                 EVAL      QueLibrary = FromLib
     C                 EVAL      MsOutQue = ToQue
     C                 EVAL      MsQueLib = ToLibrary
     C                 EVAL      Key1 = 201
     C                 EVAL      Key2 = 202
     C                 EVAL      Key3 = 203
     C                 EVAL      Key4 = 204
     C                 EVAL      Key5 = 205
     C                 EVAL      NbrOfKeys = 5
     * List spool file entries to user space
     C                 CALL      'QUSLSPL'
     C                 PARM                       UserSpace
     C                 PARM      'SPLF0200'       FormatName
     C                 PARM      FromUser         UserName
     C                 PARM                       OutSpool
     C                 PARM      '*ALL'           FormType
     C                 PARM      '*ALL'           UserData
     C                 PARM                       ErrorDs
     C                 PARM                       JobName
     C                 PARM                       Keys
     C                 PARM                       NbrOfKeys
     C                 EVAL      StartPosit = 125
     C                 EVAL      SpaceLen = 116
     C                 EVAL      SpaceName = 'SPLSPACE'
     C                 EVAL      SpaceLib = 'QTEMP'
     * Retrieve user space information
     C                 CALL      'QUSRTVUS'
     C                 PARM                       UserSpace
     C                 PARM                       StartPosit
     C                 PARM                       SpaceLen
     C                 PARM                       GeneralHed
     C                 EVAL      StartPosit = (Offset + 1)
     C                 EVAL      SpaceLen = EntrySize
     C                 EVAL      DoNbr = NumberList
B1   C                 DO        DoNbr
```

```
         C                    EVAL      SpaceName = 'SPLSPACE'
         C                    EVAL      SpaceLib = 'QTEMP'
         C                    EVAL      BytesProvd = 116
          * Retrieve user space job name information
         C                    CALL      'QUSRTVUS'
         C                    PARM                    UserSpace
         C                    PARM                    StartPosit
         C                    PARM                    SpaceLen
         C                    PARM                    Receiver
         C                    PARM                    ErrorDs
         C                    MOVEA     Retrieved     ARY(1)
         C                    EVAL      I = 1
   B2    C                    DO        5
         C                    MOVEA     ARY(I)        KeyData
   B3    C                    SELECT
         C                    WHEN      (KeyReturn = 201)
         C                    EVAL      MsSpoolNam = KeyField
         C                    WHEN      (KeyReturn = 202)
         C                    EVAL      MsJobName = KeyField
         C                    WHEN      (KeyReturn = 203)
         C                    EVAL      MsJobUsr = KeyField
         C                    WHEN      (KeyReturn = 204)
         C                    EVAL      MsJobNbr = KeyField
         C                    WHEN      (KeyReturn = 205)
         C                    EVAL      KeyField1 = KeyField
         C                    EVAL      MsSplNbr = SflNbr
   E3    C                    ENDSL
         C                    EVAL      I = I + FldRtnLen
   E2    C                    ENDDO
         C                    CALL      'QSPMOVSP'
         C                    PARM                    MoveDs
         C                    PARM      92            MoveLen
         C                    PARM      'MSPF0100'    MovFormat
         C                    PARM                    ErrorDs
         C                    EVAL      StartPosit = StartPosit + EntrySize
   E1    C                    ENDDO
         C                    EVAL      *InLr = *ON

         C        SPACE       BEGSR
          * Create a user space
         C                    CALL      'QUSCRTUS'
         C                    PARM                    UserSpace
         C                    PARM      *BLANKS       SpaceAttr
         C                    PARM      4096          SpaceLen
         C                    PARM      *BLANKS       SpaceValue
         C                    PARM      '*CHANGE'     SpaceAuth
         C                    PARM      *BLANKS       SpaceText
         C                    PARM      '*YES'        SpaceReplc
         C                    PARM                    ErrorDs
         C                    ENDSR
```

Take a look at the code in the program we used to move all spool file entries from one output queue to another. The program appears in Figure 9.14.

The program accepts the output queue name and output queue library from which to perform the move. It also accepts the user name that can be used to filter the selection. It then executes the space subroutine to create a user space into which the List Spooled File

API can put its data. See "User Spaces" in this chapter for a detailed description
of these APIs.

Next, we create a data structure of codes that indicate to the List Spooled File
(QUSLSPL) API exactly which pieces of information about the spool file we want to put
into the user space. (See Table 9.17 for a list of all of the codes that can be used.) The
List Spooled File (QUSLSPL) API is then called to get the information.

Table 9.17: Code Table for Spool File APIs

Code	Type	Description
201	Char(10)	Spooled file name
202	Char(10)	Job name
203	Char(10)	User name
204	Char(6)	Job number
205	Binary(4)	Spooled file number
206	Char(10)	Output queue name
207	Char(10)	Output queue library name
208	Char(10)	Device name
209	Char(10)	User-specified data
210	Char(10)	Status
211	Binary(4)	Total number of pages
212	Binary(4)	Current page printing
213	Binary(4)	Number of copies left to print
214	Char(10)	Form type

Code	Type	Description
215	Char(2)	Priority code
216	Char(7)	Date file was opened
217	Char(6)	Time file was opened
218	Char(16)	Internal job name (handle)
219	Char(16)	Internal spooled file identifier (handle)
220	Chart(10)	Device type

The input parameter group for the List Spooled File (QUSLSPL) API is shown in Table 9.18. All spooled files in the designated output queue are included in the list. Only the spooled file name (201), job name (202), user name (203), job number (204), and spooled file number (205) are returned for each spooled file.

Table 9.18: Input Parameter Group for List Spooled File (QUSLSPL) API

Parameter	Description	Type	Size
1	User space name	Input	Char(20)
2	Format name	Input	Char(8)
3	User name	Input	Char(10)
4	Output queue name	Input	Char(20)
5	Form type	Input	Char(10)
6	User-specified data	Input	Char(10)

Optional Parameter Group 1:

Parameter	Description	Type	Size
7	Error code	Both	Char(*)

Optional Parameter Group 2:

Parameter	Description	Type	Size
8	Job name	Input	Char(26)
9	Array of codes for return data	Input	Array(*) of Binary(4)
10	Number of fields in array in parameter 9	Input	Binary(4)

Parameter Definitions:

User space name: Object name and library name of the user space to receive the generated list. Special values for library name are Current Library (*CURLIB) or Library List (*LIBL).

Format name: The format name of the system data structure that defines the format of the returned data. Valid format name values are SPLF0100 or SPLF0200.

User name: The name of the user whose spooled files should be included in the list. Part of the filtering criteria to generate the list. It must be blank if the job name parameter is specified. Special values are All Users (*ALL) or the Current User ID (*CURRENT).

<u>Output queue name</u>: Object name and library name of the output queue whose files are to be searched to determine if they are to be included in the list. These values are used as part of the filtering criteria to generate the list. Special values are *ALL (then library part must be blank), Current Library (*CURLIB), or Library List (*LIBL) for library part of output queue name.

<u>Form type</u>: All files whose form type attribute matches this are to be included in the list. This field is also used as part of the filtering criteria to generate the list. Special values are *ALL (all form types) or *STD (the system default form type).

<u>User-specified data</u>: All files whose user-specified data attribute matches this are included in the list. Again, this value can be part of the filtering criteria to generate the list. Special value is *ALL.

<u>Error code</u>: The standard Optional Error Code Data Structure.

<u>Job name</u>: All files whose job name matches this value are to be included in the list. Job name can also be used as part of the filtering criteria to generate the list. This parameter must be blank if the user name, output queue name, form type, or user-specified data are not blank. The job name comprises three parts:

- Job Name: Char(10) - specific name or * (indicates current job).

- User ID: Char(10) - user profile name or blanks if job name is *.

- Job Number: Char(6) - specific job number or blanks if job name is specified as *.

<u>Array of codes for return data</u>: Array of codes indicating which attributes to return in format SPLF0200. Only the data represented by the codes are returned by the API. The valid codes are represented in Table 9.6. If the number of keys parameter is 0, this parameter is ignored.

<u>Number of fields in array in parameter 9</u>: The number of entries in the array of codes parameter. Must be 0 if the SPLF0100 format is being used. If this parameter is omitted, 0 is assumed.

After the call to the List Spooled File (QUSLSPL) API, the user space contains the information we are looking for. We need to use the Retrieve User Space (QUSRTVUS)

API, to get the information. As with all List APIs, the format of the data contains a generic header, an input parameter section, a specific header section, and, finally, the list data section. The generic header section contains pointers to the other sections. See List APIs in Table 9.8 for a complete description of this section.

The Retrieve User Space (QUSRTVUS) API gets us the generic header, which points us to the list section and also tells us how many entries are in the list. We use that number, NumberList, to establish a loop to walk through the user space extracting each entry in the list. See Table 9.19 for the format of the list section. Each entry in the list contains the five fields we are looking for, so we extract each field separately.

Table 9.19: Format of Lists from List Spooled File (QUSLSPL) API

SPLF0100:

Offset	Type	Description
0	Char(10)	User name
10	Char(10)	Output queue name
20	Char(10)	Library name
30	Char(10)	Form type
40	Char(10)	User specified data
50	Char(16)	Internal job identifier (handle)
66	Char(16)	Internal spooled file identifier (handle)

SPLF0200:

Offset	Type	Description
0	Binary(4)	Number of fields returned

These fields repeat for each code requested, so the offsets varies.

Offset	Type	Description
	Binary(4)	Length of field information returned
	Binary(4)	Code for data returned
	Char(1)	Type of data
	Char(3)	Reserved
	Binary(4)	Length of data returned
	Char(*)	Data returned for specified code
	Char(*)	Reserved

Having obtained all the fields necessary to move a spool file, we now call the Move Spool File (QSPMOVSP) API to actually move the spool file to the target output queue. The required input parameters for this API are shown in Table 9.20.

Table 9.20: Input Parameter Group for the Move Spool File (QSPMOVSP) API

Parameter	Description	Type	Size
1	Move information data structure	Input	Char(20)
2	Length of move data structure	Input	Binary(4)
3	Format name of data structure	Input	Char(8)
4	Standard error code data structure	Both	Char(*)

Parameter Definitions:

<u>Move information data structure</u>: The information required by the system to perform the move. It must be specified in either MSPF0100 or MSPF0200 format. See Table 9.10 for more information on these data structures.

<u>Length of move data structure</u>: The length of the information data structure. The minimum length for MSPF0100 is 92 and 144 for the MSPF0200 format.

<u>Format name of data structure</u>: The name of the format that describes the information data structure. Specify either MSPF0100 or MSPF0200 (see Table 9.21).

<u>Standard error code data structure</u>: The standard Optional Error Code Data Structure.

Table 9.21: Information Formats for the Move Spooled File (QSPMOVSP) API

MSF0100 Format:

Offset	Type	Description
0	Char(10)	From job name
10	Char(10)	From job user name
20	Char(6)	From job number
26	Char(16)	From internal job identifier (handle)
42	Char(16)	From internal spooled file identifier (handle)
58	Char(10)	From spooled file name
68	Binary(4)	From spooled file number
72	Char(10)	To output queue name
82	Char(10)	To output queue library name

MSF0200 Format:

Offset	Type	Description
0	Char(10)	From job name
10	Char(10)	From job user name
20	Char(6)	From job number
26	Char(16)	From internal job identifier (handle)
42	Char(16)	From internal spooled file identifier (handle)
58	Char(10)	From spooled file name
68	Binary(4)	From spooled file number
72	Char(10)	To job name
82	Char(10)	To job user name
92	Char(10)	To job number
98	Char(16)	To internal job identifier (handle)
114	Char(16)	To internal spooled file identifier (handle)
130	Char(10)	To spooled file name
140	Binary(4)	To spooled file number

We chose to use the MSPF0100 format, which provides the function of moving the spooled file ahead of all other spooled files on the target output queue. We are reading the source output queue in one order and moving each spooled file to the top of the target output queue, so this has the net effect of reversing the order of the spooled files on the target output queue.

If the order of the spooled files is of importance, we use the MSPF0200 format, which puts the spooled files *after* the target spooled file, thus keeping the original sequence of spooled files.

Restrictions on Moving a Spooled File

There are a number of restrictions you must consider when moving a spooled file. These are:

- You can not move a spooled file that is being held by the HLDJOB SPLFILE(*YES) command.

- A spooled file that is already printing can not be moved.

- You can not move a spooled file to follow a spooled file with an open status.

- You can not move a spooled file to follow a spooled file with a closed status, unless both spooled files are part of the same job.

- You can not move a spooled file to follow a spooled file with a deferred status, unless both spooled files are part of the same job.

- The target output queue must be defined as *FIFO (first in, first out).

- You can not move a spooled file to follow a spooled file that is printing, unless the target spooled file is the last spooled file selected by the writer. The system considers a spooled file to be printing if it is in any of the following status conditions: PND (pending), WTR (at the writer), PRT (printing), SND (being sent), or MSGW (message waiting).

- A spooled file that is at the ready, open, closed, or deferred status is changed to the held status if it is moved to follow a spooled file that is held or saved.

- A spooled file that has a status of held, open, closed, or saved is changed to ready status when it is moved to the top of an output queue.

- A spooled file that has a status of held, open, closed, or saved is changed to ready status when it is moved to follow a spooled file that has a ready status.

PROGRAM APIs FOR ILE

Modular programming has both an upside and a downside. On the upside—small, easily maintainable modules. You don't write programs anymore, you write modules and then tell the compiler to gather (bind) these modules into a program. Maintenance, as well as testing, should be easier when working with small subsections of a program.

There are two ways to gather these modules into a program, bind by reference and bind by copy. If you bind by reference, links between the module and the program are completed when the program is executed, which causes a delay the first time the program is executed. This is very similar to the Original Program Model (OPM).

If you bind by copy, a copy of the module is placed in the program, which means the module will execute as fast as if it were a subroutine. Bind by copy was not an available option in OPM. It's new for ILE.

The downside comes when you make a change to a module that has been bound by copy into more than one program. (We do not recommend that you copy a module into more than one program, but if you do, we're here to help. For more on this topic, see "Service Programs" in Chapter 13.) Unless those programs are recompiled, they will not see the change you made to the module.

For example, suppose Program A is created from Module 1, Module 2, and Module3. Program B is created from Module 2, Module 4, and Module 5. Further, assume that all modules were bound to their respective programs using bind by copy. Now, while running Program A, a user discovers and reports a bug in Module 2. Being the astute programmer that you are, you quickly discover and correct the error in Module 2. You then recreate Program A, which now works correctly. Program B however, still has the old copy of Module 2 and will not work correctly.

DISPLAY MODULE PROGRAMS (DSPMODPGM)

So the problem becomes, how do I know what programs use which modules? The Display Program (DSPPGM) command will list all modules that a program uses, but not all programs that use a given module. In Chapter 11, "Tools for the Toolbox", we have included a utility that does just that. We call it Display Module Programs or DSPMODPGM.

You can refer to Chapter 11, "Display Module Programs," for the complete code to this program. For now, we are going to take a look at the List ILE Program Information (QBNLPGMI) API. This API will list all modules that are contained in a given program. If we run this API over all programs in a given library, we will get a list of all programs and their modules. Like all list APIs, the output is produced into a user space which we then "walk through," retrieving each item in the list (the format name parameter controls the information that is contained in the list). We can then compare each item with our search criteria and display (or print) any that match.

Table 9.22 shows the input requirements to use the API. This is basically the qualified name of the user space, the format name to control the list information, the generic name of the programs to list, and the standard error code data structure. Table 9.23 shows a partial listing of the format of the returned data that we used to create this utility (for a complete listing, refer to the *System Programmer's Interface Reference Manual*, QBKA8402, SC41-8223).

Table 9.22: Required Input Parameters for the List ILE Program Information (QBNLPGMI) API

Parameter	Description	Type	Size
1	User space name	Input	Char(20)
2	Format name	Input	Char(8)
3	ILE Program Name	Input	Char(20)
4	Error data structure	Both	Char(*)

Parameter Definitions

User space name: The name and library of the user space where the requested information is to be placed. The first 10 characters are the name of the user space. The last 10 characters are the name of the library.

Format name: Format name of the system data structure that defines the format of the returned data. Valid format names are:

PGML0100 - Module listing

PGML0200 - Service program information

PGML0300 - Export information

PGML0400 - Import information

PGML0500 - Copyright information

ILE program name: The name of the program that is to be listed. The first 10 characters contain the program name and the last 10 characters contain the library name. The program name can contain *ALL or generic*. This allows us to list all programs in a particular library. If you provide the name of an OPM program, an error will be returned.

Error Code: The standard error code data structure.

Table 9.23: Format PGML0100

Offset	Type	Description
0	Char(10)	Program name
10	Char(10)	Library name
20	Char(10)	Bound module name
30	Char(10)	Bound module library name

Offset	Type	Description
40	Char(10)	Source file name
50	Char(10)	Source file library name
60	Char(10)	Source member name
70	Char(10)	Module attribute
80	Char(13)	Module created date/time

WORKING WITH SERVICE PROGRAMS

If you are using service programs in your applications and you are not using a binder language (see Chapter 13, "Integrated Language Environment (ILE) Concepts") to keep track of changes to the public interface of the service program, you can quickly find yourself in a predicament. Say you've discovered that you made a change to an existing service program that changed the public interface. You now need to know all programs that use this service program so that you can recompile them.

We have included a utility in Chapter 11 that will list all programs that use a given service program. The program performs the same function as DSPMODPGM but for service programs. In fact, it even uses the same, List ILE Program Information (QBNLPGMI) API to produce the list of programs. We simply use a different format name, PGML0200, to get a list of all service programs that the program uses. Table 9.24 shows this output format.

Table 9.24: Format PGML0200

Offset	Type	Description
0	Char(10)	Program name
10	Char(10)	Library name
20	Char(10)	Bound service program name

Offset	Type	Description
30	Char(10)	Bound service program library
40	Char(16)	Service program signature

We also thought it would be useful to show the date and time the program was created. We use the Retrieve Program Information (QCLRPGMI) API to retrieve this information. Like all retrieve APIs, this one returns the information in a variable field, not a user space. Table 9.25 shows the required Input Specifications for this API, while Table 9.26 shows a partial listing of the PGMI0100 format that our utility is using.

Table 9.25: Required Input Parameters for the Retrieve Program Information (QCLRPGMI) API

Parameter	Description	Type	Size
1	Receiver name	Output	Char(*)
2	Receiver length	Input	Binary(4)
3	Format name	Input	Char(8)
4	Qualified program name	Input	Char(20)
5	Error code	Both	Char(*)

Parameter Definitions

Receiver name: The name of the variable that is to contain the results of the call to the API. The amount of information returned is limited by the size of this variable.

Receiver length: The length of the receiver name parameter.

Format name: Format name of the system data structure that defines the format of the returned data. Valid format names are PGMI0100 (Basic OPM or ILE information), PGMI0200 (Basic plus SQL for OPM), or PGMI0300 (ILE program size).

Program name: The name of the program that is to be listed. The first 10 characters contain the program name and the last 10 characters contain the library name.

Error Code: The standard error code data structure.

Table 9.26: Format PGMI0100 (partial)

Offset	Type	Description
0	Binary(4)	Bytes returned
4	Binary(4)	Bytes available
8	Char(10)	Program name
18	Char(10)	Program library
28	Char(10)	Program owner
38	Char(10)	Program attribute
48	Char(13)	Created date/time

DON'T WORRY, BE API!

APIs provide a wide variety of functions not normally available to the RPG programmer. As with all things in life, variety breeds complexity, but that should not deter you from using these valuable tools. If you do your homework and become proficient in using APIs, you become a much better programmer in the process.

This chapter has provided you with some tools, Display Path (DSPPATH) and Move Spooled Files (MOVSPL), that can help you in your everyday tasks. Using DSPPATH improves functions already provided by the operating system. Using MOVSPL provides a way to automate spool file handling. As you become proficient in using APIs, you will generate your own tools. When you do, feel free to contact us. We would love to hear from you.

Chapter 10

Tracking Down Problems

**If none of your programs ever have bugs, you probably do not need to
read this chapter...**

but the fact that you are still reading means you probably are in the same boat as
the rest of us.

No matter how long you have been programming, how smart you are, or how carefully
you code your programs, you are going to make mistakes. We are not stating anything
that you do not already know, and it should not be discouraging to find out that you
are only human.

One of the things that separates good programmers from those who go through their professional lives in mediocrity is how quickly they can find and fix the problems that inevitably occur. The topics covered in this chapter include learning how to debug interactive and batch jobs (OPM only), using journaling as a debugging tool, and how to interpret and change the amount of information written to your job logs.

FINDING DEBUG IN DE PROGRAM

Debug is often the last place a programmer goes when trying to solve a problem in their RPG program. They look at the data and the code until their eyes are bugging out trying to solve the problem before going to that *last* resort.

We are here to tell you that this is the worst possible approach you can take. You need to make Debug your best friend. It should be the *first* step you take when trying to solve a programming problem. It is generally a good idea to place a brand new program under Debug the very first time you run it so you can step through the code and make sure the program is doing what was intended. As a matter of fact, we recommend placing *every* new program that has any degree of complexity under Debug when you first run it. This will allow you to perform the ultimate "desk check" as you step your way through your program.

Have you ever heard the expression "an ounce of prevention is worth a pound of cure?" Nothing could hit closer to home than that old adage as it applies to RPG programming. Solving a problem in a program is usually 10 times harder once the program is in production. This is especially true if the program with the error happens to update database files.

The amount of programming time lost to pride and stubbornness is simply staggering. And, if your excuse has been that you did not know how to use Debug, you are just going to have to find a new one.

DEBUG 101

AS/400 Debug is a process whereby you take a program or programs and place them under a microscope while they run. You can define points in the program where the program must take a break (cleverly called breakpoints), giving you time to examine and change variables within your program while it is running. You may also add, modify, or remove breakpoints, depending upon your needs at the time. You can *step* through the code as the program runs to see its progress. You can even run Debug on OPM (Original Program Model) programs that run in batch, but more an that later in this chapter.

Before we get too carried away, let's start at the beginning.

The first thing you must know about debugging an RPG IV program is that you must tell the system, when you compile the program, that you are want to debug it. The reason for this is that the compiler then keeps a copy of the source within the compiled object. This makes the object much bigger, but it allows you to see program variables, line statements, and so forth.

So, the recommended method of debugging is to compile your programs with the debug option enabled, then test, test, and test some more. When you are ready to put the program into production, compile it one last time with the debug option disabled. If you employ this methodology and have to debug a program while it is in production, you will need to recompile the program before you can run Debug on it.

When compiling RPG IV programs, you first set the debug option using the DBGVIEW parameter on the Create Bound RPG Program (CRTBNDRPG) command. This parameter accepts six possible options. These options are detailed in Table 10.1.

Table 10.1: DBGVIEW Options

Option	Description
*STMNT	Uses the line numbers shown on the compile listing to debug the program. This is the compile default.
*SOURCE	Uses the source member, saved at compile time, to debug the program.
*LIST	Uses the listing view to debug the program.
*COPY	Uses the source view and includes any /COPY statements.
*ALL	Uses the source, listing, and /COPY views to debug the program.
*NONE	Disables all the debug options for the program.

IN DE BEGINNING

Like most things in life, you can make the debugging process as simple or as complicated as you want to make it. But even the most simple Debug functions can offer you a tremendous amount of information and insight into the function of your programs.

When you execute the Start Debug (STRDBG) command on an RPG IV program that has been compiled with the DBGVIEW option enabled (set to anything other than *NONE), the first thing you will see is a screen similar to that shown in Figure 10.1. The Display Module Source panel will show the source for the program. This panel will appear both when you define your initial debug criteria to the system and when you actually run your program under Debug.

Figure 10.1: Display Module Source

```
                      Display Module Source

Program:   LIN001RG       Library:   REMOTE        Module:   LIN001RG
    1      *******************************************************************
    2      *   TO COMPILE:
    3      *     CRTBNDPGM PGM(XXXLIB/LIN001RG)
    4      *******************************************************************
    5      Flin001DS  CF   E               WORKSTN
    6      F                                       SFILE(SFLRECORD:SflRcdNbr)
    7      FCpuCustL1 If    e           k Disk
    8
    9      D GeneralDs       DS
   10      D  InputSize           113    116B 0
   11      D  ListOffset          125    128B 0
   12      D  ListNbr             133    136B 0
   13      D  EntrySize           137    140B 0
   14      D InputDs         DS
   15      D  UserSpace                   20
                                                              More...

Debug . . .

 F3=End program    F6=Add/Clear breakpoint    F10=Step    F11=Display variable
 F12=Resume        F13=Work with module breakpoints       F24=More keys
```

ADDING DE BREAKPOINT

The most common task to perform at this time is to set a breakpoint. The principle reason for this is that breakpoints give the programmer more control over looking at or changing variables as well as performing other debugging functions while the program is still running.

So, once you have started Debug using the Start Debug (STRDBG) command, you will be presented with the source from your module, as seen in Figure 10.1. You set the breakpoint by positioning the cursor on the line of source at which you want to set the breakpoint and then pressing Function Key 6. This will highlight the selected line, indicating where your breakpoint is set.

When you actually run the program, the breakpoint display will appear just before executing the selected line. The breakpoint display will show the module source on the screen, much like that shown in Figure 10.1. All of the Debug function keys available to you while on the Display Module Source display panel are illustrated in Table 10.2. However, far and away the most common task when defining your debug criteria is setting a breakpoint or two and getting out. We will discuss what happens to your program when it is run under Debug later in this chapter, but first let's take a look at the various debugging options that are available.

Table 10.2: Function Keys for Display Module Source Display

Function Key	Name	Description
F1	Help	Provides additional help.
F3	End	Stops the source debugger. If the program was running, the program ends.
F5	Refresh	Update the screen.
F6	Add/Remove Breakpoint	Add a breakpoint on the line at which the cursor is positioned. If a breakpoint already exists on that line, remove it.
F9	Retrieve	Retrieve last command entered on the command line.
F10	Step Over	Process 1 line and show the display module source screen again.
F11	Display Variable	Display the variable at which the cursor is now positioned.

Function Key	Name	Description
F12	Resume	Resume processing. If program is running, continue running until next breakpoint is encountered, or until end of program.
F13	Work with Module Breakpoints	Display the Work with Module breakpoints panel.
F14	Work with Module List	Display the Work with Module list panel
F15	Select View	Display the Select View panel.
F16	Set Debug Options	Display the Set Debug options panel.
F19	Left	Shift the display 40 characters to the left.
F20	Right	Shift the display 40 characters to the right.
F21	Command Line	Display the command entry line.
F22	Step Into	Process 1 line and display the Display Module Source panel again. Will execute call statements and take you into other programs.
F24	More Keys	Display more function keys

When selecting a source statement for your breakpoint, select one that you *know* will be executed. Selecting a statement that does not get executed results in no breakpoint. It is easy to add, change, or remove breakpoints later while the program is running (provided you are at a breakpoint). Also note that the breakpoint event always occurs just *prior* to the execution of the statement where you are adding the breakpoint.

DE CONDITIONAL BREAKPOINT

Sometimes, it is necessary to set what is known as a *conditional* breakpoint. This is a breakpoint that will not cause the program to stop until some condition has been met. Say, for example, the error that you are trying to fix does not occur except when a particular customer record is processed. You would want your program breakpoint to occur only when it had read that particular customer record.

To set a conditional breakpoint, you press F13 from the Display Module Source display panel. A screen similar to the one depicted in Figure 10.2 will be displayed. On the Work with Module Breakpoints display, you use the add option (option 1) to add the breakpoint to the line number that you specify. In addition, you put the condition that must exist before the breakpoint will cause the program to stop in the column headed, appropriately enough, Condition.

Figure 10.2: Work with Module Breakpoints Display

```
                       Work with Module Breakpoints
                                              System:     CPU
    Program   . . . :   LIN001RG         Library  . . . :   REMOTE
      Module . . . :      LIN001RG       Type . . . . . . :   *PGM

    Type options, press Enter.
      1=Add    4=Clear

    Opt     Line          Condition
    1        90           Account = 123

      (No breakpoints exist.)




                                                            Bottom
    Command
    ===>
```

Another wrinkle you might encounter at this time is having a program that is composed of more than one module. If this is so, then you might want to debug more than one module at a time. If you need to debug more than one module, you need the Work with Module List panel (Figure 10.3) that appears when you press F14 from the Display Module Source panel seen in Figure 10.1. From the Work with Module List panel, you can work with all the modules that comprise the program that is being debugged.

Figure 10.3: Work with Module List Display

```
                         Work with Module List
                                                   System:    CPU
Type options, press enter.
   1=Add program    4=Remove program    5=Display module source
   8=Work with module breakpoints

Opt      Program/module      Library        Type
                             *LIBL          *PGM
  _      LIN001RG            REMOTE         *PGM
  _        LIN001RG                         *MODULE      Selected




                                                              Bottom
Command
===>
F3=Exit    F4=Prompt    F5=Refresh    F9=Retrieve    F12=Cancel
```

If you compiled the program using the DBGVIEW(*ALL) option, then you could have different views to work with. Pressing function key 15 from the Display Module Source panel (Figure 10.1) will cause the Select View Display screen depicted in Figure 10.4 to appear. From the Select View Display, you can set which Debug view you want to work with.

Figure 10.4: Select View Display

```
Display Module Source
.............................................................
:                         Select View                      :
:                                                          :
:  Current View . . . :     ILE RPG/400 Source View        :
:                                                          :
:  Type option, press Enter.                               :
:    1=Select                                              :
:                                                          :
:  Opt     View                                            :
:          ILE RPG/400 Source View                         :
:          ILE RPG/400 Listing View                        :
:                                                          :
:                                                          :
:                                                          :
:                                                 Bottom   :
:                                                          :
:  F12=Cancel                                              :
:                                                          :
:.........................................................:
                                                   More...
Debug . . .

 F5=Refresh   F9=Retrieve   F14=Work with module list   F15=Select view
 F16=Set debug options   F19=Left   F20=Right   F22=Step into   F24=More keys
```

Another option that you might want to work with at this time is shown in Figure 10.5. Pressing function key 16 from the Display Module Source panel (Figure 10.1) will cause the Set Debug Options panel to appear. The Set Debug Options panel lets you toggle between update production *YES and *NO.

Figure 10.5: Set Debug Options

```
                         Display Module Source
...........................................................................
:                        Set Debug Options                 :
:                                                           : ********
: Type changes, press Enter.                                :
:                                                           :
: Update production files  . . . . . . . .   Y      Y=Yes, N=No  : ********
:                                                           :
: F12=Cancel                                                : RcdNbr)
:                                                           :
:...........................................................:
     9      D GeneralDs       DS
    10      D   InputSize           113    116B 0
    11      D   ListOffset          125    128B 0
    12      D   ListNbr             133    136B 0
    13      D   EntrySize           137    140B 0
    14      D InputDs         DS
    15      D   UserSpace                   20
                                                              More...
Debug . . .

F5=Refresh    F9=Retrieve    F14=Work with module list    F15=Select view
F16=Set debug options    F19=Left    F20=Right    F22=Step into    F24=More keys
```

If you are not familiar with this concept, read on. When you create a library on the AS/400, the Create library (CRTLIB) command has a parameter called TYPE. This parameter accepts either *TEST or *PROD. Your production libraries should be created with the parameter set to *PROD, while your testing libraries should be set to *TEST. What this type of arrangement gets you is the ability to make absolutely sure that your testing steps do not update production files.

If you set the debug option to update production *NO and then run a program that attempts to update, write, or delete a record in a file that is in a library with type *PROD, the system will not perform the function. Instead it will issue an error message. This is complete protection of your production files! Try it. You might like it.

RUNNING DE PROGRAM

Now that we have covered many of the principle Debug functions, we are ready to call our program. Unfortunately, there is no way to run the program directly from the Display Module Source display panel. You must end the task and then start the program. Press either F12 or F3 to do so. Now, call the program.

When the program reaches the point where the source statement specified in our breakpoint is about to be executed, the breakpoint display appears on our screen. It looks similar to the Display Module Source panel in Figure 10.1.

Most of the options that were available when you started Debug are still available now. However, the source shown in the panel should now be positioned to the first breakpoint that the system encountered when running the program.

DISPLAYING DE VARIABLE

Probably the most common task at this point is to display a variable. You can accomplish this in a variety of ways. The easiest way to display variable contents is to position the cursor on the field in the displayed source and press F11. This will cause the value of the field to be displayed on the line below the Debug entry line. In Figure 10.6, the Display Program Variables display panel shows the result of positioning the cursor on the field STARTLEN, referenced at statement 138, and pressing F11.

Figure 10.6: Display Program Variables

```
Display Module Source

Program:  LIN001RG        Library:   REMOTE        Module:   LIN001RG
   130    C                    EVAL      UserSpace = ('LINESSPACEQTEMP')
   131    C                    EVAL      StartPosit = ListOffset + 1
   132    C                    EVAL      StartLen = EntrySize
   133        *  Retrieve the list by walking through the user space
   134    C                    DO        ListNbr
   135    C                    CALL      'QUSRTVUS'
   136    C                    PARM                    UserSpace
   137    C                    PARM                    StartPosit
   138    C                    PARM                    StartLen
   139    C                    PARM                    CFGD0200
   140    C                    EXSR      GetUsrInfo
   141    C                    EVAL      StartPosit = StartPosit + EntrySize
   142    C                    ENDDO
   143    C                    Exsr      Display
   144    c                    If        *in05 = *ON
                                                              More...
 Debug . . .

 F3=End program     F6=Add/Clear breakpoint    F10=Step    F11=Display variable
 F12=Resume         F13=Work with module breakpoints        F24=More keys
 STARTLEN = 000000130.
```

If you display the value of a data structure, the system will return the values of all subfields in the data structure. This won't fit on a single line, so a new panel is displayed, as shown in Figure 10.7. The Evaluate Expression display panel is used to display multiple program values at once.

Figure 10.7: Evaluate Expression

```
Evaluate Expression

 Previous debug expressions

 > EVAL StartLen
   STARTLEN = 000000130.
 > EVAL GeneralDs
   INPUTSIZE OF GENERALDS = 000000100.
   LISTOFFSET OF GENERALDS = 000000384.
   LISTNBR OF GENERALDS = 000000005.
   ENTRYSIZE OF GENERALDS = 000000130.




                                                                Bottom
 Debug . . .

 F3=Exit    F9=Retrieve    F12=Cancel    F19=Left    F20=Right    F21=Command entry
```

The Debug entry line provides another method of communicating with the debugger. In Table 10.3, we see a table of the Debug Commands you can issue from this line. All of the capabilities provided by the function keys are also available via the Debug entry line. You can enter commands either by typing in the command name, or using the abbreviated version of the command.

Table 10.3: Debug Commands

Command	Abbreviation	Description
ATTR	A	Display the attributes of a variable.
BREAK	BR	Enter breakpoints.
CLEAR	C	Removes breakpoints.

Command	Abbreviation	Description
DISPLAY	DI	Display the names and definitions assigned by using the EQUATE command. Also allows you to display a different module.
EQUATE	EQ	Assign an expression, variable, or debug command to a name for shorthand use.
EVAL	EV	Display or change the value of a variable. Display the value of arrays, expressions, records, or structures.
STEP	S	Run one or more of the statements of the program being debugged.
FIND	F	Find a target line number, string, or text in the current module.
UP	U	Move the source member up the specified number of lines.
DOWN	D	Move the source member down the specified number of lines.
LEFT	L	Move the source member to the left the specified number of lines.
RIGHT	R	Move the source member to the right the specified number of lines.
TOP	T	Position the source member at the first line of source.
BOTTOM	B	Position the source member at the last line.
NEXT	N	Position the view to the next breakpoint in the source module.

Command	Abbreviation	Description
PREVIOUS	P	Position the view to the previous breakpoint in the source module.
HELP	H	Show the online help.

There are a number of commands you can use to position the source module on the screen. UP (or it's incredibly abbreviated version, U) will move the source module up X number of lines. DOWN or (D) will do the opposite. LEFT, RIGHT, TOP, and BOTTOM all do pretty much what you expect.

The FIND (F) command searches through the source module for the designated string or line number. The search begins at the current cursor location. You can add a direction indicator at the end of the command (P for Previous, N for Next), as in FIND FieldName P. Another shortcut you can use is to simply key FIND, with no parameters, and the command will use the same parameters used the last time you ran FIND.

Probably the most interesting and useful of the commands is the EVAL (E) command. This command will allow you to display the contents of a variable, exactly the same as if you had positioned the cursor on a variable field name and pressed F11. If you want to see the hexadecimal value of a field, you would key EVAL FIELDNAME: X . But it does so much more.

You use the EVAL command to change the value of a variable. Let's say that you have a program that is using a field (Index) as an index to an array. The program is blowing up when it tries to use the Index field and you can't tell why. So, you put the program under Debug and place a breakpoint on the line that is causing the error message. When the Display Module Source panel appears, you key "EVAL Index" and see that the field is 0. So now you see how to correct the code so that the Index field can never be 0, but will the program work if the index is set to the correct number? Using the EVAL command, you can set the Index to a valid number, continue the program and see if the rest of your code is correct. You simply enter "EVAL Index = 1" and then press F12 to resume the running of the program. The program will continue with the statement that had the breakpoint with the field Index set to the value of 1 (or whatever number you set it to). This is a very powerful ability for any debugging tool.

Another useful command to be aware of is the STEP command. STEP allows you to walk through a program (or section of code) stopping at each line of code. Each time it stops, it displays the Display Module Source panel, awaiting your command. If you want to stop at every fifth line, you would key STEP 5.

In addition to the number of statements to execute before stopping, the STEP command accepts two reserved words—OVER and INTO. These two reserved words refer to how to count the statements being executed. If you enter the command STEP 5 INTO and one of the lines in the next five statements calls another program, the system will go into that other program and continue counting lines until it has executed (in total) the number of lines indicated on the STEP command. It will then stop (even if it is in the called program) and display the Display Module Source panel. (This is true *only* if the called program also has debug data enabled within it.)

If you enter STEP 5 OVER and one of the lines in the next five statements calls another program, it will still execute the other program, but it will not count any of the lines in the other program. The CALL statement will count as only one line.

USING DEBUG TO DECIPHER I/O PROBLEMS

If your questions or problems involve I/O processing, you may find that running the Display Job (DSPJOB) command is useful while you are at a breakpoint. If you press F21 while on the Display Module Source panel, you will get a command line.

From the command line, key the DSPJOB command and then you will see the familiar Display Job menu of options. If you choose option 14 (Display Open Files, if active), you see all of the files that are open in your job stream.

By pressing a function key, you can see all of the I/O details for each file that is currently open (this includes your display files too!). These details include the file type, the I/O count (how many reads and writes), how the file was opened (e.g., input only, update), the relative record number of the last record read (indicating where the current file pointer is), and whether or not the file was opened with a shared data path.

Depending upon where your breakpoint is set, this information can help you solve a number of problems in your program. If the I/O count looks unusually high, you may be reading records that you did not intend to read. If the file was opened with a shared data path, you may have forgotten to reset your file pointer prior to your first read. When trying to solve data problems, this technique can often help you in your detective work.

DE SMALL PRINT

Source debugging is a powerful tool, but it has some limitations. The most serious of these is its inability to debug batch programs. It's hard to believe that IBM would leave this feature out. Hopefully it will be added by the time this book is printed. If not, this is definitely another *requirement* for your next users' group.

DEBUGGING BATCH JOBS

Now that we have discussed the basics of starting Debug, setting breakpoints, and displaying program variables, it is time to talk about batch jobs. As we stated, to our knowledge, there is currently no way to debug ILE batch programs. But if you still have batch programs written in OPM, you may find this section of the chapter useful.

As you have probably noticed, all of the Debug data we displayed was brought up to the screen. That is great when we are talking about an interactive program, but what do we do when it is a batch program that needs to be diagnosed?

Starting the Service Job

To run Debug on a batch program, you need to use a feature called a *service job*. Before initiating the service job, you need three components that describe the job you are debugging—the job name, the user, and the job number.

Finding this information is easy if the program happens to be at an error message or is already running (does the phrase *in a loop* come to mind?). You can use Work with Active Jobs (WRKACTJOB) or Work with Submitted Jobs (WRKSBMJOB) to find the job in question and then take the option that says "Work with Job." You will find all three parameters you need displayed at the top of the screen, as shown in Figure 10.8.

Figure 10.8: Work with Job Display

```
                         Work with Job
                                            System:    CPU
 Job:    ATBRPT         User:    QPGMR        Number:   541492

 Select one of the following:

      1. Display job status attributes
      2. Display job definition attributes
      3. Display job run attributes, if active
      4. Work with spooled files

     10. Display job log, if active or on job queue
     11. Display call stack, if active
     12. Work with locks, if active
     13. Display library list, if active
     14. Display open files, if active
     15. Display file overrides, if active
     16. Display commitment control status, if active
                                                        More...
 Selection or command
 ===>

 F3=Exit    F4=Prompt    F9=Retrieve    F12=Cancel
```

If the job is already running, you need to put the job on hold. This is easily accomplished while you are in the Work with Active Jobs (WRKACTJOB) or Work with Submitted Jobs (WRKSBMJOB) commands by simply following the prompts on the screen.

On the other hand, if the job you want to debug is not already running, you need to go about it a little differently. You do not want the job to begin running until you have initiated the service job.

Place the job queue on hold using the Hold Job Queue (HLDJOBQ) command and then submit the job. Placing the job queue on hold does not stop existing programs from running, but it will keep new jobs in the queue from being initiated.

The next step is to submit your job. You can then use the Work with Submitted Jobs (WRKSBMJOB) command to get the job identification parameters so you can start the service job.

By now, you should have written the job name, user, and number down. Key in:

STRSRVJOB

and press F4. You should see a screen that looks like Figure 10.9.

Figure 10.9: Starting a Service Job

```
                       Start Service Job (STRSRVJOB)
Type choices, press Enter.
Job name . . . . . . . . . . . . JOB          atbrpt
  User . . . . . . . . . . . .                qpgmr
  Number . . . . . . . . . . .                541492
                                                           Bottom
F3=Exit   F4=Prompt   F5=Refresh   F10=Additional parameters   F12=Cancel
F13=How to use this display        F24=More keys
```

You may want to use a shortcut by keying the Start Service Job (STRSRVJOB) command while you are on the Work with Job display. The parameters you need to run the STRSRVJOB command are already at the top of your screen and may be entered right to left. For example, if you are at the display seen in Figure 10.8, and you want to start your service job, key:

STRSRVJOB 541492/QPGMR/ATBRPT

Using this method, you begin your service job from the command line on the Work with Job display. Let's move on to the next step.

Starting Debug on the Batch Job

Now that you have started the service job, you need to put the program into Debug. You may now use the Start Debug (STRDBG) command just as if you are putting an interactive program into Debug, but the system will not let you add your breakpoints until the job actually begins.

It is time to release the job queue using the Release Job Queue (RLSJOBQ) command. The system sends a break message when your job is ready to begin. The message looks something like that displayed in Figure 10.10.

Figure 10.10: The Start Serviced Job Display

```
                       Start Serviced Job
                                                System:    CPU
  Job:   ATBRPT          User:   QPGMR        Number:   541580

  The serviced job has been released from the job queue.  Press Enter to
  start the job or F10 to enter debug commands for that job.






  Press Enter to continue.

  F10=Command entry
  (C) COPYRIGHT IBM CORP. 1980, 1993.
```

Defining Your Breakpoints

At this point, you must key F10 to get to a command entry screen. Your program is in Debug, but you have not told the system where you want it to break. To do that, use the Add Breakpoint (ADDBKP) or Add Trace (ADDTRC) functions to define where you want your program to stop, just as you would if debugging an interactive OPM job.

Perform the rest of the Debug functions as if the program is an interactive OPM program. That is all there is to it! When the job is complete, you get another break message informing you that the job being serviced has ended (do not confuse this with ending the service job).

Once the message has been delivered, you need to end both Debug and the service job. This can be accomplished by using End Debug (ENDDBG) and End Service Job (ENDSRVJOB) accordingly. Failure to perform these cleanup functions could result in some rather unintentional and undesirable results later in your session.

JOURNALING AS A DEBUG TOOL

Every once in a while, we hear about this data file that is mysteriously changing by itself. There seems to be no rhyme or reason to it. And, because 24 different programs in 7 different libraries are used to update this file, tracking down this anomaly is no small task. But wait! There is hope. You can use journaling to narrow down your search for the culprit.

Journaling is a process that, when employed, records changes made to a physical file in an object called (appropriately enough) a *journal receiver*. These changes are recorded as journal entries, and are much like the journal entries you would find in a general ledger. The purpose of each is the same—record a path that may be followed if you ever have to go back.

Generally speaking, journaling is used for automatic error recovery and is necessary if you use commitment control. But, for our purposes, we use it to help us track down the source of our wayward data.

Before you get too far into this subject, be aware that this technique can often take quite a bit of disk space. Depending upon how much activity occurs involving the file in question, and how long it is between the intermittent data error you are looking for, the journal of file changes can get quite large. The journal does not only record what has changed in the record, but, in fact, copies the entire record that is changed as well as recording the who, when, and where of the change. You obviously incur additional I/O while journaling is active, which may impact overall system performance. Like most things in life, you need to determine whether the potential benefits outweigh the cost.

Journaling 101

To perform journaling, you need to concern yourself with two principle components, the journal receiver and the journal itself. On the AS/400, it is the journal receiver that actually holds the journal entries (changes to the file, in our case). The journal itself is more like a directory of which file is being journaled, which receivers exist in the journal, and a variety of other information that describes the journal itself. Think of the journal as the header file when you have a system that has a header/detail record relationship (where the receiver is the detail record).

You need to create the journal receiver and then the journal. In the past, it was up to the programmers and operators to maintain the journal receivers. Failure to do so results in a situation where disk space gets gobbled up rapidly.

With the announcement of V3R1 came an improvement to the Create Journal (CRTJRN) command. Now you can elect to have the journal receivers managed by the system itself. If you specify a threshold size when the journal receiver is created, and use the Manage Receiver (MNGRCV) parameter when the journal is created, the system cleans up your journal receivers for you. The operating system checks to see if your receiver has reached its threshold size at system IPL time. If the threshold is reached, the system detaches the active receiver from the journal and automatically creates and attaches a new receiver in its place. Once this action has been performed, the freshly deactivated journal may be saved (if desired) and deleted from the system to free up valuable disk space.

Before creating the journal, we must first create the receiver that will initially contain our journal entries. In the first example, we create a journal receiver called CUSTRCV in a library called TESTLIB. This is done by keying the following command:

```
CRTJRNRCV JRNRCV(TESTLIB/CUSTRCV)
```

We then create a journal named CUSTJRN in library TESTLIB by keying the following command:

```
CRTJRN JRN(TESTLIB/CUSTJRN) JRNRCV(TESTLIB/CUSTRCV)
```

Note that we have indicated in the Create Journal (CRTJRN) command the name of the initial receiver that is used to store our journal entries.

After those two simple commands, you are ready for your detective work. All you do to activate journaling is to run the Start Journal Physical File (STRJRNPF) command. To begin journaling our file named CUSTOMER in library TESTLIB, we simply key:

```
STRJRNPF FILE(TESTLIB/CUSTOMER) JRN(CUSTJRN)
```

Now that journaling is active, our journal records everything that happens to our CUSTOMER file. That includes every time the file is opened, closed, or saved. Every time a record is written, deleted, or updated. Every time the file is touched!

Reading the Journaling Results

Anytime we want to see all of the recorded journal entries for our CUSTOMER file, we key the following command:

```
DSPJRN JRN(TESTLIB/CUSTJRN)
```

A display similar to that in Figure 10.11 appears on screen. For the purposes of our example, though, we see a little too much information. We do not really care when the file was opened, closed, or saved. We are more interested in knowing who, what, and when a program is updating our file. Thankfully, the Display Journal (DSPJRN) command allows us to filter out the journal entries we do not want to see.

Figure 10.11: Output from the Display Journal Entry (DSPJRN) Command

```
Display Journal Entries

Journal  . . . . . . . :   CUSTJRN          Library  . . . . . . :     TESTLIB

Type options, press Enter.
  5=Display entire entry


Opt     Sequence   Code   Type   Object     Library    Job          Time
               5    R     PT     CUSTOMER   TESTLIB    DEVELOP1     14:33:57
               8    R     PT     CUSTOMER   TESTLIB    DEVELOP1     14:34:10
              11    R     UP     CUSTOMER   TESTLIB    DEVELOP1     14:35:05
              14    R     UP     CUSTOMER   TESTLIB    DEVELOP1     14:36:57
              19    R     PT     CUSTOMER   TESTLIB    DEVELOP2     14:46:26
              22    R     PT     CUSTOMER   TESTLIB    DEVELOP2     14:47:34
              25    R     PT     CUSTOMER   TESTLIB    DEVELOP1     14:49:11
              28    R     PT     CUSTOMER   TESTLIB    DEVELOP2     14:50:33
              32    R     DL     CUSTOMER   TESTLIB    DEVELOP2     14:51:03
              35    R     PT     CUSTOMER   TESTLIB    DEVELOP1     14:51:28



 F3=Exit    F12=Cancel
```

To see only journal entries where a record was changed, key the following command:

```
DSPJRN JRN(TESTLIB/CUSTJRN) JRNCDE((R))
```

The output from the Display Journal (DSPJRN) command is a screen similar to the one in Figure 10.11. Note that all entries under the Code heading are an R, indicating that we are looking at journal entries where a record has been changed. Under the Type heading, you see codes specifying the type of update that was performed. PT indicates that a record was added or posted, UP indicates an update, DL indicates where a record was deleted, and so on. You can place the cursor on the Type field and press HELP to get a more complete list of the possible codes.

If you see an entry that piques your interest, you can key a 5 in front of that entry and press Enter to see a more detailed accounting of the journal entry. You are presented with a display that is similar to Figure 10.12.

Figure 10.12: Entry-specific Data Displayed with the Display Journal (DSPJRN) Command

```
                          Display Journal Entry

 Object . . . . . . . :   CUSTOMER       Library . . . . . . :   TESTLIB
 Member . . . . . . . :   CUSTOMER       Sequence . . . . . . :   11
 Code . . . . . . . . :   R  - Operation on specific record
 Type . . . . . . . . :   UP - Update, after-image

             Entry specific data
 Column       *...+....1....+....2....+....3....+....4....+....5
 00001        '0000000004Appleton, Josephine                    '
 00051        '2368 North Avenue            San Diego           '
 00101        '            CA92126000000010'



                                                           Bottom
 Press Enter to continue.

 F3=Exit   F6=Display only entry specific data
 F10=Display only entry details   F12=Cancel   F24=More keys
```

The entry-specific data that is displayed may look scrambled if packed data exists in the record. If you want your "detective" to tell you who, what, when, and where, simply press F10 (Display only entry details). You are presented with a display similar to Figure 10.13, which tells you all of the above.

Figure 10.13: Entry Details Displayed via the Display Journal (DSPJRN) Command

```
                          Display Journal Entry Details

     Journal  . . . . . . :   CUSTJRN       Library  . . . . . . :   TESTLIB
     Sequence . . . . . . :   11

     Code . . . . . . . . :   R  - Operation on specific record
     Type . . . . . . . . :   UP - Update, after-image

     Object . . . . . . . :   CUSTOMER      Library  . . . . . . :   TESTLIB
     Member . . . . . . . :   CUSTOMER      Flag . . . . . . . . :   0
     Date . . . . . . . . :   05/31/95      Time . . . . . . . . :   14:35:05
     Count/RRN  . . . . . :   5             Program  . . . . . . :   MNTCUST

     Job  . . . . . . . . :   600955/CPUPGMR/DEVELOP1
     User profile . . . . :   CPUPGMR       Ref Constraint . . . :   No
     Commit cycle ID  . . :   0             Trigger  . . . . . . :   No



     Press Enter to continue.

     F3=Exit    F10=Display entry    F12=Cancel    F14=Display previous entry
     F15=Display only entry specific data
```

It is entirely possible that your journal contains too many entries to make this particular method practical, or that the data you are looking for is contained in a packed field. If either of these situations is the case, you may want to display the information to an outfile. You could then code an RPG program that processes the outfile and, from there, narrow down your search.

When displaying a journal to an outfile, the Display Journal (DSPJRN) command puts the first 100 bytes per record of your data into a single field that is a default length of 100 bytes. If you need to see more than the first 100 bytes of your file (we need 126 bytes in our CUSTOMER file example), use the Entry Data Length (ENTDTALEN) parameter of the Display Journal (DSPJRN) command or your data is truncated automatically.

To send our CUSTOMER file journal entries to an outfile named JOURNOUT in library TESTLIB, key:

```
DSPJRN JRN(TESTLIB/CUSTJRN) JRNCDE((R)) OUTPUT(*OUTFILE)
OUTFILE(TESTLIB/JOURNOUT) ENTDTALEN(126)
```

The *after* picture of the complete record is stored in a single field named JOESD (Journal Entry Specific Data). We could use the substring function of QRYDTA to parse out the data we are looking for. But we have found that looking at individual fields in the after picture is easier if you use an RPG program.

We do this by moving the JOESD field to an external data structure of the same name as the file being journaled. For the example in Figure 10.14, we simply use our CUSTOMER physical file as an external data structure within our program. We did not code a File Specification for the customer file because our program uses the description of the customer file and not the actual file itself.

Figure 10.14: RPG Code to Process a Display Journal (DSPJRN) Outfile

```
FFilename++IPEASFRlen+LKlen+AIDevice+.Keywords++++++++++++++++++++++++++Comments++++++
FJOURNOUT  IF   E              DISK


DName++++++++++++ETDsFrom+++To/L+++IDc.Keywords++++++++++++++++++++++++++Comments++++++
D OUTFMT        E DS                   EXTNAME(CUSTOMER)


CL0N01Factor1++++++Opcode&ExtFactor2++++++Result++++++++Len++D+HiLoEq....Comments+
C                   READ     JOURNOUT                              50
C       *IN50       IFEQ     *OFF
C                   MOVEL    JOESD         OUTFMT
C                   ENDIF
```

The RPG program in Figure 10.14 could be used to read and interpret the data from the journal entries. Our example is incomplete in that you would probably want to perform some sort of selective process to narrow down your search and then either send the data to a database file or to the printer.

Changing Receivers

Receivers can have voracious appetites. If left alone, one receiver can easily eat up your disk space without even belching. You can only curb its appetite by killing it. Before you can kill it (by deleting the journal receiver), you must detach it from the journal. To do so, issue the following command:

```
CHGJRN JRN(CUSTJRN) JRNRCV(*GEN)
```

This command detaches the Current Receiver (CUSTRCV), creates a new journal receiver, and attaches the new receiver to the journal. The name of the new receiver is the name of the old receiver with a four-digit sequence number attached to the end of the name. In our example, the name of the new receiver is CUSTRC0001. Notice that the sequence number automatically replaces the last digit of the receiver name because the original receiver name was seven characters long. If you prefer, make up your own name for the new receiver and enter it instead of *GEN.

You are now free to kill the beast and get back all of the storage it ate. Issue the command:

```
DLTJRNRCV RCV(TESTLIB/CUSTRCV)
```

If you have not saved the receiver, you get the error message:

```
CPA7025 - Receiver CUSTRCV in TESTLIB never fully saved. (I
C).
```

Reply to the message with an I to ignore it, and the receiver is deleted.

Remember to Clean Up Your Mess

Once you have isolated your problem, you need to end journaling and clean up your disk. Before you can delete the journal, you must tell the system to stop journaling the file. You do that by issuing the command:

```
ENDJRNPF FILE(TESTLIB/CUSTOMER)
```

You can then delete the journal by issuing the command:

```
DLTJRN JRN(TESTLIB/CUSTJRN)
```

If you have created other receivers, do not forget to delete them.

JOB LOGS AND PROBLEM DETERMINATION

Job streams can get incredibly long and complex. Tracking down problems can become very difficult when dealing with these types of jobs. Sometimes your problem is hidden, and solving it is mostly a matter of figuring out how to retrieve more information from your system than is currently being offered. That is where the job log comes in.

Every job has a job log. If you are signed on and running an interactive session, your job log can keep track of the commands you are running, the messages you get, and the commands that are run within the CL programs you call. The amount of information written to your job log is generally controlled by the job description you are currently running (more on this later in the chapter when we discuss logging levels).

When you are in an interactive session, your job log is maintained while your session is active and then is generally deleted when you sign off (depending upon how your system is configured and the parameters specified when running the Signoff command). A batch job has its own job log that can be seen via the Work with Submitted Jobs (WRKSBMJOB) command when you choose the option to review spooled files.

The job log can be the key to solving a problem that may not result in a visible error message. To see what is in your own job log, simply key Display Job Log (DSPJOBLOG) and press Enter, as we have done in Figure 10.15. Notice that you can display additional detail by pressing F10 to see a screen similar to that in Figure 10.16. You are probably already familiar with these displays because they are accessible from so many other commands like Work with Submitted Jobs (WRKSBMJOB), Work with Active Jobs (WRKACTJOB), and Display Job (DSPJOB).

Figure 10.15: Output from the Display Job Log (DSPJOBLOG) Command

```
                        Display Job Log
                                           System:   CPU
 Job . . :    WORKSTN1      User . . :   QPGMR    Number . . . :   885343

 3>> dspjoblog




                                                           Bottom
 Press Enter to continue.

 F3=Exit     F5=Refresh    F10=Display detailed messages    F12=Cancel
 F17=Top     F18=Bottom
```

Figure 10.16: Detailed Messages Displayed from the Display Job Log
(DSPJOBLOG) Command

```
                        Display All Messages
                                           System:   CPU
 Job . . :    WORKSTN1      User . . :   QPGMR    Number . . . :   885343

      QINTER in QSYS. Job entered system on 08/26/95 at 07:38:32.
  > /*       */


 3 > DSPJOBLOG
 3 > CHGJOB
 3 > dspjoblog
 3 > wrkactjob
 3 > wrksbmjob
 3 > SAVLIB LIB(TEST)
 3 > DSPJOBLOG
 3 > wrkactjob
 5 > wrkoutq
 3>> dspjoblog
                                                           Bottom
 Press Enter to continue.

 F3=Exit    F5=Refresh    F12=Cancel    F17=Top    F18=Bottom
```

The Display Detailed Messages screen (displayed by pressing F10 on the Display Job

level is also displayed directly preceding each command. The invocation level tells you how deeply nested a command is within a job.

You can also use the DSPJOBLOG command to look at job logs of other users or jobs other than that of your current session (depending upon your security configuration) by specifying additional parameters. You can see the parameters when you press F4 after keying the command.

How Much Information is Being Recorded in My Job Log?

The level of detail recorded in your job log is primarily a function of your message logging level and whether or not your job is recording CL program commands. Most systems are configured to record relatively little information because there is a performance hit that occurs when all commands and messages are being recorded.

Finding out how much information currently is being recorded in your job log is simple. Just run the Display Job (DSPJOB) command and choose the option to Display Job Definition Attributes. You should see a display similar to Figure 10.17.

Figure 10.17: Determining Message and CL Program Command Logging Levels

```
                    Display Job Definition Attributes
                                             System:    CPU
   Job:    WORKSTN1       User:   QPGMR       Number:   885343

   Job description . . . . . . . . . . . . . . . . . :   JOBDESC
     Library . . . . . . . . . . . . . . . . . . . . :   QGPL
   Job queue . . . . . . . . . . . . . . . . . . . . :
     Library . . . . . . . . . . . . . . . . . . . . :
   Job priority (on job queue) . . . . . . . . . . . :
   Output priority (on output queue) . . . . . . . . :   5
   End severity  . . . . . . . . . . . . . . . . . . :   30
   Message logging:
     Level . . . . . . . . . . . . . . . . . . . . . :   4
     Severity  . . . . . . . . . . . . . . . . . . . :   0
     Text  . . . . . . . . . . . . . . . . . . . . . :   *SECLVL
   Log CL program commands . . . . . . . . . . . . . :   *NO
   Printer device  . . . . . . . . . . . . . . . . . :   NOPRINT
   Default output queue  . . . . . . . . . . . . . . :   NOPRINT
     Library . . . . . . . . . . . . . . . . . . . . :   QGPL
                                                            More...
   Press Enter to continue.

   F3=Exit    F5=Refresh    F12=Cancel    F16=Job menu
```

As we mentioned before, the information displayed here is a byproduct of the job description (in this case the JOBDESC job description in library QGPL). As is the case with most things on the AS/400, these parameters may be overridden. Our areas of interest for the purposes of this topic are whether or not your job records CL program commands and what the message logging level settings for your jobs happen to be.

Logging Commands within CL Programs

If your job has been defined to log CL program commands, commands within CL programs are recorded in your job log when they are encountered. This is handy because it establishes an audit trail in your job log similar to that of the trace feature of Debug.

Message Logging

The message logging settings are based on three principle components—the message logging level, message severity, and message text level. The relationship of the three components determines which messages to filter from the job log and which ones to leave in.

Parameter Definitions:

Message logging level: This parameter is used to tell the system how severe a message should be before it is logged into your job log. The possible values are 0 through 4.

0 - No messages are logged.

1 - Job start, completion, and completion status messages are logged. Also, all messages with a severity level greater than or equal to that indicated in the message severity parameter.

2 - All information recorded at level 1 plus any commands keyed or from within a CL program that result in a message with a severity level greater than or equal to that indicated in the message severity parameter.

3 - All information recorded at level 2, plus any commands keyed or called from within a CL program.

4 - All information recorded at level 3, plus any trace messages as well.

Message severity: This parameter is used in conjunction with the previous message logging level parameter to indicate how severe an error should be before it is logged into the job log.

Message text level: This parameter is used to indicate how much data should be recorded in the job log when an error occurs that meets the criteria specified with the two prior parameters. These are:

*MSG   Only the message text of the error is recorded.

*SECLVL   The message text and the help text associated with the error are recorded in the job log.

*NOLIST   A job log is not produced unless the job ends abnormally. If a job log is created, the message text and the associated help text are recorded in the job log.

Changing Job Logging Levels

The logging level of a job may be changed on a temporary or permanent basis depending upon your needs. If you want to change the logging level of your interactive session so it will record the most information possible, key:

```
CHGJOB LOG(4 0 *SECLVL) LOGCLPGM(*YES)
```

On the other hand, you can change the logging level permanently by changing the level set in the job description. To find out which job description you are running under, you can use the Display Job (DSPJOB) command, as in Figure 10.17.

Be aware that changing the job description to record more information in the job log affects the jobs of anyone who is running under the job description. System performance ultimately is affected. Obviously, system overhead is required to log additional information. On the other hand, if your system is reasonably stable, you may want to reduce your default logging levels to help enhance performance.

If your desire is for the system to record more information so you can track down problems easier, increasing the logging levels may help. You could change a job description named JOBDESC in QGPL to record the maximum information, by keying:

```
CHGJOBD JOBD(QGPL/JOBDESC) LOG(4 0 *SECLVL) LOGCLPGM(*YES)
```

Another place where you may want to change your job logging levels is with a submitted job. You can actually change them with the Submit Job (SBMJOB) command itself. To submit a job calling program XXX with the maximum logging level, key:

```
SBMJOB CMD(CALL PGM(XXX)) LOG(4 0 *SECLVL) LOGCLPGM(*YES)
```

Job logs for interactive sessions disappear when a user signs off using the default parameters of the Signoff command. The LOG parameter of the Signoff command is usually set to default to *NOLIST, which tells the system that the session job log is not needed after a user signs off. Changing the LOG parameter to *LIST causes the job log to be spooled to the printer.

Unfortunately, it is difficult to train many operators to remember to change the sign-off parameters if they had problems during their session. Consequently, the problems encountered during the session are lost forever. One solution to this problem is to change the default for the Signoff command. But this generates job logs for sessions where no problems are encountered, as well as those sessions with problems.

Perhaps a more sensible solution to this problem is a very useful program found in the *OS/400 Work Management Guide* (SC41-3306-00). The program (Figure 10.18) allows you to set up an initial menu program that only keeps the job logs if errors are encountered in the session. We find this to be a very useful program and well worth publishing again.

Figure 10.18: CL Menu Program to Help Manage Job Logs

```
PGM
           DCLF MENU
           DCL &SIGNOFFOPT TYPE(*CHAR) LEN(7)
              VALUE(*NOLIST)
               .
               .
               .
           MONMSG MSG(CPF0000) EXEC(GOTO ERROR)
PROMPT:    SNDRCVF RCDFMT(PROMPT)
           CHGVAR &IN41 '0'
               .
               .
               .
           IF (&OPTION *EQ '90'} SIGNOFF
              LOG(&SIGNOFFOPT)
               .
               .
               .
           GOTO PROMPT
ERROR:     CHGVAR &SIGNOFFOPT '*LIST'
           CHGVAR &IN41 '1'
           GOTO PROMPT
           ENDPGM
```

SOLUTIONS ARE BEST FOUND BY THOSE WHO KNOW HOW TO LOOK FOR THEM

It seems painfully obvious, but it is a constant surprise to us how many programmers fail to learn how to use the tools that are at their disposal. Programming is a lot more that just learning a programming language and writing code.

The best programmers are those who know how to use all of the tools in the toolbox. This includes the utilities that are shipped as part of the OS/400 operating system, the programming tools in this book, and the tools that are found within QUSRTOOL. The QUSRTOOL library was sent with the AS/400 operating system for all releases prior to V3R1 (when it became a product available for purchase) and should be required reading for AS/400 RPG programmers.

Take the time to learn how to use all of the tools at hand, and you just may become a master in your trade.

Chapter 11

Tools for the Toolbox

This chapter includes some of our favorite AS/400 utilities that have been developed over the years. We hope that you find them as useful as we have.

We dedicate this chapter to explaining and detailing eight of our favorite programmer utilities (Table 11.1). We think that these tools make our job easier and are hopeful that others will find this to be the case as well.

Table 11.1: A Summary of Tools for the Toolbox

Command	Description
DSPPTH	The Display Path command is designed to help you instantly find all of the various keyed access paths that exist for a specific physical file. Specify the name and library of the physical file and a display is presented that shows all of the various access paths that currently exist over the file. The utility displays the number of logical views that exist over the file and the keyed access path of each.
DSPFLD	The Display Field command gives you an instant, online look at all of the fields in a physical or logical file. The record length, number of fields, key fields, and file type are identified as well as detail information on each field. The field-level detail includes field name, buffer positions, description text, size, and data type.
RGZPFFLTR	The Reorganize Physical File Filter command is designed to free up space on your system that is occupied by deleted records. The utility looks at all physical files on your system and automatically runs the Reorganize Physical File Member (RGZPFM) command on any file where the percentage of deleted records in the file exceeds the threshold percentage you set when you run the RGZPFFLTR command.
FNDDSPLF	The Find Displaced Logical Files utility is designed to help you find logical files that do not reside in the same library as the physical file(s) they are over. This condition has the potential to be dangerous, particularly when libraries are saved or restored.
WRKOBJREF	The Work with Object Reference command is designed to allow you to display all references to a specified object in an online display. Some object types that may be displayed are files, programs, and data areas. If the object type happens to be a physical file, references to the logical files over it may be displayed as well.

Command	Description
SERPGMUSAG	The Service Program Usage command is a tool designed to help you manage programs written under the Integrated Language Environment (ILE). It is designed to help you identify those programs which were compiled referencing a specific service program.
MODUSAG	The Module Usage command is another ILE tool that will help you to identify which programs were compiled referencing a particular module (modules were formerly known as programs in the Original Program Model or OPM).
WRKFLD	The Work with Fields command will help you to identify fields in your system and their characteristics (i.e., field size, decimal positions, or name). It was originally designed to help programmers identify where date fields were being used in their systems to plan for the 21st century conversions.

THE DISPLAY PATH COMMAND

When you sit down to write a new program on the AS/400, one of the first steps is to determine which paths are available for the data you need to process. To find the existing data paths that are available over a physical file on the AS/400, you generally perform the following steps:

1. Run the Display Database Relations (DSPDBR) command over the physical file in question.

2. Write down the file and library names of each logical file found on the DSPDBR display.

3. Run the Display File Description (DSPFD) command over each logical file to see if the data path you need already exists.

These three steps can be time-consuming and cut into your productivity as a programmer. Some creative programmers have developed tools that perform these steps automatically and save much of the time required. These tools write the results of the Display Database Relations (DSPDBR) command to an *outfile* and then either print them or bring them up on a display. Our Display Path (DSPPTH) command, however, goes one step further by using the system APIs discussed in Chapter 9, bringing the information to the screen much more quickly.

The Display Path (DSPPTH) command output looks like the example in Figure 11.1. The path for the physical file is listed first. Key fields and sequence (ascending or descending) are shown, followed by any select omit statements used. Then the path information is listed for each logical file built over the physical (even if the logical file is built in a different library).

Figure 11.1: Output from the Display Path (DSPPTH) Command

```
                           Display Access Paths

    Physical File . . . . . . . . .:   CUST        Number of logicals. . . . .:   0014
    Library . . . . . . . . . . .:   *LIBL

    Library   File       Format     Key Field Seq Select/Omit Values
    TESTLIB   CUST       CUSREC     CUSNUM      A CUSTOMER NUMBER

    TESTLIB   CUSBYCLS   CUSREC     CUSCLS      A FINANCIAL CLASS

    TESTLIB   CUSBYNAM   CUSREC     CUSNAM      A CUSTOMER NAME
                                    CUSDLT      O EQ '*'

    PRODLIB   CUSBYCRD   CUSREC     CUSCRD      A CREDIT LIMIT
                                    CUSNAM      A CUSTOMER NAME
                                    CUSDLT      O EQ '*'

    PRODLIB   CUSBYPMT   CUSREC     CUSPMT      A DATE OF LAST PAYMENT
                                                                        More...



       F3=Exit       F12=Previous
```

As you can see from the preceding example, the various access paths for a file are found easily using the DSPPTH utility. Three components that make up this utility: the Display Path (DSPPTH) command in Figure 11.2, the DSPPTHDS display file in Figure 11.3, and the DSPPTHRG RPG program in Figure 11.4.

Figure 11.2: Source for the Display Path (DSPPTH) Command

```
/*================================================================*/
/* To compile:                                                    */
/*                                                                */
/*          CRTCMD      CMD(XXX/DSPPTH) PGM(XXX/FIG1104RG)      */
/*                      SRCMBR(FIG1102CM)                          */
/*                                                                */
/*================================================================*/
          CMD         PROMPT('DISPLAY ACCESS PATH')
          PARM        KWD(FILE) TYPE(NAME1) MIN(1) PROMPT('File +
                      Name:')
NAME1:    QUAL        TYPE(*NAME) LEN(10)
          QUAL        TYPE(*CHAR) LEN(10) DFT(*LIBL) SPCVAL((' ' +
                      *LIBL)) CHOICE('Name, *LIBL') +
                      PROMPT('Library Name:')
```

Figure 11.3: Source for the FIG1103DS Display File

```
     **********************************************************************
     *   TO COMPILE:
     *      CRTDSPF FILE(XXXLIB/FIG1103DS)
     **********************************************************************
     AAN01N02N03T.Name++++++RLen++TDpBLinPosFunctions+++++++++++++++++++++++++++
     A                                        CF03    CF12
     A            R SFLRCD                     SFL
     A              SFLIBRARY    10A  O  7  2
     A              SFFILENAME   10A  O  7 13
     A              SFKEYFIELD   10A  O  7 35
     A              SFFORMAT     10A  O  7 24
     A              SFASENDDEC    1   O  7 46
     A              SFTEXT       32   O  7 48
     A 59                                      DSPATR(HI)
     A            R SFLCTL                     SFLCTL(SFLRCD)
     A                                         SFLSIZ(0024)  SFLPAG(0012)
     A                                         OVERLAY
     A 21                                       SFLDSP
     A                                         SFLDSPCTL
     A 53                                       SFLEND(*MORE)
     A                                       1 29'Display Access Paths' DSPATR(HI)
     A                                       3  2'Physical File . . . . . . . . .:'
     A              OUTFILE      10A  O    3 35DSPATR(HI)
     A                                       4  2'Library . . . . . . . . . . .:'
     A              OUTLIBRARY   10A  O    4 35DSPATR(HI)
     A                                       6  2'Library  '     DSPATR(HI)
     A                                       6 13'File     '     DSPATR(HI)
     A                                       6 35'Key Field'     DSPATR(HI)
     A                                       6 49'Select/Omit Values'  DSPATR(HI)
     A                                       6 24'Format'        DSPATR(HI)
     A                                       6 45'Seq'           DSPATR(HI)
     A                                       3 47'Number of logicals. . . . .:'
     A              NBRLOGICS     4  00    3 77DSPATR(HI)
     A            R FORMAT1
     A                                      23  4'F3=Exit'    COLOR(BLU)
     A                                      23 18'F12=Previous'  COLOR(BLU)
```

Figure 11.4: Source for the FIG1104RG RPG Program

```
      ******************************************************************
      *   TO COMPILE:
      *     CRTBNDRPG PGM(XXXLIB/FIG1104RG)
      ******************************************************************
     FFilename++IPEASFRlen+LKlen+AIDevice+.Keywords+++++++++++++++++++++++++++Comments++++++
     FFig1103Ds CF   E             WORKSTN
     F                                         SFILE(SFLRCD:RelRecNbr)

     DName+++++++++++ETDsFrom+++To/L+++IDc.Keywords+++++++++++++++++++++++++++Comments++++++
     D AR              S              1    DIM(4096)
     D A2              S              1    DIM(28)
     D ARYF            S             10    DIM(1000)
     D ARYT            S             40    DIM(1000)
     D SaveStart       S              9B 0
     D SaveLen         S              9B 0
     D OutFile         S             10
     D OutLibrary      S             10
     D First           S              1
     D ObjFileFmt      S              8
     D ObjectType      S             10
     D LstOutFmt       S              8
     D Ignore          S             10
     D MessageFil      S             20
     D MessageTyp      S             10
     D MessageQue      S             10
     D FileFmt         S              8
     D RecordFmt       S             10
     D OverRide        S              1
     D System          S             10
     D FmtType         S             10
     D ListFormat      S             10
     D TestType        S              1
     D SpaceAttr       S             10
     D SpaceValue      S              1
     D SpaceText       S             50
     D SpaceAuth       S             10    INZ('*CHANGE')
     D SpaceReplc      S             10    INZ('*YES')
     D C               S              4 0
     D S               S              4 0
     D I               S              4 0
     D I1              S              4 0
     D I2              S              4 0
     D B               S              4 0
     D RelRecNbr       S              4 0
     D SfCompare       S              2
     D SfRule          S              1
     D SfValue         S             28
     D SFileLib        S             20
     D RFileLib        S             20
     D ObjReceivr      S            100
     D StartPosit      S              9B 0
     D StartLen        S              9B 0
     D ReceiveLen      S              9B 0
     D MessageKey      S              9B 0
     D MsgDtaLen       S              9B 0
     D MsgQueNbr       S              9B 0
     D FilStartP       S              9B 0
     D FilStartL       S              9B 0
     D SpaceLen        S              9B 0 INZ(1024)
     D InFileLib       S             20
     D InputDs         DS
```

```
D  UserSpace                    1     20
D   SpaceName                        10     OVERLAY(UserSpace:1)
D   SpaceLib                         10     OVERLAY(UserSpace:11)
D  OutFormat                   21     28
D  FileLib                     29     48
D   FileName                         10     OVERLAY(FileLib:1)
D   FileLibr                         10     OVERLAY(FileLib:11)
D ListDs            DS
D  MainFileLb                   1     20
D   MainFile                         10     OVERLAY(MainFileLb:1)
D   MainLib                          10     OVERLAY(MainFileLb:11)
D  DependFil                   21     30
D  DependLib                   31     40
D                  DS
D  FieldSpace                   1     20
D   FSpaceName                       10     OVERLAY(FieldSpace:1)
D   FSpaceLib                        10     OVERLAY(FieldSpace:11)
D ErrorDs          DS                       INZ
D  BytesProvd                   1      4B 0
D  BytesAvail                   5      8B 0
D  MessageId                    9     15
D  Err###                      16     16
D  MessageDta                  17    116
D KeyData          DS
D  DependKey                    1     10
D  AscendDes                   14     14
D FindSelect       DS                150     INZ
D  FindFormat                  70     79
D  NbrKeys                    117    118B 0
D  NbrSelOmit                 130    131B 0
D  OffSelOmit                 132    135B 0
D  OffSet                     136    139B 0
D KeySelect        DS                150     INZ
D  Rule                         3      3
D  Compare                      4      5
D  CompName                     6     15
D  NbrSO                       16     17B 0
D  OffsetSO                    29     32B 0
D KeySOS           DS                150     INZ
D  POffset                      1      4B 0
D  NL                           5      6B 0
D  SelectVar                   21     48
D                  DS
D  FFileLib                     1     20
D  FFileLibr                          10     OVERLAY(FFileLib:1)
D  FFileName                          10     OVERLAY(FFileLib:11)
D FGeneralDs       DS                       INZ
D  FSizeInput                 113    116B 0
D  FOffsetHed                 117    120B 0
D  FSizeHead                  121    124B 0
D  FOfftoList                 125    128B 0
D  FNbrInList                 133    136B 0
D  FSizeEntry                 137    140B 0
D FListDs          DS
D  FFieldName                   1     10
D  FFieldText                  33     82
D GenHeadDs        DS                       INZ
D  InputSize                  113    116B 0
D  ListOffset                 125    128B 0
D  NumberList                 133    136B 0
D  EntrySize                  137    140B 0
D Receiver         DS               4096     INZ
D  NbrFormats                  62     63B 0
```

```
D  DBFileOffs                 317     320B 0
D  AccessType                 337     338
D  Requester        C                         CONST('*REQUESTER*LIBL')


CL0N01Factor1++++++++Opcode&ExtFactor2++++++++Result++++++++Len++D+HiLoEq....Comments++
C           *ENTRY        PLIST
C                         PARM                      InFileLib
C                         EVAL      OutFile = %SUBST(InFileLib:1:10)
C                         EVAL      OutLibrary = %SUBST(InFileLib:11:10)
C                         EVAL      SpaceName = 'USRSPC'
C                         EVAL      SpaceLib = 'QTEMP'
C                         EVAL      FileName = OutFile
C                         EVAL      FileLibr = OutLibrary
C                         EVAL      BytesProvd = 116
C                         EVAL      MessageFil = ('QCPFMSG   ' + 'QSYS')
C                         EVAL      *IN53 = *ON
 *   Create user space
C                         CALL      'QUSCRTUS'
C                         PARM                      UserSpace
C                         PARM                      SpaceAttr
C                         PARM      1024            SpaceLen
C                         PARM                      SpaceValue
C                         PARM                      SpaceAuth
C                         PARM                      SpaceText
C                         PARM                      SpaceReplc
C                         PARM                      ErrorDs
 *   Attempt to retrieve object description
C                         CALL      'QUSROBJD'
C                         PARM                      ObjReceivr
C                         PARM      100             ReceiveLen
C                         PARM      'OBJD0100'      ObjFileFmt
C                         PARM                      InFileLib
C                         PARM      '*FILE'         ObjectType
C                         PARM                      ErrorDs
 *   If file doesn't exist, send message and get out
C                         IF        MessageId <> *BLANKS
C                         EXSR      SNDMSG
C                         GOTO      END
C                         ENDIF
 *   Create user space for fields
C                         EXSR      SPACE1
 *
C                         EVAL      SFileLib = InFileLib
C                         EVAL      First = *ON
 *   Write access path
C                         EXSR      GETFIL
C           MessageId     CABEQ     'CPF5715'       NORECS
C           MessageId     CABEQ     'CPF3210'       END
C                         EVAL      First = *OFF
C                         EVAL      SpaceName = 'USRSPC'
C                         EVAL      SpaceLib = 'QTEMP'
 * List database relations to user space
C                         CALL      'QDBLDBR'
C                         PARM                      UserSpace
C                         PARM      'DDRL0100'      LstOutFmt
C                         PARM                      SFileLib
C                         PARM      '*FIRST'        RecordFmt
C                         PARM      *BLANKS         Ignore
C                         PARM                      ErrorDs
C           MessageId     CABEQ     'CPF5715'       NORECS
C                         EVAL      StartPosit = 1
C                         EVAL      StartLen = 140
```

```
      C                    EVAL        SpaceName = 'USRSPC'

      C                    EVAL        SpaceLib = 'QTEMP'
       * Retrieve user space general information
      C                    CALL        'QUSRTVUS'
      C                    PARM                     UserSpace
      C                    PARM                     StartPosit
      C                    PARM                     StartLen
      C                    PARM                     GenHeadDs
      C                    EVAL        StartPosit = 1
      C                    EVAL        StartLen = InputSize
      C                    EVAL        SpaceName = 'USRSPC'
      C                    EVAL        SpaceLib = 'QTEMP'
       *  Retrieve user space detail information
      C                    CALL        'QUSRTVUS'
      C                    PARM                     UserSpace
      C                    PARM                     StartPosit
      C                    PARM                     StartLen
      C                    PARM                     InputDs
      C                    EVAL        StartPosit = (ListOffset + 1)
      C                    EVAL        StartLen = EntrySize
      C                    EVAL        SaveLen = EntrySize
      C                    EVAL        NbrLogics = NumberList
       *  Retrieve the list by walking through the user space
 B1   C                    DO          Nbrlogics
      C                    EVAL        SpaceName = 'USRSPC'
      C                    EVAL        SpaceLib = 'QTEMP'
      C                    EVAL        SaveStart = StartPosit
      C                    CALL        'QUSRTVUS'
      C                    PARM                     UserSpace
      C                    PARM                     StartPosit
      C                    PARM                     StartLen
      C                    PARM                     ListDs
      C     DependFil      CABEQ       '*NONE'      NORECS
      C                    EVAL        SpaceName = 'USRSPC'
      C                    EVAL        SpaceLib = 'QTEMP'
      C                    EVAL        SFileLib = DependFil
      C                    EVAL        %SUBST(SFileLib:11:10) = DependLib
      C                    EXSR        GETFIL
      C                    EXSR        CLEAR
      C                    EVAL        StartPosit = (SaveStart + SaveLen)
 E1   C                    ENDDO
      C     NORECS         TAG
      C                    IF          RelRecNbr > 0
      C                    EVAL        *In21 = *ON
 E1   C                    ENDIF
      C                    WRITE       FORMAT1
      C                    EXFMT       SFLCTL
      C     END            TAG
      C                    EVAL        *InLr = *ON
       *
      C     SNDMSG         BEGSR
       * Send error message
      C                    CALL        'QMHSNDPM'
      C                    PARM                     MessageId
      C                    PARM                     MessageFil
      C                    PARM                     InFileLib
      C                    PARM        20           MsgDtaLen
      C                    PARM        '*STATUS'    MessageTyp
      C                    PARM        '*EXT'       MessageQue
      C                    PARM        1            MsgQueNbr
      C                    PARM                     MessageKey
      C                    PARM                     ErrorDs
```

```
        C                   ENDSR

        C        GETFIL     BEGSR
        *   Retrieve key field information for each logical file
        C                   CALL      'QDBRTVFD'
        C                   PARM                    Receiver
        C                   PARM      4096          ReceiveLen
        C                   PARM                    RFileLib
        C                   PARM      'FILD0100'    FileFmt
        C                   PARM                    SFileLib
        C                   PARM                    RecordFmt
        C                   PARM      '0'           OverRide
        C                   PARM      '*LCL'        System
        C                   PARM      '*EXT'        FmtType
        C                   PARM                    ErrorDs
        C        MessageId  CABEQ     'CPF5715'     ENDGET
        C                   MOVEA     Receiver      AR(1)
        C                   IF        First = *ON
        *   File must be a physical file
        C                   MOVE      AR(9)         TestType
        C                   TESTB     '2'           TestType            01
        C                   IF        *In01 = *ON
        C                   EVAL      MessageId = 'CPF3210'
        C                   EXSR      SNDMSG
        C                   GOTO      ENDGET
 E2     C                   ENDIF
 E1     C                   ENDIF

        C                   EVAL      I = DbFileOffs
 B1     C                   DO        NbrFormats
        C                   MOVEA     AR(I)         FindSelect
        C                   EVAL      S = (Offset + 1)
        C                   IF        First = *OFF
        *   Write blank line for clarity
        C                   EXSR      CLEAR
        C                   EVAL      RelRecNbr = RelRecNbr + 1
        C                   WRITE     SFLRCD
 E2     C                   ENDIF
        C                   EVAL      SfLibrary = %SUBST(RFileLib:1:10)
        C                   EVAL      SfFileName = %SUBST(RFileLib:11:10)
        C                   EVAL      SfFormat = FindFormat
        C                   EXSR      GETTXT
 B2     C                   DO        NbrKeys
        C                   MOVEA     AR(S)         KeyData
        C                   TESTB     '0'           AscendDes           79
 B3     C                   SELECT
        C                   WHEN      *In79 = *OFF
        C                   EVAL      SfAsendDec = 'A'
        C                   WHEN      *In79 = *ON
        C                   EVAL      SfAsendDec = 'D'
 E3     C                   ENDSL
        C                   EVAL      SfKeyField = DependKey
        C                   DO        B             C
        C                   IF        ARYF(C) = DependKey
        C                   EVAL      SfValue = Aryt(C)
        C                   LEAVE
        C                   ENDIF
 E3     C                   ENDDO
        C                   EVAL      SfText = SfValue
        C                   EVAL      RelRecNbr = RelRecNbr + 1
        C                   WRITE     SFLRCD
        C                   EVAL      SfLibrary = *BLANKS
        C                   EVAL      SfFileName = *BLANKS
```

```
      C                     EVAL      SfFormat = *BLANKS
      C                     EVAL      SfValue = *BLANKS
      C                     EVAL      S = S + 32
E2    C                     ENDDO
      *    If select/omit statements exist
      C                     IF        NbrSelOmit <> *ZEROS
      C                     EXSR      SELOMT
E2    C                     ENDIF
      C                     EVAL      SfCompare = *BLANKS
      C                     EVAL      SfRule = *BLANKS
      C                     EVAL      I = I + 160
E1    C                     ENDDO
      C         ENDGET      TAG
      C                     ENDSR

      C         SELOMT      BEGSR
      C                     EVAL      I1 = (OffSelOmit + 1)
B1    C                     DO        NbrSelOmit
      C                     MOVEA     AR(I1)        KeySelect
      C                     IF        Compare = 'AL'
      C                     ITER
E2    C                     ENDIF
      C                     EVAL      SfCompare = Compare
      C                     EVAL      SfRule = Rule
      C                     EVAL      I2 = OffsetSo + 1
      C                     DO        NbrSO
      C                     MOVEA     AR(I2)        KeySOS
      C                     MOVEA     SelectVar     A2
      C                     EVAL      NL = NL - 19
      C                     IF        NL > *ZEROS
      C                     MOVEA     *BLANKS       A2(NL)
      C                     ENDIF
      C                     MOVEA     A2(1)         SfValue
      C                     EVAL      SfKeyField = CompName
      C                     EVAL      RelRecNbr = RelRecNbr + 1
      C                     EVAL      SfAsendDec = *BLANKS
      C                     EVAL      SfText = (SfRule + ' ' + SfCompare +
      C                                        ' ' + SfValue)
      C                     EVAL      *In59 = *ON
      C                     WRITE     SFLRCD
      C                     EVAL      *In59 = *OFF
      C                     EVAL      I2 = POffset + 1
      C                     ENDDO
      C                     EVAL      I1 = (I1 + 32)
E1    C                     ENDDO
      C                     ENDSR

      C         CLEAR       BEGSR
      C                     EVAL      SfLibrary = *BLANKS
      C                     EVAL      SfFileName = *BLANKS
      C                     EVAL      SfFormat = *BLANKS
      C                     EVAL      SfKeyField = *BLANKS
      C                     EVAL      SfText = *BLANKS
      C                     EVAL      SfCompare = *BLANKS
      C                     EVAL      SfRule = *BLANKS
      C                     EVAL      SfAsendDec = *BLANKS
      C                     ENDSR
      *  Get text for each field
      C         GETTXT      BEGSR
      C                     EVAL      FFileName = SfFileName
      C                     EVAL      FFileLibr = SfLibrary
      C                     EVAL      FSpaceName = 'FLDSPC'
      C                     EVAL      FSpaceLib = 'QTEMP'
```

```
         * List fields to user space
     C                    CALL      'QUSLFLD'
     C                    PARM                    FieldSpace
     C                    PARM      'FLDL0100'    ListFormat
     C                    PARM                    FFileLib
     C                    PARM      SfFormat      RecordFmt
     C                    PARM      '1'           OverRide
     C                    Z-ADD     1             FilStartP
     C                    Z-ADD     140           FilStartL
     C                    EVAL      FSpaceName = 'FLDSPC'
     C                    EVAL      FSpaceLib = 'QTEMP'
         * Retrieve user space general information
     C                    CALL      'QUSRTVUS'
     C                    PARM                    FieldSpace
     C                    PARM                    FilStartP
     C                    PARM                    FilStartL
     C                    PARM                    FGeneralDs
     C                    EVAL      FilStartP = FOffsetHed + 1
     C                    EVAL      FilStartL = FSizeHead
     C                    EVAL      FSpaceName = 'FLDSPC'
     C                    EVAL      FSpaceLib = 'QTEMP'
     C                    EVAL      FilStartP = FOfftoList + 1
     C                    EVAL      FilStartL = FSizeEntry
         * Retrieve the list by walking through the user space
  B1 C                    DO        FNbrInList
     C                    EVAL      FSpaceName = 'FLDSPC'
     C                    EVAL      FSpaceLib = 'QTEMP'
     C                    CALL      'QUSRTVUS'
     C                    PARM                    FieldSpace
     C                    PARM                    FilStartP
     C                    PARM                    FilStartL
     C                    PARM                    FListDs
     C                    EVAL      B = B + 1
     C                    EVAL      ARYF(B) = FFieldName
     C                    EVAL      ARYT(B) = FFieldText
     C                    EVAL      FilStartP = FilStartP + FSizeEntry
  E1 C                    ENDDO
     C                    ENDSR
         * Create user space for listing fields
     C        SPACE1      BEGSR
     C                    EVAL      FSpaceName = 'FLDSPC'
     C                    EVAL      FSpaceLib = 'QTEMP'
     C                    CALL      'QUSCRTUS'
     C                    PARM                    FieldSpace
     C                    PARM      *BLANKS       SpaceAttr
     C                    PARM      1024          SpaceLen
     C                    PARM      *BLANKS       SpaceValue
     C                    PARM      '*CHANGE'     SpaceAuth
     C                    PARM      *BLANKS       SpaceText
     C                    PARM      '*YES'        SpaceReplc
     C                    PARM                    ErrorDs
     C                    ENDSR
```

THE DISPLAY FIELD COMMAND

If you ever use the Display File Field Description (DSPFFD) command, you will want to take a look at this utility. The Display Field (DSPFLD) command provides an easy-to-read subfile display that shows all fields in a file. Buffer positions, key field identification, field description, record format length, and record format name are all condensed onto a single screen. The file field information can also be printed simply by pressing a function key. In Figure 11.5, we see an example of the Display Field (DSPFLD) command when it is run over our customer file.

Figure 11.5: Output from the Display Field (DSPFLD) Command

```
                          Display File Fields

                                  Position to . . . . . .:  _____
   Physical File  . . . .:  CUSTOMER     File Type . . . . . . .:        PF
   Library  . . . . . . .:  QBOOK        Record Length . . . . .:       132
   Record Format. . . . .:  CUSREC       Number of fields. . . .:         8

   Key Field      Length Dec Type From   To  Text
   K1  CUSTOMER#     10        A     1    10  CUSTOMER#
       CUSTNAME      40        A    11    50  CUSTOMER NAME
       ADDRESS       30        A    51    80  CUSTOMER ADDRESS
       CITY          30        A    81   110  CUSTOMER CITY
       STATE          2        A   111   112  CUSTOMER STATE
       ZIP            9        A   113   121  ZIP CODE
       SALESMAN       5        A   122   126  SALESMAN
       PHONENBR      10   0    P   127   132  PHONE NUMBER




                                                           Bottom


   F3=Exit        F12=Previous      F8=Print
```

The DSPFLD utility consists of three source members: The Display Field (DSPFLD) command in Figure 11.6, the DSPFLDDS display file in Figure 11.7, and the DSPFLDRG RPG program in Figure 11.8.

Figure 11.6: The Display Field (DSPFLD) Command Source

```
/*==============================================================*/
/* To compile:                                                  */
/*                                                              */
/*          CRTCMD      CMD(XXX/DSPFLD) PGM(XXX/FIG1108RG)       */
/*                      SRCMBR(FIG1106CM)                        */
/*                                                              */
/*==============================================================*/
            CMD         PROMPT('List Fields')

            PARM        KWD(FILE) TYPE(QUAL) MIN(1) PROMPT('File')
            PARM        KWD(RCDFMT) TYPE(*NAME) DFT(*FIRST) +
                          SPCVAL((*FIRST)) PROMPT('Record format')

QUAL:       QUAL        TYPE(*NAME) LEN(10)
            QUAL        TYPE(*NAME) LEN(10) DFT(*LIBL) +
                          SPCVAL((*LIBL)) PROMPT('Library')
```

Figure 11.7: The FIG1107DS Display File Source

```
     A***************************************************************
     A*   TO COMPILE:
     A*     CRTDSPF FILE(XXXLIB/FIG1107DS)
     A***************************************************************
     AAN01N02N03T.Name++++++RLen++TDpBLinPosFunctions+++++++++++++++++++++++++
     A                                          CF03 CF12
     A            R SFLRCD                       SFL
     A              SFFLD        10A  O  8  6
     A              SFLEN         5Y 0O  8 17EDTCDE(3)
     A              SFTYPE        1A  O  8 28
     A              SFFROM        5Y 0O  8 31EDTCDE(3)
     A              SFTO          5Y 0O  8 37EDTCDE(3)
     A              SFTEXT       38A  O  8 43
     A              SFDEC         1A  O  8 25
     A              SFKEY         3A  O  8  2DSPATR(HI)
     A            R SFLCTL                       SFLCTL(SFLRCD)
     A                                           SFLSIZ(0024) SFLPAG(0012)
     A                                           CF08(08 'print')
     A                                           OVERLAY
     A  21                                       SFLDSP
     A                                           SFLDSPCTL
     A  53                                       SFLEND(*MORE)
     A              RELRECPOS     4S 0H          SFLRCDNBR(*TOP)
     A                                        1 28'Display File Fields'
     A                                           DSPATR(HI)
     A                                        3  2'Physical File . . . . .:'
     A              OUTFILENAM   10A  O        3 28DSPATR(HI)
     A                                        4  2'Library . . . . . . . .:'
     A              OUTLIBNAME   10A  O        4 28DSPATR(HI)
     A                                        7  6'Field' DSPATR(HI)
     A                                        7 16'Length'  DSPATR(HI)
     A                                        7 32'From'    DSPATR(HI)
     A                                        7 43'Text'    DSPATR(HI)
     A                                        7 40'To'      DSPATR(HI)
     A                                        5  2'Record Format. . . . . .:'
     A              OUTFORMAT    10A  O        5 28DSPATR(HI)
     A                                        3 43'File Type . . . . . . .:'
     A              OUTTYPE       5A  O        3 73DSPATR(HI)
```

```
A                                        7 23'Dec'         DSPATR(HI)
A                                        4 43'Record Length . . . . . .:'
A              OUTRECLEN        6Y 0O    4 72DSPATR(HI) EDTCDE(3)
A                                        5 43'Number of fields. . . .:'
A              RELRECNBR        4Y 0O    5 74DSPATR(HI) EDTCDE(3)
A                                        7  2'Key'         DSPATR(HI)
A                                        7 27'Type'        DSPATR(HI)
A                                        2 43'Position to . . . . . .:'
A              POSITIONFL       10   B   2 68
A          R FORMAT1
A                                       23   4'F3=Exit'        COLOR(BLU)
A                                       23  18'F12=Previous'   COLOR(BLU)
A                                       23  35'F8=Print'       COLOR(BLU)
```

Figure 11.8: The FIG1108RG RPG Program Source

```
 ************************************************************
 *   TO COMPILE:
 *      CRTBNDRPG PGM(XXXLIB/FIG1108RG)
 ************************************************************
 FFilename++IPEASFRlen+LKlen+AIDevice+.Keywords++++++++++++++++++++++Comments++++++
 FFIG1107DS CF   E           WORKSTN
 F                                       SFILE(SFLRCD:RelRecNbr)
 FQSYSPRT   O    F 132        PRINTER OFLIND(*INOF)


 DName+++++++++++ETDsFrom+++To/L+++IDc.Keywords++++++++++++++++++++++++Comments++++++
     D AR            S             1     DIM(4096)
     D AKEY          S            10     DIM(20)
     D AK#           S             2   0 DIM(20)
     D J             S             2   0
     D JJ            S             2   0
     D I             S             7   0
     D S             S             7   0
     D RelRecNbr     S             4   0
     D RelRecHi#     S             4   0
     D XX            S             7   0
     D I1            S             1
     D I2            S             2
     D GENDS         DS
     D  OffsetHdr          117   120B 0
     D  SizeHeader         121   124B 0
     D  OffsetList         125   128B 0
     D  NbrInList          133   136B 0
     D  SizeEntry          137   140B 0
     D HeaderDs      DS
     D  OutFileNam           1    10
     D  OutLibName          11    20
     D  OutType             21    25
     D  OutFormat           31    40
     D  RecordLen           41    44B 0
     D InputDs       DS
     D  UserSpace            1    20
     D  SpaceName            1    10
     D  SpaceLib            11    20
     D  InpFileLib          29    48
     D  InpFFilNam          29    38
     D  InpFFilLib          39    48
     D  InpRcdFmt           49    58
```

```
D ListDs           DS
D  SfFld                        1     10
D  SfType                      11     11
D  BufferOut                   13     16B 0
D  FieldLen                    21     24B 0
D  Digits                      25     28B 0
D  Decimals                    29     32B 0
D  FieldDesc                   33     82
D ErrorDs          DS                        INZ
D  BytesPrv                     1      4B 0
D  BytesAvl                     5      8B 0
D  MessageId                    9     15
D  ERR###                      16     16
D  MessageDta                  17    116
D ReceiveVr2       S                  100
D ReceiveVar       DS                 4096
D  NbrOfFmts                   62     63B 0
D  DBFileOff                  317    320B 0
D FindSelDs        DS                  150
D  NbrOfKeys                  117    118B 0
D  KeyOffset                  136    139B 0
D KeyDataDs        DS
D  DependKey                    1     10
D                 DS
D  StartPosit                   1      4B 0
D  StartLen                     5      8B 0
D  SpaceLen                     9     12B 0
D  ReceiveLen                  13     16B 0
D  MessageKey                  17     20B 0
D  MsgDtaLen                   21     24B 0
D  MsgQueNbr                   25     28B 0
DGenSpcPtr                            *
DLstSpcPtr                            *
DHdrPtr                               *


CL0N01Factor1+++++++Opcode&ExtFactor2+++++++Result++++++++Len++D+HiLoEq....Comments+
C     *ENTRY        PLIST
C                   PARM                      FileLib          20
C                   PARM                      EntryFmt         10
C                   MOVEL(P)   'FFDSPC'       SpaceName
C                   MOVEL(P)   'QTEMP'        SpaceLib
C                   MOVEL      FileLib        InpFFilNam
C                   MOVE       FileLib        InpFFilLib
C                   EVAL       BytesPrv = 116
C     'QCPFMSG'     CAT        'QSYS':3       MSGF
C                   SETON                                      53
 * Create the user space
C                   CALL       'QUSCRTUS'
C                   PARM                      UserSpace
C                   PARM       *BLANKS        SpaceAttr        10
C                   PARM       4096           SpaceLen
C                   PARM       *BLANKS        SpaceVal          1
C                   PARM       '*CHANGE'      SpaceAuth        10
C                   PARM       *BLANKS        SpaceText        50
C                   PARM       '*YES'         SpaceRepl        10
C                   PARM                      ErrorDs
 * Attemp to retrieve object description
C                   CALL       'QUSROBJD'
C                   PARM                      ReceiveVr2
C                   PARM       100            ReceiveLen
C                   PARM       'OBJD0100'     FileFormat        8
C                   PARM                      FileLib
C                   PARM       '*FILE'        ObjectType       10
```

```
     C                    PARM                         ErrorDs
         *   If file doesn't exist, send message and get out
     C                    IF            MessageId <> *BLANKS
     C                    EXSR          SNDMSG
     C                    GOTO          END
     C                    ENDIF
         *
     C                    EXSR          GETKEY
         *   List fields to user space
     C                    CALL          'QUSLFLD'
     C                    PARM                         UserSpace
     C                    PARM          'FLDL0100'     ListFormat          8
     C                    PARM                         InpFileLIb
     C                    PARM          EntryFmt       InpRcdFmt
     C                    PARM          '1'            OverRide            1
     C                    Eval          StartPosit = 1
     C                    Eval          StartLen = 140
     C                    CALL          'QUSRTVUS'
     C                    PARM                         UserSpace
     C                    PARM                         StartPosit
     C                    PARM                         StartLen
     C                    PARM                         GENDS
     C                    EVAL          StartPosit = OffsetHdr + 1
     C                    EVAL          StartLen = SizeHeader
     C                    CALL          'QUSRTVUS'
     C                    PARM                         UserSpace
     C                    PARM                         StartPosit
     C                    PARM                         StartLen
     C                    PARM                         HeaderDs
     C                    EVAL          SpaceName = 'FFDSPC'
     C                    EVAL          SpaceLib = 'QTEMP'
     C                    EVAL          StartPosit = OffsetList + 1
     C                    EVAL          StartLen = SizeEntry
         *   Do for number of fields
  B1 C                    DO            NbrInList
     C                    CALL          'QUSRTVUS'
     C                    PARM                         UserSpace
     C                    PARM                         StartPosit
     C                    PARM                         StartLen
     C                    PARM                         ListDs
         *   Write the record to the subfile
     C                    EXSR          WRITER
     C                    EVAL          StartPosit = StartPosit + SizeEntry
  E1 C                    ENDDO
     C                    IF            RelRecNbr > 0
     C                    EVAL          *IN21 = *ON
  E1 C                    ENDIF
     C                    EVAL          OutRecLen = RecordLen
     C         ' '        CHECKR        OutType        Z                 1 0
     C                    MOVEL(P)      OutType        F5                5
     C         5          SUB           Z              Z
     C                    IF            Z < 5
     C                    EVAL          OutType = *BLANKS
     C                    CAT           F5:Z           OutType
     C                    ENDIF
     C                    WRITE         FORMAT1
     C                    EVAL          RelRecPos = 1
     C         RESHOW     TAG
     C                    EXFMT         SFLCTL
     C                    IF            PositionF1 <> *BLANKS
     C                    EXSR          REPOS
     C                    GOTO          RESHOW
     C                    ENDIF
```

```
       *  Print loop
B1     C                   IF        *IN08 = *ON
       C                   EXCEPT    HEDING
B2     C         1         DO        9998          X              4 0
       C         X         CHAIN     SFLRCD                                 68
B3     C                   IF        *IN68 = *OFF
       C                   EXCEPT    DETAIL
E3     C                   ENDIF
E2     C    N68            ENDDO
E1     C                   ENDIF
       C         END       TAG
       C                   EVAL      *INLR = *ON
       *
       C         WRITER    BEGSR
       C                   EVAL      SFLEN = Digits
       C                   MOVE      Decimals        SFDEC
       C                   IF        SFLEN = *ZEROS
       C                   EVAL      SFLEN = FieldLen
       C                   EVAL      SFDEC = *BLANKS
E1     C                   ENDIF
       C                   EVAL      SFFROM = BufferOut
       C                   EVAL      SFTO = ((SFFROM + Fieldlen) - 1)
       C                   MOVEL     FieldDesc       SFTEXT
       C                   EVAL      SFKEY = *BLANKS
B1     C                   DO        20            I
       C                   IF        AKEY(I) = SFFLD
       C                   IF        AK#(I) < 10
       C                   MOVE      AK#(I)          I1             1
       C         'K'       CAT(P)    I1:0            SFKEY
X3     C                   ELSE
       C                   MOVE      AK#(I)          I2             2
       C         'K'       CAT(P)    I2:0            SFKEY
E3     C                   ENDIF
       C                   LEAVE
E2     C                   ENDIF
E1     C                   ENDDO
       C                   EVAL      RelRecNbr = (RelRecNbr + 1)
       C                   WRITE     SFLRCD
       C                   EVAL      RelRecHi# = RelRecNbr
       C                   ENDSR
       *
       C         REPOS     BEGSR
       C                   SELECT
       C                   WHEN      PositionFl = '*TOP'
       C                   EVAL      RelRecPos = 1
       C                   WHEN      PositionFl = '*BOTTOM'
       C                   EVAL      RelRecPos = (RelRecHi# - 10)
       C                   IF        RelRecPos <= 0
       C                   EVAL      RelRecPos = 1
       C                   ENDIF
       C                   OTHER
       C                   DO        RelRecHi#     XX
       C         XX        CHAIN     SFLRCD                                 68
       C                   IF        *IN68 = *OFF
       C         ' '       CHECKR    PositionFl    P            2 0       68
       C    PositionFl:P   SCAN      SFTEXT                                 60
       C                   IF        (SFFLD = PositionFl) or (*IN60 = *ON)
       C                   EVAL      RelRecPos = XX
       C                   LEAVE
       C                   ENDIF
       C                   ENDIF
       C                   ENDDO
       C                   ENDSL
```

```
      C                     EVAL      PositionFl = *BLANKS
      C                     ENDSR
      *
      C     GETKEY          BEGSR
      * Get key field information into ReceiveVar
      C                     CALL      'QDBRTVFD'
      C                     PARM                    ReceiveVar
      C                     PARM      4096          ReceiveLen
      C                     PARM                    InpFileLib
      C                     PARM      'FILD0100'    FileFormat        8
      C                     PARM                    FileLib          20
      C                     PARM      EntryFmt      RecordFmt        10
      C                     PARM      '0'           OverRide
      C                     PARM      '*LCL'        System           10
      C                     PARM      '*EXT'        FormatType       10
      C                     PARM                    ErrorDs
      C     MessageId       CABEQ     'CPF5715'     ENDGET
      C                     MOVEA     ReceiveVar    AR(1)
      C                     EVAL      I = DBFileOff
B1    C                     DO        NbrofFmts
      C                     MOVEA     AR(I)         FindSelDs
      C                     EVAL      S = (KeyOffset + 1)
      * Don't exceed array size
      C                     IF        NbrOfKeys > 20
      C                     EVAL      NbrOfKeys = 20
E2    C                     ENDIF
      C                     EVAL      JJ = 0
      * Do for number of key fields
B2    C                     DO        NbrOfKeys
      C                     MOVEA     AR(S)         KeyDataDs
      C                     EVAL      J = (J + 1)
      C                     EVAL      JJ = (JJ + 1)
      C                     MOVEA     DependKey     AKEY(J)
      C                     MOVEA     JJ            AK#(JJ)
      C                     EVAL      S = (S + 32)
E2    C                     ENDDO
      C                     EVAL      I = (I + 160)
E1    C                     ENDDO
      C     ENDGET          TAG
      C                     ENDSR
      *
      C     SNDMSG          BEGSR
      * Send error message
      C                     CALL      'QMHSNDPM'
      C                     PARM                    MessageId
      C                     PARM                    MSGF             20
      C                     PARM                    FileLib
      C                     PARM      20            MsgDtaLen
      C                     PARM      '*DIAG'       MessageTyp       10
      C                     PARM      '*'           MessageQue       10
      C                     PARM      1             MsgQueNbr
      C                     PARM                    MessageKey
      C                     PARM                    ErrorDs
      C                     ENDSR

      O.............N01N02N03Field++++++++YB.End++PConstant/editword/DTformat++Comments+
      OQSYSPRT   E          HEDING         3 02
      O          OR   OF
      O                                        5 'DATE:'
      O                     UDATE       Y     14
      O                                       75 'PAGE:'
      O                     PAGE        Z     80
      O                                       48 'DISPLAY FIELD FOR FILE'
```

```
O                       OutFileNam           59
   *
O           E           HEDING        1
O        OR     OF
O                                         24 'PHYSICAL FILE...........'
O                       OutFileNam          35
O                                         64 'FILE TYPE..............'
O                       OutType             75
   *
O           E           HEDING        1
O        OR     OF
O                                         24 'LIBRARY................'
O                       OutLibName          35
O                                         64 'RECORD LENGTH..........'
O                       OutRecLen     Z     75
   *
O           E           HEDING        3
O        OR     OF
O                                         24 'RECORD FORMAT..........'
O                       OutFormat           35
O                                         64 'NUMBER OF FIELDS........'
O                       RelRecNbr     Z     78
   *
O           E           HEDING        1
O        OR     OF
O                                         22 'KEY     FIELD    LENGTH'
O                                         45 'DEC  TYPE FROM    TO'
O                                         75 'TEXT...................'
   *
O           EF          DETAIL        1
O                       SFKEY                4
O                       SFFLD               16
O                       SFLEN         Z     20
O                       SFDEC               27
O                       SFTYPE              32
O                       SFFROM        Z     39
O                       SFTO          Z     45
O                       SFTEXT              88
   *
```

THE REORGANIZE PHYSICAL FILE FILTER COMMAND

Those of us whose career paths closely paralleled the development of the family of IBM Midrange Systems initially found the AS/400 to be a bit of an enigma. All of the rules with which we were familiar regarding the placement of data had changed. Our trusty CATALOG was replaced with a variety of tools that we could use to determine how much disk was used and where the files were stored, but the days of using a single command to determine what had gobbled up all of our DASD were long gone.

In Search of Missing DASD...

Many improvements made to the AS/400 operating system make the task of tracking down the missing DASD easier. Print Disk Information (PRTDSKINF) can be used to help reveal some of the disk utilization. But the very nature of the AS/400 operating system can make tracking down the overall disk usage a difficult thing to expose.

One area where lost DASD can reside is in deleted records. When you delete a record on the AS/400, the record is simply blanked out or, more specifically, changed to *null* characters when the delete operation occurs. The deleted record is then ignored on subsequent I/O operations for that file. The significance of this point is that the "deleted" record still takes up the same amount of space on disk. This may not matter very much if the file was built to reuse deleted records (reusing deleted records is one of the options in the Create Physical File (CRTPF) and Change Physical File (CHGPF) commands), but most files are not configured this way because it can impact performance negatively.

Deleted records continue to take up space on the DASD until the file is reorganized. This occurs when, and if, Reorganize Physical File Member (RGZPFM) is run. Depending upon your AS/400 software, you may have hidden DASD that could be recovered on your system. Many AS/400 software packages do not reorganize physical files on a regular basis. Some do not perform this file maintenance at all.

If you are curious as to whether or not files on your system contain deleted records, you can use the Display File Description (DSPFD) command over a few of the files to find out. You may be in for a little surprise.

The Reorganize Physical File Filter (RGZPFFLTR) command identifies those files on your system that contain deleted records and automatically reorganizes them for you. It prints a status report informing you of how much DASD was regained by using the utility. You can also specify the percentage of deleted records that must exist in each file before the file reorganization occurs.

The Long and the Short of It

We employed the Reorganize Physical File Filter utility to greatly reduce the length of time that our monthend process took to complete. Our monthend used to reorganize all of the major files in the system whether they needed it or not. This was primarily because there was no easy way to tell which files had deleted records in them.

Because this utility selectively reorganizes the files based upon the percentage of deleted records, our monthend process now only reorganizes the files that need it. The amount of time our monthend process takes is reduced by more than 50 percent.

What's Under the Hood?

The command in Figure 11.9 accepts three parameters. The first, library name, also accepts the value *ALL, which causes the program to look at all files in the system. The second parameter is the percentage of deleted records that must exist in the file before the reorganization is performed. If a Y (for yes) is entered as the last parameter, the files that meet the established criteria are listed, but the reorganization is not performed.

Figure 11.9: The Reorganize Physical File Filter (RGZPFFLTR) Command Source

```
/*===============================================================*/
/* To compile:                                                   */
/*                                                               */
/*        CRTCMD      CMD(XXX/RGZPFFLTR) PGM(XXX/FIG1110RG)       */
/*                    SRCMBR(FIG1109CM)                           */
/*                                                               */
/*===============================================================*/
          CMD        PROMPT('Reorganize Files Filter)')
          PARM       KWD(LIBRARY) TYPE(*CHAR) LEN(10) MIN(1) +
                       CHOICE('Name, *ALL') PROMPT('Library  . . +
                       . . . . . . . .')
          PARM       KWD(PERCENT) TYPE(*DEC) LEN(2) DFT(10) +
                       MIN(0) PROMPT('Percent  . . . . . . . . +
                       . .')
          PARM       KWD(PRONLY) TYPE(*CHAR) LEN(1) RSTD(*YES) +
                       DFT(N) VALUES(Y N) MIN(0) +
                       PROMPT('Print only ? . . . . . . . . .') +
                       CHOICE('Y, N')
```

The RPG program for the Reorganize Physical File Filter utility is shown in Figure 11.10. The CL program is represented by Figure 11.11.

Figure 11.10: The Reorganize Physical File Filter RPG Program Source

```
************************************************************************
    *   YOU MUST BE SIGNED ON AS QSECOFR TO COMPILE:
    *
    *        CRTBNDRPG PGM(XXXLIB/FIG1110RG) USRPRF(*OWNER) ALWNULL(*YES)
    *
    *      REMEMBER, YOU MUST COMPILE AS QSECOFR  AND *OWNER
    *
    ************************************************************************
FFilename++IPEASFRlen+LKlen+AIDevice+.Keywords++++++++++++++++++++++++Comments++++++
FQADBXREF  IF   E           K DISK
FQSYSPRT   O    F 132         PRINTER OFLIND(*INOF)

DName++++++++++ETDsFrom+++To/L+++IDc.Keywords+++++++++++++++++++++++++Comments++++++
D ErrorDs         DS                    INZ
D  BytesProvd              1      4B 0
D  BytesAvail              5      8B 0
D  MessageId               9     15
D  Err###                 16     16
D  MessageDta             17    116
D                DS
D  ReceiveLen              1      4B 0
D  MessageKey              5      8B 0
D  MsgDtaLen               9     12B 0
D  MsgQueNbr              13     16B 0
D Variable        DS            500
D  TotalBytes              1      4B 0
D  AvailBytes              5      8B 0
D  NbrRecords            141    144B 0
D  NbrDeleted            145    148B 0
D  DtaStrkSiz            149    152B 0
D  AccPathSiz            153    156B 0
D AfterTotal     S             10  0
D AllTotals      S             10  0
D B4AccPath      S             10  0
D B4AccSize      S             10  0
D B4Total        S             10  0
D DiffTotal      S             10  0
D Err            S              1A
D FileFormat     S              8A
D                DS
D FileLibr                     20A
D  FLibrary                    10A     overlay(FileLibr:11)
D FormatName     S              8A
D Library        S             10A
D MemberName     S             10A
D MessageFil     S             20A
D MessageQue     S             10A
D MessageTyp     S             10A
D ObjectType     S             10A
D OverPerc       S              1A
D Percent        S              2  0
D PrintOnly      S              1A
D Reorg          S              1A
D Result         S              7  2
D TotalFile      S              7  0
D TotalOut       S              5  1
D TotalRecrd     S              9  0
D TotalReorg     S              7  0
D TotalType      S              2A
D TestPerc       S              2  0
D KeyField       S              5
```

```
CL0N01Factor1++++++Opcode&ExtFactor2+++++++Result+++++++Len++D+HiLoEq....Comments+
C          *ENTRY      PLIST
C                      PARM                      Library
C                      PARM                      Percent
C                      PARM                      PrintOnly
C                      EVAL      BytesProvd = 116
C                      SELECT
C                      WHEN      Library = '*ALL'
C          *LOVAL      SETLL     QADBXREF
C                      OTHER
C                      EXSR      EXIST
C          Library     SETLL     QADBXREF
C                      ENDSL
C                      IF        Err <> *ON
C                      EXCEPT    HEADNG
C                      DOU       *In41
C                      IF        Library = '*ALL'
C                      READ      QADBXREF                              41
C                      ELSE
C          Library     READE     QADBXREF                              41
C                      ENDIF
C                      IF        *In41 = *OFF
C                      IF        (DBXATR = 'PF') AND (DBXTYP = 'D')
C                      EVAL      Reorg = *OFF
C                      EVAL      TotalFile = TotalFile + 1
C                      EXSR      RGZCHK
C                      IF        Reorg = *ON
C                      EVAL      B4AccSize = DtaStrkSiz
C                      EVAL      B4AccPath = AccPathSiz
C                      IF        PrintOnly <> 'Y'
C                      EXSR      RGZFIL
C                      ENDIF
C                      EXSR      PRINT
C                      EVAL      TotalReorg = TotalReorg + 1
C                      ENDIF
C                      ENDIF
C                      ENDIF
C                      ENDDO
C                      IF        AllTotals > 1000000
C          AllTotals   DIV(H)    1000000        TotalOut
C                      EVAL      TotalType = 'MB'
C                      ELSE
C                      IF        AllTotals > 1024
C          AllTotals   DIV(H)    1024           TotalOut
C                      EVAL      TotalType = 'KB'
C                      ENDIF
C                      ENDIF
C                      EXCEPT    TOTAL
C                      ENDIF
C                      EVAL      *InLr = *ON
 * Ensure that requested library exists
C          EXIST       BEGSR
C                      MOVEL     Library        FileLibr
C                      MOVEL     'QSYS'         FLibrary
C                      CALL      'QUSROBJD'
C                      PARM                      Variable
C                      PARM      500            ReceiveLen
C                      PARM      'OBJD0100'     FileFormat
C                      PARM                      FileLibr
C                      PARM      '*LIB'         ObjectType
C                      PARM                      ErrorDs
C                      IF        MessageId <> *BLANKS
C          'QCPFMSG'   CAT       'QSYS':3       MessageFil
```

```
C                   CALL      'QMHSNDPM'
C                   PARM                    MessageId
C                   PARM                    MessageFil
C                   PARM                    Library
C                   PARM      10            MsgDtaLen
C                   PARM      '*STATUS'     MessageTyp
C                   PARM      '*EXT'        MessageQue
C                   PARM      1             MsgQueNbr
C                   PARM                    MessageKey
C                   PARM                    ErrorDs
C                   EVAL      Err = *ON
C                   ENDIF
C                   ENDSR
 * Call CL program to perform reorg of file
C      RGZFIL       BEGSR
C                   IF        DBXNKF = 0
C                   EVAL      KeyField = '*NONE'
C                   ELSE
C                   EVAL      KeyField = '*FILE'
C                   ENDIF
C                   CALL      'FIG1111CL'
C                   PARM                    DBXLIB
C                   PARM                    DBXFIL
C                   PARM                    KeyField
 * Get new sizes
C                   EXSR      RTVMBR
C                   ENDSR
 * See if reorg needs to be done
C      RGZCHK       BEGSR
C                   EVAL      Reorg = *OFF
C                   MOVEL     DBXFIL        FileLibr
C                   MOVE      DBXLIB        FileLibr
C                   EVAL      ReceiveLen = 500
C                   EXSR      RTVMBR
C                   IF        (NbrRecords = 0) AND (NbrDeleted <> 0)
C                   EVAL      Reorg = *ON
C                   ENDIF
C                   IF        (NbrRecords <> 0) AND (NbrDeleted <> 0)
C                   EVAL      TotalRecrd = NbrDeleted + NbrRecords
C                   IF        TotalRecrd <> 0
C      NbrDeleted   DIV       TotalRecrd    Result
C      Result       MULT      100           TestPerc
C                   IF        TestPerc > Percent
C                   EVAL      Reorg = *ON
C                   ENDIF
C                   ENDIF
C                   ENDIF
C                   ENDSR
 * Accumulate totals and print detail
C      PRINT        BEGSR
C                   EVAL      B4Total = B4AccSize + B4AccPath
C                   EVAL      AfterTotal = DtaStrkSiz + AccPathSiz
C                   EVAL      DiffTotal = B4Total - AfterTotal
C                   EVAL      AllTotals = AllTotals + DiffTotal
C                   EXCEPT    DETAIL
C                   ENDSR
 * Retreive member description
C      RTVMBR       BEGSR
C                   CALL      'QUSRMBRD'
C                   PARM                    Variable
C                   PARM                    ReceiveLen
C                   PARM      'MBRD0200'    FormatName
C                   PARM                    FileLibr
```

```
C                      PARM      '*FIRST'     MemberName
C                      PARM      '0'          OverPerc
C                      PARM                   ErrorDs
C                      ENDSR

O..............N01N02N03Field++++++++YB.End++PConstant/editword/DTformat++Comments+
OQSYSPRT    E           HEADNG         1 01
O          OR    OF
O                                             9 'LIBRARY'
O                                            18 'FILE'
O                                            39 'BEFORE SIZE'
O                                            54 'AFTER SIZE'
O                                            69 'FILE SAVED'
O                                            84 'TOTAL SAVED'
OQSYSPRT    EF          DETAIL         1
O                       DBXLIB              12
O                       DBXFIL              24
O                       B4Total        1    39
O                       AfterTotal     1    54
O                       DiffTotal      1    69
O                       AllTotals      1    84
OQSYSPRT    EF          TOTAL          2 2
O                                            24 'TOTAL BYTES SAVED.......'
O                       TotalOut       1    39
O                       TotalType           42
OQSYSPRT    EF          TOTAL          1
O                                            24 'PHYSICAL FILES PROCESSED'
O                       TotalFile      Z    39
OQSYSPRT    EF          TOTAL          1
O                                            24 'FILES REORGANIZED.......'
O                       TotalReorg     Z    39
```

Figure 11.11: The Reorganize Physical File Filter CL Program Source

```
/*******************************************************************/
/*    TO CREATE:                                                 */
/*        CRTCLPGM PGM(XXXLIB/FIG1111CL)                         */
/*******************************************************************/
PGM (&LIB &FILE &KEYFIELD)
DCL &LIB  *CHAR 10
DCL &FILE *CHAR 10
DCL &KEYFIELD *CHAR 5
MONMSG CPF0000
          RGZPFM      FILE(&LIB/&FILE) KEYFILE(&KEYFIELD)
ENDPGM
```

THE FIND DISPLACED LOGICAL FILE (FNDDSPLF) COMMAND

If a logical file resides in a different library than the physical file(s) it is over, you can end up with some rather unintentional and undesirable results. This tool helps you to identify the *outlaw logical* file and do what it takes to bring it to justice.

We all have done it at one time or another. Our object library option in PDM is not what we think it is, or our library list was messed up when we compiled that new logical file. In many cases, we end up with a job that does not complete normally and we go on to correct the situation.

But what if the conditions are such that the job does complete normally? The end result is that we create an outlaw logical file that resides in a different library than the physical file it is over.

This condition is potentially dangerous for a number of reasons. Among them are nasty little error messages that come up when a program is called that is looking for a logical file that is nowhere to be found in the library list. Your update program could inadvertently update the wrong data file! Another reason could be revealed during the Save/Restore process. If the physical file does not already reside on disk when the system attempts to restore the outlaw logical file, the system gives you an error message and the logical file is not restored.

What makes this situation alarming is that you may have an outlaw on your system and not even know it. He may be lurking around the next corner waiting to pounce upon some poor unsuspecting user at the worst possible time.

The good news is that you can do something about it. You can use this utility to sniff out those nasty varmints and put them back where they belong.

Finding the Bad Guys

The Find Displaced Logical File (FNDDSPLF) command may be run over a specific library, library list, or all libraries on your system. The program finds all outlaw logical files in the libraries specified and brings them up in a subfile display, as seen in Figure 11.12.

Figure 11.12: Output from the Find Displaced Logical File (FNDDSPLF) Command

```
                    Find Displaced Logical Files

  Physical     Library     Logical      Library      Created By   Created On
  CUST         TSTFILES    CUSTQPGMR    TESTLIB      QPGMR          8/14/95
  CUSTCRD      TSTFILES    CUSBYLIM     JOHNLIB      JOHN          11/23/94
  CUSTPLAN     TSTFILES    CUSPLAN1     JOHNLIB      JOHN          12/07/94
  TRANS        TSTFILES    TRNBYDAT     WILSONLIB    WILSON         8/04/95
  CUSXREF      TSTFILES    CUSBYZIP     WILSONLIB    WILSON         8/14/95
  TRANS        TSTFILES    TRNBYCOD     QPGMR        QPGMR          8/14/95




                                                                 Bottom


   F3=Exit
```

The program displays outlaw logical files even if the physical file they are over is not in the libraries specified. If the physical file and the logical file meet the designated search criteria, you see the record listed twice in the subfile. To give you an idea of how long this program takes to run, it ran in less than 1 minute on a fully loaded E20 with over 7,000 files filling 4.7 gigabytes of DASD.

How It is Done

The program is a simple subfile display program over the system file QADBLDNC. This file is the *Dependency logical multiple-format file* over the QADBFDEP file that can be found in library QSYS. The QADBLDNC file is used to define the relationship between all of the physical and logical files on your system.

The command (Figure 11.13), display file (Figure 11.14), and RPG program (Figure 11.15) that follow are all you need for this handy utility. Refer to the compile notes found in the source members for instructions.

Chapter 11—Tools for the Toolbox

Figure 11.13: The Find Displaced Logical File (FNDDSPLF) Command

```
/*================================================================*/
/* To compile:                                                    */
/*                                                                */
/*        CRTCMD     CMD(XXX/FNDDSPLF) PGM(XXX/FIG1115RG)         */
/*                   SRCMBR(FIG1113CM)                            */
/*                                                                */
/*================================================================*/
          CMD        PROMPT('Find Displaced Logical Files')
          PARM       KWD(LIBRARY) TYPE(*CHAR) LEN(10) DFT(*LIBL) +
                     SPCVAL((*ALL)) MIN(0) CHOICE('Name, +
                     *LIBL, *ALL') PROMPT(Library:)
```

Figure 11.14: The FIG1114DS Display File Source

```
       ****************************************************************************
       *    TO COMPILE:
       *      CRTDSPF FILE(XXXLIB/FIG1114DS)
       ****************************************************************************
     AAN01N02N03T.Name++++++RLen++TDpBLinPosFunctions++++++++++++++++++++++++++
     A                                        CA03(03 'End of Program')
     A                                        PRINT(*LIBL/QSYSPRT)
     A          R SFLRCD                       SFL
     A            DBFFIL     10A  O  4  5
     A            DBFLIB     10A  O  4 18
     A            DBFFDP     10A  O  4 31
     A            DBFLDP     10A  O  4 44
     A            CRE8BY     10   O  4 57
     A            WHEN        6Y 0O  4 70EDTCDE(Y)
     A          R SFLCTL                       SFLCTL(SFLRCD)
     A                                        SFLSIZ(0032)
     A                                        SFLPAG(0016)
     A                                        OVERLAY
     A   21                                   SFLDSP
     A                                        SFLDSPCTL
     A   41                                   SFLEND(*MORE)
     A                                      1 26'Find Displaced Logical Files'
     A                                        DSPATR(HI)
     A                                      3  5'Physical'
     A                                        DSPATR(HI)
     A                                      3 18'Library'
     A                                        DSPATR(HI)
     A                                      3 31'Logical'
     A                                        DSPATR(HI)
     A                                      3 44'Library'
     A                                        DSPATR(HI)
     A                                      3 57'Created By'
     A                                        DSPATR(HI)
     A                                      3 70'Created On'
     A                                        DSPATR(HI)
     A          R FMT1
     A                                     22  6'F3=Exit'
     A                                        COLOR(BLU)
```

Figure 11.15: The FIG1115RG RPG Program

```
**************************************************************************
*   TO COMPILE:
*       CRTBNDRPG PGM(XXXLIB/FIG1115RG)
**************************************************************************

FFilename++IPEASFRlen+LKlen+AIDevice+.Keywords+++++++++++++++++++++++++Comments++++++
FFIG1114DS CF    E                    WORKSTN
F                                              SFILE(SFLRCD:RelRecNbr)
FQADBLDNC  IF    E           K DISK


DName+++++++++++ETDsFrom+++To/L+++IDc.Keywords+++++++++++++++++++++++++++Comments++++++
D AR             S                  1    DIM(4096)
D ALIB           S                 10    DIM(50)
D ErrorDs        DS                      INZ
D  BytesProvd             1     4B 0
D  BytesAvail             5     8B 0
D  MessageId              9    15
D  Err###                16    16
D  MessageDta            17   116
D                DS
D  ReceiveLen             1     4B 0
D  MessageKey             5     8B 0
D  MsgDtaLen              9    12B 0
D  MsgQueNbr             13    16B 0
D ReceivedDs     DS            4096
D  TotalBytes             1     4B 0
D  TotalAvail             5     8B 0
D  NbrSysLibs            65    68B 0
D  NbrPrdLibs            69    72B 0
D  NbrCurLibs            73    76B 0
D  NbrUsrLibs            77    80B 0
D Receiver1      DS             460
D  WHENYR                66    67  0
D  WHENMD                68    71  0
D  CRE8BY               220   229
D                DS
D  FFileLibr                   20
D   FLibrary                   10    OVERLAY(FFIleLibr:1)
D   FSystem                    10    OVERLAY(FFileLibr:11)
D NoneFound      C                   CONST('No outlaw logicals f-
D                                    ound in')
D NowSearch      C                   CONST('Now searching files -
D                                    for outlaw logicals')
D Err            S                  1A
D FileFormat     S                  8A
D FileLibr       S                 20A
D I              S                  4  0
D PassInLibr     S                 10A
D InternlJob     S                 16A
D J              S                  4  0
D JobName        S                 26A
D Library        S                 10A
D MData          S                 50A
D MessageFil     S                 20A
D MessageQue     S                 10A
D MessageTyp     S                 10A
D ObjectType     S                 10A
D RelRecNbr      S                  4  0
```

```
CL0N01Factor1+++++++Opcode&ExtFactor2++++++Result++++++++Len++D+HiLoEq....Comments+
C          *ENTRY     PLIST
C                     PARM                      PassInLibr
C          'QCPFMSG'  CAT       'QSYS':3        MessageFil
C                     EVAL      BytesProvd = 116
C                     EVAL      Err = *OFF
C                     EVAL      Library = PassInLibr
   *  Make sure library exists
C                     IF        (Library <> '*ALL') AND (Library <> '*LIBL')
C                     EXSR      EXIST
C                     ENDIF
C                     IF        Err = *OFF
C                     EVAL      MsgDtaLen = 40
C                     EVAL      MData = NowSearch
C                     EVAL      MessageId = 'CPF9898'
C                     EVAL      MessageTyp = '*STATUS'
C                     EVAL      MessageQue = '*EXT'
C                     EVAL      MsgQueNbr = 0
C                     EXSR      SNDERR
C                     SELECT
C                     WHEN      Library = '*ALL'
C          *LOVAL     SETLL     QDBFDEP
C                     WHEN      Library = '*LIBL'
C                     EXSR      LIBLST
C          Library    SETLL     QADBLDNC
C                     OTHER
C          Library    SETLL     QADBLDNC
C                     ENDSL
C                     DOU       *In41
C                     IF        (Library = '*ALL') OR (Library = '*LIBL')
C                     READ      QDBFDEP                              41
C                     ELSE
C          Library    READE     QADBLDNC                            41
C                     ENDIF
C                     IF        *In41 = *OFF
C                     IF        DBFLIB <> DBFLDP
C                     EVAL      MessageID = *BLANKS
   * Get created information
C                     EXSR      GETCRT
C                     IF        MessageId = 'CPF9812'
C                     ITER
C                     ENDIF
C                     Z-ADD     0               WHEN
C                     MOVEL     WHENMD          WHEN
C                     MOVE      WHENYR          WHEN
C                     EVAL      RelRecNbr = RelRecNbr + 1
C                     WRITE     SFLRCD
C                     ENDIF
C                     ELSE
C                     IF        (PassInLibr = '*LIBL')
C                     EVAL      I = I + 1
C                     IF        ALIB(I) <> *BLANKS
C                     MOVEA     ALIB(I)         Library
C          Library    SETLL     QADBLDNC
C                     EVAL      *In41 = *OFF
C                     ENDIF
C                     ENDIF
C                     ENDIF
C                     ENDDO
   *
C                     IF        RelRecNbr <> 0
C                     EVAL      *In21 = *ON
C                     WRITE     FMT1
```

```
C                        EXFMT      SFLCTL
C                        ELSE
 *   No libraries found with outlaw logicals
C                        EVAL       MsgDtaLen = 38
C                        EVAL       MData = NoneFound + ' ' + Library
C                        EVAL       MessageId = 'CPF9898'
C                        EVAL       MessageTyp = '*STATUS'
C                        EVAL       MessageQue = '*EXT'
C                        EVAL       MsgQueNbr = 1
C                        EXSR       SNDERR
C                        ENDIF
C                        ENDIF
C                        EVAL       *InLr = *ON
 *  Get who created logical file and when
C        GETCRT          BEGSR
C                        EVAL       FLibrary = DBFFDP
C                        EVAL       FSystem = DBFLDP
C                        CALL       'QUSROBJD'
C                        PARM                   Receiver1
C                        PARM       460         ReceiveLen
C                        PARM       'OBJD0300'  FileFormat
C                        PARM                   FFileLibr
C                        PARM       '*FILE'     ObjectType
C                        PARM                   ErrorDs
C                        ENDSR
 *  Make sure requested library exists
C        EXIST           BEGSR
C                        EVAL       FLibrary = Library
C                        EVAL       FSystem = 'QSYS'
C                        CALL       'QUSROBJD'
C                        PARM                   ReceivedDs
C                        PARM       5000        ReceiveLen
C                        PARM       'OBJD0100'  FileFormat
C                        PARM                   FFileLibr
C                        PARM       '*LIB'      ObjectType
C                        PARM                   ErrorDs
C                        IF         MessageId <> *BLANKS
C                        EVAL       MsgDtaLen = 10
C                        EVAL       MData = Library
C                        EVAL       MessageTyp = '*DIAG'
C                        EVAL       MessageQue = '*      '
C                        EVAL       MsgQueNbr = 1
C                        EXSR       SNDERR
C                        ENDIF
C                        ENDSR
 *  Send error back to caller
C        SNDERR          BEGSR
 *  Send error message
C                        CALL       'QMHSNDPM'
C                        PARM                   MessageId
C                        PARM                   MessageFil
C                        PARM                   MData
C                        PARM                   MsgDtaLen
C                        PARM                   MessageTyp
C                        PARM                   MessageQue
C                        PARM                   MsgQueNbr
C                        PARM                   MessageKey
C                        PARM                   ErrorDs
C                        EVAL       Err = *ON
C                        ENDSR
 *  Get library list
C        LIBLST          BEGSR
C                        CALL       'QUSRJOBI'
```

```
C                         PARM                            ReceivedDs
C                         PARM          5000              ReceiveLen
C                         PARM          'JOBI0700'        FileFormat
C                         PARM          '*'               JobName
C                         PARM                            Intern1JOb
C                         MOVEA         ReceivedDs        AR(1)
C                         EVAL          I = (NbrSysLibs * 11) + 81
C                         EVAL          J = 1
 * Product libraries
C                         DO            NbrPrdLIbs
C                         MOVEA         AR(I)             ALIB(J)
C                         EVAL          J = J + 1
C                         EVAL          I = I + 11
C                         ENDDO
 * Current libraries
C                         DO            NbrCurLibs
C                         MOVEA         AR(I)             ALIB(J)
C                         EVAL          J = J + 1
C                         EVAL          I = I + 11
C                         ENDDO
 * User libraries
C                         DO            NbrUsrLibs
C                         MOVEA         AR(I)             ALIB(J)
C                         EVAL          J = J + 1
C                         EVAL          I = I + 11
C                         ENDDO
C                         MOVEA         ALIB(1)           Library
C                         EVAL          I = 1
C                         ENDSR
```

THE WORK WITH OBJECT REFERENCE COMMAND

It is a basic law of programming: Program complexity grows until it exceeds the capability of the programmer to maintain it. Change management systems have been created (costing in the tens of thousands of dollars) to help address this particular problem.

The Art of Change Management

One common problem with change management is trying to locate all the programs that reference a file, a data area, or even another program. Changing an object can be a scary thing if you do not know how many other objects in the system may be affected. Wouldn't it be nice to have a command that shows all objects that reference another?

In order to have such a command, you need to build a reference file. The Build Object Reference (BLDOBJREF) command submits a program to build an object reference file that shows all objects that reference another object. The program creates one record in the file for each reference. An inquiry program can be written to access the reference file and then you have a very useful change management tool. The Work with Object Reference (WRKOBJREF) command is designed to perform just such a function.

Before you take the time to implement this tool, be aware that it is not perfect. The reference file for this tool is created using the Display Program Reference (DSPPGMREF) command, which can not pick up programs called using the QCMDEXC API. If your programs use the QCMDEXC command extensively, this tool may not be as useful as you would like.

Running the Work with Object Reference (WRKOBJREF) Command

All you need to do to run the Work with Object Reference (WRKOBJREF) command is to key WRKOBJREF and press F4 (you must have built your object reference summary file prior to the execution of this command). You see a prompt screen similar to that in Figure 11.16.

Figure 11.16: Running the Work with Object Reference (WRKOBJREF) Command

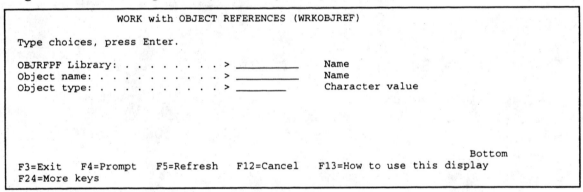

```
                    WORK with OBJECT REFERENCES (WRKOBJREF)

   Type choices, press Enter.

   OBJRFPF Library: . . . . . . . . >  _____    Name
   Object name: . . . . . . . . . . >  _____    Name
   Object type: . . . . . . . . . >  _____      Character value




                                                                    Bottom
   F3=Exit    F4=Prompt    F5=Refresh    F12=Cancel    F13=How to use this display
   F24=More keys
```

Fill in the prompt with the library name, object name, and object type (e.g., *FILE, *PGM, *DTAARA), and press Enter. If the type you specify happens to be a file, you are prompted for an extra set of parameters, shown in Figure 11.17. These parameters are necessary to determine whether or not the object you specify happens to be a physical file. If so, you may specify that the search of reference occurrences include any logical files that may be related to the physical file.

Figure 11.17: Running the Work with Object Reference (WRKOBJREF) Command on Physical Files

```
                    WORK with OBJECT REFERENCES (WRKOBJREF)

 Type choices, press Enter.

 OBJRFPF Library: . . . . . . . . > TESTLIB        Name
 Object name: . . . . . . . . . . > CUSTOMER       Name
 Object type: . . . . . . . . . . > *FILE          Character value
 Is Object a Physical File?: . .   Y               Y, N
 Include logicals over file?: . .  Y               N, Y
 Physical file library: . . . . .  *LIBL           Character value




                                                             Bottom
 F3=Exit   F4=Prompt   F5=Refresh   F12=Cancel   F13=How to use this display
 F24=More keys
```

Once you establish your search criteria and press Enter, you see an Object Reference display similar to Figure 11.18.

Figure 11.18: Sample Output from the Work with Object Reference (WRKOBJREF) Command

```
                     Work with Object References

   Object name. . . . CUSTOMER

   Type Options, press Enter.
    1=Source

 Name      Library   Text                              Useage  Logical
 CUSSUM    TESTLIB   Customer Summary Report           INPUT   CSBYNUM
 FONLST    TESTLIB   Customer Phone Book               INPUT   PHYSICAL
 LSTCUS    TESTLIB   Customer List Program             INPUT   CUSBYNAM
 QRYCUS    TESTLIB   Customer Query Program            INPUT   PHYSICAL
 RCDLCK    TESTLIB   Record lock error program         UPDATE  PHYSICAL



                                                             Bottom

    F3=Exit      F12=Previous
```

GETTING STARTED WITH WORK WITH OBJECT REFERENCE (WRKOBJREF)

Because of the number of source members required to make the Build Object Reference (BLDOBJREF) and Work with Object Reference (WRKOBJREF) commands work, we put together a CL program that builds all of the required objects for you. The first thing you need to do is get all of the source members into your desired library. Put them in a physical source file named SOURCE (you can use the CRTSRCPF command to create the file, if needed). Then compile the OBJMAKECL program, and call it. The OBJMAKECL program builds everything you need to run these two commands.

Compile the OBJMAKECL program as follows:

```
CRTCLPGM PGM(XXXLIB/OBJMAKECL) SRCMBR(FIG1123CL)
```

To run the OBJMAKECL program, simply key:

```
CALL OBJMAKECL PARM('XXXLIB')
```

Note: XXXLIB is the library where you have put the OBJREF source members.

Once the OBJMAKECL program has been run, you are ready to build your Object Reference pointer file. To do so, simply press BLDOBJREF and press F4. You are prompted for the libraries you want to include in your Object Reference pointer file and the date and time at which you want the command to execute.

How often you need to run the Build Object Reference (BLDOBJREF) command depends upon how much your programs change. If you are in a development environment like ours, you may want to incorporate this command into your daily startup programs, as we have. The data in your Object Reference pointer files can obviously only be current to the last time you ran the Build Object Reference (BLDOBJREF) command. It is important to note that BLDOBJREF will replace data from any previous BLDOBJREF jobs that met the same criteria.

THE VALUE OF WORK WITH OBJECT REFERENCE (WRKOBJREF)

We find this tool to be tremendously valuable when we have to change existing objects in our system. The command provides a quick way to determine what is involved, as well as a list of the source members that need to be changed.

There are two commands in this utility: Build Object Reference (BLDOBJREF) and Work with Object Reference (WRKOBJREF). BLDOBJREF (Figure 11.19) is used to build the work files. Figures 11.20 through 11.28 make up the display files, RPG programs, and CL programs used to build or work with the files created by the BLDOBJREF command. WRKOBJREF (Figure 11.29) is used to display the object reference instances. Even though compile notes have been added in the remarks sections of these source members, the OBJMAKECL program, described previously, should take care of all of this for you.

Figure 11.19: The Build Object Reference (BLDOBJREF) Command

```
/*================================================================*/
/* To compile:                                                    */
/*                                                                */
/*          CRTCMD       CMD(XXX/BLDOBJREF) PGM(XXX/FIG1125CL)     */
/*                       SRCMBR(FIG1119CM)                         */
/*                                                                */
/*================================================================*/
           CMD           PROMPT('BUILD OBJECT REFERENCE')
           PARM          KWD(LIB) TYPE(*NAME) PROMPT('LIBRARY FOR FILE:') MIN(1)
           PARM          KWD(LIST) TYPE(LIST1) MIN(1) MAX(100) +
                         PROMPT('LIST OF LIBRARIES:')
           PARM          KWD(JOBQ) TYPE(*CHAR) LEN(10) DFT(QBATCH) +
                         PMTCTL(*PMTRQS) PROMPT('JOB QUEUE:')
           PARM          KWD(SCDATE) TYPE(*CHAR) LEN(6) DFT(*CURRENT) +
                         SPCVAL((*CURRENT 000000)) PMTCTL(*PMTRQS) +
                         PROMPT('SCHEDULE DATE:')
           PARM          KWD(SCTIME) TYPE(*CHAR) LEN(4) DFT(*CURRENT) +
                         SPCVAL((*CURRENT 0000)) PMTCTL(*PMTRQS) +
                         PROMPT('SCHEDULE TIME (MILITARY):')
           PARM          KWD(JOBN) TYPE(*CHAR) LEN(10) DFT(BUILDREF) +
                         PMTCTL(*PMTRQS) PROMPT('JOB NAME:')
LIST1:     ELEM          TYPE(*NAME) LEN(10) MIN(1) EXPR(*YES) +
                         PROMPT('LIBRARY NAME')
```

Figure 11.20: The FIG1120CL CL Program

```
/************************************************************************/
/*     TO CREATE:                                                    */
/*         CRTCLPGM PGM(XXXLIB/FIG1120CL                             */
/************************************************************************/
PGM (&FILE &LIB)

DCL VAR(&FILE) TYPE(*CHAR) LEN(10)
DCL VAR(&LIB) TYPE(*CHAR) LEN(10)

MONMSG CPF0000

          IF          COND(&LIB *EQ '          ') THEN(DO)
          CHGVAR      VAR(&LIB) VALUE('*LIBL')
          ENDDO

          CLRPFM      FILE(QTEMP/OBJRFLOG)

          DSPDBR      FILE(&LIB/&FILE) OUTPUT(*OUTFILE) +
                        OUTFILE(QTEMP/OBJRFLOG)

ENDPGM
```

Figure 11.21: The FIG1121RG RPG Program

```
       ****************************************************************************
       *   TO COMPILE:
       *       CRTBNDRPG PGM(XXXLIB/FIG1121RG
       ****************************************************************************
       *
       *   PROGRAM NAME - FIG1121RG
       *   FUNCTION     - TAKE FILE FROM DSPPGMREF AND WRITE PERTINENT
       *                    INFO TO SCANABLE FILE.
       *

       FFilename++IPEASFRlen+LKlen+AIDevice+.Keywords++++++++++++++++++++++++++Comments+++++
       FPGMREFO   IF  E             DISK
       FOBJRFPF   O   E             DISK

       CL0N01Factor1++++++Opcode&ExtFactor2++++++Result+++++++Len++D+HiLoEq....Comments+
       C     1             SETLL     PGMREFO
B1     C                   DOU       *IN50 = *ON
       C                   READ      PGMREFO                                    50
B2     C                   IF        *IN50 = *ON
       C                   LEAVE
E2     C                   ENDIF
       C                   EVAL      OBJLIB = WHLIB
       C                   EVAL      OBJNAM = WHPNAM
       C                   EVAL      OBJTXT = WHTEXT
       C                   EVAL      OBRNAM = WHFNAM
       C                   EVAL      OBRLIB = WHLNAM
       C                   MOVEL     WHFUSG         OBRUSE
       C                   EVAL      OBRTYP = WHOTYP
       C                   WRITE     OBJREC
E1     C                   ENDDO
       *
       C                   EVAL      *INLR = *ON
```

Figure 11.22: The FIG1122CL CL Program

```
/***********************************************************************/
/*    TO CREATE:                                                       */
/*        CRTCLPGM PGM(XXXLIB/FIG1122CL                                */
/***********************************************************************/
PGM   (&LIBRARY &REPADD &REFLIB)

DCL &LIBRARY *CHAR 10
DCL &REPADD *CHAR 1
DCL &REFLIB  *CHAR 10

            DSPPGMREF  PGM(&LIBRARY/*ALL) OUTPUT(*OUTFILE) +
                         OUTFILE(QTEMP/PGMREFO) OUTMBR(*FIRST)

            OVRDBF     FILE(OBJRFPF) TOFILE(&REFLIB/OBJRFPF)
            OVRDBF     FILE(PGMREFO) TOFILE(QTEMP/PGMREFO)

IF COND(&REPADD *EQ 'R') THEN(DO)
CLRPFM &REFLIB/OBJRFPF
ENDDO

CALL FIG1121RG

            DLTOVR PGMREFO
            DLTOVR OBJRFPF

ENDPGM
```

Figure 11.23: The FIG1123CL CL Program

```
/***********************************************************************/
/*    TO CREATE:                                                       */
/*        CRTCLPGM PGM(XXXLIB/FIG1123CL)                               */
/***********************************************************************/
PGM (&LIB)

DCL &LIB *CHAR 10
DCL &MSGDTA *CHAR 50
DCL &NOADD *CHAR 1

            ADDLIBLE    &LIB
            MONMSG      MSGID(CPF2103) EXEC(DO)
            CHGVAR      &NOADD '1'
            ENDDO

            CHGVAR      VAR(&MSGDTA) VALUE('Creating OBJRFPF file')
            SNDPGMMSG   MSGID(CPF9898) MSGF(QSYS/QCPFMSG) +
                          MSGDTA(&MSGDTA) TOPGMQ(*EXT) MSGTYPE(*STATUS)
            CRTPF       FILE(&LIB/OBJRFPF) SRCFILE(&LIB/SOURCE) +
                          SRCMBR(FIG1128)

            CHGVAR      VAR(&MSGDTA) VALUE('Creating PGMREFO file')
            SNDPGMMSG   MSGID(CPF9898) MSGF(QSYS/QCPFMSG) +
                          MSGDTA(&MSGDTA) TOPGMQ(*EXT) MSGTYPE(*STATUS)
            DSPPGMREF   PGM(&LIB/*ALL) OUTPUT(*OUTFILE) +
                          OUTFILE(QTEMP/PGMREFO) OUTMBR(*FIRST)
```

```
          CHGVAR      VAR(&MSGDTA) VALUE('Creating OBJRFLOG file')
          SNDPGMMSG   MSGID(CPF9898) MSGF(QSYS/QCPFMSG) +
                        MSGDTA(&MSGDTA) TOPGMQ(*EXT) MSGTYPE(*STATUS)
          DSPDBR      FILE(&LIB/OBJRFPF) OUTPUT(*OUTFILE) +
                        OUTFILE(QTEMP/OBJRFLOG)

          CHGVAR      VAR(&MSGDTA) VALUE('Creating OBJRFDSP display file')
          SNDPGMMSG   MSGID(CPF9898) MSGF(QSYS/QCPFMSG) +
                        MSGDTA(&MSGDTA) TOPGMQ(*EXT) MSGTYPE(*STATUS)
          CRTDSPF     FILE(&LIB/FIG1127DS) SRCFILE(&LIB/SOURCE)

          CHGVAR      VAR(&MSGDTA) VALUE('Creating OBJRF RPG program     ')
          SNDPGMMSG   MSGID(CPF9898) MSGF(QSYS/QCPFMSG) +
                        MSGDTA(&MSGDTA) TOPGMQ(*EXT) MSGTYPE(*STATUS)
          CRTBNDRPG   PGM(&LIB/FIG1126RG) SRCFILE(&LIB/SOURCE)

          CHGVAR      VAR(&MSGDTA) VALUE('Creating OBJHS RPG program     ')
          SNDPGMMSG   MSGID(CPF9898) MSGF(QSYS/QCPFMSG) +
                        MSGDTA(&MSGDTA) TOPGMQ(*EXT) MSGTYPE(*STATUS)
          CRTBNDRPG   PGM(&LIB/FIG1121RG) SRCFILE(&LIB/SOURCE)

          CHGVAR      VAR(&MSGDTA) VALUE('Creating OBJCRLGL CLP program ')
          SNDPGMMSG   MSGID(CPF9898) MSGF(QSYS/QCPFMSG) +
                        MSGDTA(&MSGDTA) TOPGMQ(*EXT) MSGTYPE(*STATUS)
          CRTCLPGM    PGM(&LIB/FIG1120CL) SRCFILE(&LIB/SOURCE)

          CHGVAR      VAR(&MSGDTA) VALUE('Creating OBJHSTCL CLP program ')
          SNDPGMMSG   MSGID(CPF9898) MSGF(QSYS/QCPFMSG) +
                        MSGDTA(&MSGDTA) TOPGMQ(*EXT) MSGTYPE(*STATUS)
          CRTCLPGM    PGM(&LIB/FIG1122CL) SRCFILE(&LIB/SOURCE)

          CHGVAR      VAR(&MSGDTA) VALUE('Creating OBJREFBLDS CLP program ')
          SNDPGMMSG   MSGID(CPF9898) MSGF(QSYS/QCPFMSG) +
                        MSGDTA(&MSGDTA) TOPGMQ(*EXT) MSGTYPE(*STATUS)
          CRTCLPGM    PGM(&LIB/FIG1124CL) SRCFILE(&LIB/SOURCE)

          CHGVAR      VAR(&MSGDTA) VALUE('Creating OBJREFBSBM CLP program ')
          SNDPGMMSG   MSGID(CPF9898) MSGF(QSYS/QCPFMSG) +
                        MSGDTA(&MSGDTA) TOPGMQ(*EXT) MSGTYPE(*STATUS)
          CRTCLPGM    PGM(&LIB/FIG1125CL) SRCFILE(&LIB/SOURCE)

          CHGVAR      VAR(&MSGDTA) VALUE('Creating WRKOBJREF command      ')
          SNDPGMMSG   MSGID(CPF9898) MSGF(QSYS/QCPFMSG) +
                        MSGDTA(&MSGDTA) TOPGMQ(*EXT) MSGTYPE(*STATUS)
          CRTCMD      CMD(&LIB/WRKOBJREF) PGM(&LIB/FIG1126RG) +
                        SRCFILE(&LIB/SOURCE) SRCMBR(FIG1129CM)

          CHGVAR      VAR(&MSGDTA) VALUE('Creating BLDOBJREF command      ')
          SNDPGMMSG   MSGID(CPF9898) MSGF(QSYS/QCPFMSG) +
                        MSGDTA(&MSGDTA) TOPGMQ(*EXT) MSGTYPE(*STATUS)
          CRTCMD      CMD(&LIB/BLDOBJREF) PGM(&LIB/FIG1125CL) +
                        SRCFILE(&LIB/SOURCE) SRCMBR(FIG1119CM)

          IF          COND(&NOADD *NE '1') THEN(DO)
          RMVLIBLE    &LIB
          ENDDO

ENDPGM
```

Figure 11.24: The FIG1124CL CL Program

```
/*********************************************************************/
/*    TO CREATE:                                                     */
/*         CRTCLPGM PGM(XXXLIB/FIG1124CL)                            */
/*********************************************************************/
PGM (&LIB &LIST)

            DCL        VAR(&LIB) TYPE(*CHAR) LEN(10)
            DCL        VAR(&BLDLIB) TYPE(*CHAR) LEN(10)
            DCL        VAR(&REPADD) TYPE(*CHAR) LEN(1) VALUE('R')
            DCL        VAR(&LIST) TYPE(*CHAR) LEN(1902)
            DCL        VAR(&X) TYPE(*DEC) LEN(3 0) /* Count of nbr */
            DCL        VAR(&Y) TYPE(*DEC) LEN(5 0) VALUE(1) /* +
                         Displacement */
            DCL        VAR(&Z) TYPE(*DEC) LEN(5 0) /* Pos of values */
            DCL        VAR(&WORK) TYPE(*CHAR) LEN(2)
            DCL        VAR(&LSTCNT) TYPE(*DEC) LEN(5 0)
            DCL        VAR(&DISPCNT) TYPE(*DEC) LEN(5 0)

/*   GLOBAL MONITOR MESSAGE    */
            MONMSG     MSGID(CPF0000)

/*   IF REFERENCE FILE DOESN'T EXIST, CREATE IT FROM BASE COPY IN QGPL   */
            CHKOBJ     OBJ(&LIB/OBJRFPF) OBJTYPE(*FILE)
            MONMSG     MSGID(CPF9801) EXEC(DO)
            CRTDUPOBJ  OBJ(OBJRFPF) FROMLIB(QGPL) OBJTYPE(*FILE) +
                         TOLIB(&LIB)
            ENDDO

            OVRDBF     FILE(OBJRFPF) TOFILE(&LIB/OBJRFPF)
            CLRPFM     FILE(&LIB/OBJRFPF)

            CHGVAR     VAR(&WORK) VALUE(%SST(&LIST 1 2)) /* Nbr of +
                         lists */
            CHGVAR     VAR(&LSTCNT) VALUE(%BIN(&WORK 1 2))

/*   BEGIN LOOP FOR EACH LIST                                    */
 LOOP:
            CHGVAR     VAR(&X) VALUE(&X + 1) /* Next list */
            CHGVAR     VAR(&Y) VALUE(&Y + 2) /* Next displacement */

/*   EXTRACT DISPLACEMENT VALUE    */
            CHGVAR     VAR(&WORK) VALUE(%SST(&LIST &Y 2))
            CHGVAR     VAR(&DISPCNT) VALUE(%BIN(&WORK 1 2))

            CHGVAR     VAR(&Z) VALUE(&DISPCNT + 3) /* Bgn pos +
                         within list */

/*   GET LIBRARY NAME              */
            CHGVAR     VAR(&BLDLIB) VALUE(%SST(&LIST &Z 10))

/*   DISPLAY PROGRAM REFERENCES TO WORK FILE IN QTEMP   */
            DSPPGMREF  PGM(&BLDLIB/*ALL) OUTPUT(*OUTFILE) +
                         OUTFILE(QTEMP/PGMREFO) OUTMBR(*FIRST *ADD)

            IF         (&X *LT &LSTCNT) GOTO LOOP /* Loop back */
/*   CALL PROGRAM TO WRITE RECORDS TO REFERENCE FILE    */
```

```
        OVRDBF      FILE(OBJRFPF) TOFILE(&LIB/OBJRFPF)
        OVRDBF      FILE(PGMREFO) TOFILE(QTEMP/PGMREFO)
        CALL        PGM(FIG1121RG)
        DLTOVR PGMREFO
        DLTOVR OBJRFPF

ENDPGM
```

Figure 11.25: The FIG1125CL CL Program

```
/****************************************************************/
/*     TO CREATE:                                             */
/*        CRTCLPGM PGM(XXXLIB/FIG1125CL)                      */
/****************************************************************/
PGM (&LIB &LIST &JOBQ &SCCDATE &SCCTIME &JOBN)

            DCL         VAR(&LIST) TYPE(*CHAR) LEN(1902)
            DCL         VAR(&LIB) TYPE(*CHAR) LEN(10)
            DCL         VAR(&JOBQ) TYPE(*CHAR) LEN(10)
            DCL         VAR(&JOBN) TYPE(*CHAR) LEN(10)
            DCL         VAR(&SCCDATE) TYPE(*CHAR) LEN(6)
            DCL         VAR(&SCCTIME) TYPE(*CHAR) LEN(4)
            DCL         VAR(&SCCDATE8) TYPE(*CHAR) LEN(8) +
                          VALUE(*CURRENT)
            DCL         VAR(&SCCTIME8) TYPE(*CHAR) LEN(8) +
                          VALUE(*CURRENT)

/*    GLOBAL MONITOR MESSAGE      */
            MONMSG      MSGID(CPF0000)

/*    IF SUBMITTING ON DATE OTHER THAN CURRENT THEN USE THAT DATE    */
            IF          COND(&SCCDATE *NE '000000') THEN(DO)
            CHGVAR      VAR(&SCCDATE8) VALUE(&SCCDATE)
            ENDDO

/*    IF SUBMITTING ON TIME OTHER THAN CURRENT THEN USE THAT TIME    */
            IF          COND(&SCCTIME *NE '0000') THEN(DO)
            CHGVAR      VAR(&SCCTIME8) VALUE(&SCCTIME)
            ENDDO

/*    SUBMIT THE JOB TO CREATE THE FILE                         */
            SBMJOB      CMD(CALL PGM(FIG1124CL) PARM(&LIB &LIST)) +
                          JOB(&JOBN) JOBQ(&JOBQ) SCDDATE(&SCCDATE8) +
                          SCDTIME(&SCCTIME8)

/*    SEND JOB SUBMITTED MESSAGE BACK TO USER                   */
            SNDPGMMSG   MSGID(CPF9898) MSGF(QCPFMSG) MSGDTA('JOB' +
                          *BCAT &JOBN *TCAT ' has been submitted +
                          to batch.') MSGTYPE(*DIAG)

ENDPGM
```

Figure 11.26: The FIG1126RG RPG Program

```
    *********************************************************************
    *  TO COMPILE:
    *     CRTBNDRPG PGM(XXXLIB/FIG1126RG)
    *********************************************************************
   FFilename++IPEASFRlen+LKlen+AIDevice+.Keywords++++++++++++++++++++++++Comments++++++
   FFIG1127DS CF   E             WORKSTN
   F                                          SFILE(SFLRCD:RelRecNbr)
   F                                          INFDS(InfoDs)
   FOBJRFPF    IF   E           K DISK        USROPN
   FOBJRFLOG   IF   E             DISK        USROPN

   DName++++++++++ETDsFrom+++To/L+++IDc.Keywords+++++++++++++++++++++++++Comments++++++
   D InfoDs          DS
   D  WorkStatID            197    206
   D  FirstLine             378    379B 0
   D ErrorDs         DS                   INZ
   D  BytesProv               1      4B 0
   D  BytesAval               5      8B 0
   D  MessageId               9     15
   D  ERR###                 16     16
   D  MessageDta             17    116
   D                 DS
   D  MsgDtaLen               1      4B 0
   D  MsgQueNbr               5      8B 0
   D  MsgKey                  9     12B 0
   D  RelRecNbr     S                4  0
   D  Found         S                1
   D  Duplicate     S               20
   D  PassLibNam    S               10
   D  PassObjNam    S               10
   D  PassType      S                8
   D  PhysicalFl    S                1
   D  LogicalYN     S                1
   D  LogicalLib    S               10
   D  ProgramQue    S               10
   D  Command       S               50
   D  Length        S               15     5 INZ(50)
   D  F20           S               20
   D  MoreLogics    S                1
   D               SDS
   D  UserName              254    263
   D  NbrParms            *PARMS
   D RestOfCmd      C                      CONST('OVRDBF FILE(OBJRFPF)-
   D                                        TOFILE(')
   D FileNamCon     C                      CONST('/OBJRFPF)')
   D NoRefernce     C                      CONST('NO REFERENCES EXIST -
   D                                       FOR THIS OBJECT  - P-
   D                                       RESS ENTER')

   CL0N01Factor1++++++Opcode&ExtFactor2++++++Result+++++++Len++D+HiLoEq....Comments+
   C     *ENTRY      PLIST
   C                 PARM                    PassLibNam
   C                 PARM                    PassObjNam
   C                 PARM                    PassType
   C                 PARM                    PhysicalFl
   C                 PARM                    LogicalYN
   C                 PARM                    LogicalLib
   C                 MOVEL     '*'           ProgramQue
   C                 MOVEL(P)  RestOfCmd     Command
   C                 CAT       PassLibNam:0  Command
   C                 CAT       FileNamCon:0  Command
```

```
        C                    CALL      'QCMDEXC'
        C                    PARM                        Command
        C                    PARM                        Length
        C                    OPEN      OBJRFPF                              99
        C                    Eval      ScanName = PassObjNam
        C                    IF        (PassType = '*FILE') and (LogicalYN = 'Y')
        C                              and (PhysicalFl = 'Y')
        C                    CALL      'OBJCRLGL'
        C                    PARM                         ScanName
        C                    PARM                         LogicalLib
        C                    OPEN      OBJRFLOG                             99
        C                    If        *IN99 = *OFF
        C                    EVAL      *IN82 = *ON
E2      C                    ENDIF
E1      C                    ENDIF
        C      ScanName      SETLL     OBJRFPF
        C                    EXSR      LODSFL
        C                    EVAL      *IN21 = *OFF
        C                    If        RelRecNbr <> 0
        C                    EVAL      *IN21 = *ON
        C                    EVAL      PosRelRec = 1
X1      C                    ELSE
        C                    EXSR      ERRSR
        C                    WRITE     MSGCTL
        C                    EVAL      *IN03 = *ON
E1      C                    ENDIF
        C                    DOU       (*IN03 = *ON) or (Found <> 'Y')
        C                    IF        *IN03 = *OFF
        C                    WRITE     FORMAT1
E2      C                    ENDIF
        C                    EXFMT     SFLCTL
        C                    EVAL      Found = *Blanks
E1      C                    ENDDO
        C                    EVAL      *INLR = *ON
        * Load the subfile
        CSR    LODSFL        BEGSR
        C                    DOU       MoreLogics = *blanks
        C                    EVAL      MoreLogics = *blanks
        C                    DOU       (*IN51 = *ON)
        C      ScanName      READE     OBJRFPF                              51
        C                    IF        *IN51 = *ON
        C                    LEAVE
E3      C                    ENDIF
        *
        * If object referenced more than once in same progeram, only want it shown
        *   in the subfile once
        *
        C                    MOVEL     OBJLIB      F20            20
        C                    MOVE      OBJNAM      F20
        C                    IF        F20 = Duplicate
        C                    ITER
E3      C                    ENDIF
        C                    EVAL      Duplicate = F20
        C                    MOVE      OBJNAM         DOBJNM
        C                    MOVE      OBJLIB         DOBJLB
        C                    MOVEL     OBJTXT         DOBJTX
        C                    MOVE      *BLANKS        DUSEDS
        C                    IF        ObrTyp = '*FILE'
        C                    MOVEL(P)  'UNKNOWN'      DUSEDS
B4      C                    SELECT
        C                    WHEN      ObrUse = '01'
        C                    MOVEL(P)  'INPUT'        DUSEDS
        C                    WHEN      ObrUse = '02'
```

```
     C                   MOVEL(P)   'OUTPUT'        DUSEDS
     C                   WHEN       ObrUse = '03'
     C                   MOVEL(P)   'WRKSTN'        DUSEDS
     C                   WHEN       ObrUse = '04'
     C                   MOVEL(P)   'UPDATE'        DUSEDS
     C                   WHEN       ObrUse = '06'
     C                   MOVEL(P)   'UPD/ADD'       DUSEDS
     C                   WHEN       (ObrUse = '09') or (ObrUse = '11')
     C                   MOVEL(P)   'DEL/CRT'       DUSEDS
E4   C                   ENDSL
E3   C                   ENDIF
     C                   IF         (DLogNm = *blanks) and (*IN82 = *ON)
     C                   MOVEL      'PHYSICAL'      DLOGNM
E3   C                   ENDIF
     C                   EVAL       RelRecNbr = (RelRecNbr + 1)
     C                   WRITE      SFLRCD
E2   C                   ENDDO
      * If logicals are included in search, put next logical name and loop to th
     C                   IF         *IN82 = *ON
     C                   READ       OBJRFLOG                              52
     C                   IF         *IN52 = *OFF
     C                   MOVEL(P)   WHREFI          ScanName
     C                   MOVEL(P)   WHREFI          DLOGNM
     C                   EVAL       MoreLogics = 'X'
     C       ScanName    SETLL      OBJRFPF
E3   C                   ENDIF
E2   C                   ENDIF
E1   C                   ENDDO
     C                   ENDSR
     C       ERRSR       BEGSR
     C                   EVAL       BytesProv = 116
     C       'QCPFMSG'   CAT        'QSYS':3        MSGF
     C                   MOVE       'CPF9898'       MessageId
     C                   MOVEL(P)   NoRefernce      MessageDta
     C                   Z-ADD      60              MsgDtaLen
     C                   Z-ADD      0               MsgQueNbr
      * Send error message
     C                   CALL       'QMHSNDPM'
     C                   PARM                       MessageId
     C                   PARM                       MSGF         20
     C                   PARM                       MessageDta
     C                   PARM                       MsgDtaLen
     C                   PARM       '*DIAG'         MessageTyp   10
     C                   PARM       '*'             MessageQue   10
     C                   PARM                       MsgQueNbr
     C                   PARM                       MsgKey
     C                   PARM                       ErrorDs
     C                   ENDSR
```

Figure 11.27: The FIG1127DS Display File

```
A************************************************************************
A*   TO COMPILE:
A*     CRTDSPF FILE(XXXLIB/FIG1127DS)
A************************************************************************
AAN01N02N03T.Name++++++RLen++TDpBLinPosFunctions++++++++++++++++++++++++++
A                                       DSPSIZ(24 80 *DS3)
A                                       PRINT
A                                       CA03(03)
A                                       CA12(03)
A          R SFLRCD                     SFL
A   40                                  SFLNXTCHG
A            DOBJNM      10A  O  9  4
A            DOBJLB      10A  O  9 15
A            DOBJTX      38A  O  9 26
A            DUSEDS       7A  O  9 65
A            DLOGNM       8A  O  9 73
A          R SFLCTL                     SFLCTL(SFLRCD)
A                                       CHGINPDFT
A                                       SFLSIZ(0024)
A                                       SFLPAG(0012)
A                                       OVERLAY
A   21                                  SFLDSP
A                                       SFLDSPCTL
A   51                                  SFLEND(*MORE)
A            POSRELREC    4S 0H         SFLRCDNBR
A                                    1 26'Work with Object References'
A                                       DSPATR(HI)
A                                       DSPATR(UL)
A                                    3  3'Object name. . . . .'
A N21                                   DSPATR(ND)
A            SCANNAME    10A  O  3 22
A N21                                   DSPATR(ND)
A   21N82                            8  2' Name        Library     Text      -
A                                         Useage-
A                                         '
A                                       DSPATR(HI)
A   21 82                            8  2' Name        Library     Text      -
A                                         Useage-
A                                         Logical'
A                                       DSPATR(HI)
A          R FORMAT1
A                                       TEXT('Command keys')
A                                   23  4'F3=Exit'
A                                       COLOR(BLU)
A                                   23 17'F12=Previous'
A                                       COLOR(BLU)
A          R MSGSFL                     SFL
A                                       SFLMSGRCD(24)
A            MESSAGEKEY                 SFLMSGKEY
A            PROGRAMQUE                 SFLPGMQ
A          R MSGCTL                     SFLCTL(MSGSFL)
A                                       OVERLAY
A                                       ALARM
A                                       SFLSIZ(3) SFLPAG(1)
A                                       SFLDSP SFLINZ
A   90                                  SFLEND
A            PROGRAMQUE                 SFLPGMQ
```

Figure 11.28: The OBJRFPF Physical File

```
A*****************************************************************
A*   TO COMPILE:
A*     CRTPF FILE(XXXLIB/OBJRFPF) SRCMBR(FIG1128)
A*****************************************************************
AAN01N02N03T.Name++++++RLen++TDpBLinPosFunctions+++++++++++++++++++++++++++
A          R OBJREC
A            OBJNAM        10            COLHDG('OBJECT NAME')
A            OBJLIB        10            COLHDG('OBJECT LIBRARY')
A            OBJTXT        40            COLHDG('OBJECT TEXT')
A            OBRNAM        10            COLHDG('REFERENCED OBJECT')
A            OBRLIB        10            COLHDG('REFERENCED LIBRARY')
A            OBRTYP        10            COLHDG('REFERENCED TYPE')
A            OBRUSE         2            COLHDG('FILE USEAGE')
A          K OBRNAM
A          K OBRLIB
A          K OBJNAM
A          K OBJLIB
```

Figure 11.29: The Work with Object Reference (WRKOBJREF) Command

```
/*===============================================================*/
/* To compile:                                                   */
/*                                                               */
/*          CRTCMD     CMD(XXX/WRKOBJREF) PGM(XXX/FIG1126RG)      */
/*                     SRCMBR(FIG1129CM)                          */
/*                                                               */
/*===============================================================*/
           CMD        PROMPT('WORK with OBJECT REFERENCES')
           PARM       KWD(LIB) TYPE(*NAME) PROMPT('OBJRFPF Library:') +
                        MIN(1)
           PARM       KWD(NAME) TYPE(*NAME) PROMPT('Object name:') +
                        MIN(1)
           PARM       KWD(TYPE) TYPE(*CHAR) LEN(8) PROMPT('Object type:') +
                        MIN(1)
           PARM       KWD(PHYFIL) TYPE(*CHAR) LEN(1) RSTD(*YES) +
                        VALUES(Y N) DFT(N) PMTCTL(TYPE) PROMPT('Is +
                        Object a Physical File?:')
           PARM       KWD(LOGYN) TYPE(*CHAR) LEN(1) RSTD(*YES) +
                        DFT(Y) VALUES(N Y) PMTCTL(ATTR) +
                        PROMPT('Include logicals over file?:')
           PARM       KWD(LOGLIB) TYPE(*CHAR) LEN(10) DFT(*LIBL) +
                        PMTCTL(ATTR) PROMPT('Physical file library:')
TYPE:      PMTCTL     CTL(TYPE) COND((*EQ *FILE))
ATTR:      PMTCTL     CTL(PHYFIL) COND((*EQ Y))
```

THE SERVICE PROGRAM USAGE COMMAND

Service programs were introduced as part of ILE. We will be discussing the pros and cons of service programs in Chapter 13. In the mean time, suffice it to say that this command will help you to identify all programs in your system that call a service program.

This tool will list all programs in a given library that use the given service program. When running this tool, you will enter the search library name and optionally a generic program name. In addition, you will specify the service program and library that is the object of the search. The library name accepts the special value *ANY, which means exactly what it says. The tool will look for *any* program that uses a service program with the indicated name, regardless of the library that the service program is in.

You can see an example of the output from this command in Figure 11.30. The display file, RPG program, and command that make it all work are in Figures 11.31 through 11.33, respectively.

Figure 11.30: Output from the Service Program Usage (SERPGMUSAG) Command

```
                        Programs with Service Program

Requested Service Program: QRNXIE       *ANY
Search parameters:            *ALL       APPLIB

Library      Program      Created    Time    Owner
APPLIB       DBG002RG     05/14/96    7:56   QPGMR
APPLIB       INU001RG     05/01/96   14:41   QPGMR
APPLIB       LIL001RG     05/16/96   13:38   JOE
APPLIB       MOD001RG     02/06/96   13:27   QPGMR
APPLIB       MOD005RG     03/06/96    9:18   QPGMR
APPLIB       MOD007RG     03/10/96   13:31   QPGMR
APPLIB       SRV005RG     03/07/96    9:55   QPGMR
APPLIB       TSTBND       03/07/96   12:35   BILLO
APPLIB       TSTCAT       05/21/96   11:18   QPGMR
APPLIB       TSTPGM2      03/10/96   13:55   QPGMR
APPLIB       TSTPGM3      03/10/96   13:34   QPGMR
APPLIB       TSTSIZ       05/21/96   13:12   QPGMR
                                                          More...


   F3=Exit
```

Figure 11.31: The FIG1131DS Display File

```
A*****************************************************************
A*   TO COMPILE:
A*      CRTDSPF FILE(XXXLIB/FIG1131DS)
A*****************************************************************
AAN01N02N03T.Name++++++RLen++TDpBLinPosFunctions++++++++++++++++++++++++++++++
A                                        DSPSIZ(24 80 *DS3)
A                                        CF03(03)
A           R SFLRECORD                  SFL
A             LIBRARYNAM    10A  O  7  2
A             PROGRAMNAM    10A  O  7 14
A             DCREATEMDY     8A  O  7 27
A             DCREATETIM     4Y 0O  7 36EDTWRD('  :  ')
A             PGMOWNER      10A  O  7 43
A           R SFLCONTROL                 SFLCTL(SFLRECORD)
A                                        SFLSIZ(0024)
A                                        SFLPAG(0012)
A                                        OVERLAY
A   21                                   SFLDSP
A   22                                   SFLDSPCTL
A   23                                   SFLCLR
A   24                                   SFLEND(*MORE)
A                                      1 25'Programs with Service Program'
A                                        DSPATR(HI)
A                                        DSPATR(UL)
A                                      6  2'Library'
A                                        DSPATR(HI)
A                                        DSPATR(UL)
A                                      6 14'Program'
A                                        DSPATR(HI)
A                                        DSPATR(UL)
A                                      3  2'Requested Service Program:'
A             TARGETNAME    10A  O  3 29
A             TARGETLIB     10A  O  3 40
A                                      4  2'Search parameters:'
A             SEARCHOBJ     10A  O  4 29
A             SEARCHLIB     10A  O  4 40
A                                      6 44'Owner'
A                                        DSPATR(HI)
A                                        DSPATR(UL)
A                                      6 27'Created'
A                                        DSPATR(HI)
A                                        DSPATR(UL)
A                                      6 37'Time'
A                                        DSPATR(HI)
A                                        DSPATR(UL)
A           R FMT1
A                                     22  3'F3=Exit'   COLOR(BLU)
```

Figure 11.32: The FIG1132RG RPG Program

```
     *************************************************************************
     *   TO COMPILE:
     *      CRTBNDPGM PGM(XXXLIB/FIG1132RG)
     *************************************************************************
    FFilename++IPEASFRlen+LKlen+AIDevice+.Keywords+++++++++++++++++++++Comments+++++
    FFIG1131DS CF   E                    WORKSTN
    F                                    SFILE(SFLRECORD:SflRcdNbr)
    FQSYSPRT   O    F 132                PRINTER OFLIND(*INOA) USROPN

    DName+++++++++++ETDsFrom+++To/L+++IDc.Keywords+++++++++++++++++++++++Comments+++++
    D GeneralDs       DS
    D  InputSize            113    116B 0
    D  ListOffset           125    128B 0
    D  ListNbr              133    136B 0
    D  EntrySize            137    140B 0
    D InputDs         DS
    D  UserSpace                    20
    D TarNamLib       S             20
    D TargetName      S             10
    D TargetLib       S             10
    D PrintOrDsp      S              1
    D SrvListDs       DS
    D  PgmNameLib             1     20
    D   ProgramNam                  10       OVERLAY(PgmNameLib:1)
    D   LibraryNam                  10       OVERLAY(PgmNameLib:11)
    D  SrvPgmNam             21     30
    D  SrvPgmLib             31     40
    D ErrorDs         DS                     INZ
    D  BytesProvd             1      4B 0    INZ(116)
    D  BytesAvail             5      8B 0
    D  MessageId              9     15
    D  Err###                16     16
    D  MessageDta            17    116
    D                DS                     INZ
    D  StartPosit             1      4B 0
    D  StartLen               5      8B 0
    D  SpaceLen               9     12B 0
    D  NbrEntries            29     32B 0
    D  LenEntry              37     40B 0
    D  NbrReturn             41     44B 0
    D  MaxEntries            45     48B 0
    D  ReceiveLen            49     52B 0    INZ(100)
    D SrchNamLib      S             20
    D SpaceAtrib      S             10
    D SpaceValue      S              1
    D SpaceAuth       S             10
    D SpaceText       S             50
    D SpaceReplc      S             10
    D FormatName      S              8
    D TotalNbr        S              7   0
    D SflRcdNbr       S              4   0
    D DoRrn           S              4   0
    D Index           S              4   0
    D                DS
    D  Receiver                    100
    D  PgmOwner                     10       OVERLAY(Receiver:28)
    D  CrtDatTim                    13       OVERLAY(Receiver:49)
    D   CreateYMD                    6   0   OVERLAY(CrtDatTim:2)
    D   CreateTime                   4   0   OVERLAY(CrtDatTim:8)
    D  SourceFile                   10       OVERLAY(Receiver:62)
    D  SourceLib                    10       OVERLAY(Receiver:72)
```

```
D LibLstCon         C                    CONST('*LIBL      ')
D DateCreate        S            D       DATFMT(*YMD)
D CreateMDY         S            D       DATFMT(*MDY)
D DCreateMDY        S            8


CL0N01Factor1+++++++Opcode&ExtFactor2+++++++Result+++++++++Len++D+HiLoEq....Comments+
C        *ENTRY      PLIST
C                    PARM                        SrchNamLib
C                    PARM                        TarNamLib
C                    PARM                        PrintOrDsp
C                    EVAL        UserSpace = ('BNDSPC     QTEMP')
C                    EVAL        TargetName = TarNamLib
C                    EVAL        TargetLib = %SUBST(TarNamLib:11:10)
C                    EVAL        SearchObj = SrchNamLib
C                    EVAL        SearchLib = %SUBST(SrchNamLib:11:10)
 *     Create user space
C                    CALL        'QUSCRTUS'
C                    PARM                        UserSpace
C                    PARM        *BLANKS         SpaceAtrib
C                    PARM        2048            SpaceLen
C                    PARM        *BLANKS         SpaceValue
C                    PARM        '*CHANGE'       SpaceAuth
C                    PARM        *BLANKS         SpaceText
C                    PARM        '*YES'          SpaceReplc
C                    PARM                        ErrorDs
 *     List service programs in all programs to the user space
C                    CALL        'QBNLPGMI'
C                    PARM                        UserSpace
C                    PARM        'PGML0200'      FormatName
C                    PARM                        SrchNamLib
C                    PARM                        ErrorDs
C                    EVAL        StartPosit = 1
C                    EVAL        StartLen = 140
 *     Retrieve user space general information
C                    CALL        'QUSRTVUS'
C                    PARM                        UserSpace
C                    PARM                        StartPosit
C                    PARM                        StartLen
C                    PARM                        GeneralDs
C                    EVAL        StartPosit = 1
C                    EVAL        StartLen = InputSize
 *     Retrieve user space detail information
C                    CALL        'QUSRTVUS'
C                    PARM                        UserSpace
C                    PARM                        StartPosit
C                    PARM                        StartLen
C                    PARM                        InputDs
C                    EVAL        UserSpace = ('BNDSPC     QTEMP')
C                    EVAL        StartPosit = ListOffset + 1
C                    EVAL        StartLen = EntrySize
 *     Retrieve the list by walking through the user space
C                    DO          ListNbr
C                    CALL        'QUSRTVUS'
C                    PARM                        UserSpace
C                    PARM                        StartPosit
C                    PARM                        StartLen
C                    PARM                        SrvListDs
C                    IF          (SrvPgmNam = TargetName)
C                    IF          (TargetLib = '*ANY')
C                                 or (SrvPgmLib = *blanks)
C                                 or (SrvPgmLib = TargetLib)
C                    EXSR        GETPROGRAM
C                    EVAL        SflRcdNbr = SflRcdNbr + 1
```

```
C                    WRITE     SFLRECORD
C                    ENDIF
C                    ENDIF
C                    EVAL      StartPosit = StartPosit + EntrySize
C                    ENDDO
C                    IF        PrintOrDsp = 'D'
C                    EXSR      DISPLAY
C                    ELSE
C                    EXSR      PRINT
C                    ENDIF
C                    EVAL      *InLr = *ON
C     GETPROGRAM     BEGSR
C                    CALL      'QCLRPGMI'
C                    PARM                    Receiver
C                    PARM                    ReceiveLen
C                    PARM      'PGMI0100'    FormatName
C                    PARM                    PgmNameLib
C                    PARM                    ErrorDs
C     *YMD           MOVEL     CreateYMD     CreateMDY
C                    MOVE      CreateMDY     DCreateMDY
C                    EVAL      DCreateTim = CreateTime
C                    ENDSR
C     DISPLAY        BEGSR
C                    IF        SflRcdNbr > 0
C                    EVAL      *In21 = *ON
C                    ENDIF
C                    EVAL      *In22 = *ON
C                    EVAL      *In24 = *ON
C                    WRITE     FMT1
C                    EXFMT     SFLCONTROL
C                    ENDSR
C     PRINT          BEGSR
C                    OPEN      QSYSPRT
C                    EXCEPT    HEADING
C                    EVAL      DoRrn= SflRcdNbr
C                    DO        DoRrn         Index
C     Index          CHAIN     SFLRECORD                           68
C                    IF        *In68 = *OFF
C                    EXCEPT    DETAIL
C                    ENDIF
C                    ENDDO
C                    ENDSR

O..............N01N02N03Field++++++++YB.End++PConstant/editword/DTformat++Comments+
OQSYSPRT   E            HEADING        3 02
O          OR   OA
O                                            5 'DATE:'
O                       UDATE       Y       14
O                                           75 'PAGE:'
O                       PAGE        Z       80
O                                           48 'Programs with Service'
O                                         +001 'Programs'
O          E            HEADING        1
O          OR   OA
O                                           30 'Requested Service Program'
O                       TargetName          42
O                       TargetLib           54
O          E            HEADING        3
O          OR   OA
O                                           30 'Search Parameters........'
O                       SearchObj           42
O                       SearchLib           54
O          E            HEADING        1
```

```
O           OR    OA
O                                            12 'Library'
O                                            27 'Program'
O                                            47 'Created On'
O                                            54 'Time'
O                                            63 'Owner'
O           EF         DETAIL       1
O                      LibraryNam            15
O                      ProgramNam            30
O                      DcreateMDY            47
O                      DcreateTim            54
O                      PgmOwner              68
```

Figure 11.33: The Service Program Usage (SERPGMUSAG) Command

```
/*===============================================================*/
/* To compile:                                                   */
/*                                                               */
/*        CRTCMD     CMD(XXX/SERPGMUSAG) PGM(XXX/FIG1132RG)       */
/*                   SRCMBR(FIG1133CM)                            */
/*                                                               */
/*===============================================================*/
           CMD        PROMPT('Service Program Useage')
           PARM       KWD(SEARCH) TYPE(QUAL) MIN(1) PROMPT('Search +
                      Program:')
           PARM       KWD(FOR) TYPE(QUAL1) MIN(1) PROMPT('Find +
                      Program:')
           PARM       KWD(DSPPRINT) TYPE(*CHAR) LEN(1) RSTD(*YES) +
                      DFT(D) VALUES(D P) PROMPT('Display or +
                      Print:')
QUAL:      QUAL       TYPE(*GENERIC) LEN(10) DFT(*ALL) SPCVAL((*ALL))
           QUAL       TYPE(*NAME) LEN(10) DFT(*LIBL) +
                      SPCVAL((*LIBL) (*CURLIB)) PROMPT('Library')
QUAL1:     QUAL       TYPE(*NAME) LEN(10)
           QUAL       TYPE(*NAME) LEN(10) DFT(*LIBL) +
                      SPCVAL((*LIBL) (*CURLIB) (*ANY)) +
                      PROMPT('Library')
```

THE MODULE USAGE COMMAND

What we have always referred to as programs in the OPM became *Modules* when we went to ILE. One or more *modules* are used to make a *program* under ILE.

Whatever confusion you may have over this issue will be cleared up when you get to Chapter 13. Once you have read that chapter, it will become apparent that you are going to need some way to identify which programs use a particular module (depending upon how you choose to do your program binding). We have written a tool that will allow you to identify all programs that use a particular module. We call the tool the *Module Usage (MODUSAG) Command*.

The MODUSAG command shows all programs that use a specified module. You specify the generic program name to search (or *ALL) and the library. You indicate the module name and library that you are interested in researching. In addition, you have the option of printing or displaying the results of the search.

You will find that this command is useful when you have more than one program using the same module. If you then need to make a change to the module, it would be useful to know the other programs that need to be recompiled in order to see the changed module. Again, the need for this tool is predicated on how you will be performing your program binding, which we will discuss in Chapter 12.

You can see an example of the output from the MODUSAG command in Figure 11.34. The display file, RPG program, and the MODUSAG command can be seen in Figures 11.35 through 11.37, respectively.

Figure 11.34: Output from the MODUSAG Command

```
                    Programs using Requested Module

Requested Module:    INU001RG    *LIBL
Search parameters:   *ALL        APPLIB

Library      Program      Created  Time   SourceFile  Source Lib  Source Mbr
APPLIB       INU001RG     05/01/96 14:40  QRPGLESRC   APPLIB      INU001RG
APPLIB       INU014RG     05/05/96 15:22  QRPGLESRC   APPLIB      INU014RG
APPLIB       INU015RG     05/02/96 09:17  QRPGLESRC   APPLIB      INU015RG
APPLIB       INU022RG     05/02/96 10:55  QRPGLESRC   APPLIB      INU022RG




                                                              Bottom

 F3=Exit
```

Figure 11.35: The FIG1135DS Display File

```
A*******************************************************************
A*   TO COMPILE:
A*      CRTDSPF FILE(XXXLIB/FIG1135DS)
A*******************************************************************
AAN01N02N03T.Name++++++RLen++TDpBLinPosFunctions++++++++++++++++++++++++++++
A                                       CF03(03)
A           R SFLRECORD                 SFL
A             LIBRARYNAM    10A  O   7  2
A             PROGRAMNAM    10A  O   7 14
A             DCREATEMDY     8A  O   7 26
A             DCREATETIM     4Y 0O   7 35EDTWRD('   :   ')
A             SOURCEFILE    10   O   7 42
A             SOURCELIB     10   O   7 54
A             SOURCEMBR     10   O   7 66
A           R SFLCONTROL                SFLCTL(SFLRECORD)
A                                       SFLSIZ(0024)
A                                       SFLPAG(0012)
A                                       OVERLAY
A   21                                  SFLDSP
A   22                                  SFLDSPCTL
A   23                                  SFLCLR
A   24                                  SFLEND(*MORE)
A                                     1 25'Programs using Requested Module'
A                                       DSPATR(HI)
A                                       DSPATR(UL)
A                                     6  2'Library'
A                                       DSPATR(HI)
A                                       DSPATR(UL)
A                                     6 14'Program'
A                                       DSPATR(HI)
A                                       DSPATR(UL)
A                                     3  2'Requested Module:'
A             TARGETNAME    10A  O   3 22
A             TARGETLIB     10A  O   3 33
A                                     4  2'Search parameters:'
A             SEARCHOBJ     10A  O   4 22
A             SEARCHLIB     10A  O   4 33
A                                     6 26'Created'
A                                       DSPATR(HI)
A                                       DSPATR(UL)
A                                     6 35'Time'
A                                       DSPATR(HI)
A                                       DSPATR(UL)
A                                     6 42'SourceFile'
A                                       DSPATR(HI)
A                                     6 54'Source Lib'
A                                       DSPATR(HI)
A                                     6 66'Source Mbr'
A                                       DSPATR(HI)
A           R FMT1
A                                    22  3'F3=Exit'  COLOR(BLU)
```

Figure 11.36: The FIG1136RG RPG Program

```
**********************************************************************
*   TO COMPILE:
*      CRTBNDPGM PGM(XXXLIB/FIG1136RG)
**********************************************************************
FFilename++IPEASFRlen+LKlen+AIDevice+.Keywords+++++++++++++++++++++++Comments+++++
FFIG1135ds CF   E              WORKSTN
F                                       SFILE(SFLRECORD:SflRcdNbr)
FQSYSPRT   O    F  132         PRINTER OFLIND(*INOA) USROPN

DName+++++++++++ETDsFrom+++To/L+++IDc.Keywords+++++++++++++++++++++++Comments+++++
D GeneralDs       DS
D  InputSize            113    116B 0
D  ListOffset           125    128B 0
D  ListNbr              133    136B 0
D  EntrySize            137    140B 0
D InputDs         DS
D  UserSpace                    20
D TarNamLib       S             20
D TargetName      S             10
D TargetLib       S             10
D PrintOrDsp      S              1
D                 DS
D ModListDs                    508
D  PgmNameLib             1     20
D   ProgramNam                  10     OVERLAY(PgmNameLib:1)
D   LibraryNam                  10     OVERLAY(PgmNameLib:11)
D  ModuleName                   10     OVERLAY(ModListDs:21)
D  ModuleLib                    10     OVERLAY(ModListDs:31)
D  SourceFile                   10     OVERLAY(ModListDs:41)
D  SourceLib                    10     OVERLAY(ModListDs:51)
D  SourceMbr                    10     OVERLAY(ModListDs:61)
D  CrtDatTim                    13     OVERLAY(ModListDs:81)
D   CreateYMD                    6   0 OVERLAY(CrtDatTim:2)
D   CreateTime                   4   0 OVERLAY(CrtDatTim:8)
D ErrorDs         DS                   INZ
D  BytesProvd             1      4B 0 INZ(116)
D  BytesAvail             5      8B 0
D  MessageId              9     15
D  Err###                16     16
D  MessageDta            17    116
D                 DS                   INZ
D  StartPosit             1      4B 0
D  StartLen               5      8B 0
D  SpaceLen               9     12B 0
D  NbrEntries            29     32B 0
D  LenEntry              37     40B 0
D  NbrReturn             41     44B 0
D  MaxEntries            45     48B 0
D SrchNamLib      S             20
D SpaceAtrib      S             10
D SpaceValue      S              1
D SpaceAuth       S             10
D SpaceText       S             50
D SpaceReplc      S             10
D FormatName      S              8
D TotalNbr        S              7   0
D SflRcdNbr       S              4   0
D DoRrn           S              4   0
D Index           S              4   0
```

```
D DateCreate      S              D   DATFMT(*YMD)
D CreateMDY       S              D   DATFMT(*MDY)
D DCreateMDY      S              8

CL0N01Factor1+++++++Opcode&ExtFactor2+++++++Result+++++++++Len++D+HiLoEq....Comments+
C     *ENTRY      PLIST
C                 PARM                         SrchNamLib
C                 PARM                         TarNamLib
C                 PARM                         PrintOrDsp
C                 EVAL       UserSpace = ('MODSPACE  QTEMP')
C                 EVAL       TargetName = TarNamLib
C                 EVAL       TargetLib = %SUBST(TarNamLib:11:10)
C                 EVAL       SearchObj = SrchNamLib
C                 EVAL       SearchLib = %SUBST(SrchNamLib:11:10)
 *   Create user space
C                 CALL       'QUSCRTUS'
C                 PARM                         UserSpace
C                 PARM       *BLANKS           SpaceAtrib
C                 PARM       2048              SpaceLen
C                 PARM       *BLANKS           SpaceValue
C                 PARM       '*CHANGE'         SpaceAuth
C                 PARM       *BLANKS           SpaceText
C                 PARM       '*YES'            SpaceReplc
C                 PARM                         ErrorDs
 *   List all programs matching search criteria to user space
C                 EVAL       UserSpace = ('MODSPACE  QTEMP')
C                 CALL       'QBNLPGMI'
C                 PARM                         UserSpace
C                 PARM       'PGML0100'        FormatName
C                 PARM                         SrchNamLib
C                 PARM                         ErrorDs
C                 EVAL       StartPosit = 1
C                 EVAL       StartLen = 140
 *   Retrieve user space general information
C                 EVAL       UserSpace = ('MODSPACE  QTEMP')
C                 CALL       'QUSRTVUS'
C                 PARM                         UserSpace
C                 PARM                         StartPosit
C                 PARM                         StartLen
C                 PARM                         GeneralDs
C                 EVAL       StartPosit = 1
C                 EVAL       StartLen = InputSize
 *   Retrieve user space detail information
C                 EVAL       UserSpace = ('MODSPACE  QTEMP')
C                 CALL       'QUSRTVUS'
C                 PARM                         UserSpace
C                 PARM                         StartPosit
C                 PARM                         StartLen
C                 PARM                         InputDs
C                 EVAL       StartPosit = ListOffset + 1
C                 EVAL       StartLen = EntrySize
 *   Retrieve the list by walking through the user space
C                 DO         ListNbr
C                 EVAL       UserSpace = ('MODSPACE  QTEMP')
C                 CALL       'QUSRTVUS'
C                 PARM                         UserSpace
C                 PARM                         StartPosit
C                 PARM                         StartLen
C                 PARM                         ModListDs
C                 IF         (ModuleName = TargetName)
C     *YMD        MOVEL      CreateYMD         CreateMDY
C                 MOVE       CreateMDY         DCreateMDY
C                 EVAL       DCreateTim = CreateTime
```

```
C                       EVAL      SflRcdNbr = SflRcdNbr + 1
C                       WRITE     SFLRECORD
C                       ENDIF
C                       EVAL      StartPosit = StartPosit + EntrySize
C                       ENDDO
C                       IF        PrintOrDsp = 'D'
C                       EXSR      DISPLAY
C                       ELSE
C                       EXSR      PRINT
C                       ENDIF
C                       EVAL      *InLr = *ON
C     DISPLAY           BEGSR
C                       IF        SflRcdNbr > 0
C                       EVAL      *In21 = *ON
C                       ENDIF
C                       EVAL      *In22 = *ON
C                       EVAL      *In24 = *ON
C                       WRITE     FMT1
C                       EXFMT     SFLCONTROL
C                       ENDSR
C     PRINT             BEGSR
C                       OPEN      QSYSPRT
C                       EXCEPT    HEADING
C                       EVAL      DoRrn= SflRcdNbr
C                       DO        DoRrn           Index
C     Index             CHAIN     SFLRECORD                           68
C                       IF        *In68 = *OFF
C                       EXCEPT    DETAIL
C                       ENDIF
C                       ENDDO
C                       ENDSR

O..............N01N02N03Field++++++++YB.End++PConstant/editword/DTformat++Comments+
OQSYSPRT   E            HEADING        3 02
O         OR   OA
O                                               5 'DATE:'
O                       UDATE       Y          14
O                                              75 'PAGE:'
O                       PAGE        Z          80
O                                              48 'Programs with Modules'
O          E            HEADING        1
O         OR   OA
O                                              30 'Requested Module:'
O                       TargetName             42
O                       TargetLib              54
O          E            HEADING        3
O         OR   OA
O                                              30 'Search Parameters........'
O                       SearchObj              42
O                       SearchLib              54
O          E            HEADING        1
O         OR   OA
O                                              12 'Library'
O                                              27 'Program'
O                                              46 'Created On'
O                                              53 'Time'
O                                              67 'SourceFile'
O                                              80 'Source Lib'
O                                              93 'Source Mbr'
```

```
O              EF           DETAIL            1
O                           LibraryNam              15
O                           ProgramNam              30
O                           DcreateMDY              46
O                           DcreateTim              53
O                           SourceFile              67
O                           SourceLib               80
O                           SourceMbr               93
```

Figure 11.37: The MODUSAG Command

```
/*================================================================*/
/* To compile:                                                    */
/*                                                                */
/*         CRTCMD     CMD(XXX/MODUSAG)       PGM(XXX/FIG1136RG)    */
/*                    SRCMBR(FIG1137CM)                           */
/*                                                                */
/*================================================================*/
           CMD        PROMPT('Module Useage)')
           PARM       KWD(SEARCH) TYPE(QUAL) MIN(1) PROMPT('Search +
                        Program:')
           PARM       KWD(FOR) TYPE(QUAL1) MIN(1) PROMPT('Find +
                        Program:')
           PARM       KWD(DSPPRINT) TYPE(*CHAR) LEN(1) RSTD(*YES) +
                        DFT(D) VALUES(D P) PROMPT('Display or +
                        Print:')
QUAL:      QUAL       TYPE(*GENERIC) LEN(10) DFT(*ALL) SPCVAL((*ALL))
           QUAL       TYPE(*NAME) LEN(10) DFT(*LIBL) +
                        SPCVAL((*LIBL) (*CURLIB)) PROMPT('Library')
QUAL1:     QUAL       TYPE(*NAME) LEN(10)
           QUAL       TYPE(*NAME) LEN(10) DFT(*LIBL) +
                        SPCVAL((*LIBL) (*CURLIB) (*ANY)) +
                        PROMPT('Library')
```

THE WORK WITH FIELDS COMMAND

Although it may be used for a variety of other things as well, we originally wrote the Work with Fields command as a tool to help convert legacy systems into systems capable of handling the 21st century. It became apparent to us that there were no tools available to help programmers identify where the date fields in their systems were. So, to address this issue we wrote the Work with Fields command.

The Work with Fields command allows you to display a subfile of all programs that contain a field with a specified length or name. For instance, if the size of your date fields are generally six digits with zero decimal positions, you can use this command to list every program that has a six-digit field and no decimal positions in it.

On the other hand, if all date fields in your system have DAT or DTE in the field name, we have provided a wild card search capability. If all of your date fields have the characters DAT (or any characters you specify), you can filter the search to include only programs with field names that have the specified characters embedded in them.

When the subfile of program names is displayed, you can edit, browse, or print the source members that include the search criteria you specified. We designed this command so it will work on either OPM or ILE programs.

Due to the nature of this type of application, you must first build a work file over the programs before you can search for a field. The Build Work with Fields (BLDWRKFLD) command will build the work file for you. The command works by compiling a source member into the QTEMP library and directing its output into a file.

> **Note:** When you run the build command, you must be sure to have the library that contains the source to all of the utilities in your library list.

The BLDWRKFLD command may take some time to complete, so we have ensured that it runs in batch. If you run the command interactively, it will submit itself to batch.

When running the Work with Fields (WRKFLD) command, you can elect to search for fields based upon field characteristics (size and decimal positions) and field name. When specifying the field name, you can use an asterisk (*) as a wild card character, as we have done in Figure 11.38. As you can see, any field with six digits and no decimal positions that happened to have the characters DAT anywhere in the field name would be displayed in the subfile. Note that the date and time the command was run (and the work file was built) is prominently displayed on the screen.

Figure 11.38: Output from the Work with Fields (WRKFLD) Command

```
                      Work with Fields

  Holding file to search in. . . . . . FIELDS      Created: 14:38  5/22/1996
   Library of holding file . . . . . . APPLIB
  Size of search field . . . . . . . .  00006 00
  Only include field named . . . . . . *DAT*

  Type options, press enter.
     1=Edit source    2=Browse    6=Print

   Opt   Field      Program    Opt   Field      Program
    _    ACADAT     ACTCHG      _    OMDATE     ACTCHG
    _    ACCDAT     ACTCHG      _    RGLDAT     ACTCHG
    _    ACFDAT     ACTCHG      _    RGTDAT     ACTCHG
    _    ACODAT     ACTCHG      _    TIDAT2     ACTCHG
    _    ACPDAT     ACTCHG      _    TIIDAT     ACTCHG
    _    FLDATA     ACTCHG      _    TMDATE     ACTCHG
    _    FLDATC     ACTCHG      _    TMSDAT     ACTCHG
    _    MBEDAT     ACTCHG      _    TRLDAT     ACTCHG
    _    MMDATE     ACTCHG      _    TRPDAT     ACTCHG
    _    OHTDAT     ACTCHG      _    TRSDAT     ACTCHG
                                                        More...
   F3=Exit      F12=Previous
```

Figures 11.39, 11.40, and 11.41 represent the physical files required for the Build Work with Fields (BLDWRKFLD) and Work with Fields (WRKFLD) commands. Figure 11.42 shows the code for the BLDWRKFLD command. Figures 11.43 and 11.44 represent the CL and RPG programs that are behind the BLDWRKFLD command.

Figure 11.39: The FIELDSPF Physical File

```
     A*****************************************************************
     A*   TO COMPILE:
     A*     CRTPF FILE(XXXLIB/FIELDSPF) SRCMBR(FIG1139)
     A*****************************************************************
     AAN01N02N03T.Name++++++RLen++TDpBLinPosFunctions+++++++++++++++++++++++++++++
     A          R FIELDSREC
     A            FIELDNAME     10          COLHDG('FIELD NAME')
     A            PROGRAMNAM    10          COLHDG('PROGRAM NAME')
     A            NBRDIGITS      5 0        COLHDG('NBR OF DIGITS')
     A            NBRDECIMLS     2 0        COLHDG('NBR OF DECIMALS')
     A            SOURCELIB     10          COLHDG('SOURCE LIB')
     A            SOURCEFILE    10          COLHDG('SOURCE FILE')
     A            CREATEDATE     8          COLHDG('CREATED DATE')
     A            CREATETIME     4          COLHDG('CREATED DATE')
     A          K NBRDIGITS
     A          K NBRDECIMLS
```

Figure 11.40: The SPLDTAILE Physical File

```
A******************************************************************
A*    TO COMPILE:
A*      CRTPF FILE(XXXLIB/SPLDTAILE) SRCMBR(FIG1140)
A******************************************************************
AAN01N02N03T.Name+++++RLen++TDpBLinPosFunctions++++++++++++++++++++++++
A          R ILESPLRCRD
A            ILBLANK9        9         COLHDG('BLANKS')
A            ILFLDNAME      10         COLHDG('FIELD NAME')
A            ILFILLER8       8         COLHDG('FILLER')
A            ILFLDSIZE      10         COLHDG('FIELD SIZE')
A            ILFILLER       95         COLHDG('FILLER')
```

Figure 11.41: The SPLDTAOPM Physical File

```
A******************************************************************
A*    TO COMPILE:
A*      CRTPF FILE(XXXLIB/SPLDTAOPM) SRCMBR(FIG1141)
A******************************************************************
AAN01N02N03T.Name+++++RLen++TDpBLinPosFunctions++++++++++++++++++++++++
A          R OPMSPLRCRD
A            PMBLANK8        8         COLHDG('BLANKS')
A            PMFLDNAME      10         COLHDG('FIELD NAME')
A            PMFILLER2       2         COLHDG('FILLER')
A            PMFLDTYPE      10         COLHDG('FIELD TYPE')
A            PMFILLER      102         COLHDG('FILLER')
```

Figure 11.42: The BLDWRKFLD Command

```
/*===============================================================*/
/* To compile:                                                   */
/*                                                               */
/*          CRTCMD      CMD(XXX/BLDWRKFLD) PGM(XXX/FIG1143CL)     */
/*                      SRCMBR(FIG1142CM)                         */
/*                                                               */
/*===============================================================*/
           CMD          PROMPT('BUILD WORK FIELDS')
           PARM         KWD(SRCFILE) TYPE(NAME1) MIN(1) +
                          PROMPT('Source File Name:')
           PARM         KWD(HOLDFILE) TYPE(NAME1) MIN(1) +
                          PROMPT('Holding File Name:')
NAME1:     QUAL         TYPE(*NAME) LEN(10)
           QUAL         TYPE(*CHAR) LEN(10) DFT(*LIBL) SPCVAL((' ' +
                          *LIBL)) CHOICE('Name, *LIBL') +
                          PROMPT('Library Name:')
```

Figure 11.43: The FIG1143CL CL Program

```
/********************************************************************/
/*    TO CREATE:                                                    */
/*        CRTCLPGM PGM(XXXLIB/FIG1143CL)                            */
/********************************************************************/
PGM    (&SRCIN  &HLDIN)

            DCL        VAR(&SRCIN) TYPE(*CHAR) LEN(20)
            DCL        VAR(&HLDIN) TYPE(*CHAR) LEN(20)
            DCL        VAR(&SRCLIB) TYPE(*CHAR) LEN(10)
            DCL        VAR(&HLDFIL) TYPE(*CHAR) LEN(10)
            DCL        VAR(&HLDLIB) TYPE(*CHAR) LEN(10)
            DCL        VAR(&SRCFIL) TYPE(*CHAR) LEN(10)
            DCL        VAR(&SRCTYP) TYPE(*CHAR) LEN(10)
            DCL        VAR(&MEMBR) TYPE(*CHAR) LEN(10)
            DCL        VAR(&JOBTYPE) TYPE(*CHAR) LEN(1)
            DCL        VAR(&MSGDTA) TYPE(*CHAR) LEN(512)
            DCL        VAR(&MSGID) TYPE(*CHAR) LEN(7)

            CHGVAR     &SRCFIL VALUE(%SST(&SRCIN 1 10))
            CHGVAR     &SRCLIB VALUE(%SST(&SRCIN 11 10))
            CHGVAR     &HLDFIL VALUE(%SST(&HLDIN 1 10))
            CHGVAR     &HLDLIB VALUE(%SST(&HLDIN 11 10))

/*  MAKE SURE SOURCE FILE/LIBRARY EXISTS             */

            CHKOBJ     OBJ(&SRCLIB/&SRCFIL) OBJTYPE(*FILE)
            MONMSG     MSGID(CPF0000) EXEC(DO)
            RCVMSG     MSGDTA(&MSGDTA) MSGID(&MSGID)
            SNDPGMMSG  MSGID(&MSGID) MSGF(QCPFMSG) MSGDTA(&MSGDTA)
            RETURN
            ENDDO

            IF         (&SRCIN = &HLDIN) THEN(DO)
            SNDPGMMSG  MSGID(CPF9898) MSGF(QCPFMSG) MSGDTA('Source FILE/LIBRARY
                         AND holding FILE/LIBRARY cannot be the same name.')
            RETURN
            ENDDO

/*  IF NOT RUNNING IN BATCH, SUBMIT IT AND GET OUT  */

            RTVJOBA    TYPE(&JOBTYPE)
            IF         COND(&JOBTYPE *EQ '1') THEN(DO)
            SBMJOB     CMD(CALL PGM(FIG1143CL) PARM(&SRCIN &HLDIN)) +
                         JOB(BLDWRKFLDS)
            SNDPGMMSG  MSGID(CPF9898) MSGF(QCPFMSG) MSGDTA('JOB +
                         BLDWRKFLDS has been submitted +
                         to batch.') MSGTYPE(*DIAG)

            GOTO       ENDPGM
            ENDDO

/*  CREATE TEMPORARY WORK FILE FOR COMPILES  */

            CHKOBJ     QTEMP/FLDSPOOL *FILE
            MONMSG     MSGID(CPF9801) EXEC(DO)
            CRTPF      FILE(QTEMP/FLDSPOOL) RCDLEN(132) +
                         OPTION(*NOSRC) MAXMBRS(*NOMAX) +
                         SIZE(*NOMAX) LVLCHK(*NO)
            ENDDO
            CLRPFM     QTEMP/FLDSPOOL
```

```
            CHKOBJ      &HLDLIB/&HLDFIL *FILE
            MONMSG      MSGID(CPF9801) EXEC(DO)
            CRTPF       FILE(&HLDLIB/&HLDFIL) SRCFILE(SOURCE) +
                          SRCMBR(FIG1139) SIZE(*NOMAX) LVLCHK(*NO)
            ENDDO
            CLRPFM      &HLDLIB/&HLDFIL
            OVRDBF      FILE(FIELDSPF) TOFILE(&HLDLIB/&HLDFIL)

    /*   GET THE FIRST SOURCE MEMBER TO COMPILE   */

            RTVMBRD     FILE(&SRCLIB/&SRCFIL) MBR(*FIRSTMBR) +
                          RTNMBR(&MEMBR) SRCTYPE(&SRCTYP)
            MONMSG      MSGID(CPF3049) EXEC(GOTO ENDPGM)
            GOTO        FIRST

LOOP:
            RTVMBRD     FILE(&SRCLIB/&SRCFIL) MBR(&MEMBR *NEXT) +
                          RTNMBR(&MEMBR) SRCTYPE(&SRCTYP)
            MONMSG      MSGID(CPF3049) EXEC(GOTO ENDPGM)
FIRST:
            IF          COND((&SRCTYP *NE 'RPG') *AND (&SRCTYP *NE +
                          'RPGLE')) THEN(GOTO CMDLBL(LOOP))

            ADDPFM      FILE(QTEMP/FLDSPOOL) MBR(&MEMBR)
            MONMSG      MSGID(CPF0000)
            OVRDBF      FILE(QSYSPRT) TOFILE(QTEMP/FLDSPOOL) MBR(&MEMBR)
            IF          COND(&SRCTYP *EQ 'RPG') THEN(DO)
            CRTRPGPGM   PGM(QTEMP/&MEMBR) SRCFILE(&SRCLIB/&SRCFIL) +
                          OPTION(*NOGEN *SRC) GENOPT(*XREF)
            ENDDO
            IF          COND(&SRCTYP *EQ 'RPGLE') THEN(DO)
            CRTRPGMOD   MODULE(QTEMP/&MEMBR) SRCFILE(&SRCLIB/&SRCFIL)
            MONMSG      MSGID(RNS9309)
            ENDDO
            OVRDBF      FILE(FLDSPOOL) TOFILE(QTEMP/FLDSPOOL) MBR(&MEMBR)
            CALL        FIG1144RG  (&SRCTYP &SRCLIB &SRCFIL)
            RMVM        FILE(QTEMP/FLDSPOOL) MBR(&MEMBR)
            MONMSG      MSGID(CPF0000)
            GOTO        LOOP

ENDPGM:

            DLTOVR      *ALL
ENDPGM
```

Figure 11.44: The FIG1144RG RPG Program

```
     ***********************************************************************
     *   TO COMPILE:
     *      CRTBNDRPG PGM(XXXLIB/FIG1144RG)
     ***********************************************************************
     *
     FFilename++IPEASFRlen+LKlen+AIDevice+.Keywords++++++++++++++++++++++++++Comments+++++
     FFldspool  IF   F 132        Disk    INFDS(InfoDs)
     FFieldsPf  O    e            Disk

     DName++++++++++ETDsFrom+++To/L+++IDc.Keywords++++++++++++++++++++++++++Comments+++++
     DSplDtaOpm       E DS                EXTNAME(SplDtaOpm)
     DSplDtaILE       E DS                EXTNAME(SplDtaILE)
     DSpoolType         S         10
     DSourceLib         S         10
     DSourceFile        S         10
     DWorkNumber        S          3 0
     DWrkDigits         S          5
     DFldLen1           S          1
     DFldLen2           S          2
     DTimeField         S          6 0
     DInfoDs            DS
     D MemberName              129   138
     DDateDs            DS
     DWorkDate                        D
     D Year4                          4   OVERLAY(WorkDate:1)
     D Month                          2   OVERLAY(WorkDate:6)
     D Day                            2   OVERLAY(WorkDate:9)

     CL0N01Factor1++++++Opcode&ExtFactor2++++++Result+++++++Len++D+HiLoEq....Comments+
     C           *ENTRY        PLIST
     C                         PARM                    SpoolType
     C                         PARM                    SourceLib
     C                         PARM                    SourceFile
     C           *MDY          MOVE      UDATE         WorkDate
     C                         TIME                    TimeField
     C           1             SETLL     FLDSPOOL
B1   C           SpoolType     Caseq     'RPG'         ProcessOpm
     C           SpoolType     Caseq     'RPGLE'       ProcessILE
E1   C                         ENDCS
     C                         Eval      *inlr = *ON
     * Process original program model source members
     C           PROCESSOPM    BEGSR
B1   C                         DOU       *in50 = *ON
     C                         READ      FLDSPOOL      SplDtaOpm                50
B2   C                         IF        *in50
     C                         LEAVE
E2   C                         ENDIF
     * Filter out none field name records
B2   C                         IF        PmBlank8 <> *blanks
     C                         ITER
E2   C                         ENDIF
B2   C                         IF        PmFldName = *BLANKS
     C                         ITER
E2   C                         ENDIF
     C                         MOVEL     PmFldType     TST2           2
B2   C                         IF        (Tst2 <> 'A(') and
     C                                   (Tst2 <> 'P(') and
     C                                   (Tst2 <> 'B(') and
     C                                   (Tst2 <> 'S(')
     C                         ITER
E2   C                         ENDIF
```

```
        *   Strip out size of field digits and decimals
        C                   EVAL      WrkDigits = *blanks
        C                   eval      NbrDigits = 0
        C                   eval      NbrDecimls = 0
B2      C                   If        Tst2 = 'A('
        C         ')'       Scan      PmFldType:3    G              2 0      02
        C                   Eval      WrkDigits = %SUBST(PmFldType:3:(G-3))
X2      C                   else
        C         ','       Scan      PmFldType:3    F              2 0      01
B3      C                   If        *in01 = *on
        C                   Eval      WrkDigits =  (%SUBST(PmFldType:3:(F-3)))
        C         ')'       Scan      PmFldType:F    G                       02
B4      C                   If        *in02 = *on
        C                   Eval      WorkNumber = (G-F) - 1
B5      C                   If        WorkNumber = 1
        C                   Eval      FldLen1 = %subst(IlFldSize:G+1:1)
        C                   MOVE      FldLen1        NbrDecimls
X5      C                   ELSE
        C                   EVAL      FldLen2 = %subst(IlFldSize:G+1:2)
        C                   MOVE      FldLen2        NbrDecimls
E5      C                   ENDIF
E4      C                   ENDIF
E3      C                   ENDIF
E2      C                   ENDIF
        *   Right justify and replace blanks with 0's
B2      C                   IF        WrkDigits <> *blanks
        C                   EVAL      WrkDigits = %Trimr(WrkDigits)
        C         ' ':'0'   XLATE     WrkDigits      WrkDigits
        C                   Move      WrkDigits      NbrDigits
E2      C                   ENDIF
        C                   EVAL      FieldName = PmFldName
        C                   EVAL      ProgramNam = MemberName
        C                   EVAL      CreateDate = Year4 + Month + Day
        C                   MOVEL     TimeField      CreateTime
        C                   WRITE     FieldsRec
E1      C                   ENDDO
        C                   ENDSR
        C         PROCESSILE BEGSR
B1      C                   DOU       *in50 = *ON
        C                   READ      FLDSPOOL       SplDtaILE               50
B2      C                   IF        *in50
        C                   LEAVE
E2      C                   ENDIF
        *   Filter out none field name records
B2      C                   IF        ILBlank9 <> *blanks
        C                   ITER
E2      C                   ENDIF
B2      C                   IF        ILFldName = *BLANKS
        C                   ITER
E2      C                   ENDIF
        C                   EVAL      WrkDigits = *blanks
        C                   MOVEL     IlFldSize      TST2           2
        C                   MOVEL     IlFldSize      TST3           3
B2      C                   IF        (Tst2 <> 'A(') and
        C                             (Tst2 <> 'P(') and
        C                             (Tst2 <> 'B(') and
        C                             (Tst2 <> 'S(') and
        C                             (Tst3 <> 'DS(')
        C                   ITER
E2      C                   ENDIF
        *   Strip out field size digits and decimals
        C                   EVAL      NbrDecimls = 0
B2      C                   IF        (Tst2 = 'A(') or (Tst3 = 'DS('
```

```
B3    C                    IF         Tst2 = 'A('
      C                    EVAL       F = 3
X3    C                    ELSE
      C                    EVAL       F = 4
E3    C                    ENDIF
      C         ')'        SCAN       IlFldSize:F   G                      2 0    02
      C                    EVAL       WrkDigits = %SUBST(IlFldSize:F:(G-F))
E2    C                    ENDIF
      C                    EVAL       F = 3
      C         ','        SCAN       IlFldSize:F   G                      2 0    01
B2    C                    IF         *in01 = *on
      C                    EVAL       WrkDigits = %SUBST(IlFldSize:F:(G-F))
      C         ')'        SCAN       IlFldSize:G   H                      2 0    02
B3    C                    IF         *in02 = *on
      C                    EVAL       WorkNumber = (H-G) - 1
B4    C                    IF         WorkNumber = 1
      C                    EVAL       FldLen1 = %subst(IlFldSize:G+1:1)
      C                    MOVE       FldLen1          NbrDecimls
X4    C                    ELSE
      C                    EVAL       FldLen2 = %subst(IlFldSize:G+1:2)
      C                    MOVE       FldLen2          NbrDecimls
E4    C                    ENDIF
E3    C                    ENDIF
E2    C                    ENDIF
      * Right justify the size field and replace *blanks with 0's
B2    C                    IF         WrkDigits <> *blanks
      C                    EVAL       WrkDigits = %Trimr(WrkDigits)
      C         ' ':'0'    XLATE      WrkDigits        WrkDigits
      C                    Move       WrkDigits        NbrDigits
E2    C                    ENDIF
      C                    EVAL       FieldName = IlFldName
      C                    EVAL       ProgramNam = MemberName
      C                    EVAL       CreateDate = Year4 + Month + Day
      C                    MOVEL      TimeField        CreateTime
      C                    WRITE      FieldsRec
E1    C                    ENDDO
      C                    ENDSR
```

Figures 11.45, 11.46, 11.47, and 11.48 are the display file, RPG program, CL program, and command that make up the Work with Fields (WRKFLD) command.

Figure 11.45: The FIG1145DS Display File

```
A*****************************************************************
A*   TO COMPILE:
A*      CRTDSPF FILE(XXXLIB/FIG1145DS)
A*****************************************************************
AAN01N02N03T.Name+++++RLen++TDpBLinPosFunctions++++++++++++++++++++++++++++
A                                          DSPSIZ(24 80 *DS3)
A                                          CF03(03)
A                                          CF12
A              R FORMAT2                   SFL
A                SFLSELECT     1A  B 12   7DSPATR(HI)
A                HDNSRCLIB    10A  H
A                HDNSRCFIL    10A  H
A                FIELDNAME    10A  O 12 11
A                PROGRAMNAM   10A  O 12 22
A              R FORMAT2C                  SFLCTL(FORMAT2)
A                                          SFLLIN(0005)
A                                          SFLSIZ(0040)
A                                          SFLPAG(0020)
A                                          ROLLUP(27)
A                                          OVERLAY
A   21                                     SFLDSP
A                                          SFLDSPCTL
A   25                                     SFLCLR
A   41                                     SFLEND(*MORE)
A                RRNRCD        4S 0H       SFLRCDNBR
A                                         1 30'Work with Fields'
A                                          DSPATR(HI)
A                                          DSPATR(UL)
A                                         5  4'Size of search field . . . . . . .-
A                                          .'
A                                         9 23'2=Browse'
A                                          COLOR(BLU)
A N21                                      DSPATR(ND)
A                                         9 34'6=Print'
A                                          COLOR(BLU)
A N21                                      DSPATR(ND)
A                                         9  7'1=Edit source'
A                                          COLOR(BLU)
A N21                                      DSPATR(ND)
A                                         8  3'Type options, press enter.'
A                                          COLOR(BLU)
A N21                                      DSPATR(ND)
A                                        11  6'Opt'
A                                          DSPATR(HI)
A N21                                      DSPATR(ND)
A                                        11 11'Field'
A                                          DSPATR(HI)
A N21                                      DSPATR(ND)
A                                        11 22'Program'
A                                          DSPATR(HI)
A N21                                      DSPATR(ND)
A                                         3  4'Holding file to search in. . . . .-
A                                          .'
A                SEARCHFILE   10A  B  3 41
A   21                                     DSPATR(PR)
A                                         4  5'Library of holding file . . . . . -
A                                          .'
A                SEARCHLIB    10A  B  4 41
A   21                                     DSPATR(PR)
A                SRCHDIGITS    5D 0B  5 43CHGINPDFT
A                                          CHECK(RZ)
```

```
A  21                                   DSPATR(PR)
A            SRCHDECIML     2D 0B  5 49CHGINPDFT
A                                       CHECK(RZ)
A  21                                   DSPATR(PR)
A                                    3 54'Created:'
A N60                                   DSPATR(ND)
A            HOLDDATE       8Y 0O  3 69EDTWRD('  /  /    ')
A N60                                   DSPATR(ND)
A            HOLDTIME       4Y 0O  3 63EDTWRD('  :  ')
A N60                                   DSPATR(ND)
A                                   11 36'Opt'
A                                       DSPATR(HI)
A N21N61                                DSPATR(ND)
A                                   11 41'Field'
A                                       DSPATR(HI)
A N21N61                                DSPATR(ND)
A                                   11 52'Program'
A                                       DSPATR(HI)
A N21N61                                DSPATR(ND)
A            FILTERNAME    10A  B  6 41
A  21                                   DSPATR(PR)
A                                    6  4'Only include field named . . . . . .-
A                                        .'
A          R FORMAT1
A                                   23  4'F3=Exit'
A                                       COLOR(BLU)
A                                   23 16'F12=Previous'
A                                       COLOR(BLU)
```

Figure 11.46: The FIG1146RG RPG Program

```
    **********************************************************************
    *   TO COMPILE:
    *      CRTBNDPGM PGM(XXXLIB/FIG1146RG)
    **********************************************************************
FFilename++IPEASFRlen+LKlen+AIDevice+.Keywords+++++++++++++++++++++++++Comments++++++
FFig1145DS CF   E              WORKSTN
F                                        SFILE(Format2:RelRecNbr)
F                                        INFDS(InfoDs)
FFIELDSPF   IF   E            K DISK     USROPN

DName++++++++++++ETDsFrom+++To/L+++IDc.Keywords+++++++++++++++++++++++++Comments++++++
DOverrideC       c                       'OVRDBF FILE(FIELDSPF) TOFILE('
DSearchSize       S              7
DSaveFile         S             21
DHoldFile         S             21
DCommand          S             55
DCommandLen       S             15  5
DRelRecNbr        S              4  0
DTestWild         S              1
DOkToGoON         S              1
DIndex            S              2  0
DWildSearch       S             10
DTestField        S             10
DDataField        S             10
DX                S              2  0
DI                S              2  0
DSearchLen        S              2  0
DFound            S              2  0
```

```
         DEight           S              8  0
         DIsoDate         S                 D    datfmt(*iso)
         DUsaDate         S                 D    datfmt(*usa)
         DInfoDs          DS
         D FirstLine               378    379B 0

         CL0N01Factor1++++++Opcode&ExtFactor2++++++Result++++++++Len++D+HiLoEq....Comments+
         C                   DOU        *IN03 = *on
         C                   SETOFF                                           216061
         C                   WRITE      FORMAT1
         C                   EXFMT      FORMAT2C
         C                   IF         *in03 = *on
         C                   GOTO       endpgm
         C                   ENDIF
          * Clear the subfile
         C                   EVAL       *in25 = *on
         C                   WRITE      Format2C
         C                   EVAL       *in25 = *off
         C                   EVAL       RelRecNbr = 0
          * Override to requested fields holding file
         C                   EVAL       Holdfile=%Trim(SearchLib) +
         C                                '/' + SearchFile
         C                   IF         Holdfile <> Savefile
         C                   IF         SaveFile <> *blanks
         C                   CLOSE      FIELDSPf
         C                   ENDIF
         C                   EVAL       Command = OverrideC +
         C                                       %Trim(HoldFile) + ')'
         C                   CALL       'QCMDEXC'
         C                   PARM                   Command
         C                   PARM       55          CommandLen
         C                   OPEN       FIELDSPf
         C                   ENDIF
         C                   EVAL       SaveFile = HoldFile
         C      SizeKey      KLIST
         C                   KFLD                   SrchDigits
         C                   KFLD                   SrchDeciml
          *   Read requested records
         C      SizeKey      SETLL      FIELDSPf
         C                   DOU        *IN27 = *OFF
         C                   EVAL       X = 0
B1       C                   DOU        (*In41 = *on) or (X = 20)
         C      SizeKey      READE      FIELDSPF                             41
B2       C                   IF         *In41 = *ON
         C                   LEAVE
E2       C                   ENDIF
         C                   IF         FilterName <> *blanks
         C                   MOVEL      FilterName   TestWild
         C                   IF         TestWild = '*'
         C                   EXSR       WildSR
         C                   IF         OkToGoOn <> 'Y'
         C                   ITER
         C                   ENDIF
         C                   ENDIF
         C                   EVAL       Found = 0
         C                   EVAL       SearchLen = 0
         C                   IF         OkToGoOn <> 'Y'
         C      '*'          CHECKR     FilterName   Found
         C                   IF         Found <> 0
         C                   EVAL       SearchLen = Found - 1
         C      SearchLen    SUBST      FilterName:1 TestField
         C      SearchLen    SUBST      FieldName:1  DataField
         C                   IF         DataField <> TestField
```

```
       C                    ITER
       C                    ENDIF
       C                    ENDIF
       C                    ENDIF
       C                    IF         FieldName <> FilterName
       C                                 and TestWild <> '*'
       C                                 and SearchLen = 0
       C                    ITER
       C                    ENDIF
       C                    ENDIF
       C                    EVAL       RelRecNbr = RelRecNbr + 1
       C                    EVAL       HdnSrcLib = SourceLib
       C                    EVAL       HdnSrcFil = SourceFile
       C                    EVAL       RrnRcd = RelRecNbr
       C                    EVAL       X = X + 1
       C                    WRITE      FORMAT2
E1     C                    ENDDO
          * Only display subfile if records were written
B1     C                    IF         RelRecNbr <> 0
       C                    EVAL       *in21 = *on
       C                    ENDIF
          * Display heading for secondary columns if enough records
B1     C                    IF         RelRecNbr > 20
       C                    EVAL       *in61 = *on
       C                    ENDIF
       C                    MOVE       CreateDate   Eight
       C         *ISO       TEST(D)                 Eight              68
       C                    IF         *IN68 = *OFF
       C         *ISO       MOVE       Eight        IsoDate
       C                    MOVE       IsoDate      UsaDate
       C                    MOVE       UsaDate      HoldDate
       C                    Else
       C                    MOVE       *zeros       HoldDate
       C                    ENDIF
       C                    MOVE       CreateTime   HoldTime
       C         Reshow     TAG
       C                    EVAL       *in60 = *on
       C                    WRITE      FORMAT1
       C                    EXFMT      FORMAT2C
       C         *INKC      CABEQ      *ON          ENDPGM
       C                    ENDDO
          * Back up and input new request
       C                    IF         *INKL = *ON
       C                    ITER
       C                    ENDIF
          * Look for requests to edit,view, or print the source members
B2     C                    DOU        *in55 = *On
       C                    READC      FORMAT2                         55
B3     C                    IF         *in55 = *ON
       C                    LEAVE
E3     C                    ENDIF
B3     C         SflSelect  CASEQ      '1'          SOURCE
B3     C         SflSelect  CASEQ      '2'          SOURCE
B3     C         SflSelect  CASEQ      '6'          SOURCE
E3     C                    ENDCS
       C                    MOVE       ' '          SflSelect
       C                    UPDATE     FORMAT2
       C                    EVAL       RRNRCD = RelRecNbr
E2     C                    ENDDO
B2     C                    IF         Looked = 'Y'
       C                    MOVE       ' '          Looked             1
       C                    GOTO       RESHOW
E2     C                    ENDIF
```

```
C                     ENDDO
C        ENDPGM       TAG
C                     EVAL        *inlr = *ON
 * Call program to edit,view or print the requested source member
C        SOURCE       BEGSR
C                     CALL        'FIG1147CL'
C                     PARM                    HdnSrcLib
C                     PARM                    HdnSrcFil
C                     PARM                    ProgramNam
C                     PARM                    SflSelect
C                     MOVE        'Y'         Looked
C                     ENDSR
 * Look for wildscan if search field
C        WILDSR       BEGSR
C                     EVAL        OkTOGoON = 'Y'
C        '*'          SCAN        FilterName:2  Found
C                     IF          Found <> 0
C                     EVAL        Index = Found - 2
C        Index        SUBST(P)    FilterName:2  WildSearch
C        ' '          CHECKR      WildSearch    I
C        WildSearch:I SCAN        FieldName                      05
C                     IF          *in05 = *oFF
C                     EVAL        OkTOGOON = 'N'
C                     ENDIF
C                     ENDIF
C                     ENDSR
```

Figure 11.47: The FIG1147CL CL Program

```
/*****************************************************************************/
/*    TO CREATE:                                                            */
/*       CRTCLPGM PGM(XXXLIB/FIG1147CL)                                     */
/*****************************************************************************/
            PGM        PARM(&TOLIB &TOFILE &PASMBR &FUNC)

            DCL        VAR(&PASMBR) TYPE(*CHAR) LEN(10)
            DCL        VAR(&TOLIB)  TYPE(*CHAR) LEN(10)
            DCL        VAR(&TOFILE) TYPE(*CHAR) LEN(10)
            DCL        VAR(&FUNC)   TYPE(*CHAR) LEN(1)
            DCL        VAR(&OPTION) TYPE(*CHAR) LEN(1)

            IF         COND(&FUNC *EQ '1') THEN(DO)
            CHGVAR     &OPTION '2'
            ENDDO
            IF         COND(&FUNC *EQ '2') THEN(DO)
            CHGVAR     &OPTION '5'
            ENDDO
            IF         COND(&FUNC *EQ '6') THEN(DO)
            CHGVAR     &OPTION '6'
            ENDDO
            STRSEU     SRCFILE(&TOLIB/&TOFILE) SRCMBR(&PASMBR) +
                         TYPE(*SAME) OPTION(&OPTION)
            ENDPGM
```

Figure 11.48: The WRKFLD Command

```
/*================================================================*/
/* To compile:                                                    */
/*                                                                */
/*          CRTCMD       CMD(XXX/WRKFLD) PGM(XXX/FIG1146RG)        */
/*                       SRCMBR(FIG1148CM)                         */
/*                                                                */
/*================================================================*/
          CMD           PROMPT('WORK FIELDS')
```

FINAL WORDS ABOUT TOOLS IN THE TOOLBOX

We have not observed any programmers whom we feel had too many tools in their toolbox. It is our position that you simply can not have too many weapons in your arsenal.

If a tool can improve your productivity enough that the amount of time saved by the tool surpasses the amount of time spent developing it, the development time was time well spent. If a tool eliminates or helps to reduce certain errors from getting into production, implementation of the tool should be considered seriously.

Chapter 12

Date Handling and the Change of the Century

Most programming shops that support AS/400 legacy systems are looking towards January 1, 2000, with nervous anticipation. You see, the odds are pretty good that the systems they support are among the estimated 90 percent of existing business systems considered to be *calendrically challenged*. These systems were simply not designed to handle the transition to the 21st century.

The problem with making this transition exists primarily because most business systems have dates stored in six-digit formats. They are not capable of handling the change in century. This change creates a situation where the date simply has too many zeros! These legacy applications will interpret the two-digit year 00 as 1900, not 2000. As a result, many programs will begin to "crash and burn" on or before January 1, 2000, if they are left unchanged.

So, if you think that you can wait until 1998 or 1999 to start thinking about the problem, think again. Many systems have routines that calculate *projected* dates or *follow-up* dates years into the future. These routines could begin to have problems long before the year 2000. The magnitude of the problem can be mind boggling.

Of equal importance is cost. The cost of implementing the corrective measures necessary to keep these systems up and running has been estimated as high as 600 billion dollars (yes, you read that right, that's *billion* with a *B*).

The fact that you are reading this chapter at all tells us that you are probably a programmer who will not be retiring anytime soon. However, you are an *AS/400 programmer*, so not all of this is doom and gloom. The introduction of RPG IV includes the ability to work with the date data type. As you will soon see, this is very good news indeed!

This chapter will introduce you to the *date data type* and teach you how to take advantage of it. We will then show you how to use this new technology to help bring those old legacy systems up to speed without a major overhaul. We will give you some sample code to replace your old, clunky, RPG date routines. We will introduce you to a new tool that can be used to help you plan for the transition to the 21st century. We will teach you how to convert your data so it will incorporate the new date data type. And finally, we will help you develop a strategy to implement the changes required.

THE DATE DATA TYPE

Even though date data types have been around since V2R1M1, we had to wait until V3R1 before we could begin using them in RPG. The good news is that it may have been worth the wait, especially if you have not begun planning for the change in century. Careful implementation of this new technology can offer us old "green-screeners" some pretty significant short cuts that will take our software well into the 21st century.

Data fields may be designated as having *date* data types when they are defined in DDS or RPG IV Definition Specifications. Along with this new data type, we also have been introduced to a series of new RPG op codes designed to help us manipulate dates. Routines that use a series of moves or math routines to switch the format of our dates from month-day-year to year-month-day are a thing of the past. As you will see, complicated routines to increment or decrement dates have gone the way of the dinosaurs, too.

The date data type allows you to store data in a number of six- and eight-digit date formats (Table 12.1) all of which include the century. The date separator is automatically stored with your data making the field lengths appear to be either 6, 8, or 10 characters. In other words, you will see your date fields in the date format you defined with the separator characters already in place when you print or look at your data on the screen. The number and style of the separator character that appears depends upon the date format chosen, as seen in Table 12.1.

Table 12.1: An Example of the Date Data Types

Format	DATFMT Parameter	Separator Character	Field Length	Example
Month, Day, Year	*MDY	/	8	12/31/96
Day, Month, Year	*DMY	/	8	31/12/96
Year, Month, Day	*YMD	/	8	96/21/31
Julian	*JUL	/	6	96/366 [1]
International Standards Organization	*ISO	-	10	1996-12-31
IBM USA Standard	*USA	/	10	12/31/1996
IBM European Standard	*EUR	.	10	31.12.1996
Japanese Industrial Standard Christian Era	*JIS	-	10	1996-12-31
[1] The Julian date of 96/366 is a valid translation of December 31, 1966, because 1996 is a leap year.				

One of the cool things about the date data type is that, regardless of the date format chosen, DB2/400 stores the new date data type fields in only 4 bytes on disk, which happens to be the same amount of storage required to store a six-digit date in packed format. So as you convert your six-digit date fields from numeric or packed data types to the new date data types, you should not notice any increase in DASD utilization.

Date fields are compared based upon their *chronological* value. You can compare a date stored in month-day-year format to a date stored in Julian date format without performing any kind of conversion and still get your desired results. You will not need to convert the month-day-year report dates keyed before comparing them to dates that are stored in your database in a year-month-day format.

YEAR-MONTH-DAY FORMAT NO LONGER NECESSARY

You may find that there is no longer a reason to store dates in your database in year-month-day format just to get the key sequence you want. Because date fields are stored and compared based upon their chronological value, you may even want to store the dates in a month-day-year format. Doing so means that you would not need to convert the date when you print it on a report. As a matter of fact, you would not even need to use an edit code or an edit word when printing dates. Fields defined with a date data type will print with the date separator characters (seen in Table 12.1) already in place.

But before you run off to reformat all of your date fields into month-day-year format, you need to be aware that the six-digit date fields (*YMD and *MDY) *only* cover the years from 1940 to 2039. This should be ample for most transaction dates, but may be unacceptable in systems that perform some type of forecasting function or that record birth dates, which could easily be prior to 1940.

The reason for this anomaly is the way IBM employed its *date windowing* algorithms as they apply to the six-digit date. The system automatically assumes that, when this format is used, the two-digit years between 40 and 99 are for the 20th century and the years between 00 and 39 belong in the 21st century. Consequently, the system-defined *LOVAL for a date field differs, depending upon the date format chosen. If a date is defined with the eight-digit *ISO format type, *LOVAL is going to be 0001-01-01. If a date field is defined with the six-digit *YMD format, *LOVAL is going to be 40/01/01, and so on.

Date fields are very particular about data validity. If you define a field as a date data type, the system expects to see a valid date in that field. If there is any question about the content of the data you are going to place in a date field, you should use the TEST op code, described below, to check the field prior to placing it in the date field. If you think you can just leave zeros in a date field, forget it. The system will insist that you only allow valid dates in a field defined with a date data type (a nasty run-time error will occur if the data is not deemed valid).

Date fields are entirely interchangeable. Moving a date stored in the *ISO format to a date field defined with a *MDY date format (or any other format, for that matter) requires only a simple move operation. The conversion of the data will be performed for you automatically.

Another slick thing about working with the new date data types is the new RPG IV op codes. There are four new op codes (as illustrated in Table 12.2), which allow you to perform a variety of date manipulation functions. It should be noted that these op codes were designed to work with the date, time, and timestamp data types that are all part of the DB2/400 database.

Table 12.2: New Op Codes for Date and Time Manipulation

Op Code	Purpose
ADDDUR	Adds the duration specified in Factor 2 to a date or time field and places the outcome of the operation in the Result field. Factor 2 contains both the number to add as well as the duration type you want to add.
EXTRCT	Extracts part of a date, time, or timestamp field and places the outcome in the Result field. The second part of Factor 2 is used to designate what type of information you want to extract.
SUBDUR	Subtracts a duration (specified in Factor 2) from a date or time field and places the outcome of the operation in the result field.

Op Code	Purpose
TEST	Tests a date, time, or timestamp field for validity according to the indicated data type. The field being tested is stored in the Result field and does not necessarily need to be a date, time, or timestamp element. If you use the TEST op code on a numeric or alphanumeric field, you must indicate the data type you are testing for in the op code extender field, and the desired field format must be indicated in Factor 1. All of the criteria required for the indicated data type must be met or the test will fail. When testing alphanumeric fields, the data keyed must include the separator characters that coincide with the format indicated in Factor 1 or the data will be deemed invalid.

WHAT IS THE DOWNSIDE?

You knew it sounded too good to be true, didn't you? The bad news about the date data type is that V3R1 does not support it for display files. "Why," you ask? We wish we knew. But it really is not much of an obstacle, as you will see in our first example.

We put together a simple RPG IV program (Figures 12.1 and 12.2) that will test dates keyed at a workstation. The program will accept input and send back a message as to whether or not the date keyed was valid (see Figure 12.3). It will also allow the operator to press F6 to add a day to the date currently displayed, or press F5 to subtract a month. While this program is not very useful, it does give us a chance to see how a few of the new date op codes function.

Figure 12.1: The FIG1201DS Display File

```
A***********************************************************************
A*    TO COMPILE:
A*      CRTDSPF FILE(XXXLIB/FIG1201DS)
A***********************************************************************
AAN01N02N03T.Name++++++RLen++TDpBLinPosFunctions++++++++++++++++++++++++++
A             R FORMAT1
A                                          CF03
A                                          CF05
A                                          CF06
A                                        1 30'Date Test'
A                                          DSPATR(HI)
A                                        9 29'Date:'
A             DATE           6D 0B  9 35
A  98                                      ERRMSG('You keyed a Valid Date!')
A  99                                      ERRMSG('Invalid Date!')
A                                       22  5'F3=Exit'
A                                          COLOR(BLU)
A                                       22 15'F5=Subtract a month'
A                                          COLOR(BLU)
A                                       22 37'F6=Add a day'
A                                          COLOR(BLU)
```

Figure 12.2: The FIG1202RG RPG IV Program

```
***********************************************************************
*    TO COMPILE:
*      CRTBNDRPG PGM(XXXLIB/FIG1202RG)
***********************************************************************
FFilename++IPEASF.....L.....A.Device+.Keywords+++++++++++++++++++++++++++++++++Comments
FFIG1201DS CF   E             Workstn

DName+++++++++++ETDsFrom+++To/L+++IDc.Keywords+++++++++++++++++++++++++++++++++Comments
d Workdate        S             D   Datfmt(*MDY)

CL0N01Factor1++++++Opcode&ExtExtended-factor2+++++++++++++++++++++++++++++++++Comments
c                   DOU       *Inkc = *on
c                   EXFMT     Format1
c                   MOVEA     '00'          *In(98)
c     *MDY          TEST(D)                 Date                    99
c                   IF        *In99
 * Test failed, date is invalid. Display error message
c                   ITER
c                   ENDIF
 * If no function keys were pressed, just send the message
c     *Inke         IFEQ      *off
c     *Inkf         ANDEQ     *off
c                   EVAL      *In98 = *on
c                   ITER
c                   ENDIF

c                   MOVE      Date          WorkDate
c                   SELECT
 * If F5 was pressed, decrement date and re-display screen
c                   WHEN      *Inke = *on
c                   SUBDUR    1:*M          WorkDate
 * If F6 was pressed, increment date and re-display screen
```

```
c                 WHEN       *Inkf = *on
c                 ADDDUR     1:*D          WorkDate
c                 ENDSL
c                 MOVE       WorkDate      Date
c                 ENDDO

c                 EVAL       *Inlr = *on
```

Figure 12.3: Example of the FIG1202RG RPG IV Program

```
                        Date Test




                  Date: 123196




    F3=Exit    F5=Subtract a month    F6=Add a day

 You keyed a Valid Date!
```

The display file in Figure 12.1 has a six-digit numeric field called DATE. We added two error messages that will be used to reflect whether or not the date keyed was valid. The program in Figure 12.2 first tests the date field to see if it is valid based upon the *MDY format specified in Factor 1 of the TEST op code.

We could have made the date field an alphanumeric field, but the system would have insisted that the date keyed include the date separator characters before it would be considered valid. As a general rule, operators do not want to key separator characters or the century digits.

You can see an example of the output from our simple program in Figure 12.3.

If the date keyed is valid and function key F5 is pressed, the new Subtract Duration (SUBDUR) op code is used to subtract one month from the date currently on the screen. If the date test is passed and function key F6 is pressed, the ADDDUR op code is used to increment the displayed date by one day. In both of the examples for these new op codes, the value to increment or decrement is specified in Factor 2 as well as the duration interval for which the date is to be changed.

Valid duration intervals for date data types include *D or *DAYS (days), *M or *MONTHS (months), and *Y or *YEARS (years). Other duration types are *H or *HOURS (hours), *MN or *MINUTES (minutes), *S or *SECONDS (seconds), and *MS or *MSECONDS (microseconds).

You will notice in Figure 12.2 that we had to move the DATE field to a field defined with a date type before we could perform the ADDDUR or SUBDUR operations. While TEST may be performed on fields that are not defined with a date data type, that is not the case with the ADDDUR, SUBDUR, or EXTRCT op codes.

DATE ARITHMETIC

As you have surmised by now, all of those fancy RPG II and RPG III routines we developed through the years to validate dates, calculate follow-up dates, or detect how old a particular transaction is have now gone the way of the dinosaur. But do not lament the fact that they have become extinct, because the replacement routines are simple and very easy to code.

In Figure 12.4, indicator 99 is going to come on if the data in the Date field does not represent a valid date in the month-day-year format that was specified in Factor 1. Remember, the reason this technique is important is because display files do not support the date data type. When dates are entered, you will need to validate the data prior to putting it into fields with a date data type. Failure to do so will result in a nasty little run-time error.

Figure 12.4: Validating a Six-digit Numeric Date

```
CLON01Factor1++++++Opcode&ExtFactor2+++++++Result+++++++Len++D+HiLoEq....Comments++++++
c     *MDY         TEST(D)            Date                        99
```

In Figure 12.5, we wanted to calculate a 15-day follow-up date. After applying the code in this example, the resulting follow-up date in the FollowDate field would be 15 days after the date specified in the Factor 1 Date field. We no longer need to worry about whether or not the results of our actions will cause a change in the month or year. The system now handles all of that for you!

Figure 12.5: Calculating a 15-day Follow-up Date

```
CLON01Factor1+++++++Opcode&ExtFactor2+++++++Result++++++++Len++D+HiLoEq....Comments++++++
c     Date          ADDDUR   15:*DAYS        FollowDate
```

Figure 12.6 illustrates how you would calculate the age of a particular sales transaction. By moving the current system date (stored in month-day-year format) into a date data type work field we called Today, we are able to use the new field in our date math calculations.

Figure 12.6: Calculating the Age of a Transaction

```
DName++++++++++++ETDsFrom+++To/L+++IDc.Keywords++++++++++++++++++++++++Comments++++++++++++
D Today           S                 D   Datfmt(*MDY)
D DaysOld         S                 4 0
D MonthsOld       S                 4 0
D YearsOld        S                 4 0

CLON01Factor1+++++++Opcode&ExtFactor2+++++++Result++++++++Len++D+HiLoEq....Comments++++++
c                   Move     Udate           Today
c     Today         SUBDUR   SaleDate        DaysOld:*Days
c     Today         SUBDUR   SaleDate        MonthsOld:*M
c     Today         SUBDUR   SaleDate        YearsOld:*Y
```

If our system date format (DATFMT) was *YMD, we would want to define Today as *YMD too. You can use Display Job (DSPJOB) to tell what your system default is. You can use Change Job (CHGJOB) if you want to change it for the current session, or the DATEEDIT Control Specification keyword within your program.

The SaleDate field in our database file could be in any format, as long as it is a date data type. The SaleDate field in our file might be in *YMD or *ISO format, but it will not affect the math, because each date is evaluated on its chronological value.

Finding the last day of the month has been made easy, as we can see in Figure 12.7. We took the current date and reset it to the beginning of the month. By using a data structure to overlay the Today date field with the day portion (CurrentDay) of the date, we were able to reset the date by simply moving '01' to the CurrentDay field. Notice that we specified that the overlap position begins in the fourth position of the field because the *MDY format is stored as MM/DD/YY.

Figure 12.7: Finding the Last Day of the Month

```
DName++++++++++ETDsFrom+++To/L+++IDc.Keywords++++++++++++++++++++++++Comments+++++++++++
D                       DS
D Today                           D     Datfmt(*MDY)
D   CurrentDay                    2     Overlay(Today:4)

D EndofMonth       S              D     Datfmt(*MDY)

CLON01Factor1++++++++Opcode&ExtFactor2++++++++Result++++++++Len++D+HiLoEq....Comments++++++
C                       Move      Udate             Today
C                       Move      '01'              CurrentDay
C           Today       ADDDUR    1:*Months         EndOfMonth
C                       SUBDUR    1:*Days           EndOfMonth
```

Once we reset the date to the beginning of the current month, we used the Add Duration (ADDDUR) op code to add one month to the date so the result would be the first day of next month. Then we simply used the Subtract Duration (SUBDUR) to subtract one day from the date to get the desired result. This relieves us from having to keep track of leap years or how many days are in each month.

Finding the day of the week can be simple too. The code in Figure 12.8 may be used to calculate the day of the week for any date beyond January 1, 1901.

Figure 12.8: Calculating the Day of the Week (simple method)

```
DName++++++++++ETDsFrom+++To/L+++IDc.Keywords++++++++++++++++++++++++++Comments++++++++++
d BaseDate        S                    D    INZ(D'1901-01-01')
d Workdate        S                    D

d TempField       S              7  0  INZ
d WeekDay         S             10A

CL0N01Factor1++++++++Opcode&ExtFactor2+++++++Result++++++++Len++D+HiLoEq....Comments++++++
 * Calculate day of the week
c      WorkDate       SUBDUR    BaseDate       TempField:*D
c                     DIV       7              TempField
c                     MVR                      Index
c                     SELECT
c                     WHEN      Index = 0
c                     EVAL      WeekDay = 'Tuesday'
c                     WHEN      Index = 1
c                     EVAL      WeekDay = 'Wednesday'
c                     WHEN      Index = 2
c                     EVAL      WeekDay = 'Thursday'
c                     WHEN      Index = 3
c                     EVAL      WeekDay = 'Friday'
c                     WHEN      Index = 4
c                     EVAL      WeekDay = 'Saturday'
c                     WHEN      Index = 5
c                     EVAL      WeekDay = 'Sunday'
c                     WHEN      Index = 6
c                     EVAL      WeekDay = 'Monday'
c                     ENDSL
```

The key to calculating the day of the week in the example in Figure 12.8 is to define a base date where you know what the day of the week is. In our example, we defined a base date of Tuesday, January 1, 1901. We then used the SUBDUR op code to subtract the base date from the WorkDate variable. The result of this operation is the number of days since the base date, which is then divided by 7 (the number of days in a week). The remainder of the division operation is the number of days after Tuesday.

While this method is simple, it may not be flexible enough for your needs. It assumes that the input date is already in a date data type. It is also only valid for dates after January 1, 1901.

The program in Figure 12.9 uses APIs to calculate the day of the week from a wide variety of date input pictures (as seen in Table 12.3). It first uses the CEEDAYS API to convert the input date to a Lilian date. The program then uses the CEEDYWK API to convert the Lilian date to the day of the week. The input date, the picture format describing the input date (see Table 12.3), and the day of the day of the week to be returned to the calling program are the three parameters used in this program. If you need to utilize other date formats that are not included in the table, refer to the *System API*

Reference manual (SC41-3801-00) for a complete description of the formats that the CEEDAYS API can handle.

Figure 12.9: Calculating the Day of the Week (industrial strength)

```
************************************************************************
*   TO COMPILE:
*      CRTBNDRPG PGM(XXXLIB/FIG1209RG) DFTACTGRP(*NO) ACTGRP(QILE)
************************************************************************

DName++++++++++++ETDsFrom+++To/L+++IDc.Keywords+++++++++++++++++++++++++++++Comments+++++++++++
DInDate           s                25
DPictureFmt       s                25
DFeedBack         s                12
DLilianDate       s                 9B 0
DDayOfWeek        s                 9B 0
DWeekDay          s                10
DIndex            s                 1  0

CL0N01Factor1++++++Opcode&ExtFactor2++++++Result+++++++Len++D+HiLoEq....Comments+++++
C      *ENTRY      PLIST
C                  PARM                    InDate
C                  PARM                    PictureFmt
C                  PARM                    WeekDay
 *    Convert input date to lilian date format
C                  CALLB(D)   'CEEDAYS'
C                  PARM                    InDate
C                  PARM                    PictureFmt
C                  PARM                    LilianDate
C                  PARM                    FeedBack
 *    Convert lilian date to day of week
C                  CALLB(D)   'CEEDYWK'
C                  PARM                    LilianDate
C                  PARM                    DayOfWeek
C                  PARM                    FeedBack
C                  move       DayOfWeek    Index
 *    Convert index field to day of week description
c                  SELECT
c                  WHEN       Index = 0
c                  EVAL       WeekDay = 'Error'
c                  WHEN       Index = 1
c                  EVAL       WeekDay = 'Sunday'
c                  WHEN       Index = 2
c                  EVAL       WeekDay = 'Monday'
c                  WHEN       Index = 3
c                  EVAL       WeekDay = 'Tuesday'
c                  WHEN       Index = 4
c                  EVAL       WeekDay = 'Wednesday'
c                  WHEN       Index = 5
c                  EVAL       WeekDay = 'Thursday'
c                  WHEN       Index = 6
c                  EVAL       WeekDay = 'Friday'
c                  WHEN       Index = 7
c                  EVAL       WeekDay = 'Saturday'
c                  ENDSL
c                  eval       *inlr = *on
```

Table 12.3: Some of the Date Input Pictures Allowed for Program FIG1209RG

Date Input Picture	Sample Input Date	Description
YYMMDD	961201	Must include all six digits of the date (including leading zeros).
YYYYMMDD	19961201	Same as above, except the entire year, including century, is specified.
YYYY-MM-DD	1996-12-1	Eight-digit date is specified with the dash (-) as the separator character. Leading zeros are not mandatory for month and day.
MMDDYY	120196	Month-day-year six-digit date format, requires leading zeros on month and day.
MM/DD/YY	12/01/96	Same as above, except slash (/) is included as the separator character. Leading zeros on month and day must be specified.
ZM/ZD/YY	12/1/96	Same as above, except leading zeros on month and day may be suppressed.
MM/DD/YYYY	12/01/1996	Eight-digit date is specified with the slash (/) as the separator character. Leading zeros are required on month and day.
DD.MM.YY	01.12.96	Six-digit day-month-year format with the decimal (.) as the separator character. Leading zeros are required on month and day.

Date Input Picture	Sample Input Date	Description
DD MMM YY	01 DEC 96	Date is entered as day-month-year. Day is entered as two-digit numeric (including leading zeros). Month is entered as the three-character abbreviation. Year is entered as two-digit numeric.
DD Mmmmmmmmmm YY	01 December 96	Day-month-year format. Day is entered as two digits (leading zeros included). Month is specified as the full 10-character description (including blanks). Year is specified as two-digit numeric.
ZD Mmmmmmmmmz YY	1 December 96	Same as above, except leading zeros and trailing blanks are suppressed.
Mmmmmmmmmmz ZD, YYYY	December 1, 1996	Same as above except input date is specified as month-day-year. A comma is specified to separate day and year, and the year is specified as four digits (including the century).
YY.DDD	96.336	Julian date with the decimal (.) as the separator character.
YYDDD	96366	Same as above, except no separator characters.

DATE FORMATTING

As we have mentioned, if you have defined a field in your database file as a date data type, it will appear and print in the format specified in the DDS. So if the sales date in your transaction file was defined in an *ISO format, it will print and display as YYYY-MM-DD. For example, a sales date of December 1, 1996, would appear as 1996-12-01 if you were to print the field in a report or view it on the screen. Note that no edit code is required when the date is printed or displayed, because the separator character is now part of the field.

But this can cause problems if your screens and reports were all designed to output a six-digit date field. Reworking all of the screens and reports to fit the new field sizes could require a great deal of work just to get you back to where you were in the first place. And what if your program specifications called for using a slash (/) as a separator character instead of a dash (-)? And wouldn't those same specifications probably require that dates be month-day-year instead of year-month-day?

Rather than redesign your reports and screens, we recommend that you simply move the date fields from your database file to a date field defined with the desired format prior to printing or displaying them.

Using the scenario we just described, let's say that our sales date is defined in our database file as an *ISO date data type. If we were to print the sales date of December 1, 1996, as defined, it would appear as 1996-12-01. But if we were to move the SalesDate field into the DateOfSale output field, as defined in Figure 12.10, it would appear as 12-01-96. If we wanted it to appear as 12/01/96, we would define the DateOfSale field with a date format of *MDY/ or *MDY (slash is the default separator for the *MDY format).

Figure 12.10: Changing the Output Format of Date Fields

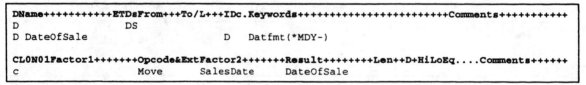

```
DName++++++++++ETDsFrom+++To/L+++IDc.Keywords+++++++++++++++++++++++++++Comments++++++++++
D                         DS
D DateOfSale                     D    Datfmt(*MDY-)

CLON01Factor1+++++++Opcode&ExtFactor2+++++++Result++++++++Len++D+HiLoEq....Comments++++++
C                   Move      SalesDate      DateOfSale
```

By performing this simple move operation prior to output, we have eliminated the need to redefine our print or display output. Our database will be able to handle the change in century (because the date is stored with the century digits), but our output does not need to be redesigned. The date of January 1, 2000, will appear as 01/01/00, but people looking at a report will know that a sales date of 01/01/00 represents the year 2000 and not the year 1900.

What about date input field, you ask? Pretty much the same rules apply. Why would you want to change all of your display files if you do not need to? If you refer back to the example we saw in Figures 12.1 through 12.3, you will see how we defined a date input field as a simple six-digit numeric field. We tested the field for validity (using the new TEST op code) prior to moving it to a field defined with a date data type. If an error was found during the test operation, an error was displayed and the field was not moved to the date data type field.

There are a few things to consider when it comes to date input fields, however. The first is whether or not there is any possibility that the date could be outside of the date "window" range we discussed earlier. If the input date keyed could *ever* be outside of the date range of 01/01/1940 and 12/31/2039, you should include the century as part of your input field. When this is the case, a six-digit numeric field is probably not going to work for you. A common example of where the six-digit date does not work is date of birth. People can live longer than 100 years, so a six-digit date could never work for date-of-birth data.

Another thing you need to think about when coding date input fields is whether or not you want to use a numeric field or an alphanumeric field. Both can be used and both can be validated using the new TEST op code. A numeric input date is easy to code because there are no separator characters to contend with. But if you choose to use an alphanumeric input field, there may be some additional work on your part.

In Figure 12.11, we see an example of the code required to test an alphanumeric date field that will be keyed as month-day-year, as specified in Factor 1 of the TEST op code statement. The trick with the TEST op code is that, if the date is not keyed in the exact format that the code in Factor 1 specifies, indicator 99 is going to be turned on. *This includes separator characters!* So an alphanumeric date keyed as 120196 or 12-01-96 would not be considered valid when used with the code in Figure 12.11. The operator would have to key December 1, 1996, as 12/01/96 because a slash (/) is the appropriate separator character for the *MDY date format (as we saw in Table 12.1).

Figure 12.11: Validating a Six-digit Alphanumeric Date

```
CL0N01Factor1+++++++Opcode&ExtFactor2+++++++Result++++++++Len++D+HiLoEq....Comments++++++
c     *MDY          TEST(D)             AlfaDate                99
```

Once again, changing date formats is a simple move operation when you are utilizing fields with date data types. Moving a date defined with an *MDY (month-day-year) format to a date defined with a *YMD (year-month-day) format is a simple move operation. The system does all of the conversion work for you. Converting keyed input dates to the format you desire is now a simple, single-statement move operation.

IDENTIFYING THE DEPTH OF THE PROBLEM

The first step in converting your system over so it will accommodate the 21st century is to identify where your problem areas are. Doing so will require that you find all of the database files, display files, and programs that work with dates. This may be no small task if your system is very large. Going through it one line of code at a time can be time-consuming, and it would be easy to miss something. It is for that reason that we wrote the Work with Fields tool (found in Chapter 11, "Tools for the Toolbox") to help you with this task.

The Work with Fields programmers' tool was designed to help you find date fields in your system. It does this by allowing you to identify fields in your system that have specific characteristics.

The Work with Fields (WRKFLD) command lets you search for fields based upon field characteristics (size and decimal positions) and also on field name. When specifying the field name, you can use an asterisk (*) as a wild-card character, as we have done in Figure 12.12. As you can see, any field with six digits and no decimal positions that happened to have the characters DAT anywhere in the field name would be displayed in the subfile.

Figure 12.12: The Work with Fields (WRKFLD) Programmers' Tool

```
                          Work with Fields

   Holding file to search in. . . . . . FIELDS      Created: 14:38  5/22/1996
    Library of holding file . . . . . . APPLIB
   Size of search field . . . . . . . .  00006 00
   Only include field named . . . . . . *DAT*

 Type options, press enter.
     1=Edit source    2=Browse    6=Print

   Opt   Field      Program       Opt   Field      Program
    _    ACADAT     ACTCHG         _    OMDATE     ACTCHG
    _    ACCDAT     ACTCHG         _    RGLDAT     ACTCHG
    _    ACFDAT     ACTCHG         _    RGTDAT     ACTCHG
    _    ACODAT     ACTCHG         _    TIDAT2     ACTCHG
    _    ACPDAT     ACTCHG         _    TIIDAT     ACTCHG
    _    FLDATA     ACTCHG         _    TMDATE     ACTCHG
    _    FLDATC     ACTCHG         _    TMSDAT     ACTCHG
    _    MBEDAT     ACTCHG         _    TRLDAT     ACTCHG
    _    MMDATE     ACTCHG         _    TRPDAT     ACTCHG
    _    OHTDAT     ACTCHG         _    TRSDAT     ACTCHG
                                                          More...
     F3=Exit      F12=Previous
```

As you have probably already guessed, before you can run the Work with Fields (WRKFLD) command, you must first build a work file for your system using the Build Work Fields (BLDWRKFLD) command. You will note that the date and time the Build Work Fields (BLDWRKFLD) command was run is displayed on the screen in Figure 12.12.

The tool works by compiling all of the programs in your system into QTEMP (a temporary work library for each session) and then analyzing the output to create the work file that will be processed by the Work with Fields (WRKFLD) command. The end result will be that all fields in your database files, display files, and RPG programs will be placed in the work file that the WRKFLD command processes as long as those fields are referenced by at least one RPG program in your system.

It should be noted that the Work with Fields (WRKFLD) command is not to be considered the panacea for identifying all of your areas of concern. The tool works by compiling all of the RPG programs in your system, so it obviously does not address programs written in other languages (like CL). It also will not show you where you have date fields in your database if they are not touched by an RPG program somewhere in your system.

DATE CONVERSION

Speaking of conversion... What would you think if we told you that the system will convert the date fields in your database files from non-date data types to date data types for you? Well, it will, and we are going to show you how.

Any programmer who has worked on the AS/400 for a while is familiar with the Copy File (CPYF) command. It is great for performing a variety of copy functions, but you are probably aware that it will not usually allow you to convert the data type of fields. One exception to this rule, however, is when converting dates in your database files to fields that have a date data type, as long as you follow a very specific set of rules.

Let's look at an example of how the Copy File (CPYF) command can be used to convert the data type of your date fields. Figure 12.13 shows us an example of the DDS of a sales transaction file.

Figure 12.13: DDS for FIG1213PF Transaction File with a Six-digit Date Field

```
A****************************************************************************
A*   TO COMPILE:
A*      CRTPF FILE(XXXLIB/FIG1213PF) SRCMBR(FIG1213PF)
A****************************************************************************
AAN01N02N03T.Name++++++RLen++TDpBLinPosFunctions++++++++++++++++++++++++++++
A                                       UNIQUE
A             R TRANSREC                TEXT('Sales Transactions')
A               TRCUSTNO      5A        TEXT('Customer Number')
A               TRSALEDATE    6S  0     TEXT('Sales Date')
A               TRTRANSNO     5S  0     TEXT('Sales Transaction ID#')
A               TRSKU#       23A        TEXT('SKU Number')
A               TRAMOUNT      7S  2     TEXT('Sales Amount')
 *
A             K TRCUSTNO
A             K TRSALEDATE
A             K TRTRANSNO
```

The DDS in Figure 12.13 defines a simple Sales Transaction file. In the file, we have defined a customer number, sales date, transaction ID number, SKU number, and transaction amount. Note that the TRSALEDATE field is defined as a six-digit, numeric, signed field.

In Figure 12.14, we have taken the same Sales Transaction file definition and modified it so the TRSALEDATE field would be defined with a date data type. For our example, we chose to use the *ISO format. However, we could use any of the date data type formats we saw in Table 12.1 and still end up with our desired results.

Figure 12.14: DDS for FIG1214PF Sales Transaction File with a Date Data Type

```
A*******************************************************************
A*   TO COMPILE:
A*     CRTPF FILE(XXXLIB/FIG1214PF) SRCMBR(FIG1214PF)
A*******************************************************************
AAN01N02N03T.Name+++++RLen++TDpBLinPosFunctions++++++++++++++++++++++++
A                                   UNIQUE
A          R TRANSREC                TEXT('Sales Transactions')
A            TRCUSTNO      5A        TEXT('Customer Number')
A            TRSALEDATE    L         DATFMT(*ISO)
A                                    DFT('0001-01-01')
A                                    TEXT('Sales Date')
A            TRTRANSNO     5S 0      TEXT('Sales Transaction ID#')
A            TRSKU#        23A       TEXT('SKU Number')
A            TRAMOUNT      7S 2      TEXT('Sales Amount')
 *
A          K TRCUSTNO
A          K TRSALEDATE
A          K TRTRANSNO
```

In our examples here, we are converting a sales transaction file with the six-digit date (FIG1213PF) to a new file (FIG1214PF), which we created with a sales date defined with an *ISO date data type. Notice that the differences between the two files are the size, data type, and default value of the TRSALEDATE field.

For our purposes here, the date in the FIG1213PF file was stored in a YYMMDD (year-month-day) format. This is important because it has a direct bearing on how the Copy File (CPYF) command will work.

We created a sample CL program in Figure 12.15 that will be used to convert our file without the date data type (FIG1213PF) to the new file with the date data type (FIG1214PF). Because we perform a Change Job (CHGJOB) command in this CL program (we will explain why in the next few pages), it is important to submit this job rather than run it interactively. Failure to do so could result in subsequent interactive jobs that do not perform as expected.

*Figure 12.15: CL Program to Convert Six-digit Numeric Date to *ISO Date Data Type*

```
/*******************************************************************/
/*   TO CREATE:                                                    */
/*       CRTCLPGM PGM(XXXLIB/FIG1215CL)                            */
/*******************************************************************/
PGM
            CHGJOB      DATFMT(*YMD)
            CPYF        FROMFILE(FIG1213PF) TOFILE(FIG1214PF) +
                          MBROPT(*REPLACE) FROMRCD(1) FMTOPT(*MAP)
ENDPGM
```

Figure 12.16 reflects what the data in our sample sales transaction file might look like. Note that the data in the column titled TRSALEDATE shows our dates formatted as YYMMDD (year-month-day). The sales date in the first record, January 15, 1996, appears as 960115 (note that query added the extra comma to our six digit numeric field in an attempt to make it easier to read).

Figure 12.16: Example of FIG1213PF Sales Data Prior to Conversion

```
                          Display Report
                                   Report width . . . . . :      68
     Position to line  . . . . .  ____    Shift to column  . . . . .      ___
     Line      ....+....1....+....2....+....3....+....4....+....5....+....6....+...
               TRCUSTNO   TRSALEDATE   TRTRANSNO   TRSKU#                TRAMOUNT
     000001    1000        960,115           1    00056405578902130456821   1,500.00
     000002    1000        960,119           4    56408798701234564021131    895.00
     000003    1001        960,120          15    56408798732165490780322    805.00
     000004    1001        960,120          17    21345054897012345648970    950.00
     000005    1002        960,120           7    54089790812318654987012   1,325.00
     000006    1005        960,115           6    87089798701234564078966   1,725.33
     000007    1005        960,121           8    56456489789012316549821   1,880.25
     000008    1010        960,118           9    56408798321045897634156    155.00
     000009    1010        960,118          12    54098780456105645644506    909.00
     000010    1010        960,120           2    56405487905315879012213    211.15
     000011    1010        960,120           6    78901231657498078970123    753.33
     000012    1010        960,120          14    87098756410321546548970    500.50
     000013    1010        960,120          18    54089702314567804564022    750.00
     000014    1010        960,120          21    54870231549870545640822     69.96
     000015    1010        960,121          16    54089703131564087086454    800.48
     000016    1011        960,115          10    79802134564897083213215    649.60
                                                                          More...
     F3=Exit      F12=Cancel      F19=Left      F20=Right      F24=More keys
```

Prior to conversion, the data reflected in Figure 12.16 was stored in the FIG1213PF physical file. The CL conversion program in Figure 12.15 converted the data in the FIG1213PF physical file and placed the results in the FIG1214PF physical file. Figure 12.17 shows the results after our conversion program was run.

Figure 12.17: Example of FIG1214PF Sales Data after Conversion

```
                         Display Report
                                    Report width . . . . . :       68
     Position to line  . . . . . ____      Shift to column  . . . . . .      ____
     Line    ....+....1....+....2....+....3....+....4....+....5....+....6....+...
             TRCUSTNO  TRSALEDATE  TRTRANSNO  TRSKU#                      TRAMOUNT
     000001  1000      1996-01-15         1   00056405578902130456821    1,500.00
     000002  1000      1996-01-19         4   56408798701234564021131      895.00
     000003  1001      1996-01-20        15   56408798732165490780322      805.00
     000004  1001      1996-01-20        17   21345054897012345648970      950.00
     000005  1002      1996-01-20         7   54089790812318654987012    1,325.00
     000006  1005      1996-01-15         6   87089798701234564078966    1,725.33
     000007  1005      1996-01-21         8   56456489789012316549821    1,880.25
     000008  1010      1996-01-18         9   56408798321045897634156      155.00
     000009  1010      1996-01-18        12   54098780456105645644506      909.00
     000010  1010      1996-01-20         2   56405487905315879012213      211.15
     000011  1010      1996-01-20         6   78901231657498078970123      753.33
     000012  1010      1996-01-20        14   87098756410321546548970      500.50
     000013  1010      1996-01-20        18   54089702314567804564022      750.00
     000014  1010      1996-01-20        21   54870231549870545640822       69.96
     000015  1010      1996-01-21        16   54089703131564087086454      800.48
     000016  1011      1996-01-15        10   79802134564897083213215      649.60
                                                                            More...
     F3=Exit      F12=Cancel      F19=Left      F20=Right      F24=More keys
```

Note that the same sales date (under the column titled TRSALEDATE in Figure 12.17) , January 15, 1996, now shows as 1996-01-15. The Copy File (CPYF) command in our FIG1215CL conversion program automatically added the century and the date separator characters for us when the copy was performed!

Now that we have whet your appetite, there are some pretty strict rules that *must* be adhered to if you are going to use this method to convert your database files. These rules are illustrated in Table 12.4.

Table 12.4: Rules Regarding Date Conversion Using the Copy File (CPYF) Command

Rule	Description
No packed dates allowed.	While the Copy File (CPYF) command works great when converting six-digit numeric signed fields, it will give you an error if you try to use packed fields. If your dates are packed, simply change your DDS so the fields are signed numeric, recompile, and copy the file with packed dates into the one that no longer has packed dates. Then you will be ready to convert to a file with the date data types.
Alphanumeric dates require separator characters.	The Copy File (CPYF) command *will* convert alphanumeric data into fields with a date data type, but the preconverted data *must* include the separator characters that match the date format of the date data type to which you are converting.
Specify a default value for the new date data type.	If your DDS for the new date data type does not have a default value specified (see Figure 12.14), the system will automatically use the current date as the default date when it experiences a mapping error. A preconverted date with zeros in it will experience a mapping error when it is copied to a field with a date data type (zeros are not a valid value in date data fields), and the current date will be placed in the converted data. Imagine an accounts receivable detail file with payment dates that are zero being converted into a new file with all of the payment dates filled in with the current date. What a mess!

Rule	Description
The date format of your session must match the date format of the file you are trying to convert.	You will note that, in our sample conversion program (Figure 12.15), we performed a Change Job (CHGJOB) command to change the date format to *YMD (year-month-day). That is because the format of our preconverted date field was in the *YMD format. The Copy File (CPYF) command will not perform the conversion if the session date format and the preconverted date format do not match. If you are unlucky enough to have two date fields in the same file that have *different* date formats, you will need to perform your conversion in multiple passes (changing the DDS of your file to a date data type for one date, performing the conversion, and then repeating the process for the next date). Use the Display Job (DSPJOB) command to see what your session date format is currently. The safest method is to simply perform the Change Job (CHGJOB) command every time you convert a file, regardless of your default setting.
The name of the new field with the date data type must match the name of the one without the date data type.	This one is rather obvious. If you use the *MAP option of the Copy File (CPYF) command, the system uses the field names to map the data. If the field names do not match, no mapping can occur.
Copy the records in arrival sequence.	Anytime you perform a Copy File (CPYF) function, you should copy the records using the arrival access path unless there is a compelling reason not to. By specifying the FROMRCD(1) parameter in the Copy File (CPYF) command as we did in Figure 12.15, the system will copy the records in arrival sequence instead of by key. You will notice that the performance is considerably better than when you copy a file using a keyed access path.

In our sample conversion program (Figure 12.15), we chose to use two different source members to describe our sample sales transaction file. This is probably not practical in most programming environments.

A better approach for the purposes of conversion would be to move the physical file to a different library using the Move Object (MOVOBJ) command, then recompile the DDS for the file (assuming that it has been updated with the date data type), and then run your conversion program. In this scenario, the Copy File (CPYF) command in the conversion program would be a little different than the one we used in Figure 12.15 because the file names would be the same, but they would be qualified with the library name.

You should not expect good performance with this type of conversion. It will help significantly if you copy the file using the arrival sequence access path but, anytime you use the *MAP option on the Copy File (CPYF) command, you are looking at a pretty slow process.

DEVELOPING A STRATEGY TO TAKE YOU INTO THE 21ST CENTURY

Obviously, the transition to the 21st century is going to be no small feat. But that does not mean that you need to fulfill the doom-and-gloom prophecies that have been tossed around by various techno-pundits either.

A typical knee-jerk reaction to this type of change might be to begin looking at your screens and reports to see what type of design changes are necessary to add the two century digits to all of your dates. But let's talk about that.

Users of your software have been working with six-digit dates for years. They know that a date that appears as 01/15/96 is in the year 1996. Logic tells them that, unless the date in question can actually span the century mark (a birth date, for instance), the last two digits of the year are going to be whichever century happens to bring the date closest to the current date. When they begin to see transaction dates like 01/15/00, are they going to freak out thinking that the computer system has run amok? Probably not.

With that said, we would like to propose that you *do not* change your reports and screens at all. Does anyone really think that a data entry operator who keys thousands of transactions a day is going to appreciate having to key two extra digits for every date field encountered? Of course not. Especially when it is not necessary.

If you have date fields like birth dates that can span the century mark, they are already eight-digit dates or you would have no way to accommodate them. There is really no compelling reason to change your reports and screens. You should focus your energies instead toward the data that is "under the covers." If the changes you make are invisible to the user, your transition to date data types will give you fewer headaches. Change is well received when there are obvious benefits to be gained, but not so when you are simply trying to maintain the status quo.

CAREFUL PLANNING IS REQUIRED FOR ANY BIG DATE...

Our advice is to change the data in your database and not in your user interface. The old adage "if it ain't broke, don't fix it" comes to mind.

We have tried to show you throughout this chapter, how easy the new date data type is to deal with. In Figures 12.1 through 12.3, we saw how easy it was to put a six-digit date on the screen and convert it to a field with a date data type behind the scenes. Even though the format chosen in our example happened to be *MDY, it could have been any date format.

We have taught you how to replace existing date routines with a variety of new code that will handle a broader range of situations. We have introduced you to a tool that will help you to identify your trouble spots. We have shown you that printing a date in a month-day-year, six-digit format can be performed with a simple move operation regardless of which date data type format the data is stored in. Finally, we have shown you how easy it will be to convert your data from your legacy system to a new and improved database that is ready to take you into the next millennium.

Entering the next century is going to be an E-ticket ride for most of us in data processing. But if you plan carefully and far enough ahead, you just may avoid many of the pitfalls that your counterparts are certain to experience. Borrow from the Boy Scouts. Be prepared.

Chapter 13

Integrated Language Environment
(ILE) Concepts

There has been much confusion over the announcement of RPG IV and the Integrated Language Environment (ILE for short). Because they were announced in the same time frame, many MIS professionals were confused into thinking that they were one and the same. In reality, the two are distinctly different.

RPG IV is simply the newest generation of the RPG programming language. ILE, on the other hand, is not a programming language at all. It is an environment that was designed to enhance (speed up) calls between programs, especially if those programs are created from different languages. In the Original Program Model (OPM), programs have been able to call other programs that were created in different languages, but the performance has always been less than desirable. With ILE, you have the option of creating the program so that it will run as fast as if called programs were simply subroutines of the calling program.

To begin with, we need to understand two new concepts that are introduced with ILE. The first is the concept of *binding*. Binding is the process the compiler goes through when linking modules together to create a program. And, as with most everything else on the AS/400, binding comes in more than one flavor. We'll cover the types of binding later in the chapter.

The second concept we need to comprehend is *activation groups*. An activation group is a subset of a job that is used to control the resources of that job. You may or may not be aware of this, but all jobs run in an activation group, even OPM programs! Activation groups can be used to control memory, file overrides, commitment control, and more. We'll take a good look at activation groups later in this chapter.

In addition to these two main concepts, there are some other new concepts that support them. These include *modules*, *service programs*, *exports*, *imports*, *program interfaces*, and even a new language—*binder language*. We'll cover all of these topics, and maybe a few more. Let's begin our journey through ILE by discussing the basic building block of programs—*modules*.

MODULES

This may come as a shock to some of you, but we do not write programs anymore. Instead, we write nice, neat, little modules. The theory here is that a module is generally smaller than a program, so it is easier to code, test, and debug. A module is not a program. You can not execute a module directly. Instead, we tell the system to gather these modules into a program (or a service program) that can be executed. Once the program has been created, the modules used to create the program are no longer needed or used. The module may then be deleted to save disk space.

In simple terms, a module is like a program that you can not run. It is produced from the ILE compiler, but it is nonexecutable. It is a building block for programs, in that programs are compiled by gathering modules together.

Chapter 13—Integrated Language Environment (ILE) Concepts

EXPORTS

Modules can contain *procedures* that are available to other ILE objects. A procedure is a set of instructions that performs a task and returns to the caller. Procedures that exist in one module, but are available to other ILE objects, are called *exports*.

A data item (field) can also be made available to ILE objects outside of the module and, therefore, can also be called an *export*. Use the keyword EXPORT on the Data Definition Specification to designate a field as an export.

Exports are identified by name and type (procedure or data).

IMPORTS

Items that have been exported from one module can be imported into another module. An *import* is simply a reference to a procedure or data item not defined in the current module.

Imports are identified by name and type.

Modules are created from your source code using the Create XXX Module (CRTXXXMOD) command, where *XXX* represents the programming language. To create an RPG module, you run the CRTRPGMOD command.

PROGRAMS

Programs are created using the Create Program (CRTPGM) command. Notice that you do not specify a language when creating a program. This is because programs can be created from modules that in turn were created using different programming languages. (We are only going to cover ILE RPG/400 characteristics.)

If your program has only one module, you can use the Create Bound RPG (CRTBNDRPG) command instead of the Create Program (CRTPGM) command. This command combines the Create Module (CRTMOD) and the Create Program (CRTPGM) commands into a single step. The module is created in library QTEMP, used in the compilation of the program, and then discarded.

As with OPM programs, ILE programs have only one program entry point (PEP). PEPs are coded in modules, and programs can consist of more than one module, so programs could conceivably have more than one PEP. Because this is not allowed, you control which PEP is used via the ENTMOD parameter on the Create Program (CRTPGM) command. You designate which module is used as the entry point. All other PEPs in other modules in the program are ignored (as program entry points).

BINDING

As we have already said, programs are created by binding modules together to form a program. By using a parameter on the Create Program (CRTPGM) command, you can list each module to be included in the program. As a convenient alternative, you can specify that the binder search a *binder directory* to find the modules to include in the program.

A binding directory is a list of modules and service programs that you may need when creating a program. You can create a directory of all modules that provide a similar function (math, for instance). Then you simply specify the math function binding directory and the binder will go find the ones you used.

There are two methods of binding, bind by copy and bind by reference. Which method you use can have enormous performance and maintenance consequences.

Bind by Copy

When the program is compiled, all of the modules identified on the module parameter of the Create Program (CRTPGM) command are copied into the program being created. The binding directory is searched if there are any unresolved imports, and if a match is found that provides a corresponding export, then that module is also copied into the program. Physical addresses that the system needs to access these parts are established now, when the program is compiled.

Bind by copy creates a program that executes very quickly. In fact, all of the called modules that have been bound to the program will execute almost as quickly as if they were coded as subroutines. But this speed is bought at the expense of maintenance.

Because of the maintenance considerations involved, bind by copy is best suited for code used in only one or two programs.

Bind by Reference

When the program is compiled, no copying of any modules is performed. Instead, symbolic links to the service programs that provide the services are saved in the program. These symbolic links are converted to the real addresses that the system needs when the program is activated.

Bind by reference is best suited for code used in many programs, such as utility functions, or for general application functions.

SERVICE PROGRAMS

A service program is a collection of procedures (programs or modules) that are directly accessible by other ILE programs. They provide common services that other programs may need. For those of you who are familiar with Microsoft Windows concepts, they are similar in concept to Dynamic Link Libraries (DLLs).

Some of the characteristics of a service program are as follows:

- One or more modules (from any language) are copied to make a service program.

- No Program Entry Procedure is associated with a service program. PEPs in modules that are contained in the service program are ignored.

Suppose for a minute that you had different modules that performed different math functions. One module did addition, another square roots, while still another did percentage calculations. All of these different modules could be pulled into a single service program to provide math functions. Thereafter, any program that needs a math function only needs to have the service program made available to it in order to gain access to the required function.

Why not have any program that needs a math function call the corresponding module directly? Why go through a service program to access the function? Doesn't this just add another layer of complexity? The answer to all of these questions lies in that dreaded word—maintenance. But before we can show you how adding another layer of complexity actually simplifies maintenance, we must briefly examine how programs are put together.

Modules are bound to programs using the bind-by-copy method. Service programs are bound to programs using the bind-by-reference method. Modules that are bound into programs using the bind-by-copy method will be much more difficult to maintain than those that are bound by reference. Think about it for a minute. Suppose one little line of code needs to be changed in a module. If that module has been bound by copy into 50 other programs, you will need to find all those other programs and then recompile them.

Service programs are not bound by copy into other programs. Therefore, it is possible to make a change to a service program and not be required to recompile all the programs that access it. If all you are doing is fixing a bug or changing some logic in the program, you will not have to recompile any of the programs that use the service program. This is true as long as you do not change the *public interface* to the program in a way that makes it incompatible with the existing programs. The public interface to a service program consists of the names of the exported procedures and data items accessible to other ILE programs.

The system uses these procedures and data items to generate what is called a *signature*. A signature provides a quick and easy method to validate the public interface to a service program. If you add procedures to a service program, this would normally change the signature and any programs that access that service program would have to be recompiled. But, through the use of a binder language, you can tell the system to keep multiple signatures (both the new one as well as any signature previously generated). Then you do not need to recompile any of the existing programs that access the service program (unless you wanted them to access the new procedure added to the service program).

BINDER LANGUAGE

The binder language consists of a small set of commands that define the exports for a service program. You enter these commands into a source member (type BND) using SEU. This member is not compiled. The default file for the member is QSRVSRC.

To create a service program, you use the Create Service Program (CRTSRVPGM) command. One of the parameters available on this command is the EXPORT/SRCFILE/SRCMBR. This parameter directs the binder to a source file and member that contain the binder statements that the binder will use to generate one or more signatures for the program.

It is possible to change this parameter to *ALL, in which case all symbols are exported from the service program and no binder language is necessary. This option is the easiest to use but can be a nightmare to maintain. If the order or number of exports change (due to maintenance of the service program), then the signature would change and all programs or service programs that use the changed service program would have to be recompiled. This is why *ALL is not the default on the CRTSRVPGM command.

THE COMMANDS

The commands are Start Program Export (STRPGMEXP), End Program Export (ENDPGMEXP), and EXPORT. Let's examine each command in detail, after which you should be an expert binder language programmer.

The Start Program Export (STRPGMEXP) command identifies the beginning of a list of exports from a service program. One of the parameters of this command is PGMLVL (program level), which accepts either the value *CURRENT or *PRV. This parameter allows us to define multiple export lists, each with a Start Program Export (STRPGMEXP) and a corresponding End Program Export (ENDPGMEXP) command. This is the secret to maintaining multiple signatures (multiple lists of exports).

There can be only one STRPGMEXP(*CURRENT) statement in the member, but there can be multiple STRPGMEXP(*PRV) statements.

One of the other parameters on the STRPGMEXP command is the level check LVLCHK. This performs the same function as level checking for files. Turn this off, LVLCHK(*NO), and no signature checking will be performed. If you go there, beware. The maintenance you save now by turning this off will undoubtedly have to be repaid in triplicate later on when the users begin to experience run time errors.

There is one other parameter on the Start Program Export (STRPGMEXP) command, namely the SIGNATURE parameter. This allows you to explicitly specify a signature for the program. The default is *GEN, which causes the binder to generate a signature based on the export statements.

There are two instances where you might consider specifying your own signature.

- The binder could generate a duplicate signature if two export blocks have the same exports in the same order. But you know that the two interfaces are not really compatible (different number of parameters perhaps) and should not generate the same signature.

- The binder could generate a new signature when you want it to remain the same. For instance, you change the name of a procedure, but it is still the same function.

The EXPORT command identifies the symbol name to be exported from the service program. An *export* is either a program or data to which the service program provides access. You should note that, if the exported symbol is to contain lowercase letters, the symbol should be enclosed in apostrophes (''). Otherwise, the symbol name is converted to all uppercase letters.

The End Program Export (ENDPGMEXP) command simply identifies the end of the list of exports.

Figure 13.1 shows a sample of the binder language program. It shows that, originally, this service program contained two exports, Program1 and Program2. A third program, Program3, has been added and a new signature has been generated with it. Because the original signature is still being maintained (STRPGMEXP PGMLVL(*PRV)), any programs that were compiled using this service program and expecting two exports will still work and do not have to be recompiled. If you do recompile any of the programs that use this service program, they will get a signature assigned based on the current three exports.

Figure 13.1: Sample Binder Language Program

```
STRPGMEXP PGMLVL(*CURRENT) LVLCHK(*YES)
EXPORT SYMBOL(Program1)
EXPORT SYMBOL(Program2)
EXPORT SYMBOL(Program3)
ENDPGMEXP
STRPGMEXP(PGMLVL(*PRV)
EXPORT SYMBOL(Program1)
EXPORT SYMBOL(Program2)
ENDPGMEXP
```

SERVICING THE SERVICE PROGRAM

So now you have created a service program that contains seven or eight modules and shipped it out to all of your customers. One of those customers complains about a problem in module number 6, which you quickly locate and correct. To recompile that service program on all of your accounts' machines requires you to send them the source for all eight modules. Obviously, this could become a time-consuming and expensive endeavor. All you really want to do is ship module number 6 and update the service program to include the corrected module. That is exactly what the Update Service Program (UPDSRVPGM) command allows you to do.

The UPDSRVCMD command will not work on programs that have been compiled with *NO specified on the Allow Update (ALWUPD) parameter. Why you would want to shut this fantastic function down is beyond us, but you can if you want to.

For most quick fixes, the command is very simple. You specify the module or modules being replaced. Only existing modules with the same name will be replaced. You can not use the command to add new modules to a service program.

Sometimes the update function is not so simple. There are extra parameters on the command to account for these times. Let's examine these parameters.

Parameter Definitions:

RPLLIB: Replacement library. Allows you to specify how to handle the update when more that one module contained in the service program has the same name. The default for this parameter is *ONLY, and an error will be generated if the same name appears more than once in the module list. FIRST (use the first module found with this name) or *MODULE (use the module that comes from the same library as the specified module) are two other options available.

BNDSRVPGM: Bound Service Programs. If you have changed the number of imports or exports in the module being updated, then you may need more service programs to resolve those imports. This parameter allows you to specify additional service programs that will be bound to this service program to handle those imports.

BINDIR: Binding Directory. Provides another method of specifying modules or service programs that will handle extra imports.

CASCADING REFERENCES

When a service program is activated, all programs that are in the service program are also activated. This can be a major performance hit, so be aware.

Let's go back to our example of the "math" service program. Let us assume that this service program uses modules to add, divide, multiply, and so on. If we run a program that calls the module to add, the system will also have to load all of the modules to subtract, divide, multiply, and so on, into memory when the program is run, whether we are using them or not.

Even worse, if any math modules that are not being used happen to call other modules, they will be loaded into memory as well. Those unneeded modules could reference other unneeded modules, and this could go on and on. Hence the term "cascading references."

TIPS FOR GOOD SERVICE

Use a naming convention with a common prefix. This will help prevent modules with the same name being in different programs. It will also make it easier to specify modules generically on the module parameter of the Create Program (CRTPGM) command.

Keep the number of programs that use a particular module low. We recommend that modules not be copied into multiple programs. If a module must be used by more than one program, put the module in a service program.

Use the binder language for all service programs. Although you can create service programs without using the binder language, maintenance will be much simpler if you do.

You must continue (or start, if you are not already doing so) to use shared file opens in your programs. We discussed this in Chapter 1, but we can not stress the importance of this enough.

LIP SERVICE

Congratulations! In an industry that is defined as service, you have mastered the fine art of service programs. In the process, you have added another language to your ever-growing list of languages. Never mind that there are only three statements in the language. It's the size of the list that matters.

Service programs are an important aspect of ILE. They should be used both when creating new applications and when converting existing OPM applications to ILE.

ACTIVATION GROUPS

An *activation group* is a substructure of a job into which all programs are activated. It has two main functions. It is a method of grouping system resources (e.g., static variables, dynamic storage, open files) necessary to run the programs. This separation of resources effectively isolates a set of programs from other users on the system. This is great if your AS/400 runs software from different vendors (and whose doesn't?). It is also a method of cleaning up storage (that used to be done when a program ended, but is now done when an activation group ends).

An activation group is created when the first program that needs the activation group is called. Thereafter, any programs that use the same activation group will use the same resources.

When you create a program, you specify the activation group in which the program is to run. You use the ACTGRP parameter on the Create Program (CRTPGM) or CRTSRVPGM commands to accomplish this. This parameter allows three options.

- You name the activation group. This allows you to isolate your application from others.

- The system names the activation group. You specify ACTGRP(*NEW) for this option, which indicates to the system that it is to generate a new activation group whenever this program is called. The system will assign a unique name to the activation group.

- Use the activation group of the calling program. You specify ACTGRP(*CALLER) for this option. The system will never generate a new activation group, but will instead use the activation group of the program calling this program.

Default Activation Group

The default activation group is created whenever an OS/400 job is started. This is the default activation group used by all OPM programs.

It is also possible (but not intended) for ILE programs to run in this default activation group. If you specify ACTGRP(*CALLER) when you create the ILE program and then call the program from a program that is already running in the default activation group (OPM program), the ILE program will run in the default activation group. This situation should be avoided because the default activation group can not be deleted .

Named Activation Group

A named activation group is created by explicitly naming the activation group where the program is to run. This is done via the ACTGRP parameter of the Create Program (CRTPGM) command.

Named activation groups are persistent. This means that they exist until the end of the job or until they are explicitly destroyed. Because they are persistent and there is a tremendous overhead in creating activation groups, this is the recommended option to use when creating programs.

New Activation Group

The other option available for activation groups is the ACTGRP(*NEW) option. This is the default when creating programs, but it is most definitely **NOT** the best option for you to use (if performance is a consideration).

New activation groups are not persistent. Every time a program with this option is called, a new activation group is created and named by the system. When the program ends, the activation group is destroyed. If the program is called again, a new activation group is created. Creating (and to some degree destroying) activation groups is a resource hog. If you are continually doing this, you will notice a response problem.

SCOPING

Activation groups support another concept called *scoping*. There is a new parameter on the Open Database File (OPNDBF) and Open Query File (OPNQRYF) commands, called OPNSCOPE, which can be used to limit your file resources to an activation group. There is an OVRSCOPE parameter on all OVRxxxF commands to do the same thing. This means that file overrides used in one activation group will not be used if you call another program that runs in another activation group.

Scoping can have a big effect on commitment control. Commitment control has been with us for a long time. It is a method of controlling a block of file updates so that, if an error occurs while updating one of the files in the block, none of the updates will actually take effect.

Let's say Program A presents a screen for the user to enter some information and then updates five files based on the information entered. The program updates file 1, then updates file 2, and then an error occurs. If the updates are performed under commitment control, the changes that were made to files 1 and 2 would be undone or "rolled back" to their original state. This is true with either ILE programs or OPM.

But now, let's complicate matters a little bit and say that, after updating files 1 and 2, and before updating the other files, Program A calls Program B. Program B also is under commitment control and executes some code that ends the commit block. What happens to the updates that were performed to file 1 and 2 in Program A? In OPM, the updates are committed and, if an error occurs during the update to file 3, the updates to file 1 and 2 will not be rolled back. In ILE, because the commitment control was scoped to an activation group, the end commit block in Program B will not affect the commitment control in Program A. The new Commit Scope (CMTSCOPE) parameter on the Start Commitment Control (STRCMTCTL) command can be used to control scoping.

Another important aspect of activation groups to be aware of is the way that activation groups control memory allocation. In OPM, when a program ends with the Last Record indicator ON, the storage is released. In ILE, the storage is not released until the activation group ends.

The Reclaim Resource (RCLRSC) command will not clean up the storage left by a program, but Reclaim Activation Group (RCLACTGRP) will. However, you can not run the RCLACTGRP command from within the activation group you are attempting to reclaim (there had to be a catch didn't there?).

ILE BE *GOOD*

ILE has introduced us to some new concepts. Some of these we can choose to ignore and some we cannot. Creating service programs may not be necessary for every shop. On the other hand, every program runs in an activation group, so you can't get around understanding these critters. Furthermore, the default for creating programs is to use the *NEW parameter, so you might want to consider changing the default on this command.

ILE, as it exists today, simply sets the stage for the future. Programs created from different vendors in different languages that provide interconnected functions (with subsecond response) could be a not-too-distant reality. Hopefully, we have given you a good understanding of the concepts. It is up to you to take it from here.

Appendix A

Companion Diskette Contents

The companion diskette, which accompanies this book, contains source code for many of the figures. Table A.1 represents a cross reference for the figures and files on the diskette.

Table A.1: Diskette Cross-reference Information

Figure	File Name	Description
2.8	FG208DS	DDS for "Customer Subfile"
2.9	FG209RG	RPG Program for "Customer Subfile"
2.10	FG210DS	DDS for State Lookup Window Subfile
2.11	FG211RG	RPG for State Lookup Window Subfile Program
2.12	FG212DS	DDS for Message Subfile
2.13	FG213RG	RPG for Message Subfile
2.15	FG215	DDS for Physical File PRINTER
2.16	FG216	DDS for Logical File PRINTERS
2.17	FG217DS	DDS for Printer Lookup
2.18	FG218RG	RPG Specifications for Printer LOOKUP
3.3	FG303DS	Sample DDS for Menu Bar in Figures 3.1 and 3.2
3.4	FG304RG	RPG Program to Present a Menu Bar
3.7	FG307RG	RPG for the System Request Window
3.8	FG308DS	DDS for the System Request Window
4.3	FG403RG	Common Fields in the File Information Data Structure
4.4	FG404RG	Open Feedback Area File Information Data Structure
4.5	FG405RG	I/O Feedback Area File Information Data Structure
4.6	FG406RG	Device-specific Feedback Area—Printers

Figure	File Name	Description
4.7	FG407RG	Device-specific Feedback Area—Database File
4.8	FG408RG	Device-specific Feedback Area—Workstation
4.9	FG409RG	Device-specific Attributes: Workstation
4.10	FG410RG	Device-specific Attributes: ICF Session
4.11	FG411RG	Program Status Data Structure
4.12	FG412RG	Defining Subfields with Special Keywords
4.13	FG413DS	DDS for Sample Record Lock Program
4.14	FG414RG	Sample RPG Program for Record Locks
6.2	FG602RG	Using QCMDEXC to Run OPNQRYF from within an RPG Program
6.3	FG603RG	Using QCMDEXC to Override Printer Attributes
6.4	FG604DS	Customer List Prompt Screen Display File
6.6	FG606RG	Using QCMDEXC to Submit Jobs from within an RPG Program
6.7	FG607RG	RPG API Program to Validate Printer Existence
7.3	FG703RG	Using Sort Array (SORTA) to Resequence Array Elements
7.4	FG704RG	Multicolumn Customer Phone List Using Arrays to Format Output
9.2	FG902RG	Sample of the Retrieve Object Description API
9.3	FG903RG	Sample RPG Program to Validate Object Existence

Figure	File Name	Description
9.4	FG904RG	Sample RPG Program Using the Send Program Message (QMHSNDPM) API
9.5	FG905DS	DDS for the MSGEX RPG Program Using the QMHSNDPM Send Program Message API
9.6	FG906RG	RPG Program to Create a User Space
9.7	FG907RG	RPG Program to Retrieve User Space
9.10	FG910RG	RPG Program to Retrieve File Access Paths
9.11	FG911DS	DDS for the DSPPATH Command
9.12	FG912CM	DSPPATH Command
9.13	FG913RG	Retrieve and Add Size of Documents in a Folder
9.14	FG914RG	Move Spool File Entries
11.2	FG1102CM	DSPPATH Command to Display File Access Paths
11.3	FG1103DS	DSPPTH Display File
11.4	FG1104RG	DSPPTH RPG Program
11.6	FG1106CM	Display Field (DSPFLD) Command
11.7	FG1107DS	Display Fields Display File
11.8	FG1108RG	Display Fields RPG Program
11.9	FG1109CM	RGZPFFLTR Command Source
11.10	FG1110RG	RGZPFFLTR RPG Program
11.11	FG1111CL	RGZPFFLTR CL Program

Figure	File Name	Description
11.13	FG1113CM	FNDDSPLF Command
11.14	FG1114DS	FNDDSPLF Display File
11.15	FG1115RG	FNDDSPLF RPG Program
11.19	FG1119CM	BLDOBJREF Command
11.20	FG1120CL	BLDOBJREF CL Program
11.21	FG1121RG	BLDOBJREF RPG Program
11.22	FG1122CL	BLDOBJREF CL Program
11.23	FG1123CL	BLDOBJREF CL Program
11.24	FG1124CL	BLDOBJREF CL Program
11.25	FG1125CL	BLDOBJREF CL Program
11.26	FG1126RG	WRKOBJREF RPG Program
11.27	FG1127DS	WRKOBJREF Display File
11.28	FG1128	WRKOBJREF Work File
11.29	FG1129CM	WRKOBJREF Command
11.31	FG1131DS	Display Service Program Usage Display File
11.32	FG1132RG	Display Service Program Usage RPG Program
11.33	FG1133CM	Display Service Program Usage Command
11.35	FG1135DS	Display Module Usage Display File
11.36	FG1136RG	Display Module Usage RPG Program

Figure	File Name	Description
11.37	FG1137CM	Display Module Usage Command
11.39	FG1139	Work with Fields Physical File
11.40	FG1140	Work with Fields Physical File
11.41	FG1141	Work with Fields Physical File
11.42	FG1142CM	BLDWRKFLD Command
11.43	FG1143CL	BLDWRKFLD CL Program
11.44	FG1144RG	BLDWRKFLD RPG Program
11.45	FG1145DS	WRKFLD Display File
11.46	FG1146RG	WRKFLD RPG Program
11.47	FG1147CL	WRKFLD CL Program
11.48	FG1148CM	WRKFLD Command
12.1	FG1201DS	Date Test Display File
12.2	FG1202RG	Date Test RPG Program
12.8	FG1208RG	Find Day of the Week RPG Program (simple method)
12.9	FG1209RG	Find Day of the Week RPG Program (industrial strength)
12.13	FG1213PF	Sample Sales Transaction File without Date Data Type
12.14	FG1214PF	Sample Sales Transaction File with Date Data Type
12.15	FG1215CL	Date Data Type Conversion CL Program

Also on the diskette is the source code for files used in the examples.

FILE: CUSTOMER   Customer File

FILE: PRINTER   Printer Description File

FILE: PRINTERS   Printer File by Description

FILE: REQUEST   Request File

FILE: STATES   States Description File

TRANSFERRING THE SOURCE

The companion diskette includes source code for program samples and utilities listed in this appendix. Because the diskette is a PC diskette, you need a PC and PC Support (or another file-transfer utility) to transfer the source to the AS/400. In addition, your system needs the RPG compiler.

To transfer the source, follow these steps:

1. Sign on to the AS/400 with a user profile that has *PGMR user class.

2. If you want, create a library to contain all the software you're about to install. For example, you could call it POWERRPG for ease of identification:

    ```
    CRTLIB LIB(POWERRPG)
    ```

3. Create a source physical file called SOURCE in the library of your choice. You MUST name this file SOURCE:

    ```
    CRTSRCPF FILE(POWERRPG/SOURCE) RCDLEN(112) TEXT('Power
    RPG/IV source')
    ```

    where *POWERRPG* is the name of the library selected.

4. Transfer all source code to the source file just created. The preceding cross-reference table is provided to allow you to match the figures in the book to the file names found on the diskette.

COMPILING THE POWER TOOLS

Almost all of the objects in Chapter 11, "Tools for the Toolbox," may be created automatically by running the MAKECL program.

Compile the MAKECL program as follows:

```
CRTCLPGM PGM(POWERRPG/MAKECL) SRCFILE(POWERRPG/SOURCE)
SRCMBR(MAKECL)
```

To run the MAKECL program, submit the following to the job queue:

```
CALL MAKECL PARM('POWERRPG')
```

The only object that could not be compiled by the MAKECL program must be compiled by QSECOFR. The FG1110RG RPG program is part of the Reorganize Physical File Filter (RGZPFFLTR) command which references the QADBXREF file. This file resides in library QSYS and may only be accessed by QSECOFR.

To compile this program, sign on as QSECOFR and key:

```
CRTBNDRPG PGM(POWERRPG/FIG1110RG) USRPRF(*OWNER)
ALWNULL(*YES) SRCFILE(POWERRPG/SOURCE) SRCMBR(FG1110RG)
```

COMPILING THE REST OF THE SOURCE

Some of the source members on the diskette that are not from the "Tools for the Toolbox," chapter may be compiled individually. In these instances, you will find instructions on how to compile each source member in the first few lines of each source member itself. For the most part, the compiles are very straightforward.

In the example below, POWERRPG represents the name of the library where the source members reside and *XXX* is the name of the source member to compile.

For CL programs:

```
CRTCLPGM PGM(POWERRPG/XXX) SRCFILE(POWERRPG/SOURCE)
```

For display files:

```
CRTDSPF FILE(POWERRPG/XXX) SRCFILE(POWERRPG/SOURCE)
```

For RPG programs:

```
CRTBNDRPG PGM(POWERRPG/XXX) SRCFILE(POWERRPG/SOURCE)
```

Index

Reader's Comment Form for Power RPG IV

Please feel free to copy this form. Use it to identify any errors in this book, make any comments about this book, or request information about Midrange Computing products. We will attempt to maintain the content and do our best to assure its accuracy. If you would like a reply, please indicate that in your comments.

Snail Mail	FAX	E-mail	Ordering Information
Doug Pence & Ron Hawkins c/o Midrange Computing 5650 El Camino Real, Suite 225 Carlsbad, CA 92008-7128 Attn: Book Editor	(619) 931-9935	pence@as400.com	(800) 477-5665

Your Name: _____

Company: _____

Phone: _____

Fax: _____

E-mail: _____

Address: _____

_____

_____

❑ Please send me a free Midrange Computing Education and Product Training Catalog

❑ Please send me Information on Midrange Computing Seminars and Conferences

Comments:

_____

_____

_____

_____

_____

_____

_____

_____